LEGAL STUDIES

```
DIVISION OF COMMUNITY EDUCATION
BOSSIER PARISH COMMUNITY COLLEGE
2719 AIRLINE DRIVE, NORTH
BOSSIER CITY, LA  71111
```

BASIC LEGAL RESEARCH

Edward A. Nolfi
Attorney-at-Law
Akron, Ohio

GLENCOE
Macmillan/McGraw-Hill

New York, New York
Columbus, Ohio
Mission Hills, California
Peoria, Illinois

Library of Congress Cataloging-in-Publication Data

Nolfi, Edward A.
    Basic legal research / Edward A. Nolfi.
      p. cm.—(Legal studies series)
    Includes bibliographical references and index.
    ISBN 0-02-800286-5
    1. Legal research—United States. I. Title. II. Series.
KF240.N65 1993
349.73′072—dc20
[347.30072]
                                                                                                                                                  92–974
                                                                                                                                                  CIP

Copyright © 1993 by the Glencoe Division of Macmillan/McGraw-Hill School Publishing Company.
All rights reserved. Except as permitted under the United States Copyright Act, no part of this
publication may be reproduced or distributed in any form or by any means, or stored in a database
or retrieval system, without prior written permission of the publisher.

Send all inquiries to:
GLENCOE DIVISION
Macmillan/McGraw-Hill
936 Eastwind Drive
Westerville, OH 43081

ISBN 0-02-800286-5

Printed in the United States of America

1 2 3 4 5 6 7 8 9 POH 99 98 97 96 95 94 93 92

OTHER TITLES IN THE LEGAL STUDIES SERIES

Basic Law Office Management

Basic Legal Writing

Basic Family Law

Introduction to Legal Assisting

Basic Civil Litigation

Defining the Law: A Basic Legal Dictionary

ABOUT THE AUTHOR

As an associate editor with the Lawyers Co-operative Publishing Company in the mid-1980s, Edward A. Nolfi learned legal research from the inside out. While preparing annotations for American Law Reports, Federal, and case-noting the Internal Revenue Code for the United States Code Service, he researched the knowledge, wisdom, tips, and tricks of current and former editors, establishing ties back to the founding of the company and beyond.

In 1988, he brought his wealth of knowledge to the paralegal and court reporting classroom, teaching over 1,800 student-classes in three years as Professor of Law at the Academy of Court Reporting, in Akron, Ohio.

As a general practice attorney, Edward Nolfi has handled a wide variety of civil and criminal matters and has done legal research for a U.S. congressman. He is admitted to the bar in New York and Ohio, the U.S. Tax Court, the U.S. District Court for the Northern District of Ohio, the U.S. Court of Appeals for the Sixth Circuit, and the U.S. Supreme Court.

Edward Nolfi's educational background includes receiving an A.B. with Honors Thesis (religious studies) from Brown University and a J.D. (law) from the University of Akron School of Law.

This book is dedicated to my students at the Academy of Court Reporting, who proved that paralegals and legal secretaries can master legal research, and proclaimed that I was their teacher.

CONTENTS

Preface _____ xiii

PART ONE

PRELIMINARY MATTERS

CHAPTER 1 Introduction to Legal Research _____ 2

1-1 The U.S. Legal System _____ 3

    Law Is the Command of a Sovereign _____ 3
    Common-Law Origins _____ 3
    The Constitution of the United States _____ 5

1-2 The Business of Law Publishing _____ 8

    Law Publishing in the United States _____ 8
    Why Master Legal Researchers Know "Who
    Publishes What" _____ 9

1-3 The Purpose of Legal Research _____ 10

    The Court May Be Ignorant _____ 10
    The Way to Win _____ 10
    What Aaron Burr Said About the Law _____ 11
    Authority: Primary and Secondary _____ 11

1-4 Law Books and Law Libraries _____ 13

How to Judge a Law Book by Its Cover, and Other Parts 13
Visit Law Libraries 14

PART TWO

RESEARCHING PRIMARY AUTHORITY

CHAPTER 2 Case Law 20

2–1 Judicial Power 21

Court Sovereignty 21
Legal Reasoning 22

2–2 Judicial Opinions 25

Parts of an Opinion 25
Types of Opinions 30

2–3 Judicial Reports 30

Reported Opinions 32
National Reporter System 33
Federal Court Reports 36
State Court Reports 40
Unreported Opinions 43

CHAPTER 3 Case Finders 48

3–1 Case Finders Generally 49

Citations 49
Casebooks 50
Lawyers 51
Memorandums 52
Briefs 52

3–2 Digests 52

How a Digest Is Like an Index 59
A Digest Walk-Through 60
West's American Digest System 72
Other Digests 73
The Limitations of Digests 74

3–3 Other Case Finders 77

A.L.R. Annotations 77
Computer-Assisted Legal Research 77

Shepard's Citations ———— 77
Secondary Authority ———— 77

CHAPTER 4 Annotations ———— 80

4-1 Annotations Generally ———— 81
Where Annotations Came From ———— 81
When to Use Annotations ———— 84

4-2 A.L.R. Annotations ———— 84
Series ———— 84
Parts and Sections ———— 86
How an A.L.R. Annotation Is Prepared ———— 93

4-3 A.L.R. Annotation Finders ———— 94
A.L.R. Indexes ———— 94
A.L.R. Digests ———— 96
A.L.R. Help Line ———— 96
Total Client Service Library ———— 96
Case & Comment Magazine ———— 97
Shepard's Citations ———— 97
Auto-Cite and LEXIS ———— 97

4-4 A.L.R. Annotation Supplementation ———— 97
Blue Books ———— 98
Later Case Service ———— 98
Pocket Supplementation ———— 98
A.L.R. Latest Case Service ———— 98
Annotation History Table ———— 98

4-5 The Limitations of A.L.R. Annotations ———— 99

CHAPTER 5 Statutory Law ———— 103

5-1 Legislation ———— 104
Legislative History ———— 105
After a Bill Becomes Law ———— 107

5-2 Federal Codes ———— 108
United States Code (U.S.C.) ———— 110
Annotated Codes ———— 111
United States Code Annotated (U.S.C.A.) ———— 113
United States Code Service (U.S.C.S) ———— 114
The Limitations of Codes ———— 114

5-3 State Codes ———— 114

5-4 Local Codes ———— 124

CHAPTER 6 Constitutional Law, Court Rules, and Other Promulgations — 127

6-1 Constitutional Law — 128
- Federal Constitution — 128
- Annotated Constitutions — 129
- State and Local Constitutions — 130

6-2 Court Rules — 131
- Annotated Court Rules — 132

6-3 Treaties — 132

CHAPTER 7 Administrative Law — 137

7-1 Administrative Agencies and Executive Departments — 137
- Administrative Regulations — 140
- Administrative Codes — 143
- Administrative Orders and Executive Orders — 145
- Administrative Decisions — 146
- Attorney General Opinions — 146

7-2 Looseleaf Services — 146
- Tax Services — 148

PART THREE

RESEARCHING SECONDARY AUTHORITY

CHAPTER 8 General Works — 154

8-1 Encyclopedias — 155
- Guide to American Law — 156
- Corpus Juris Secundum — 156
- American Jurisprudence 2d — 156
- State Encyclopedias — 159
- Law Outlines — 161

8-2 Dictionaries — 161
- Black's Law Dictionary — 163
- Ballentine's Law Dictionary — 165
- Gifis' Law Dictionary — 165
- Other Dictionaries — 165

8-3 Directories — 165

Martindale-Hubbell Law Directory	167
Other National Directories	168
State, Local, and Specialized Directories	168

CHAPTER 9 Specialized Works — 171

9–1 Textbooks and Treatises — 172

Hornbooks and Nutshells — 174
Restatements — 174
Uniform Laws — 177

9–2 Form Books — 178

Legal Forms — 178
Pleading and Practice Forms — 178
Trial and Practice Books — 181

9–3 Periodicals — 182

Law Reviews — 182
Law Journals — 185
Newsletters — 186
Newspapers — 186
Periodical Indexes — 186

PART FOUR

CITING THE LAW

CHAPTER 10 A Uniform System of Citation — 192

10–1 Citation Style — 193

The Bluebook: A Uniform System of Citation — 193
Other Systems of Citation — 195

10–2 Technical Rules — 195

Citing Cases — 195
Citing Statutes — 197
Citing Other Primary Sources — 198
Citing Secondary Sources — 198
Computer-Assisted Citation Style — 199

10–3 Citation Requirements — 199

CHAPTER 11 *Shepard's Citations* and Other Citators — 202

11–1 *Shepard's Citations* — 203

Using Shepard's as a Case Reviewer —— 209
Using Shepard's as a Case Finder —— 211
Shepard's on LEXIS or WESTLAW —— 211

11–2 Other Citators —— 211

Parallel Cites —— 212
Auto-Cite —— 212
Insta-Cite —— 214
LEXIS or WESTLAW as a Citator —— 214

PART FIVE

USING COMPUTERS AND OTHER TECHNOLOGIES

CHAPTER 12 Computer-Assisted Legal Research —— 218

12–1 Understanding Computer-Assisted Legal Research —— 219

The Data Corporation's Concordance —— 219
Computer-Assisted Legal Research Takes Off —— 220

12–2 LEXIS —— 222

12–3 WESTLAW —— 223

12–4 Other Databases —— 224

12–5 The Advantages and Disadvantages of Computer-Assisted Legal Research —— 225

CHAPTER 13 Microforms, Floppy Disks, CD-ROM, and Computer-Organized Legal Research —— 230

13–1 Microforms —— 231

13–2 Floppy Disks —— 231

13–3 CD-ROM —— 233

13–4 Computer-Organized Legal Research —— 234

Searching and Sorting a Database —— 235
Word Processing —— 237
The Advantages of Information on Computer —— 237
COLR Products —— 238

PART SIX

RESEARCH STRATEGIES

CHAPTER 14 Legal Research Strategies — 242

14-1 Ready for Legal Research — 243
- *Get the Facts* — 244
- *Analyze the Facts* — 244

14-2 Basic Search Strategy — 245
- *Select the Sovereign* — 245
- *Search Mandatory "Statutory" Authority* — 246
- *Search Mandatory Case Authority* — 246
- *Search Persuasive Case Authority* — 247
- *Search Persuasive Secondary Authority* — 247

14-3 Basic Search Procedure — 247
- *Find the Law* — 248
- *Read the Law* — 250
- *Review the Law* — 250
- *Stop the Search* — 251

14-4 Comprehensive Search Strategy — 252
- *Background and Citations* — 252
- *Quick Read and Outline* — 253
- *Second Read and First Draft* — 254
- *Review and Final Draft* — 254

14-5 Limited Search Strategies — 254
- *Instant Answers* — 254

14-6 Mastering Legal Research — 255

Appendix I The Constitution of the United States — 259

Appendix II Table of Parallel Volume References, U.S. Supreme Court Reporters — 270

Appendix III Table of Selected State Law Sources — 280

Appendix IV Law Library Classification — 301

Glossary — 311

Index — 323

PREFACE

Legal research is an art. It is a specialized knowledge blended with specialized skills. It is the knack for the effective use of law books and other media. The key to its mastery is acquiring a knowledge of the true nature of law books, accompanied by significant experience with their use.

In a candid speech to the Los Angeles Bar Association in 1932, William Mark McKinney, then Editor-in-Chief of the Bancroft-Whitney Company, spoke eloquently about the great value of law books, but tempered his remarks with an admission: "There is no such thing as a one hundred per cent perfect law book." At the end of an unprecedented career with all of the leading law publishers of his time, McKinney explained:

> The lawyer's books! What a part they play in his career, from the time he begins his law school studies to the day when he writes his last brief! What struggles and sacrifices he makes in early days to satisfy his need for these indispensable tools! What hours of intense perusal he gives them when great results hang on his investigation! What problems they solve for him, and what disappointment they sometimes bring when preconceived views are shattered by their cold light! The lawyer does indeed live by his books. Use of them marks nearly every step taken in his journey through professional life. The day when practice could be conducted with only a copy of the Revised Statutes, if it ever existed, is gone forever. In these days the law office without books is but a naked pretense—a hollow shell.
>
> . . . The bar by intelligent criticism can do much to improve the character of its books. A reviewer can only superficially appraise them. The test of their accuracy and value is made by actual use in study, practice and briefing. It is then that the authorities cited are looked up, that the soundness of propositions is determined, that the completeness with which the decisions are cited is ascertained, and that clerical and printers' errors are found. Praise your books when they are found worthy of compliment, for the publisher is eager to learn of satisfaction with his wares. But damn the books heartily when they fail. By judicious praise and hearty blame, when either is deserved, you will earn the lasting gratitude of those who make the lawyer's books.

The law is embodied in words and contained in countless books and other media. But it is a serious mistake to believe that all law books are created equal. They are not. They must be carefully examined and questioned, and used creatively, if their full value is to be obtained.

Most legal research books are sonorous legal bibliographies. They read like publishing house catalogs. The reader is introduced to one book after another, and one feature after another, with little or no attempt to make sense of the books as a whole. The value of each book and each feature is never questioned.

The reader is left with no sense of what books are good and what books are bad; no sense of what books are easy to use and what books are difficult to use; no sense of what books are worth reading, and when, and what books should be left on the shelf.

This book is an "insider's guide" to the art of legal research. I have endeavored to rate fairly the principal books and features I discuss. In general, I have endeavored to describe how these books are actually written, rather than merely parroting the self-serving descriptions of the publishers. In particular, I have drawn on my experience and knowledge acquired inside the Lawyers Co-operative Publishing Company. I know that *no publisher publishes a superior set of law books.*

Inside knowledge is invaluable. In the same way that a navigator's chart is a map of the sea, a law book is a map of the law. If navigators fail to take into account the distortions inherent in their charts, they may go off course and not reach the destination they desire. Similarly, if legal researchers fail to take into account the distortions inherent in the books, they may be deceived and not find the law they are looking for.

This book does not cover every law book. No one can claim an intimate knowledge of every law book. Yet, experienced legal researchers know that some law books are used repeatedly, or should be, while others stay on the shelf, to be used only rarely, if at all. This book, *Basic Legal Research*, covers the principal law books and other media used by general practice lawyers and paralegals in the United States, with a decided emphasis on national sources. If, after reading this book, you want to know more, you can always consult a sonorous legal bibliography, local guide, or specialized text.

Organization of the Text

The text has six parts and four appendixes. Part One, "Preliminary Matters," includes a chapter that introduces legal research through a summary of the U.S. legal system, law publishing, law books, and law libraries, with a section on the purpose of legal research. Appendix I gives the text of the most fundamental document in U.S. legal research, the Constitution of the United States.

The six chapters in Part Two, "Researching Primary Authority," cover the principal sources of the law: cases, statutes, constitutions, court rules, and administrative regulations. Appendix II gives parallel volume references for the U.S. Supreme Court reporters, useful in the study of case law. Part Three, "Researching Secondary Authority," includes two chapters that cover the miscellaneous publications used in legal research. Appendix III gives selected references to law sources in the various states, and Appendix IV presents the Library of Congress Classification system used in most law libraries. Student access to a law library, or to samples of each source discussed, is vital during the study of Parts Two and Three.

Part Four, "Citing the Law," includes a chapter on citation style (emphasizing *The Bluebook: A Uniform System of Citation*, 15th edition, 1991) and a chapter on citators. Access to *The Bluebook* and to a complete set of *Shepard's Citations* would be useful during the study of Part Four. The two chapters in Part Five, "Using Computers and Other Technologies," address the use of high technology in legal research. Finally, Part Six, "Research Strategies," consists of a chapter that puts everything together in a practical format.

Text Design

Each chapter begins with a topic outline followed by a commentary that presents a sample situation in which the student is introduced to the information discussed in the chapter. Chapter objectives follow.

This text was designed to be user-friendly. The lined margins provide ample space for both instructors and students to make notes within each chapter. Key terms are boldfaced and defined at first use, with an alphabetical list of these terms at the end of each chapter.

Further, each chapter contains assessments and other activities to amplify the legal research concepts presented, thus enhancing the learning process. Students are encouraged to write in these books, to complete all assessments and activities, and to keep this text at home or in the office as a handy desk reference.

Other Learning and Teaching Resources

The accompanying *Study Guide* is designed as student support in the study of legal research. Performing its numerous exercises will help the student achieve the objectives of this course.

Each chapter begins with a fill-in Chapter Outline followed by a Before and After section, a Legal Research Concepts activity, a Language of Legal Research vocabulary review, an Applying Principles section, and Research Exercises. Each activity reinforces the information presented in the text and relates it to real-life situations. In addition, systematic review and use of the *Study Guide* may help the student improve test scores and develop critical thinking skills.

To facilitate the teaching and learning process, an *Instructor's Manual* accompanies this text. Included are model course syllabi for classes that meet on the quarter system and for those on semester schedules. In addition, there are answer keys to all review and discussion questions contained in the text, along with tests and answers for each chapter including true/false, multiple-choice, and short-answer problems.

Computer-Assisted Legal Research Tutorial

The software component available with this textbook, *Computer Assisted Legal Research Tutorial*, is designed to instruct each student in using LEXIS and WESTLAW. The software covers basic principles of on-line bibliographic database searching, such as Boolean operators (AND and OR) and correcting over- and under-inclusion. The techniques used in each service are illustrated by escorting the student through specific search simulations. The simulations are off-line, eliminating connect-time charges and the need for a modem.

The software has been written to create and display screens, graphics, and instructional text windows. The tutorial includes a pulldown menu structure which is fully mouse-supported, though a mouse-supported system is not required to operate the software.

The software contains eight lessons which appear in a single scrolling list box. When the student logs onto the program, the Lessons menu scrollbar is positioned at the last lesson accessed. This allows the student to continue easily from where he or she left off.

The eight lessons in the CALR software are:

1. Introduction to CALR
2. Introduction to Searching
3. Searching LEXIS
4. LEXIS Advanced Search Techniques
5. Searching WESTLAW
6. WESTLAW Advanced Search Techniques
7. Shepard's
8. Legal Periodicals

Each lesson contains review questions, and the software will display and print a student report. This report lists the date, lesson name, number of questions answered, and score.

The software also features LEXIS and WESTLAW Search Planners which allow students to enter their search terms and connectors on a fill-in-the-blanks form. The software then displays the proper statement syntax for LEXIS or WESTLAW. The Planners are a valuable educational component in the software, and students will be able to use them separately from the tutorial. In this manner, the Planners will help students formulate their own searches while on the job.

Acknowledgments

The author wishes to acknowledge the contributions of the following reviewers, without whose efforts, suggestions, ideas, and insights this text would not be as valuable a tool as it is.

Susan Dunn, Esq., Coordinator of Legal Research and Writing, Adelphi University Lawyer's Assistant Program, West Hempstead, NY

Jeffrey A. Helewitz, Esq., Adjunct Faculty, Paralegal Programs at New York University, Queens College & Baruch College, New York, NY

Aletha L. Honsowitz, Esq., Lawyer/Librarian, Thomas M. Cooley Law School Library; CALR Instructor, Thomas M. Cooley Law School, Lansing, MI

Honorable Richard D. Huffman, Academic Coordinator, Evening Division, University of San Diego Lawyer's Assistant Program, San Diego, CA

Kathleen Mercer Reed, Esq., Instructor, Legal Assisting Technician Program, University of Toledo Community and Technical College, Toledo, OH

Barbara J. Young, Esq., Academic Coordinator, Legal Assistant Studies, San Jose State University, San Jose, CA

The author also wishes to acknowledge the assistance of Paul Richert, Librarian, for granting special access to the University of Akron Law Library; Doug Martin, for his photography; Paula Grant, for her copyediting; Sue Diehm, for her production editorial assistance; and Ed Huddleston, for his publishing services.

In addition, the author acknowledges the support, friendship, and guidance received throughout this project from Editor Rick Adams. The author gives special thanks to his wife, Sheri, and his sons, Anthony and Brian, for enduring everything.

PART ONE

PRELIMINARY MATTERS

Chapter 1
Introduction to Legal Research

CHAPTER 1 Introduction to Legal Research

OUTLINE

1-1 The U.S. Legal System
    Law Is the Command of a Sovereign
    Common-Law Origins
    The Constitution of the United States
1-2 The Business of Law Publishing
    Law Publishing in the United States
    Why Master Legal Researchers Know "Who Publishes What"
1-3 The Purpose of Legal Research
    The Court May Be Ignorant
    The Way to Win
    What Aaron Burr Said About the Law
    Authority: Primary and Secondary
1-4 Law Books and Law Libraries
    How to Judge a Law Book by Its Cover, and Other Parts
    Visit Law Libraries

COMMENTARY

Your child was born at City Hospital last week, and your father has given you $100 to open a bank account in your child's name. The clerk at the bank says you need a Social Security number to open the account. The clerk at the Social Security Administration says you need a birth certificate to get a number. The clerk at the Health Department says you can't get the birth certificate because City Hospital hasn't filed it yet. The clerk at City Hospital says it takes eight weeks to process the birth certificate, because it is necessary to get the doctor's signature. What are you going to do? Who are you going to believe? What is the law regarding birth certificates? How do you find out?

OBJECTIVES

In this chapter you will learn about the origins and nature of the U.S. legal system, the business of law publishing, and what ties them together: the need to do legal research. You will also learn about law books and law libraries. After reading this chapter, you should be able to:

1. Identify the origins of the U.S. legal system in English history.
2. Explain what the "common law" is.
3. Describe the basic structure of the U.S. legal system.
4. Understand the significance of "federalism" for legal research.

5. Understand the significance of the "separation of powers" for legal research.
6. Appreciate why master legal researchers know "who publishes what."
7. Explain why legal research is necessary.
8. Explain the purpose of legal research.
9. Distinguish "primary" authority from "secondary" authority.
10. Explain why law librarians avoid giving patrons *the* answer to legal questions.

1-1 The U.S. Legal System

It is evident that to do legal research you must have an adequate understanding of the legal system. It is also evident that to have an adequate understanding of the legal system, you must be able to recognize the law in all its forms. In short, you must know the "sources of the law."

The U.S. legal system is complex. We inherited the sophisticated legal system of medieval England, and, to avoid the tyranny of a king, modified it with the Constitution of the United States. As a result, to research U.S. law effectively, a legal researcher must know and appreciate a few fundamental facts, myths, and legends from world, English, and American history.

Law Is the Command of a Sovereign

What is the law? There are many answers to this question, and, together, the answers form our **jurisprudence,** a term used to describe both the philosophy of law and the law collectively. Indeed, one of the encyclopedias covering "all the law of America" is entitled *American Jurisprudence.* (See Chapter 8.) Fortunately, among all the answers, there is one that serves as a beacon for lawyers, law students, paralegals, and legal researchers of all kinds. To paraphrase the great English jurist Sir Edward Coke, *law is the command of a sovereign*.

What a command is, is easy to understand—someone telling you what you can or cannot do—but what is a sovereign? By definition, a **sovereign** is an entity with the power to command. The classic sovereign is the king. Who makes the laws, the commands, that people must follow? The classic answer, still true in many parts of the world today, is that the most powerful person, the one who can enforce obedience, is sovereign.

World history is replete with the conquests, crusades, and wars of men and women who have struggled to rule. These leaders have followed a variety of philosophies and religions. What is the taproot of the U.S. legal system? There is a specific time and place in world history to which it can be traced. The year is 1066 A.D., and the place is England.

Common-Law Origins

On Christmas Day, 1066, William the Conqueror was crowned King of England. It was the climax of the **Norman Conquest,** in which William, living on the Normandy coast of France, crossed the English Channel with his army and deposed the reigning king, Harold.

The Norman Conquest is significant because as sovereign, William exercised his powers in unprecedented ways. Unlike the previous kings of England, who allowed local disputes to be resolved by local officials, William decreed that he alone would resolve all disputes. Among other things, William declared that all of the land of England would be titled "of the King," and he parceled out the use of the land in exchange for services to his kingdom, establishing a system known as **feudalism.**

At first, William personally decided disputes all over England. He soon discovered, however, that he couldn't continue to do so, because he couldn't be in two places at once. He couldn't handle important national and international affairs in London, and at the same time be in Scotland to hear various disputes there. William therefore delegated some of his power to decide domestic disputes to representatives by giving them—the first **judges**—the power to decide disputes in his name, subject to his review.

The judges were given large territories to cover on horseback. Each judge would ride into a town and announce that he had come to decide disputes on behalf of the King. After hearing and deciding all the disputes in that town, he announced when he expected to return and rode on to the next town. Each judge went from town to town deciding disputes, "riding a circuit" around and back to the first town.

While on the road, these judges would often pass by each other. They would stop and invite each other to a roadside inn to talk about the cases they had decided. In discussing their cases, they discovered that each of them had, given a similar set of facts, decided the outcome of a case differently.

The judges realized that their comfortable jobs—riding around hearing and deciding cases on behalf of the King—were in jeopardy. They had observed that people have a sense of *simple justice:* that persons in like circumstances should be treated alike. If the peasants complained to the King that his judges were not treating them fairly, because they were not treating persons in like circumstances alike, the King would have their heads! The judges realized that more important than the merits of their individual decisions, their decisions as a whole had to be consistent from territory to territory, from circuit to circuit, across all of England.

The judges agreed to continue to meet regularly. They would keep a record of the facts they found in each case, their reasoning in deciding the case, and their decision. At the inn, they would report and study each other's cases. If they had a case that presented a similar fact pattern or issue, they would follow the reasoning and rule of law laid down by the judge in the case that had already been decided.

Following the rule established for the preceding similar case, the **precedent,** is known as the doctrine of *stare decisis* (Latin for "stand by that decided"). By following precedent, the rules of law made by judges in deciding actual cases, the judges, over time, made rules of law common to all of England, known as the **common law.** Restated, the common law is the law made by judges in deciding actual cases—a legal system emphasizing case law.

For example, the judges, not the King, made the "mailbox rule" of contracts: that if a contract offer invites acceptance by mail, a contract is created when the acceptance is mailed. Later judges followed the reasoning of the first judges to decide the issue: that the offeror who invites acceptance by mail should bear the risk of the acceptance being lost in the mail, and be bound by the contract, even if the offeror doesn't actually receive the acceptance.

By following the doctrine of *stare decisis*, the judges put some predictability into their decisions: they would follow the reasoning of the most similar past case, unless they decided that its reasoning would not apply.

Although, since 1066, the kings of England gradually lost most of their sovereign powers to the English legislature (i.e., the Parliament), for over 700 years there were two main sources of law in England: the commands of the king and the rules of law—the common law—made by judges. (See Figure 1-1.) The sovereignty of the king and the common law were carried to English colonies.

The Constitution of the United States

By the mid-1700s, the English had colonized the eastern coast of North America, displacing claims of sovereignty by the native American Indians. The colonists were subjects of the King of England and subject to the common law.

The American colonists, however, saw the tyranny inherent in the sovereignty of a king. They wanted to start new lives in America, yet they were controlled by a King who reigned over 3,000 miles away. Having little or no voice in their government, they were taxed, without representation, mostly for the benefit of the King. Finding this sovereignty intolerable, they revolted. On July 4, 1776, they declared their independence and fought until their colonies were recognized as sovereign states.

In 1787, delegates from the states met in Philadelphia to organize a powerful government to unite the states. Throughout the summer, the delegates, mostly lawyers trained in English law, debated various plans and political theories, and reached a consensus. The result was the Constitution of the United States. (See Figure 1-2 and Appendix I.)

Ratified on June 21, 1788, and put into effect on April 30, 1789, the **Constitution of the United States** is the fundamental law of the land. Two aspects of the Constitution, two aspects of **constitutional law,** are of great significance to the legal researcher: federalism and the separation of powers. Both were designed, in part, to prevent any one person from attaining the power, and the inevitable tyranny, of a king.

Federalism The preamble of the Constitution of the United States proclaims: "We the People of the United States . . . do ordain and establish this Constitution." Ultimate sovereignty was placed in the people, but immediately expressed in the Constitution. The Constitution created a new sovereign—the federal government of the United States of America. Under **federalism,** the federal government is a limited sovereign, having only the powers explicitly or implicitly granted it in the Constitution, primarily the powers granted the Congress in Article I, Section 8.

As the Tenth Amendment reflects, the states retained sovereignty over all powers not granted to the federal government. Thus, the person researching

Figure 1-1 The Medieval English Legal System

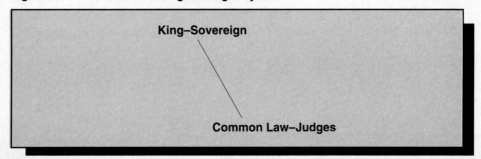

Figure 1-2 The Origins of the Constitution of the United States

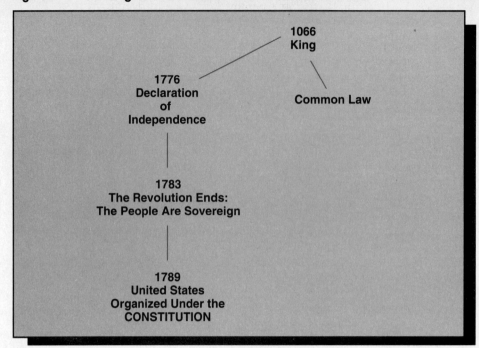

U.S. law must be aware that there are 51 sovereigns in the United States: the federal government (including the District of Columbia) and 50 state governments. (See Figure 1-3.) The first step in legal research is to determine if the subject to be researched is a matter of federal law or state law, and if state law, of what state.

Separation of Powers As Articles I, II, and III reflect, the powers of the federal government, under the Constitution, are divided into three branches: legislative, executive, and judicial. This division, maintained by checks and balances, is the **separation of powers.**

Under Article I, the **legislative** branch, headed by Congress, makes the law. The legislative branch makes new laws. When it passes a law, it makes a reality in the future. Indeed, the *ex post facto* ("after the fact") clauses of the Constitution prohibit criminal laws from having a retroactive effect. **Statutes** are

Figure 1-3 The Federalism Compromise

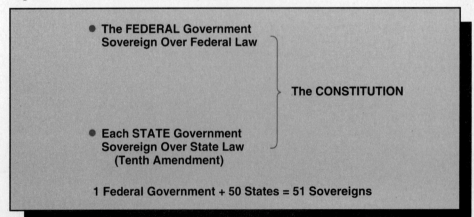

the laws the legislative branch makes, and law from the legislative branch is generally known as **statutory law.**

Under Article II, the **executive** branch, headed by the President, enforces the law. The executive branch sees that the laws are "faithfully executed." When the executive branch enforces a law, it is a reality in the present. To announce the exercise of a discretionary power, the executive may issue an **executive order.** The President, with the advice and consent of the Senate, also negotiates nation-binding agreements with foreign countries, known as **treaties.**

Under Article III, the **judicial** branch, headed by the Supreme Court, interprets the law. The judicial branch reviews the law, and makes law only in deciding actual legal controversies, known as **cases.** When the judicial branch interprets a law, its reality applies to events in the past, and a precedent is laid down for the future. Law from the judicial branch is generally known as **case law.**

Unstated in the Constitution, but understood by the lawyers at the time the Constitution was written and today, is the fact that the Constitution did not displace the common law of England and colonial America. Unless a federal or state constitution or statute changed the common law, U.S. judges continued, and continue today, to apply the common law, as developed in the United States since the American Revolution.

In addition, under the legislative and executive branches, **administrative agencies** have been created. Since the typical legislator or executive does not have sufficient expertise to regulate a specialized area of the law such as aviation or radio transmission, administrative agencies, such as the Federal Aviation Administration (FAA) and the Federal Communications Commission (FCC), have been created and staffed by experts in the field. Within their specialized area of the law, administrative agencies may perform analogous legislative, executive, and judicial functions by making, enforcing, and interpreting their own **regulations.** (See Figure 1–4.)

Although the Constitution does not require the states to establish separation

Figure 1–4 The Separation of Powers Compromise

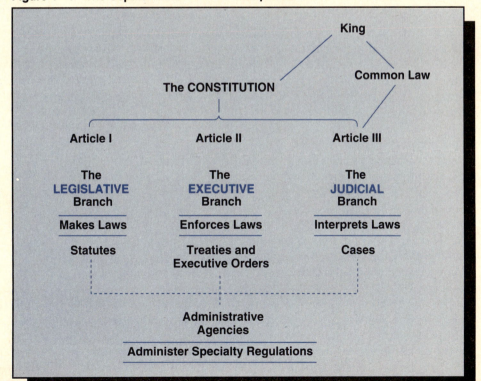

of powers in their constitutions, all the states have governments resembling the federal government. Thus, for the person researching U.S. law, there is another complexity. Not only are there 51 sovereigns, but each sovereign has its own constitution, three branches, and administrative agencies. In a real sense, then, there are 204 significant sources of law in the United States; 51 sovereigns, times four governmental units each: legislative, executive, and judicial branches, and administrative agencies.

1–2   The Business of Law Publishing

Who keeps track of the law coming from 51 sovereigns and the countless entities and subdivisions within them? The federal government and state governments publish some materials, but for a number of reasons, most legal publications are prepared by a private law publishing industry. First, the law in its various forms—statutes, cases, regulations, and the like—is public property, free to be published by anyone. Second, since private publishers are closer to, and more responsive to, the legal marketplace, they can get better products to the market quicker and at less cost than the government does. Third, private publishers may hire better writers and editors, invest more time and money, and advertise more effectively. Finally, private publishers have the incentive of making a profit.

Law Publishing in the United States

After the printing press was brought to England in the 1400s, it became practical to publish court decisions and other laws. However, in medieval England, and later in colonial America, law books were few and far between. Law publishing was not a major industry because the legal profession was not yet a major industry.

In the late 1800s, as the United States experienced the Industrial Revolution, the legal profession grew in stature. By the mid-1800s, U.S. courts had decided hundreds of thousands of cases, thereby developing their own common law. The number of decisions handed down by the U.S. courts grew steadily. Entrepreneurs saw the opportunity to sell "U.S. law" back to lawyers and other interested parties, and the U.S. law publishing industry was born.

In 1856, Hubert Howe Bancroft saw the need for law books in the growing West and founded the Bancroft-Whitney Company. In 1873, Frank Shepard had the idea of creating books that systematically listed when judges had cited other cases and founded the Frank Shepard Company. In 1876, John B. West recognized the need for the systematic publication of state court decisions and founded the West Publishing Company (West). In 1882, James E. Briggs found a better way to publish the decisions of the U.S. Supreme Court and established the Lawyers Co-operative Publishing Company (LCP). In 1887, Matthew Bender had the vision to publish practice-oriented materials written by acknowledged experts, and thus he founded Matthew Bender & Company. And so on.

The late 1800s and early 1900s saw fierce competition for market share and even lawsuits between major competitors. In particular, West established a monopoly in the publishing of court decisions, and LCP established a monopoly in the publishing of selected decisions with analysis. After West sued LCP in 1892, alleging copyright infringement, the companies became testy, if not bitter, rivals.

The Great Depression of the 1930s, and World War II in the 1940s, matured the law publishing industry. During the 1960s, 1970s, and 1980s, when the nation entered the "information age," the legal profession grew rapidly, and the established law publishers reaped the profits. Besides hundreds of thousands of pages of statutes and regulations, there are now over three million cases in U.S. case law, and the flood continues.

Today, the law publishing industry can be analogized to the rental car industry. The "Hertz" of the industry, the largest company and the established leader, is West Publishing Company (West), of St. Paul, Minnesota. The "Avis" is the former Lawyers Co-operative Publishing Company (LCP) of Rochester, New York, now the Lawyers Cooperative Publishing division of Thomson Legal Publishing Inc. (TLPI). TLPI includes LCP's former subsidiary, now a co-division, the Bancroft-Whitney Company of San Francisco, California, and LCP's former subsidiary, now a division of Thomson Professional Publishing, the Research Institute of America (RIA) of New York, New York. TLPI also includes the Clark Boardman Callaghan (CBC) division, a combination of the former Clark Boardman Co. Ltd. of New York, New York, and the former Callaghan & Company of Wilmette, Illinois. TLPI and Thomson Professional Publishing are subsidiaries of Thomson U.S. Inc.

At the heels of the leaders is a group of major competitors, the "Budget," "Dollar," and "Thrifty" types. These competitors include the Bureau of National Affairs, Inc. (BNA), of Washington, D.C.; Commerce Clearing House, Inc. (CCH), of Chicago, Illinois; Matthew Bender & Co. (MB) of New York, New York; Mead Data Central (MDC) of Dayton, Ohio, and its subsidiary The Michie Company (Michie) (pronounced Mickey) of Charlottesville, Virginia; Prentice-Hall Information Services (P-H), a division of Simon & Schuster, Inc., Paramus, New Jersey; and Shepard's/McGraw-Hill, Inc. (Shepard's), of Colorado Springs, Colorado.

There are also hundreds of smaller companies filling the gaps; e.g., Anderson Publishing Company of Cincinnati, Ohio; Banks-Baldwin Law Publishing Co. of Cleveland, Ohio; Business Laws, Inc., of Chesterland, Ohio; Foundation Press, Inc., of Westbury, New York; Little, Brown and Company of Boston, Massachusetts; Pike & Fischer, Inc., of Bethesda, Maryland; and many more.

Law publishing is a multimillion-dollar industry. West's sales are about half a billion dollars a year. In 1989, International Thomson Organization Ltd. purchased LCP for $810 million in cash, to acquire LCP's $200 million in yearly revenue. Several other companies are owned by giant media conglomerates and/or have nine-figure incomes.

Why Master Legal Researchers Know "Who Publishes What"

This book carefully identifies "who publishes what." Why should you care who publishes what? Aren't all law books the same? The answer is "No!"

Law publishing is highly competitive and profitable. Therefore, law publishers usually do not acknowledge their competitor's works in their publications, even if the competitor covers the same law source, no matter how useful such references might be to the legal researcher. Yet, to paraphrase William Mark McKinney, law publishers are human. They miss cases, exclude them, or include them but index them poorly. There is no such thing as a perfect law book. If you can't find what you are looking for in one publisher's book, you need to know the alternatives. You need to know the competitor's book that covers the same law source, so you can use it instead.

As you become experienced in legal research, you will find that different law publishers have different publishing styles: aggressive or cautious, comprehensive or selective, fast or thoughtful, self-supporting or thoroughly cross-referenced. You get more out of a publication when you understand the style it reflects.

Perhaps the best reason why you should know who publishes what is simply this: Every master in the art of legal research knows who published what.

1–3 The Purpose of Legal Research

There's a legal system, and a legal publishing industry to cover it, but why do legal research at all? What's the big deal? Doesn't the judge know all the law anyway? It can't be that complicated, can it?

Legal research is a big deal because the law is a big deal. The law is complicated, but legal research will allow you to cut through it and make effective arguments to the judge. Ethical codes and rules require legal professionals to be competent, and legal research ability is part of that competence.

The Court May Be Ignorant

One of the biggest misconceptions about the law is the notion that the courts know everything there is to know about the law. Courts are run by judges, who are human beings. No one has ever read and digested all of the millions of existing cases, statutes, regulations, and other sources of the law. Moreover, the law is always changing. It is so vast that no one person can ever know all of it. The best one can do is research the law, thoroughly.

Just because judges can't know everything, however, doesn't mean they don't know anything. Just as the average paralegal knows more law than the average layman, and the average lawyer knows more law than the average paralegal, so the average judge knows more law than the average lawyer, and so is worthy of respect. However, because judges don't know every law, they can be convinced by an effective argument. The wise advocate tactfully makes the judge aware of the law, to the advocate's—and the advocate's client's—advantage.

The Way to Win

What is the goal of legal research? It relates to the goal of any advocate in any case: to get the judge to say, "You win."

Stop and think. Why should a judge rule in your favor? *What is the strongest argument you can make to a judge?*

Recall what the first judges realized. Human beings have a sense of simple justice: *that persons in like circumstances should be treated alike*. The challenge is to make the judge's basic sense of justice work in your favor.

The strongest argument you can make to a judge begins with someone else. Someone else was once in circumstances—whether factually, legally, or both—just like yours. If that person went to court and the judge said that he won, you can argue simple justice: persons in like circumstances should be treated alike. That person was in circumstances like yours, and he won. Since he won, the judge should say you win, because persons in like circumstances should be treated alike.

Don't lose sight of the purpose of legal research: *to find a case like yours, where the person like you won*. That is the strongest argument you can make to a judge. It's the way to get the judge to say, "You win." (See Figure 1–5.)

What Aaron Burr Said About the Law

Aaron Burr said, "The law is what's boldly asserted and plausibly maintained." In every case, competent advocates boldly assert the law in their favor. The winner is the advocate who most plausibly maintains what he or she boldly asserts. The most plausible and maintainable assertion you can make is one backed by sound legal research. Tell the judge about the cases like yours, where people like you won. If your research is superior, the judge should conclude either that the cases you found are more like the case at hand than the cases your opponent found, where people like your opponent won, or that the cases cited are equally relevant, but more cases have gone your way. Either way, the judge should say, "You win."

Authority: Primary and Secondary

Law is not only commands argued about, it is also something decided and commanded anew by the sovereign. You should understand the difference between the law itself—firmly rooted in and established by the sovereign—and a mere "bold assertion" of the law, however plausibly maintained by a nonsovereign.

At its best, law is a bold assertion plausibly maintained because a sovereign said it. **Law** is the command of a sovereign. In the United States, no man,

Figure 1–5 Why Do Legal Research?

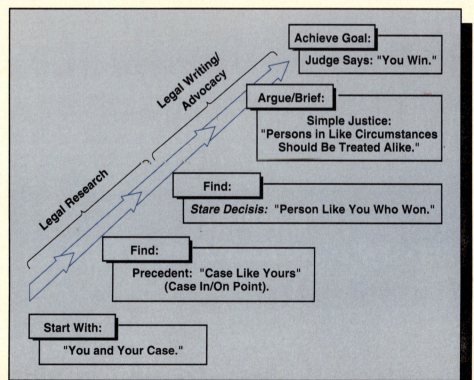

woman, or business is above the law. The Constitution of the United States is the supreme law of the land. As a result of federalism, law can come only from the federal government or from a state government. As a result of the separation of powers, law can come only from the appropriate branch or agency of the sovereign. Only what the appropriate branch or agency of the sovereign commands is the law.

The Constitution is the fundamental law. The legislature makes statutes. The executive issues executive orders. The courts decide cases. Administrative agencies regulate special areas of the law. These acts—the Constitution, statutes, executive orders, court decisions, and administrative regulations—are authoritative acts of the sovereign and are known as **primary authority**. Primary authority is the law itself.

Everything else is **secondary authority**. Everything else includes encyclopedias, law review articles, newspaper polls, personal opinions, company policies, and teacher's assertions.

Any assertion of the law, no matter how bold, made by someone who is not the appropriate representative of the sovereign, acting in that capacity, is not the law. It may be a fine expression of the law, it may explain the law and give it meaning, but it is not the law. (See Figure 1–6.)

Suppose you decide to put an item on layaway at a department store. The clerk says you must deposit 25% of the purchase price. You ask the clerk to accept 20% of the purchase price, which is all you have with you. The clerk snaps, "You must put 25% down, that's the law." Is it? Unless there is a statute, case, or regulation of the sovereign that says so, or a judge who will say so if you take the matter to court, it's not the law. The 25% requirement, however boldly asserted, is just a store *policy*, a guide to decision making, but not the law. The store, perhaps through the manager, could simply decide to change its policy and accept your 20% deposit, and no law would be broken.

Suppose your instructor tells you that you can't successfully be sued for negligence if you didn't proximately cause the harm, but the hurt person sues

Figure 1–6   Legal Authority: Primary and Secondary

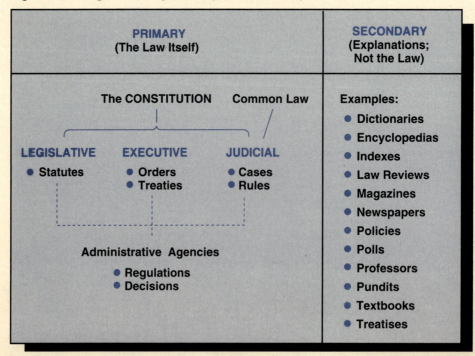

you anyway. The judge will not be impressed if you say: "My instructor said I can't lose." Your instructor is not a sovereign, nor is he the appropriate representative of a sovereign, acting in that capacity, for deciding negligence law. The judge will be impressed if you say something like: "Your honor, may I tell you about several cases like mine, where the persons like me won?"

Does secondary authority have any value? Yes. Courts consider primary authority first and foremost, but if the primary authority is unclear, or if there is no primary authority on the issue at hand, the courts will consider secondary authority. The law in a given circumstance may have been better expressed by a law book writer than by a representative of a sovereign. One might read a book, such as this one, because the author—a teacher—can explain the law better than any representative of a sovereign. In a law review article, a law professor may describe the best laws for the future and suggest a course for the development of those laws that a court would be wise to follow.

As a legal researcher, you must know how to research both primary authority and secondary authority. When you report the results of your research, however, cite to primary authority whenever and wherever possible. Primary authority is the law itself.

1–4 Law Books and Law Libraries

When people with no legal training enter a law library for the first time, they are awed and overwhelmed. They find themselves surrounded by row upon row of impressive-looking books lining the shelves. Earth-tone colors—lime, green, brown, tan, black, and blue—predominate, occasionally splashed with reds and maroons. The titles are mysterious—codes and coordinators; reporters and reviews; statutes and citators—and imposing.

This book explains those impressive-looking books. In particular, it introduces you to the jargon of legal research. Legal research terms are explained and used, because once you understand the jargon of legal research, you can, very often, judge a law book by its cover.

How to Judge a Law Book by Its Cover, and Other Parts

The title of a law book usually reflects its contents. Once you know the jargon, you know what's in the book. For example, books that collect the opinions written by judges are called **reports.** Thus, if you see a book entitled *United States Reports*, you can reasonably infer that it contains opinions written by the appellate judges, the **justices,** on the U.S. Supreme Court.

You should carefully examine every law book the first time you use it. If a book's title is not specific, examine the cover page. The cover page of the *South Western Reporter*, for example, indicates that it collects opinions from courts in Arkansas, Kentucky, Missouri, Tennessee, and Texas.

One part of a law book frequently neglected but well worth reading is the "foreword" or "preface." In prefaces, law book authors and editors often explain with great accuracy what is and what isn't in the book. Many law books have guides explaining how to use the book.

You should also examine tables of contents. Like almanacs, dictionaries, encyclopedias, and other reference books, law books frequently contain more information than you might at first expect. Many law books have two tables of

Rows of "Impressive-Looking" Law Books

Source: © Doug Martin.

contents: one that summarizes the book in breadth and one that outlines the book in depth.

You should be especially alert to law books containing tables of information, which are valuable tools for legal research. For example, some books covering federal law have "code" finding tables. If you know that your legal research problem involves a specific section of the *United States Code,* you can quickly find out if it is referred to in a given book by looking up that "code" section in the code-finding table for that book and consulting the references, if any, listed there.

You should also examine a law book's index. Most indexes are prepared directly from the text, so if a topic is in the index, it, or something about it, is in the book. If it's not in the index, it's probably not in the book. The quality of a book can often be determined by the depth and quality of its index.

Visit Law Libraries

Legal researchers do their best work in law libraries. Like all artists, you should develop a "professional curiosity" about your work. Just as musicians attend concerts and sculptors visit museums to gain more insight into their work, you should visit law libraries whenever possible. In exploring a law library, and in considering the opportunities for doing research there, you will inevitably increase your knowledge and sharpen your skills.

This is not to say, however, that it will be easy to get in. Most law libraries are private, members-only operations.

Most county or court law libraries were created for the use of the judges in that county or court. The judges decide who can use their library, and they usually limit use to attorneys in the local bar association and their employees.

Some law libraries are run by associations of attorneys that limit use to attorneys who are dues-paying members and their employees. Most law firms limit use of their libraries to their own partners, associates, and employees. Most law schools limit the use of their libraries to their own students and faculty.

Fortunately the situation is not as bleak as it may at first appear. Private libraries are gradually opening up their memberships to law and paralegal students. The main branches of many college and public libraries are increasing their law book collections, so you may find the law book you are looking for there. In addition, more and more legal material is being put on computer, accessible to any authorized user.

Your best bet, however, to get into a law library for free is to find the law libraries in your area that are members of the Federal Depository Library Program. (See Figure 1–7.) Under this program, the library gets copies of federal government publications at little or no cost. In return, by federal law, the library must be open to the public.

Even if a law library you wish to use is a Federal Depository Library, you may run into obstacles. Since most books in a law library require training for effective

Figure 1–7 Federal Depository Library Logo

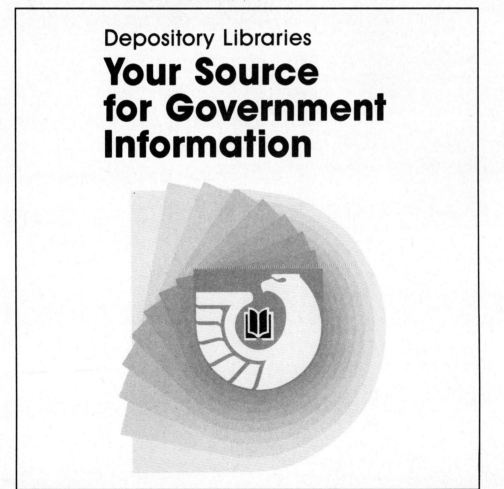

use, law librarians don't welcome the idea of having their doors open to everyone. Regular patrons of law libraries, trained in legal research, are generally quiet, responsible people who don't cause trouble.

For example, a state university law school library may be a Federal Depository Library. But the library may be on the second floor of the law school building and accessible only from within the building. There may be no first-floor signs to direct visitors to the entrance of the library or even mention its existence, let alone announce that it is open to the public.

Outside the entrance, there may be prominent signs indicating that the library is for the use of law school students and faculty only. Again, there may be nothing to indicate that the library is open to the public, except, perhaps, a small sign reading, "Visitors must register."

Inside the library, the desk clerks may question and discourage those who enter who do not look like they belong there. If visitors insist on staying, they are asked to register not just once, but every time they enter the library (which may be unconstitutional). In addition, some staff may refuse to assist patrons who are not law school students.

Thus, you may have to be a detective to find the library, and brave and tactful to get in. It is important that you act and dress appropriately, obey reasonable requests, and cultivate the impression that you belong there by your effective use of the library's resources.

Once librarians become used to your presence, they will be friendlier. If you need help finding what you are looking for, ask the reference librarian. If the librarian doesn't help you find exactly what you are looking for, the librarian's suggestions will usually lead you in the right direction, at least by getting you to think of a solution to your problem yourself.

There is one more thing that you should be aware of when you visit a law library. Law librarians are concerned that their reference advice not be construed as legal advice. Don't ask a law librarian to find "the" answer to your legal problem. That's what lawyers do. Law librarians know that people do not ordinarily ask legal questions out of idle curiosity, and they are wary of accusations of unauthorized law practice, or legal malpractice, being made against them. A law librarian can suggest sources for you to use, but you have to do the research yourself.

SUMMARY

1-1

Law is the command of a sovereign. The classic sovereign is the king. In the Norman Conquest of 1066 A.D., William the Conqueror became King of England. William appointed the first judges, who rode circuits in England. By following precedent, the judges made rules of law common to all of England, known as the common law. The common law is the law made by judges in deciding actual cases, and it was brought to America. In the United States, however, the U.S. Constitution is the supreme law of the land, and the federal government and each state are sovereign; thus, there are 51 sovereigns. The powers of the federal government are divided into three branches: legislative, executive, and judicial. The legislative branch makes the law in the form of statutes. The executive branch enforces the law. The judicial branch interprets the law and makes law—the common law—in deciding cases. Administrative agencies regulate specialized areas of the law.

1-2

Most legal publications are prepared by the private law publishing industry. Many law publishers were founded in the late 1800s. When the nation entered the "information age" in the 1900s, the established law publishers reaped the profits. The largest law publisher is West Publishing Company, of St. Paul, Minnesota. The next largest is the Lawyers Cooperative Publishing division of Thomson Legal Publishing Inc., Rochester, New York. There are several other major law publishers, and, together, they make up a multimillion-dollar industry. In view of the competitiveness of these publishers, good legal researchers know the importance of "who publishes what."

1-3

Courts are run by judges, who are human beings. To get the judge to say, "You win," the strongest argument you can make is that persons in like circumstances should be treated alike. The purpose of legal research, then, is to find a case like yours where the person like you won, and tactfully point it out to the judge. Legal research is how the law, boldly asserted, is plausibly maintained. It is important to distinguish primary authority, the law itself, from secondary authority. You must know how to research both, but when you report the results of your research, cite to primary sources whenever and wherever possible.

1-4

This text explains the books found in law libraries. Once you understand the jargon of legal research, you can, very often, judge a law book by its cover. You should check the title, the cover page, the table of contents, the preface, the tables, and the index. You should visit law libraries whenever possible. Most law libraries, however, are private, members-only operations. Thus, your best bet to get into a law library for free is to find the law libraries in your area that are members of the Federal Depository Library Program and, by federal law, must be open to the public. Act and dress appropriately, obey reasonable requests, and cultivate the impression that you belong by your effective use of the library's resources. Finally, be aware that law librarians are concerned that their reference advice not be construed as legal advice. A law librarian can suggest sources for you use, but you have to do the research yourself.

REVIEW

Key Terms

Before proceeding, review the key terms listed below to be sure you understand each one. If necessary, read over the corresponding section of the chapter. When you are ready to test your understanding, answer the Review Questions.

administrative agencies
case law
cases
common law
Constitution of the United States
constitutional law
executive
executive order
ex post facto
federalism
feudalism
judges
judicial
jurisprudence
justices
law
legislative
Norman Conquest
precedent
primary authority
regulations
reports
secondary authority
separation of powers
sovereign
stare decisis
statutes
statutory law
treaties

Questions for Review and Discussion

1. To what event in 1066 A.D. can the U.S. legal system be traced?
2. Who makes the "common law," and what does it have in common?
3. What is the fundamental law in the United States?
4. How many sovereigns are there in the United States?
5. How are the powers of the federal government divided?
6. Why do master legal researchers know "who publishes what"?
7. Why is legal research necessary?
8. What is the purpose of legal research?
9. Why is primary authority more important than secondary authority?
10. Why do law librarians avoid giving patrons "the" answer to legal questions?

Activities

1. Using an almanac, general encyclopedia, or history book, bone up on American history. Review the circumstances that lead to the writing of documents like the Declaration of Independence, the Constitution, and the Bill of Rights. Understand that the fundamentals of legal research come directly out of American history.
2. Develop the habit of knowing "who publishes what." Take the time to note the name of the publisher of each law book, which is usually found at the bottom of the spine of the book and at the bottom of the title page.
3. Find and visit the nearest law library that is a member of the Federal Depository Library Program. Although to most people the law is foreign and mysterious, to those who know where to look, the law is readily available. The law of the United States is probably the most recorded, organized, and analyzed body of knowledge in the world. Relatively speaking, it's almost as available as it could possibly be. Once you find the law, all you have to do is read it—carefully.

PART TWO

RESEARCHING

PRIMARY AUTHORITY

Chapter 2
Case Law

Chapter 3
Case Finders

Chapter 4
Annotations

Chapter 5
Statutory Law

Chapter 6
Constitutional Law, Court Rules, and Other Promulgations

Chapter 7
Administrative Law

CHAPTER 2 Case Law

OUTLINE

2-1 Judicial Power
    Court Sovereignty
    Legal Reasoning
2-2 Judicial Opinions
    Parts of an Opinion
    Types of Opinions
2-3 Judicial Reports
    Reported Opinions
    National Reporter System
    Federal Court Reports
    State Court Reports
    Unreported Opinions

COMMENTARY

While at the court house, filing suit against City Hospital, you see a notice announcing an opening for a "legal assistant/paralegal" for the City Law Department. Among the duties listed is "some legal research." After determining that City Hospital is privately owned, you apply for the job. During your interview the law director is impressed, but skeptical of your ability to do legal research. Nonetheless, you're hired, called in, and given your first assignment. The mayor wants to display a nativity scene in Central Park during the Christmas holiday season. The law director feels this would violate the establishment clause of the First Amendment, but a book the law director used in law school mentions a case, *Lynch v. Donnelly* [465 U.S. 668 (1984)], that allowed it. You are to locate the case and find out why the nativity scene was allowed in that case.

OBJECTIVES

In this chapter you will learn when the courts have power, how that power is exercised, and how the exercise of that power is explained by the courts in written opinions. Court opinions, the backbone of the common law, are found in a variety of books. After reading this chapter, you should be able to:

1. Accurately describe a court's power to make law.
2. Explain what the *ratio decidendi* of a case is.
3. Explain what the "holding" of a case is.
4. Identify the parts of a judicial opinion.
5. Understand the types of judicial opinions.
6. Describe the courts in a three-level court system.
7. Identify the federal reporters in the National Reporter System.

8. Recognize the regional reporters in the National Reporter System.
9. Identify major reporters outside the National Reporter System.
10. Understand the significance of "unreported" opinions.

2–1 Judicial Power

As discussed in Chapter 1, the U.S. legal system has roots in the common law. The common law is made and maintained by the courts. In a common-law system, the best argument you can make to a judge to win your case is that there was a case like yours where the person like you won.

Court Sovereignty

Under the Constitution of the United States and under state constitutions, the power to interpret the law is given to the courts. In a common-law system, where the doctrine of *stare decisis* is followed, the interpretations themselves become precedents for future cases. Thus, in a sense, the courts not only interpret the law, they also make the law.

It is important at this point not to lose sight of the constitutional separation of powers. The courts do not have sovereign power to simply "dream up" the law like the legislative branch. The courts have sovereign power only when they interpret the law. A court must be confronted with a legal controversy, a case, in order to exercise sovereign power. Only in interpreting the law to decide a case can a court make the law. The court makes precedent.

Not only must a court be confronted with a legal controversy to interpret and make law, it must also be confronted with an *actual* legal controversy. Courts do not hear hypothetical or pretended controversies. Unless an actual case is filed and an actual legal controversy exists, the courts are without power to act. Otherwise, the courts would be "dreaming up" the law like the legislature, which would be fundamentally illegal. A fundamentally illegal act is **unconstitutional.** (See Figure 2–1.)

An infamous case, *In re Copland* [66 Ohio App. 304, 33 N.E.2d 857 (Cuyahoga County Ct. App. 1940)], serves as a memorable example of the limits of judicial power. In *Copland*, the appellate court was asked to review the disbarment of a judge:

> who was found guilty of having written, and caused to be published in a legal journal, an opinion in a fictitious cause purporting to have been heard and decided by him when he well knew that its published report would be relied upon by lawyers and judges as the decision of a court in a litigated controversy.

The judge said:

> [I]t was his purpose to edify the Bench and Bar by his thesis published under the guise of an authentic court finding . . . [and that] he employed this means for the purpose of stating his personal views on a hypothetical legal question for the benefit of the legal professional and the exaltation of his ego [66 Ohio App. at 305, 306].

Maintaining the distinction between primary authority and secondary authority, the appellate court noted that the judge "by deception and concealment would foist his legal views upon his brethren as the judgment of a court of law," and said "[h]is effrontery in so doing is monstrously astounding." [66 Ohio App. at 305.]

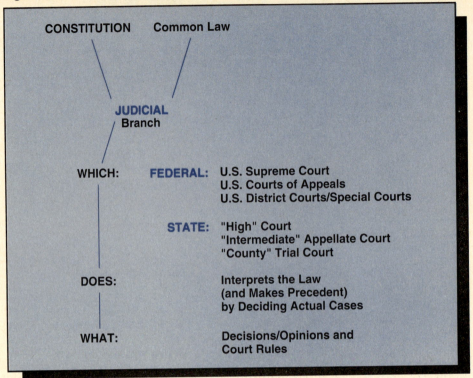

Figure 2-1 The Judicial Branch

In upholding the disbarment of the judge, the appellate court took care to point out that it was acting appropriately within the law: "We have pursued the authorities for like situations. We find none and none are necessary." [66 Ohio App. at 307.] It was a deft declaration that the court, confronted by a real case, had dutifully searched for precedents under the doctrine of *stare decisis* and, finding none, exercised its sovereign power in its best judgment.

Legal Reasoning

In a common-law system, legal reasoning is often reasoning by analogy. When a court is called on to decide a case, it must compare the case to similar cases already decided and follow the most analogous case as precedent. Under the doctrine of *stare decisis*, if the court does not follow the precedent from the most analogous case, it must find a good reason for not doing so.

In deciding a case, a court is confronted with an actual legal controversy, known as the **case at bar.** Ordinarily, there is both a **plaintiff** (i.e., the person or legal entity that sought relief in the trial court) and a **defendant** (i.e., the person or legal entity responding to the plaintiff's claim). A plaintiff, especially a "plaintiff" expecting to be unopposed, may be termed a **petitioner,** and a defendant, especially a "defendant" opposing a petitioner, may be termed a **respondent.** The court must reason out the **decision,** the outcome of the case, declaring whether the plaintiff (or petitioner) wins or the defendant (or respondent) wins. A preliminary decision (e.g., a ruling on a motion) is known as an **order.** The final decision of a court entered into its records is its **judgment.** A determination of the rights and duties of the parties (e.g., in a divorce) is known as a **decree.** A judgment or decree is an **adjudication** of the case.

In deciding a legal controversy, a court usually weighs two types of authority: mandatory authority and persuasive authority. A court must follow **mandatory authority** (also referred to as **binding authority**), which consists of the laws properly enacted by its sovereign's legislature, and the law found in the opinions of its sovereign's next higher or highest court, if any. If mandatory authority is lacking in any way, a court may consider **persuasive authority,** which consists of nonmandatory court opinions within its sovereign, opinions by any other court tracing its origins to the Norman Conquest of 1066, and secondary authority.

The court must reason its way through the legal controversy and arrive at a decision. The basic technique, honed over the centuries, is for the court to determine the point on which the case will turn, known as the *ratio decidendi,* and, if necessary, make a **holding,** a rule of law, upon which to decide the case.

Let's consider an example. Suppose that a power failure causes the traffic light at an intersection to go out. Subsequently, two cars collide head-on, because both drivers, one driving on a two-lane highway and the other driving on a four-lane highway, each thought he had the legal right to proceed through the intersection. (See Figure 2–2.) If the drivers sue each other, how does the court decide who wins?

The parties and the court do legal research. If there is a previous case like this one, known as a **case in point,** it is a simple matter to decide who wins. If a court in a previous case held that at an intersection a driver must yield to the car on the driver's right, then the driver of the car on the right wins.

If there is no previous case like the case at bar, if it is a case without precedent, known as a **case of first impression,** the matter is much more complicated. Suppose that there was no "right-of-way" rule in the sovereign or that the legislature had said that right-of-way does not apply at an intersection with a traffic light. Then what?

If there is no previous case like the case at bar, the court must, nonetheless, analogize from the case, however distant, most like the case at bar. To make a

Figure 2–2 Intersection Example

distinction that master legal researchers recognize, there is often a case **"on point"** that covers the issue implicitly, or by analogy, even if there is no case **"in point"** that covers the issue explicitly, or exactly.

Suppose that in an earlier railroad crossing case, a court had reasoned that the driver of a car must yield to a train because trains are bigger and heavier than cars, more difficult to stop, and, in a sense, a train's railroad is a "bigger" road than a car's highway. If the court in the case at bar decides that the relative size of the roads is the key to deciding which driver must yield at a highway intersection, that becomes the *ratio decidendi* of the case. Making a new rule of law for highway intersections, the court holds that in the event of a traffic light failure, the driver on the smaller highway must yield to the driver on the bigger highway. Following the new rule, the court "logically" decides that the driver on the four-lane highway wins.

Of course, this kind of reasoning by analogy is subject to argument. The court could have ruled that the smaller car must yield to the larger car or that the legislature meant the right-of-way rule to not apply only where there was an *operating* traffic light, and so on. The *ratio decidendi* of a case, the distinction made, is crucial. A different *ratio decidendi* will lead to a different holding and may result in a different decision in the case.

A court may also make extra comment in its opinion, not necessary to the decision, known as *dicta* (plural of *dictum*). Not being necessary to the decision, *dicta* are only secondary authorities. Irrelevant comment (e.g., the judge mentioning that as she decided the case it was snowing outside) is known as **obiter dicta**. Serious comment, however, comment of importance to potential litigants, is known as **considered dicta** and has persuasive authority. For example, the court confronted with the highway intersection case might discuss how it would rule in a rail-rail crossing case. The comment is *dicta*, because it is not about the highway intersection case at bar, but it is serious comment because the court's discussion gives guidance to potential litigants in a future rail-rail crossing case. (See Figure 2–3.)

The nature of legal reasoning can also be understood with a nonlegal example. Suppose a parent must decide which of two children gets the last cookie in the cookie jar. How does the parent decide who eats the cookie?

The parent will decide after first making some distinction—a *ratio decidendi*—in the controversy. For example, the parent might decide that the child who eats the cookie should have clean hands and rule that the first child to wash

Figure 2–3 Legal Reasoning

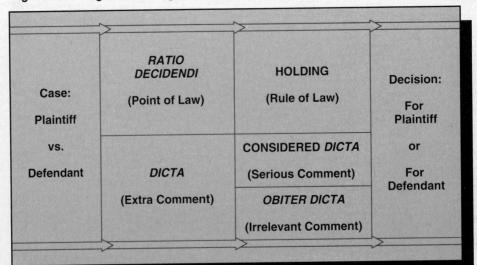

his hands gets the cookie. Or the parent might decide that the child who gets the cookie should first eat all her vegetables and rule that the first child to eat all her vegetables gets the cookie. Or the parent might decide that the children should be treated equally whenever possible and split the cookie in half. In any event, once a distinction is made, a rule can be formulated and a decision easily made. With a precedent established, it will be easier for the parent to decide later who gets the last piece of pie.

2–2 Judicial Opinions

When confronted with a legal controversy, a court has the power to decide who wins. In the course of reasoning out a decision, a court ordinarily develops a *ratio decidendi* and a holding, but, from the winner's point of view, there is no necessity for the court to explain its reasoning. The winner has achieved the goal: the judge said to the winner, "You win."

For the loser, however, a decision that "you lose" without explanation is not emotionally or intellectually satisfying. From the loser's point of view, simple justice requires that persons in like circumstances be treated alike, and the loser believes that in past cases most like his, the persons like him won. The loser wants to know why the judge disagreed. To feel that justice has been done, the loser must be able to see how the judge based the decision against him on other more analogous precedents.

Moreover, for other persons like the winner and loser, the decided case like theirs is a precedent. They want to understand why the winner won and to change their situation, if necessary, to assure themselves that they will win if their case goes to court in the future. In addition, other judges have an interest in understanding why the winner won in the event they must decide a case like that case.

Because of the need for a just explanation, and for the establishment of *ratio decidendi*, holdings, and precedent, it is customary for a court, especially an appellate court reviewing a lower court case, to explain its reasoning and its decision in writing. A court's written explanation of its decision is known as its **opinion**.

Parts of an Opinion

A published appellate judicial opinion customarily consists of the following parts, in the order discussed. (See the case illustrated in Figure 2–4.)

A published appellate judicial opinion begins with the title of the case. Cases are usually titled in the names of the lead parties. The plaintiff, or plaintiffs, are separated from the defendant, or defendants, by *v.* for *versus*, meaning against. Thus, if John Doe and Richard Roe sue Sammy Smith, the title of the case, abbreviated, is *Doe v. Smith*. In a few states, the case title is reversed if and when the defendant appeals.

In criminal cases, the plaintiff is the sovereign. Criminal cases are titled "United States of America" or "State of," "People of" or "Commonwealth of" a state, versus the defendant or defendants (e.g., "United States of America v. Oliver North" is cited *United States v. North*). In forfeiture cases, the case is titled in the name of the sovereign and the contraband seized (e.g., *One 1958 Plymouth Sedan v. Pennsylvania*).

Figure 2–4 Illustrative Case

*See Chapter 3

Figure 2-4 cont.

UNITED STATES v. SHOVEA
Cite as 580 F.2d 1382 (1978)

methamphetamine, and agents observed co-defendant leave residence, carrying suitcase in careful manner, drive to airport in elusive manner, fly to another city where he was met by defendant and drive to defendant's residence. 18 U.S.C.A. § 2; Comprehensive Drug Abuse Prevention and Control Act of 1970, § 401(a)(1), 21 U.S.C.A. § 841(a)(1); U.S.C.A.Const. Amend. 4.

5. Criminal Law ⇐1144.13(3, 5)

On appeal from jury conviction, Court of Appeals must view evidence, both direct and circumstantial, and all reasonable inferences to be drawn therefrom in light most favorable to Government in determining its sufficiency.

6. Conspiracy ⇐47(12)

Evidence supported conviction of conspiracy to manufacture and possess with intent to distribute methamphetamine, a schedule II controlled substance. 18 U.S.C.A. § 2; Comprehensive Drug Abuse Prevention and Control Act of 1970, § 401(a)(1), 21 U.S.C.A. § 841(a)(1).

7. Criminal Law ⇐696(1)

Trial court did not err in failing to grant defense motion to strike testimony of DEA agent, although all of agent's investigatory notes had been destroyed after being turned over to another agent who incorporated the notes into a report.

8. Criminal Law ⇐1171.3

Although evidence did not support assistant United States attorney's closing argument that it was possibility that defendant had given another the idea to use fictitious name of defendant's employer in ordering chemical used to make controlled substance, since defendant's participation in conspiracy to manufacture was substantial, error, if present, was harmless. 18 U.S.C.A. § 2; Comprehensive Drug Abuse Prevention and Control Act of 1970, § 401(a)(1), 21 U.S.C.A. § 841(a)(1).

9. Criminal Law ⇐728(2)

Where defense was aware that comment unsupported by evidence was made in prosecution's closing argument, but defense attorney opted, as trial tactic, not to move court for corrective action at that time and the comment was relatively harmless, trial court properly refused to grant defendant's motion for mistrial.

Jonathan L. Olom, Denver, Colo. (Stanley H. Marks, Denver, Colo., on brief) for appellant Shovea.

Edward L. Kirkwood, Asst. Federal Public Defender, Denver, Colo. (Daniel J. Sears, Federal Public Defender, Denver, Colo., on brief) for appellants Robba and Gaias.

Edward W. Nottingham, Asst. U. S. Atty., Denver, Colo., for appellee (Joseph F. Dolan, U. S. Atty., Denver, Colo., with him on brief for Shovea and Robba, Cathlin Donnell, U. S. Atty., Denver, Colo. (Interim) with him on brief for Gaias.

Before BARRETT, and McKAY, Circuit Judges, and BRATTON, District Judge.*

BARRETT, Circuit Judge.

Scott Shovea (Shovea), Gebbie Robba (Robba) and Stephen Gaias (Gaias) appeal their jury convictions of conspiracy to manufacture and possess with intent to distribute methamphetamine, a schedule II controlled substance, in violation of 18 U.S.C.A. § 2 and 21 U.S.C.A. § 841(a)(1).

Appellants were originally indicted with Geoffrey Hungerford (Hungerford). At the commencement of the trial, the Government dismissed its charges against Hungerford. Thereafter, a mistrial was declared as to Gaias. The trial proceeded as to Shovea and Robba. They were convicted. Subsequent thereto, Gaias was tried individually and convicted. A detailed recitation of the pertinent facts should facilitate our review.

Gaias originally ordered a chemical, phenyl-2-proponone (p–2–p), a primary precursor of methamphetamine, from a New York chemical company under the name of "Jay Edwards." The order was submitted on behalf of "Royce International, 315

---

* Of the District of New Mexico, sitting by designation.

Figure 2-4 cont.

UNITED STATES v. SHOVEA 1391
Cite as 580 F.2d 1382 (1978)

In determining whether the "clear error" rule should be invoked, the entire record must be reviewed and considered. *Adams v. United States,* 375 F.2d 635 (10th Cir. 1967), cert. denied, 389 U.S. 880, 88 S.Ct. 117, 19 L.Ed.2d 173 (1967); *Jennings v. United States,* 364 F.2d 513 (10th Cir. 1966), cert. denied, 385 U.S. 1030, 87 S.Ct. 760, 17 L.Ed.2d 677 (1967). And in weighing whether there was a clear error the most significant factor to be considered is the strength of the case against the defendant. *United States v. Williams,* 445 F.2d 421 (10th Cir. 1971). The evidence against Stevens is substantial; the testimony concerning other stolen vehicles could not have had a significant effect in influencing the jury verdict. *Kotteakos v. United States,* 328 U.S. 750, 66 S.Ct. 1239, 90 L.Ed. 1557 (1946).

452 F.2d, at p. 635.

We hold that the prosecutor's comment did not give rise to clear error. Shovea's participation in the conspiracy was substantial. Error, if present, was harmless. In *United States v. Guerrero,* 517 F.2d 528 (10th Cir. 1975), we stated:

We recently noted in *Young v. Anderson,* 513 F.2d 969 (10th Cir. 1975), citing to *Donnelly v. DeChristoforo,* 416 U.S. 637, 94 S.Ct. 1868, 40 L.Ed.2d 431 (1974):

. . . not every trial error or infirmity which might call for application of supervisory powers correspondingly constitutes a "failure to observe that fundamental fairness essential to the every concept of justice." *Lisenba v. California,* 314 U.S. 219, 236 [62 S.Ct. 280, 290, 86 L.Ed. 166] (1941).

416 U.S. 637, at 642, 94 S.Ct. 1868, at 1871, 40 L.Ed.2d 431.

517 F.2d, at p. 531.

See also: United States v. Hall, 536 F.2d 313 (10th Cir. 1976), cert. denied, 429 U.S. 919, 97 S.Ct. 313, 50 L.Ed.2d 285 (1976); *Sanchez v. Heggie,* 531 F.2d 964 (10th Cir. 1976); cert. denied, 429 U.S. 849, 97 S.Ct. 135, 50 L.Ed.2d 122 (1976).

[9] Shovea's trial attorney was aware that the comment was made. He opted, as a matter of trial tactic, not to move the court for corrective action at that time. Under these circumstances and in view of the relative harmless nature of the comment, the trial court properly refused to grant Shovea's motion for mistrial.

(d), (e) and (f)

Shovea's remaining allegations of error do not merit further detailed discussion. The evidence obtained by the search following execution of the search warrant was proper, as discussed under Robba, *supra;* the trial court's instructions relating to possession were proper; and the Government's experts were properly qualified.

III.

Gaias' sole allegation of error is that the trial court erred in allowing in evidence that which the Government obtained by search and seizure at 3352 West Gill Place following the execution of the search warrant, since "that search warrant was substantially based upon a previous unconstitutional search of . . . [his] . . . suitcase." This contention is without merit. *See Robba (a), supra.*

WE AFFIRM.

*See Chapter 3

Source: Federal Reporter, Second Series, vol. 580 (St. Paul, MN: West Publishing Company, 1978), pp. 1382–1391. Reprinted with permission.

Not all cases are contested. Some cases, such as bankruptcy, probate, and guardianship cases, are simply titled *"In the Matter of (whatever)"* or, in Latin, *"In re (whatever)."* Some cases can be brought on the application of one party and may be titled *"Ex parte (whoever)."*

If a person can sue as a named plaintiff with a collateral benefit to the general public, the case title may begin *"State ex rel. (whoever v. whoever),"* indicating "State on the relation of the named plaintiff v. defendant." In maritime law, a case title may be simply the name of the affected ship (e.g., *The Titanic*).

The case title usually indicates who appealed, known as the **appellant** or **petitioner,** and who answered the appeal, known as the **appellee** or respondent. In some states a defendant-appellant may be known as the **plaintiff in error.**

Next, the court opinion contains the case's trial or appellate court docket number. The **docket number** is the court's serial number. There are two types of docket numbers. In most courts, the docket number indicates the year the case was filed and when it was filed in relation to the other cases filed that year. In abbreviations, the docket number may also indicate the month filed or the type of case (e.g., civil, criminal, or domestic relations). For example, "CV 92-3-120" might indicate "the 120th civil case filed in the third month of 1992." In some courts, the docket number indicates the sequence of filing from the day the court first opened for business. For example, "No. 12984" might mean "the 12,984th case filed in this court since it opened for business."

If necessary to avoid confusion, the opinion next states the name of the court deciding the case. The date of the decision is listed next, sometimes after the date the case was argued before the court.

Some publishers prepare a short paragraph summary of the entire case, known as the **synopsis** of the case, which appears next. Following that, most publishers prepare brief summaries of the major legal points made in the opinion, known as **headnotes,** because they are editor-made notations that appear before the court's opinion, often at the "head," or top, of the page. Also, the court, or a court employee known as the "Reporter of Decisions," may prepare an official summary or list of the major legal points in the opinion, known as the **syllabus.**

Next, the names (and sometimes the firms) of the attorneys who argued the case are listed. This information can be extremely valuable to a legal researcher because many attorneys, if asked, will share their advice, wisdom, insight—even research references—gained from actually litigating their case like yours.

The justices who decided the case are usually listed next. Note that the abbreviations C.J., JJ., and J. indicate "Chief Justice," "Justices," and "Justice," and are not abbreviations for the first name of a justice.

Next comes the opinion of the court, explaining the decision in the case. Most opinions begin with a brief overview of the case. The classic opinion then goes through the facts of the case in detail, the law that the court deemed applicable, the court's reasoning, and, finally, its decision.

An appellate court can make three kinds of decisions, in whole or in part, for or against the plaintiff, defendant, or both. The appellate court can **affirm,** which means it agrees with the decision of the lower court and that the party who won in the lower court wins. The appellate court can **reverse,** which means it disagrees with the decision of the lower court and that either the party who lost in the lower court wins **(reversal)** or the case itself is dismissed **(vacated).** Or, the appellate court can **remand,** which means it found that the proceedings in a lower court were not fair or complete, so it could not determine who should win and is therefore returning the case to lower court for a new decision to be made after a fair and complete proceeding.

Types of Opinions

An appellate court opinion may consist of several opinions. Appellate courts consist of panels of three to nine justices. Each justice may have his own reasoning for voting to decide a case one way or the other, and each justice may write an opinion explaining his reasoning for voting the way he did.

For example, the custom in the U.S. Supreme Court is for the Justices to hear a case and then to meet in a private conference to vote on and decide the case. If the Chief Justice is in the majority, the Chief Justice assigns one of the Justices in the majority to write the opinion of the Court. If the Chief Justice is not in the majority, the Senior Associate Justice in the majority assigns one of the Justices in the majority to write the opinion of the Court.

If the other Justices who agree with the decision agree with the reasoning written by the assigned Justice, they simply "join" in the opinion of the Court. If a majority of the Justices join together in the opinion of the Court, the opinion is known as a **majority opinion,** and it, along with the decision, is considered precedent. If a Justice agrees with the decision but does not fully agree with the opinion of the Court, the Justice may write a separate opinion, known as a **concurring opinion,** in which other Justices may join.

On occasion, a majority of the Justices may agree on a decision, but a majority is unable to agree on the reasoning. The opinion of the Court is then known as a **plurality opinion,** in which other Justices who agree with the decision may join.

A Justice who disagrees with the decision of the Court may write an opinion explaining the disagreement, known as a **dissenting opinion,** in which other Justices who disagree with the decision may join.

There are two other types of opinions. To signal unity (or to disguise differences), the majority agreeing with the decision may write a joint anonymous opinion, known as a *per curiam* ("by the court") **opinion.** If the court does not deem it necessary to write a full opinion, it may prepare a brief opinion, known as a **memorandum opinion.** Memorandum opinions are ordinarily used for the granting or denial of an application for a writ of *certiorari* (e.g., "cert. granted" or "cert. denied"). A **writ of *certiorari*** is the written order of an appellate court with discretionary jurisdiction (usually the highest court in a three-level court system) stating that it chooses to review a lower court decision and directing the lower court to produce its records for review.

2–3 Judicial Reports

Court opinions (technically, copies of court opinions) are collected and published in books known as **reports.** (See Figure 2–5.) A set of reports is known as a **reporter.** Not all opinions are published in reports, for a number of reasons, including the level of the court involved, discussed next. Unreported decisions and the danger of decisions flooding the U.S. legal system are discussed in the final part of this section.

The federal court system and most state court systems are three-level court systems. (See Figure 2–6.) Some states, having less legal business, have a two-level court system.

The first level in both systems consists of trial courts. The purpose of the trial court is to determine the facts and make the original application of the law. Evidence is presented to a fact finder, judge or jury, and after a verdict is reached, judgment is entered. In the vast majority of cases, the disagreement between the parties is much more a disagreement about the facts than a disagreement about the law. When a trial court applies the law as understood by

Figure 2–5 Case-Decision-Opinion-Report

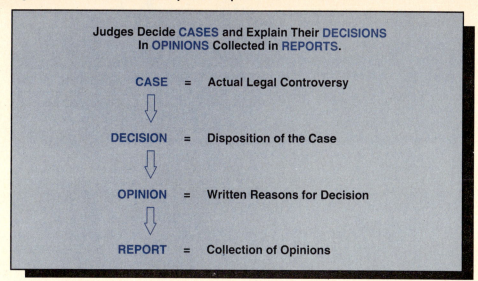

both parties, no new precedent is made. Since there is no new law to be found by researching such a case, they are generally not reported. Trial court opinions are reported only if the trial judge takes the time to write an opinion to explain a novel application of the law in an unusual or unusually significant case.

The second and third levels of a three-level court system (combined in a two-level court system) consist of appellate courts. By reviewing the trial court record, weighing arguments presented in written briefs, and, if necessary, hearing oral argument, appellate courts review the decisions of the trial courts, and in so doing, determine whether the trial courts properly applied the law. Appellate court opinions are generally reported because their opinions must be researched in order to find the law.

The second level of a three-level court system consists of intermediate appellate courts. Generally, the parties to a trial have a right to appeal, to have the acts of the trial judge reviewed, because of the broad discretionary powers given to the trial judge. However, experience shows that many appeals to intermediate appellate courts are without merit. Whether the result of bitterness, confusion, desperation, ignorance, or simply a dramatic attempt to

Figure 2–6 Three-Level Court System

	EXAMPLES	Federal Courts	Illinois Courts	New York Courts
Appellate Courts	"High," or "Supreme," Court	U.S. Supreme Court	Illinois Supreme Court	New York Court of Appeals
	Intermediate Appellate Court	U.S. Court of Appeals (by Circuit)	Illinois Appellate Court	Appellate Term, N.Y. Supreme Court
Trial Courts		U.S. District Court (by District)	Illinois Circuit Court	New York Supreme Court

establish a new precedent, parties often appeal even though the precedents are against them. There is an increasing tendency among the intermediate appellate courts to discourage publishers from reporting opinions in appeals having little or no merit, if only by not recommending certain opinions for publication. Sometimes, to conceal misdeeds by lawyers and judges, even meritorious appeals are not reported.

The third level of a three-level court system consists of the "high," or final, court, usually named the supreme court. The supreme court manages the lower courts and generally has discretion to accept for review only cases involving significant legal issues. Because of their inherent significance, virtually all supreme court opinions are reported.

Reported Opinions

Although the details vary with the sovereign, the court, and the publisher, the publication of court opinions does follow a general pattern.

Court opinions are released chronologically, as the courts decide the cases filed chronologically. The opinion is typed or printed and made part of the court's official record.

Because it is impractical for everyone interested in knowing the law to travel to every courthouse in the country to read every opinion in every court's official record, supreme courts (or the legislature) usually arrange for one government agency or private publisher to publish the **official reports** for the court system. The opinions, however, are not copyrightable. They are public records that anyone is free to publish. Opinions are often published without special authority in books known as **unofficial reports.** The only significance of the official version is that it controls if the unofficial version conflicts with the official version. Since publishers know that nobody would want to buy an inaccurate unofficial version, this rarely happens. "Unofficial" versions are carefully checked against the original and official versions, and they can, in fact, be more reliable than the "official" version. For example, when the editors of the Lawyers Cooperative Publishing Company (LCP) were preparing to reprint the company's unofficial *United States Supreme Court Reports, Lawyers' Edition* (L. Ed.) in 1905, they found many differences between the official records of the court and the court's "official" reports. On the advice of the court that the court records were "more official" than the "official" reports, the editors "reported from the records" to give lawyers the correct version.

If an individual court opinion is published separately, it is known as a **slip opinion.** Court opinions are first collected for reporters in temporary pamphlets, known as **advance sheets,** quickly assembled and distributed to customers to use until enough opinions have been released, and enough time has passed, for the publisher to be able to make a permanent bound volume. The advance sheets usually have the same pagination as the bound volume.

A reporter is a set of bound volumes that publish court opinions. When the features of a reporter change, or the marketing of the set changes, publishers sometimes start a new or higher numerical series of the reporter. For example, when West Publishing Company no longer reported U.S. District Court opinions in its *Federal Reporter* (F.), it started the *Federal Reporter, Second Series* (F.2d).

Court reports collect court opinions in a variety of combinations. Most reporters collect opinions by sovereign and court. LCP's *United States Supreme Court Reports, Lawyers' Edition, Second Series* (L. Ed. 2d), for example, collects the opinions of the U.S. Supreme Court. Some reporters collect opinions by geographic area or region. West's *South Eastern Reporter* (S.E.), for example, collects opinions from the southeastern states of Georgia, North Carolina, South Carolina, Virginia, and West Virginia. Some reporters collect opinions by subject. For example, *United States Tax Cases* (U.S.T.C.), published by Commerce Clearing House, Inc. (CCH), collects opinions in cases deciding federal tax law.

A bound reporter volume ordinarily contains several useful features. The full names and titles of the justices whose opinions appear in the volume may be listed. (See Figure 2–7.) If the bound volume is unofficial, there may be a cross-reference table showing where the official version of an opinion appears in the volume and vice versa. A table, in alphabetical order by case title, may indicate the opinions reported in the volume and the page on which they can be found. (See Figure 2–8.) Other tables may list and cross-reference statutes, court rules, and "words and phrases" interpreted by the opinions in the volume, and where those interpretations can be found. Finally, as will be discussed in Chapter 3, there may be a "digest" for the volume collecting by topic the legal points made in the opinions in the volume.

As we will learn in Chapter 10, reporters are customarily identified by conventional abbreviations, so that a particular opinion can be simply cited by volume number, reporter abbreviation, and page number. For example, the famous U.S. Supreme Court opinion in *Marbury v. Madison,* decided in 1803, can be found in the first volume published by reporter William Cranch, which became the fifth volume of the Government Printing Office's official reporter, the *United States Reporter,* wherein the opinion begins on page 137. It can also be found in the second volume of the *United States Supreme Courts Reports, Lawyers' Edition,* an unofficial reporter published by LCP, wherein the opinion begins on page 60. By custom, all of that can be said as follows: *Marbury v. Madison*, 5 U.S. (1 Cranch) 137, 2 L. Ed. 60 (1803). Being part of the jargon of legal research, reporter abbreviations are noted and used in this book wherever appropriate.

National Reporter System

As discussed in Chapter 1, law publishing was not a major industry in the United States through the early 1800s. Law books, published by local publishers widely scattered around the country, were scarce and did not systematically report the opinions of all appellate courts. The change started in 1879, in St. Paul, Minnesota.

In 1876, John B. and Horatio D. West began publishing a weekly newsletter for Minnesota attorneys that included all the opinions of the Supreme Court of Minnesota. Attorneys in neighboring states, who also received the newsletter, asked the West brothers to include opinions from their states in the newsletter. In 1879, the West brothers began publishing a new set of books, the *North Western Reporter* (N.W.), that included opinions from the states of Iowa, Michigan, Minnesota, Nebraska, North Dakota, South Dakota, and Wisconsin.

The *North Western Reporter* was a hit. It was the only complete and reliable source of appellate court opinions in the region. The concept was quickly applied in other parts of the country. By 1888, the West brothers, incorporated as West Publishing Company, had seven regional reporters covering the states (discussed below under "State Court Reports") and two federal reporters covering the federal courts (discussed below under "Federal Court Reports"), and had achieved a monopoly in publishing all of the appellate court opinions in the country. The system, known as the National Reporter System, remains, with a few additions, the backbone of legal research in the United States. Because of its national scope, the National Reporter System reporters are the most important for a legal researcher to be familiar with. A reference to a National Reporter System volume has meaning throughout the country.

Figure 2–7 Table of Judges

JUDGES
OF THE
FEDERAL COURTS

With Date of Appointment

DISTRICT OF COLUMBIA CIRCUIT

Warren E. Burger,
  Circuit Justice .... 6-23-69 .... Washington, D. C.

CIRCUIT JUDGES

Judge	Date	Location
Spottswood W. Robinson, III, C. J.*	11- 3-66	Washington
J. Skelly Wright*	3-30-62	Washington
Patricia M. Wald	7-26-79	Washington
Abner J. Mikva	9-26-79	Washington
Harry T. Edwards	2-20-80	Washington
Ruth Bader Ginsburg	6-18-80	Washington
Robert H. Bork	2-12-82	Washington
Antonin Scalia	8-17-82	Washington
Kenneth W. Starr	9-20-83	Washington
Laurence H. Silberman	10-28-85	Washington

SENIOR CIRCUIT JUDGES

Judge	Date	Location
David L. Bazelon	2-10-50	Washington
John A. Danaher	3-31-54	West Hartford, Conn.
Carl McGowan	3-27-63	Washington
George E. MacKinnon	5- 6-69	Washington
Roger Robb	5- 6-69	Washington
Malcolm Richard Wilkey	2-25-70	Washington

DISTRICT JUDGES

Judge	Date	Location
Aubrey E. Robinson, Jr., C. J.	11- 3-66	Washington
Gerhard A. Gesell	12- 7-67	Washington
John H. Pratt	6- 7-68	Washington
Barrington D. Parker	12-19-69	Washington
Charles R. Richey	5- 5-71	Washington
Louis F. Oberdorfer	11- 1-77	Washington
Harold H. Greene	5-19-78	Washington
John Garrett Penn	3-23-79	Washington
Joyce Hens Green	5-11-79	Washington
Norma Holloway Johnson	5-12-80	Washington

* Former U. S. District Judge.
617 F.Supp.   VII

Source: Federal Supplement, vol. 617 (St. Paul, MN: West Publishing Company, 1986), p. vii. Reprinted with permission.

Figure 2-8 Table of Cases

CASES REPORTED

ARRANGED UNDER THEIR RESPECTIVE CIRCUITS

DISTRICT OF COLUMBIA CIRCUIT

	Page		Page
Adams v. Hodel—D.C.D.C.	359	McCall v. Shields Associates, Inc.—D.C.D.C.	244
Amdahl Corp. v. Baldrige—D.C.D.C.	501	National Clients Council, Inc. v. Legal Services Corp.—D.C.D.C.	480
Anonymous v. Federal Deposit Ins. Corp.—D.C.D.C.	509	National Coal Ass'n v. Hodel—D.C.D.C.	584
Bartel v. F.A.A.—D.C.D.C.	190	National Treasury Employees Union v. Cornelius—D.C.D.C.	365
Bartel v. U.S. (Two Cases)—D.C.D.C.	190	SDS Biotech Corp. v. E.P.A.—D.C.D.C.	319
Chase v. Pan-Pacific Broadcasting, Inc.—D.C.D.C.	1414	Shurberg Broadcasting of Hartford, Inc. v. F.C.C.—D.C.D.C.	825
Crane v. Dole—D.C.D.C.	156	Slade v. United States of Mexico—D.C.D.C.	351
Endres v. Helms—D.C.D.C.	1260	Sullivan v. Veterans Admin.—D.C.D.C.	258
Hirschfeld v. S.E.C.—D.C.D.C.	262	Texasgulf, Inc. v. United Gas Pipe Line Co. (Mem.)—D.C.D.C.	41
Informatics General Corp. v. Weinberger—D.C.D.C.	331	United Church Bd. for World Ministries v. S.E.C.—D.C.D.C.	837
Kas v. Financial General Bankshares, Inc.—D.C.D.C.	288	Washington Post Co. v. U.S. Dept. of Air Force—D.C.D.C.	602
Lapin v. U.S.—D.C.D.C.	167		
Ledgerwood v. State of Iran—D.C.D.C.	311		

FIRST CIRCUIT

	Page		Page
Bank of New York v. Hoyt—D.C.R.I.	1304	Morgan v. Nucci—D.C.Mass.	1316
Bielass v. New England Safe System, Inc.—D.C.Mass.	682	Perez v. Secretary of Health and Human Services—D.C.Puerto Rico	36
Briggs v. U.S.—D.C.R.I.	1399	Rodriguez v. Muñoz—D.C.Puerto Rico	518
Bulpett v. Heckler—D.C.Mass.	850	Roig Commercial Bank v. Dueño—D.C. Puerto Rico	913
Doe by Roe v. Gaughan—D.C.Mass.	1477	Sands v. Cunningham—D.C.N.H.	1551
Hooksett, Town of, School Dist v. W.R. Grace and Co.—D.C.N.H.	126	Small v. Inhabitants of City of Belfast—D.C.Me.	1567
Local No. 6, Indus. Union of Marine Shipbuilding Workers of America, AFL-CIO v. Bath Iron Works Corp.—D.C.Me.	1046	Stitzer v. University of Puerto Rico—D.C. Puerto Rico	1246
McCormack v. Abbott Laboratories—D.C. Mass.	1521	Town of Hooksett School Dist. v. W.R. Grace and Co.—D.C.N.H.	126

617 F.Supp. XLIII

Source: Federal Supplement, vol. 617 (St. Paul, MN: West Publishing Company, 1986), p. xliii. Reprinted with permission.

Federal Court Reports

The federal court system is a three-level court system with specialized courts.

The highest level in the federal court system, the court of last resort, is the U.S. Supreme Court, located, since 1800, in Washington, D.C. The Court assembled in 1790 in New York City, moved to Philadelphia later that year, and released its first opinions in 1792. A private individual, Alexander J. Dallas, who had published a volume of Pennsylvania state court reports, decided to report the opinions of the other "Pennsylvania" court. Covering the period from 1792 to 1800, Volumes 2, 3, and 4 of Dallas contained the first opinions of the Court. Dallas was succeeded by William Cranch and Henry Wheaton, and, beginning in 1828, a series of private individuals were hired to be the Court's official reporter: Richard Peters, Benjamin C. Howard, J. S. Black, and John William Wallace. The volumes of these early reporters were published by a variety of publishers.

In 1875, the reporter volumes compiled by individuals (known as **nominative reporters**) from Dallas to Wallace were renumbered sequentially and became Volumes 1–90 of the official *United States Reports* (U.S.), published by the U.S. Government Printing Office. (See Appendix II.) Advance sheets for *United States Reports* are available, but they are not published as fast as the advance sheets for the two unofficial reporters discussed next.

Two problems that were encountered with the early Supreme Court reports were availability and price. In 1882, James E. Briggs, attorney for a railroad, was practicing law with his son, William H. Briggs, and an associate, Ernest Hitchcock, in Newark, New York. Briggs needed access to the opinions of the U.S. Supreme Court but was tired of driving his buggy all the way to the library in Rochester (over 30 miles away) to review the opinions. Upon investigation, Briggs and his associates determined that because of the economies of mass production, if 2,500 lawyers subscribed in advance, the reports of the Supreme Court, then selling for as much as $15 per volume, could be published and sold at one dollar per volume.

Briggs and his associates sent out circulars asking lawyers if they would subscribe in advance to a Supreme Court reporter at one dollar per volume. They got back over 3,500 orders. The project was undertaken under the name of the Lawyers Co-operative Publishing Company, because lawyers, with their advance subscriptions, cooperated in the company's initial venture. Ironically, just three years later, Briggs, as president, moved the company to Rochester.

LCP's first publication was the *United States Supreme Court Reports, Lawyers' Edition* (L. Ed.), reporting the decisions of the court from 1792. In 1896, LCP added notations by Professor Walter Rose to the set, and L. Ed with "Rose's Notes" became the constitutional scholar's reporter. Over time, LCP's editors added their own commentary to the set, and, by 1957, under the guidance of Ernest Hugo Schopler, a second series was begun (L. Ed. 2d), regularly featuring in-depth collections of cases known as annotations. (See Chapter 4.) Advance sheets report cases until a bound volume can be published with annotations, a table of cases, and other similar editorial features. The bound volumes also include, where available, summaries of the briefs filed in each case. One advantage of L. Ed. 2d is its inclusion in LCP's Total Client Service Library. (See Chapter 4.)

The third principal source of the opinions of the U.S. Supreme Court is the *Supreme Court Reporter* (S. Ct.) published by West Publishing Company. The *Supreme Court Reporter* was begun in 1882, starting with Volume 106 of the official reports. (See Appendix II.) Advance sheets report cases until a bound volume can be published with a table of cases and other similar editorial features. One advantage of the *Supreme Court Reporter* is its inclusion in West's National Reporter System and West's Topic and Key Number digests. (See Chapter 3.)

The Supreme Court Reporters

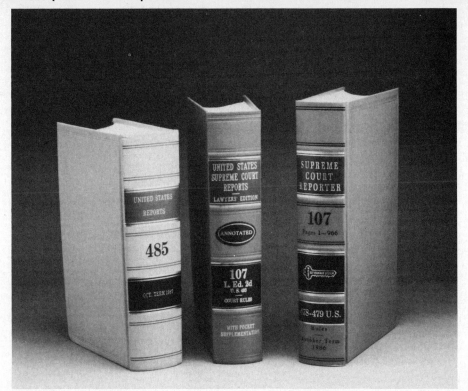

Source: © Doug Martin.

Both L. Ed. 2d and the *Supreme Court Reporter* indicate on their spines the volumes of the *United States Reports* covered in the volume. (See Appendix II.) Both L. Ed. 2d and the *Supreme Court Reporter* have in their volumes exact cross-reference tables to and from the *United States Reports*. Both L. Ed. 2d and the *Supreme Court Reporter* note with an asterisk and page number the pagination of the official reporter in the text of their report of the opinion, a device known as **star pagination,** so that any passage in L. Ed. 2d or in the *Supreme Court Reporter* can be cited to the *United States Reports*. One subtle distinction, that may be important to a legal researcher, can be made between the sets. The *Supreme Court Reporter* never cites L. Ed. 2d, whereas L. Ed. 2d's running heads give the three principal parallel cites for a United States Supreme Court case: *United States Reports* (U.S.), L. Ed. 2d, and the *Supreme Court Reporter*.

Two other publications, both emphasizing the speedy publication of Supreme Court opinions via weekly publication of slip opinions, are worthy of note. The Bureau of National Affairs (BNA) publishes *United States Law Week* (U.S.L.W.) and CCH publishes the *United States Supreme Court Bulletin* (S. Ct. Bull. [CCH]).

The opinions of the Supreme Court are also available on the LEXIS (GENFED;US file) and WESTLAW (SCT and SCT-OLD databases) computer-assisted legal research systems, which will be discussed in Chapter 12.

Most of the opinions of the lower federal courts are not officially reported. Fortunately, in 1880, West undertook the systematic unofficial publication of lower federal court opinions in units of its National Reporter System. First, however, to cover the 18,000 federal cases decided from 1789 to 1879, the cases were arranged alphabetically and numbered in that order, and published in a 31-volume set, *Federal Cases* (F. Cas.). The 31st volume contains cross-reference tables to the reporters in which the cases were originally reported.

In 1879, West began the federal portion of its National Reporter System with the *Federal Reporter* (F.), reporting, chronologically, until 1932, opinions designated for publication by the intermediate courts of appeals and selected trial court opinions from the district courts. In 1932, West began a new series, the *Federal Reporter, Second Series* (F.2d), to include only U.S. Court of Appeals opinions. West started a new unit of the National Reporter System, the *Federal Supplement* (F. Supp.), to report U.S. District Court opinions. (See Figure 2–9.) Advance sheets are published for F.2d and F. Supp. to report cases until a bound volume can be published.

The federal courts of appeals are divided into 11 multistate circuits, the District of Columbia Circuit, and the "Federal Circuit" created in 1982. (See Figure 2–10.) The U.S. Court of Appeals for the Federal Circuit took over the functions of the former U.S. Court of Patent Appeals and the appellate division of the former U.S. Court of Claims. Along with the opinions of the geographic circuit courts of appeals, F.2d now contains the opinions of the U.S. Court of Appeals for the Federal Circuit and the Temporary Emergency Court of Appeals. F.2d also lists decisions without a published opinion.

The opinions of the federal courts of appeals are also available on the LEXIS (GENFED;USAPP and other files) and WESTLAW (CTA, CTA-OLD, and other databases) computer-assisted legal research systems, to be discussed in Chapter 12.

In addition to district court opinions, F. Supp. now includes U.S. Claims Court (Cl. Ct.), Judicial Panel on Multidistrict Litigation (J.P.M.L.), and Special Court Regional Rail Reorganization Act (Regional Rail Reorg. Ct.) opinions.

West also publishes *Federal Rules Decisions* (F.R.D.), a collection of district court opinions not designated for publication, that, since 1939, involve the Federal Rules of Civil Procedure, or, since 1946, involve the Federal Rules of Criminal Procedure. LCP provides similar coverage in *Federal Rules Service* (Fed.

Figure 2–9 West's Leading Federal Reporters

Figure 2-10 U.S. Federal Judicial Circuits

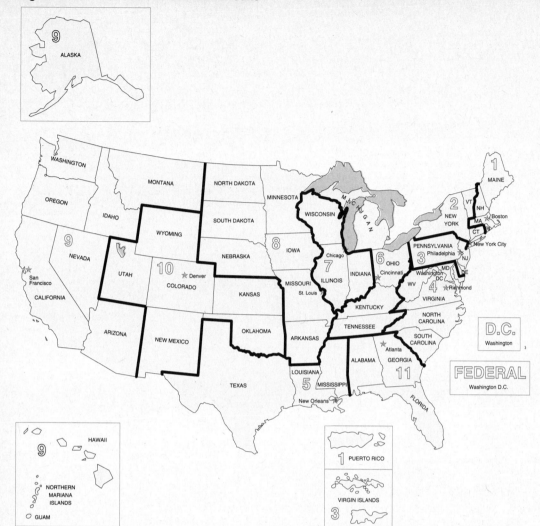

Source: Sample Pages (St. Paul, MN: West Publishing Company, 1986), p. 200. Reprinted with permission.

R. Serv.) and *Federal Rules Service, Second Series* (Fed. R. Serv. 2d) (formerly published by Callaghan & Company).

The opinions of the federal district courts are also available on the LEXIS (GENFED;DIST and other files) and WESTLAW (DCT, DCT-OLD, and other databases) computer-assisted legal research systems, which will be discussed in Chapter 12.

Beyond the reporters already discussed, there are a number of reporters currently covering the specialized federal courts.

Started in 1975, West's *Military Justice Reporter* (M.J.) reports opinions of the U.S. Court of Military Appeals, the various Courts of Military Review, and the Court of Veterans Appeals.

Started in 1979, West's *Bankruptcy Reporter* (Bankr.) reports opinions from the U.S. Bankruptcy Courts and other cases involving bankruptcy law not reported in F. Supp.

West's *United States Claims Court Reporter* (Cl. Ct.) reports opinions of the U.S. Claims Court since 1982, and opinions in cases on appeal from that court.

The Government Printing Office officially publishes the designated opinions of the U.S. Tax Court (formerly the Board of Tax Appeals) in its *Reports of the United States Tax Court* (T.C.). CCH unofficially covers these opinions, along with U.S. Supreme Court, Court of Appeals, and District Court tax opinions in its *United States Tax Cases* (U.S.T.C.). Prentice-Hall (P-H) unofficially covers the same courts in its *American Federal Tax Reports* (A.F.T.R.) and *American Federal Tax Reports, Second Series* (A.F.T.R.2d). CCH and P-H also each publish the Tax Court's undesignated opinions in a set entitled *Tax Court Memorandum Decisions* (T.C.M. [CCH]; T.C.M. [P-H]).

Finally, among federal reports, the Government Printing Office also officially publishes the opinions of the U.S. Court of International Trade (formerly the U.S. Customs Court) in its *Court of International Trade Reports* (Ct. Int'l Trade), also published officially in the *Customs Bulletin and Decisions* (Cust. B. & Dec.), which BNA unofficially covers in its *International Trade Reporter Decisions* (I.T.R.D. [BNA]).

The opinions of the specialized federal courts are also available on the LEXIS and WESTLAW computer-assisted legal research systems to be discussed in Chapter 12.

LEXIS and WESTLAW also cover the federal courts generally. On LEXIS, the GENFED;COURTS2 file contains opinions from all federal courts. On WESTLAW, the ALLFEDS and ALLFEDS-OLD databases contain opinions from all federal courts.

State Court Reports

The reports of state court opinions can be briefly summarized as follows. Every state, at one time or another, has arranged for the official publication of the opinions of its highest court, if not all appellate courts, by a local publisher. West's National Reporter System, which unofficially reports all the appellate court opinions of all the states in a regional or specialized reporter, has become so prevalent, however, that several states have eliminated one or more of their little-used official state reporters, and most of them recognize the appropriate unit of the National Reporter System for their state as their official reporter. In the larger states, there may also be a market for a local publisher to publish the state's court opinions unofficially. The variety of reports for a state can become bewildering.

For example, in 1911, E. A. Feazel of the Cleveland Law Library Association, writing in the *Law Library Journal,* lamented:

> This paper is to be neither a defense of, nor apology for the abominable system, or rather lack of system which has prevailed in reporting the decisions of Ohio courts, especially inferior courts, for the writer has never been connected with any of the publishing houses whose misguided enterprise is responsible for the present conditions, nor with the legislative branch of the state government with which is lodged the power to correct those conditions.
>
> The excuse for this paper is the fact that Ohio reports are so confusing that only a small percentage of Ohio lawyers understand them, coupled with a desire on the writer's part to be of some assistance in helping lawyers and librarians outside the state to comprehend the scope and relative value of the various series of reports. [Feazel, *Ohio Case Law,* 4 LAW LIBR. J. 2 (1911)]

Fortunately, over time, the situation in Ohio improved, and now it is almost simple. In 1982, Anderson Publishing Company (Anderson), which had published the unofficial *Ohio Opinions* (Ohio Op.), *Ohio Opinions, Second Series* (Ohio Op. 2d), and *Ohio Opinions, Third Series* (Ohio Op. 3d), became Ohio's official reporter and started a new set, *Ohio Official Reports.* The only complication with *Ohio Official Reports* is that the State's supreme court opinions are cited as if they were a continuation of the former official set, *Ohio State Reports;* court of appeals opinions are cited as if they were a continuation of the former official set, *Ohio Appellate Reports;* and other law courts are cited as if they were a continuation of the former official, *Ohio Miscellaneous.* Thus, opinions in *Ohio Official Reports* are cited to Ohio St. 3d, Ohio App. 3d, and Ohio Misc. 2d. A final twist occurred in 1991, when Anderson's contract expired, and West became Ohio's official reporter, taking over publication of *Ohio Official Reports.*

West's National Reporter System covers the states with seven regional reporters. (See Figure 2–11.) Starting in 1879 with the *North Western Reporter* (N.W., N.W.2d) covering Iowa, Michigan, Minnesota, Nebraska, North Dakota, South Dakota, and Wisconsin, West added the *Pacific Reporter* (P., P.2d) in 1883, now covering Alaska, Arizona, California, Colorado, Hawaii, Idaho, Kansas, Montana, Nevada, New Mexico, Oklahoma, Oregon, Utah, Washington, and Wyoming. In 1885, West added the *North Eastern Reporter* (N.E., N.E.2d), covering Illinois, Indiana, Massachusetts, New York, and Ohio, and the *Atlantic*

Figure 2–11 National Reporter System Map

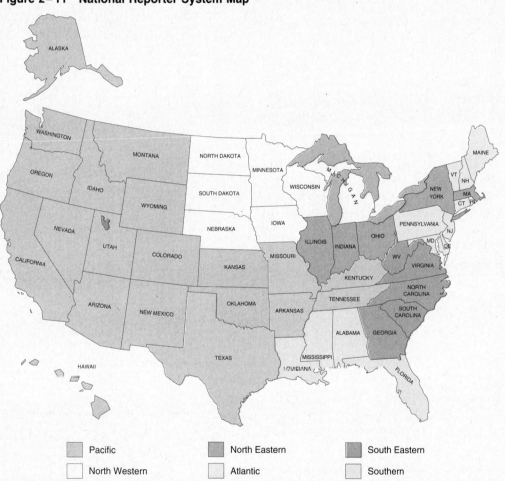

The National Reporter System also includes the Supreme Court Reporter, the Federal Reporter, the Federal Supplement, Federal Rules Decisions, West's Bankruptcy Reporter, the New York Supplement, West's California Reporter, West's Illinois Decisions, West's Military Justice Reporter, and the United States Claims Court Reporter.

Source: West's Law Finder (St. Paul, MN: West Publishing Company, 1990), p. 2. Reprinted with permission.

Reporter (A., A.2d), now covering Connecticut, Delaware, Maine, Maryland, New Hampshire, New Jersey, Pennsylvania, Rhode Island, Vermont, and the District of Columbia. In 1886, West added the *South Western Reporter* (S.W., S.W.2d), covering Arkansas, Kentucky, Missouri, Tennessee, and Texas. In 1887, West added the *Southern Reporter* (So., So. 2d), covering Alabama, Florida, Louisiana, and Mississippi, and the *South Eastern Reporter* (S.E., S.E.2d), covering Georgia, North Carolina, South Carolina, Virginia, and West Virginia. (See Figure 2–12.)

Recognizing the large amount of legal business in one of the nation's most populous states, in 1888, West added a specialized unit to the National Reporter System, the *New York Supplement* (N.Y.S., N.Y.S.2d) to cover New York. Similarly, in 1959, West added *West's California Reporter* (Cal. Rptr.) to cover California. And in 1976, West added *West's Illinois Decisions* to cover Illinois.

The abbreviation of the current official reporter, if any, for the highest court in each state, or the current National Reporter System reporter covering the state, is as follows:

State	Reporter Abbreviation	State	Reporter Abbreviation
Alabama	So. 2d	Montana	Mont.
Alaska	P.2d	Nebraska	Neb.
Arizona	Ariz.	Nevada	Nev.
Arkansas	Ark.	New Hampshire	N.H.
California	Cal. 3d	New Jersey	N.J.
Colorado	P.2d	New Mexico	N.M.
Connecticut	Conn.	New York	N.Y.2d
Delaware	A.2d	North Carolina	N.C.
Florida	So. 2d	North Dakota	N.W.2d
Georgia	Ga.	Ohio	Ohio St. 3d
Hawaii	Haw.	Oklahoma	P.2d
Idaho	Idaho	Oregon	Or.
Illinois	Ill. 2d	Pennsylvania	Pa.
Indiana	N.E.2d	Rhode Island	A.2d
Iowa	N.W.2d	South Carolina	S.C.
Kansas	Kan.	South Dakota	N.W.2d
Kentucky	S.W.2d	Tennessee	S.W.2d
Louisiana	So. 2d	Texas	S.W.2d
Maine	A.2d	Utah	P.2d
Maryland	Md.	Vermont	Vt.
Massachusetts	Mass.	Virginia	Va.
Michigan	Mich.	Washington	Wash. 2d
Minnesota	N.W. 2d	West Virginia	S.E. 2d
Mississippi	So. 2d	Wisconsin	Wis. 2d
Missouri	S.W. 2d	Wyoming	P. 2d

State court opinions are also available on the LEXIS and WESTLAW computer-assisted legal research systems, which will be discussed in Chapter 12. On LEXIS, the STATES;OMNI2 file contains court opinions from all the states, and the STATES;HIGHCT file contains opinions from the highest courts in all the states. On WESTLAW, the ALLSTATES and ALLSTATES-OLD databases contain court opinions from all the states, and the ATL, NE, NW, PAC, SE, and SO databases contain the opinions reported in the Atlantic, North Eastern,

Figure 2–12 States Covered in Specific West Regional Reporters

Regional Reporter	States Covered
Atlantic	Connecticut, Delaware, Maine, Maryland, New Hampshire, New Jersey, Pennsylvania, Rhode Island, Vermont; also District of Columbia
North Eastern	Illinois, Indiana, Massachusetts, New York, Ohio
North Western	Iowa, Michigan, Minnesota, Nebraska, North Dakota, South Dakota, Wisconsin
Pacific	Alaska, Arizona, California, Colorado, Hawaii, Idaho, Kansas, Montana, Nevada, New Mexico, Oklahoma, Oregon, Utah, Washington, Wyoming
South Eastern	Georgia, North Carolina, South Carolina, Virginia, West Virginia
South Western	Arkansas, Kentucky, Missouri, Tennessee, Texas
Southern	Alabama, Florida, Louisiana, Mississippi

North Western, Pacific, South Eastern, and Southern regional reporters, respectively. (See Appendix III for a collection of selected state law sources, including selected state-specific LEXIS files and WESTLAW databases.)

Unreported Opinions

Appellate courts, both intermediate and supreme, are becoming increasingly concerned about the burdens placed on the legal system by an ever-growing flood of appellate court opinions. There are now three million to four million reported cases in U.S. case law, and the number grows by more than 60,000 cases per year. Some argue that the information content of the average case has decreased to the point that the value to society of reporting every case is less than its cost in the forests cut down to make the paper to make the books and the valuable library and office space used to shelve it all.

Many appellate courts have sought to limit the number of their opinions that are reported. With increasing frequency, appellate courts are disposing of cases with memorandum opinions or without opinions. Most appellate courts require attorneys who cite unreported opinions (which should be considered only persuasive authority) to include a copy of the opinion in their briefs to the court. Some appellate courts have gone so far as to prohibit the citing of opinions in briefs where the opinions have not been specifically marked by the appellate court as being "for publication."

As a practical matter, legal researchers must try to find cases like theirs where the persons like them won even if those cases are unreported. Nothing tells the legal researcher what the law is on a topic better than the reasoned opinion of a court, whether or not that opinion is reported. If a copy must be obtained of the unreported case in order to cite it, so be it. Even if a court prohibits the citation of an unreported case, one would be foolish not to tactfully make an argument—based on the unreported case—known to have worked in the past.

So how does the legal researcher find unreported cases on a given topic? Beyond the methods that can also be used for finding reported cases (see Chapter 3), there are three principal methods.

First, some publishing companies, recognizing the importance of unreported opinions, publish summaries and indexes to unreported decisions. For example, in Ohio, the Banks-Baldwin Law Publishing Company publishes the *Ohio Appellate Decisions Index*, which notes the key issues and facts in each case. As the publisher's catalog notes, there are "nearly 8,000 decisions issued each year by Ohio's twelve District Courts of Appeals, less than 10% of which are officially reported." Summaries of unreported decisions may also be found in local bar association newsletters.

Second, most "unreported" opinions, by definition not published in books, have nonetheless been entered into computer databases. Unreported cases can be searched and found on both the LEXIS and WESTLAW computer-assisted legal research systems, to be discussed in Chapter 12.

Third, as a last resort, an "unknown" unreported opinion can sometimes be obtained from the court through a clerk familiar with the case.

SUMMARY

2–1

Under the Constitution of the United States and under state constitutions, the sovereign power to interpret the law, and in so doing make the law, is given to the courts. A court must be confronted with an *actual* legal controversy, a case, in order to exercise sovereign power. When a court is called on to decide a case, it must compare the case to similar cases already decided and follow the most analogous case as precedent. A court must follow mandatory authority, but it may consider persuasive authority. In making a decision, the court will determine the point on which the case will turn, known as the *ratio decidendi*, and, if necessary, make a holding, a rule of law, upon which to decide the case.

2–2

Because of need for a just explanation and for the establishment of *ratio decidendi*, holdings, and precedent, it is customary for a court, especially an appellate court reviewing a lower court case, to explain its reasoning and its decision in writing. A court's written explanation of its decision is known as its opinion. A published appellate judicial opinion customarily consists of the following parts: title of the case, docket number, name of court, date of decision, synopsis, headnotes, syllabus, attorneys' names, justices' names, overview of the case, the facts, the law, the court's reasoning, and the court's decision. The appellate court can affirm, which means it agrees with the decision of the lower court, it can reverse, which means it disagrees with the decision of the lower court, or it can remand, which means it found that the proceedings in a lower court were not fair or complete, and so it is returning the case to lower court. The types of opinions include the majority opinion, the concurring opinion, the plurality opinion, and the dissenting opinion, as well as the *per curiam* opinion, and the memorandum opinion.

2–3

Court opinions are collected and published in books known as reports. A set of reports is known as a reporter. Trial court opinions are reported only if the trial judge takes the time to write an opinion to explain a novel application of the law in an unusual or unusually significant case. Appellate court opinions are generally reported, because their opinions must be researched in order to find the law. Nevertheless, there is an increasing tendency among the intermediate appellate courts to discourage publishers from reporting opinions in appeals having little or no merit. Court opinions are released chronologically. Supreme courts will usually arrange for one government agency or private publisher to publish the official reports for the court system. However, opinions are often published without special authority in unofficial reports. Court reports collect court opinions in a variety of combinations, but most collect opinions by sovereign and court. A bound reporter volume ordinarily contains several useful features, including the full names and titles of the justices, cross-reference tables, alphabetical tables of cases, and tables of statutes construed. Of all the reporters, the National Reporter System reporters are the most important for a legal researcher to be familiar with. Currently, the United States Supreme Court is reported officially in the *United States Reports* (U.S.), published by the Government Printing Office. Unofficially, Supreme Court cases are reported in the *United States Supreme Court Reports, Lawyers' Edition, Second Series* (L. Ed. 2d), published by LCP and the *Supreme Court Reporter* (S. Ct.) published by West. Federal court of appeals cases are reported only in the *Federal Reporter, Second Series* (F.2d), published by West, and federal trial court opinions are reported in the *Federal Supplement* (F. Supp.) published by West. The specialized federal courts are covered by a variety of reporters. As for the state courts, every state, at one time or another, has arranged for the official publication of the opinions of its highest court, if not all appellate courts, by a local publisher. West's National Reporter System, which unofficially reports all the appellate court opinions of all the states in a regional or specialized reporter, has become so prevalent, however, that several states have eliminated one or more of their little-used official state reporters, and most of them recognize the appropriate unit of the National Reporter System for their state as their official reporter. The seven current regional reporters in the National Reporter System, each in their second series, are the *North Western Reporter* (N.W.2d), the *Pacific Reporter* (P.2d), the *North Eastern Reporter* (N.E.2d), the *Atlantic Reporter* (A.2d), the *South Western Reporter* (S.W.2d), the *Southern Reporter* (So. 2d), and the *South Eastern Reporter* (S.E.2d). There are now three million to four million reported cases in U.S. case law, and the number grows by more than 60,000 cases per year. In recent years, however, unreported cases outnumber reported cases by a wide margin.

REVIEW

Key Terms

Before proceeding, review the key terms listed below to be sure you understand each one. If necessary, read over the corresponding section of the chapter. When you are ready to test your understanding, answer the Review Questions.

adjudication
advance sheets
affirm
appellant
appellee
binding authority
case at bar
case in point
case of first impression
certiorari, writ of
concurring opinion
considered *dicta*
decision
decree
defendant
dicta, dictum
dissenting opinion
docket number
headnotes
holding
in point
judgment
majority opinion
mandatory authority
memorandum opinion
nominative reporters
obiter dicta
official reports

on point
opinion
order
per curiam opinion
persuasive authority
petitioner
plaintiff
plaintiff in error
plurality opinion
ratio decidendi
remand
reporter
reports
respondent
reversal
reverse
slip opinion
star pagination
syllabus
synopsis
unconstitutional
unofficial reports
vacated

Questions for Review and Discussion

1. What can a legislature do in making law that a court cannot do in making precedents?
2. What is the *ratio decidendi* of a case?
3. What is the "holding" of a case?
4. Are headnotes written by the court?
5. How is a plurality opinion different from a majority opinion?
6. How are appellate courts different from trial courts?

7. Name the current National Reporter System reporters that cover the U.S. Supreme Court, the U.S. Courts of Appeal, and the U.S. District Courts.
8. Name the seven regional reporters in the National Reporter System.
9. Name the reporter for the U.S. Supreme Court published by LCP.
10. How many "unreported" opinions are there?

Activities

1. Read through a recent opinion of the U.S. Supreme Court. Notice the Court's concern for detail in stating the facts, its citation of authority in stating the law, and its careful reasoning in reaching a decision.
2. Examine a recent opinion reported in the National Reporter System. Identify the parts of the opinion. Was there a dissenting opinion in the case?
3. Compare and contrast a volume of L. Ed. 2d with a volume of S. Ct. Did you find the cross-reference tables to the *United States Reports*?

CHAPTER 3 Case Finders

OUTLINE

3–1 Case Finders Generally
    Citations
    Casebooks
    Lawyers
    Memorandums
    Briefs
3–2 Digests
    How a Digest Is Like an Index
    A Digest Walk-Through
    West's American Digest System
    Other Digests
    The Limitations of Digests
3–3 Other Case Finders
    A.L.R. Annotations
    Computer-Assisted Legal Research
    Shepard's Citations
    Secondary Authority

COMMENTARY

After receiving your oral report about the *Lynch v. Donnelly* case and discussing your findings with the mayor, the law director asks you to prepare a memorandum on the subject of public religious displays. The law director wants you to find as many cases as you can and focus the memorandum on the facts of each case. Heading out of the office on the way to court, the law director mentions that "we" have only the state digest in the office, so you'll have to go down to the County Law Library to use federal digests. Before you realize it, the law director is gone. What digests are you going to use?

OBJECTIVES

In this chapter you will begin to learn how lawyers and legal researchers "find a case like yours where the person like you won." This chapter gives an overview of all the methods of finding cases, with an emphasis on searching specialized indexes known as digests. In particular, you will learn about the digest method of West Publishing Company. After reading this chapter, you should be able to:

1. Identify the essential parts of a case citation.
2. Describe how law students find cases when they begin law school.
3. Explain the purpose of a memorandum of law and its use in finding cases.
4. Recognize briefs as potential case finders.

5. Compare and contrast a digest with an index.
6. Explain "digest topics" and "key numbers."
7. Describe the digest method in detail.
8. Identify the units in the American Digest System.
9. Recognize the limitations of digests as case finders.
10. List the major case finders discussed in other chapters of this book.

3–1 Case Finders Generally

As discussed in Chapter 1, courts have power only to decide actual cases. Actual cases occur **chronologically,** in real-time sequence. As noted in Chapter 2, most reporters report cases chronologically as the courts decide them. Yet, as discussed in Chapter 1, the goal of legal research is to find cases like yours, where the person like you won. In other words, the goal of legal research is to find cases on your topic, or **topically.** If the cases are reported chronologically, how do you find them topically? This is the most fundamental problem in legal research. The solution is using a case finder.

There are two types of case finders: indexes and collections. The value of an index is that the publisher has taken the time to systematically record the location of cases by topic to speed up your research. The value of a collection is that the publisher has taken the time to arrange the cases by topic to reduce the amount of your research. The law's unique indexing case finder, the digest, is discussed in this chapter. The law's unique collection case finder, the annotation, will be discussed in Chapter 4.

Citations

As noted in Chapter 2, case reporters are customarily identified by conventional abbreviations. No matter what type of case finder you use, the reference to the location at which a case opinion may be found in a reporter is customarily given by a **citation** (or **cite**). The citation is usually a reference to the first page of the report of an opinion in a reporter, but it may also be a reference to a specific succeeding page of the opinion, known as a **jump cite** or **pinpoint cite.** Since an opinion may be reported in more than one reporter (e.g., in an official reporter and in an unofficial reporter), it may be found in more than one location. An alternate location reference for a case opinion is known as a **parallel citation** (or **parallel cite**).

As will be discussed in Chapter 10, there are a variety of styles for citing cases and other sources, but one convention is universal. Cases are always cited by volume number, reporter abbreviation, and page (or paragraph) number, in that order. For example, instead of referring to "the U.S. Supreme Court opinion in the case of Moore against the City of East Cleveland, decided in 1977, starting on page 494 of Volume 431 of the *United States Reports,* published by the U.S. Government Printing Office," the custom is to cite the case as follows: *Moore v. City of East Cleveland,* 431 U.S. 494 (1977). An example of a jump cite to the portion of the *Moore* opinion on page 497 of Volume 431 of the *United States Reports* would be as follows: *Moore v. City of East Cleveland,* 431 U.S. 494, 497 (1977). As an example of a citation including a parallel cite, instead of referring to "the New York Court of Appeals opinion in the case of Palsgraf against the Long Island Railroad Co., decided in 1928, starting on page 339 of Volume 248 of the *New York Reports,* and also starting on page 99 of Volume 162 of the *North Eastern Reporter,* the custom is to cite the case as follows: *Palsgraf v. Long Island Railroad Co.,* 248 N.Y. 339, 162 N.E. 99 (1928).

Giving conventional legal citations to legal authorities is important because of the distinction between primary authority and secondary authority. Unless you are an official representative of a part of a sovereign acting in that capacity (i.e., a legislator, executive, judge, or administrator), what you say about the law is not the law itself. It's not primary authority. It is, at best, only secondary authority. When you make a bold assertion about the law, a lawyer or legal researcher will want you to give at least one conventional reference to a primary authority, or a respected secondary authority, that also said so, or implied so. Then, if the lawyer or legal researcher has any doubt as to whether you have stated or interpreted the law accurately, he can look up your reference (made according to the style that will be discussed in Chapter 10) and decide for himself. Get in the habit of citing legal authority, especially primary authority, for your legal assertions.

Casebooks

The case finder lawyers first learn about in law school, and the case finder lawyers in practice most frequently forget about, is the law school casebook.

Most U.S. law schools claim to teach the law by the so-called Socratic method first introduced at Harvard Law School by Christopher Columbus Langdell in 1871. Teaching a course in contract law, Langdell provided his students with a book, now known as a **casebook,** containing a series of carefully selected cases on each topic he covered. Langdell had his students read the cases he collected in his book, then, in class, he carefully questioned them in order to teach them to discover for themselves the rules of law that could be found in the cases.

Langdell's teaching method caught on and became the standard in law schools across the nation. The method has been severely criticized at times, and properly so, because if not properly done, if the questioning is not carefully built around the student's knowledge, the students are tortured and not taught. Nevertheless, the method, in some form or another, has remained a part of the law school experience.

Because of the Socratic, or "casebook," method, professors and scholars at leading law schools have, over the years, written hundreds of casebooks for use in law school courses in almost every subject. What better way is there to find a case on your topic than to use the work of a scholar committed to studying the law? The only limit is that a given casebook may not cover your particular topic or the casebook may be more time-consuming to use than other case finders.

For example, three renowned professors of criminal law, Yale Kamisar, Wayne R. LaFave, and Jerold H. Israel, have co-authored *Modern Criminal Procedure: Cases, Comments and Questions,* published as part of the "American Casebook Series" by West Publishing Company (West). It is an excellent source of significant and instructive cases on the topics that have arisen in modern criminal procedure.

The principal publishers of casebooks are West, Foundation Press, and Little, Brown and Company. Casebooks may be purchased from the publisher or from a law school bookstore. Most lawyers keep at least some of their casebooks from

Casebooks

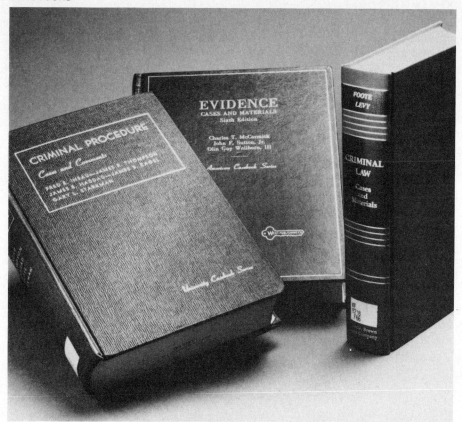

Source: © Doug Martin.

law school. Casebooks may also be found in law libraries according to the Library of Congress Classification system. (See Appendix IV.)

Lawyers

Like a professor or scholar, whose business is it to keep up to date on the law? The answer, of course, is a lawyer. By definition, a **lawyer** is a legal expert. The "average" lawyer has gone to law school, studied for a bar exam, performed legal research, given advice, and handled—through negotiations, hearings, trials, and appeals—a variety of cases. Another obvious and frequently forgotten potential case finder is the "average" lawyer.

Suppose you work in a large law firm and have been given an extensive legal research project. One way to get started is to ask the lawyers in the firm what they know about your topic. There is a good chance that somewhere in their past or in their law practice, at least one of them had a reason to become familiar with your topic. In fact, some lawyers, just to stay current in the law, read advance sheets religiously. Lawyers may, at times, astonish you with what they know "off the tops of their heads." They remember case names, cites, relevant books, their notes from a continuing education seminar, and other similar sources that they can and will refer you to. This information might have taken you hours to discover on your own or you might have missed some of it completely.

In short, lawyers are generally well-trained and experienced legal experts. Use their expertise to help you find your case.

Memorandums

In a well-run law office, the discoveries of the firm's lawyers and legal researchers may already be recorded and relevant to your topic. When a client comes into a law office for advice, it is a common and sensible practice for a lawyer to have the client's legal questions thoroughly researched before any "100%" advice is given.

The usual scenario is for a partner to pose the client's legal question to an associate or paralegal and to have the associate or paralegal research the question in detail. So as to not prejudice the research, the associate or paralegal is not told who in the fact pattern the partner represents.

The associate or paralegal is then directed to prepare a **memorandum of law,** a written discussion of a legal question, objectively reporting the law favoring each side in the fact pattern, as found after researching the topic. The "memo" may also include the researcher's opinion as to who, based on her research, she believes will win if the case goes to court. With a well-written memo in hand, a lawyer can confidently advise the client of the arguments pro and con and the likelihood of the client winning in court.

To avoid duplicating research that has already been done by someone else in the firm, well-run law offices keep a copy of every memorandum ever prepared by lawyers in their offices, indexed by topic. If you work in such a firm, you should check if your topic has already been researched and written up in a memo. If so, all you may have to do is update it.

Briefs

When a case is appealed, appellate courts ordinarily require the lawyers to present their arguments to the court in writing. A formal written argument to a court is known as a **brief.** A brief, as the name suggests, should be brief, because concise arguments are usually more powerful and persuasive than extended arguments. However, because lawyers often deal with complex legal issues and complicated fact patterns, a well-written brief may turn out to be quite lengthy.

Unlike a memorandum, which is objective in nature and intended to be used only within the firm, a brief is public advocacy. In a brief, lawyers argue their client's cause, putting forth the best arguments available for the client: cases like their client's where the person like their client won. Unlike a memorandum, a brief is filed with the court and available to the public. (See Figure 3-1.)

Libraries that serve appellate courts frequently collect the briefs and records filed in the cases before the court. In some states, the briefs and records are microfilmed and available in other libraries as well. If you know a case is relevant to your case, you can often find cases not only by reading the court's opinion, but also by reading the briefs filed by each party's lawyer in the case. You can find cases by using the work of a lawyer doing what a lawyer does best: arguing a client's cause.

3-2 Digests

Soon after West began publishing cases chronologically in the various units of the National Reporter System, its editors realized that lawyers and legal researchers needed a way of finding the cases reported by topic. Their solution was to create a specialized index of the reported cases and the rules of law found therein, known as a **digest.**

Figure 3-1 Excerpts From Two Briefs

Brief #1

IN THE UNITED STATES COURT OF APPEALS
SIXTH CIRCUIT
CINCINNATI, OHIO

JAMES A. TRAFICANT, JR.   )
)
          Petitioner/Appellant   )
) CASE NO: 88-1271
     -vs-   )
) Tax Court
COMMISSIONER OF INTERNAL REVENUE SERVICE) No: 37845-84
)
          Respondent/Appellee   )

BRIEF OF PETITIONER/APPELLANT JAMES A. TRAFICANT, JR.

MATTHEW FEKETE   WILLIAM S. ROSE, JR.,
Attorney for Appellant   Assistant Attorney General
11 Overhill Road   Tax Division
Youngstown, Ohio 44512   c/o GARY R. ALLEN, CHIEF
                                Appellate Section, Tax Division
                                Department of Justice
                                P. O. Box 502
                                Washington, D.C. 20044

3-2 Digests

Figure 3-1 cont.

The Tax Court's reasoning is flawed. The Tax Court cites <u>Helvering v. Mitchell</u>, 303 U.S. 391 (1938). <u>Helvering,</u> at 303 U.S. 397, explains that ordinarily:

> "The difference in degree of the burden of proof in criminal and civil cases precludes application of the doctrine of res judicata. [In the case at bar, the] acquittal was 'merely . . . an adjudication that the proof was not sufficient to overcome all reasonable doubt of the guilt of the accused. '. . .That acquittal on a criminal charge is not a bar to a civil action by the Government, remedial in its nature, arising out of the same facts on which the criminal proceeding was based has long been settled."

Unfortunately for Petitioner, the Tax Court applied this rule without reason.

The criminal case was, by far, no ordinary case. The Petitioner, a public figure, without legal training, acting pro se, and opposed by the Justice Department of the United States, successfully vindicated himself from charges that he accepted bribes in violation of the Racketeer Influenced and Corrupt Organizations Act, 18 U.S.C. §1961 et seq, and charges that he willfully filed a false tax return in violation of §7206(1) of the Internal Revenue Code.

In an ordinary criminal case the jury receives general instructions on the burden of proof (i.e. the burden is on the prosecution to prove each element of the case beyond a reasonable doubt, and if the prosecution does not, the jury is to find for the defendant, whether or not he may be "innocent"). However, in Petitioner's case, Petitioner, a public figure, sought vindication from the charge that he had received a bribe. Acting pro se the Petitioner asked for and received from a judge a special instruction that the

Figure 3-1 cont.

jury was to determine whether <u>or</u> <u>not</u> there was a bribe, not merely whether there was "proof beyond a reasonable doubt" that there was a bribe. Accordingly, the judge specifically instructed the jury on issue of bribery:

> "Ladies and gentlemen of the jury, Count II of the indictment alleges the defendant knowingly signed and filed a false income tax return. If you find that the defendant did receive the bribes alleged in Count I of the indictment, you must consider whether he failed to report the bribes as income on his 1980 income tax return. Even if you find that there was no conspiracy, and that the defendant is not guilty of the RICO offense, you must consider the offense alleged in Count II of the indictment if you find that he accepted the bribes.
>
> However, <u>if you find that the defendant did not receive the bribes alleged in Count I of the indictment, you shall find the defendant not guilty of Count II</u>." [Emphasis Added; Criminal Transcript at p. 3369, lines 8-22. Quoted in Petitioner's Trial Brief, p. 40].

When the jury acquitted the Petitioner on all counts they did not determine "only that reasonable doubt existed that the accused was guilty of the offenses charged." The jury determined that there were <u>no</u> <u>bribes</u>.

Furthermore, the Tax Court ignored the remainder of the Supreme Court's analysis in <u>Helvering v. Mitchell</u>. On the very next page of the official reporter, at 303 U.S. 398, the Supreme Court declared:

> "<u>Where the objective of the subsequent action is punishment, the acquittal is a bar</u>, because to entertain the second proceeding for punishment would subject the defendant to double jeopardy; and double jeopardy is precluded by the Fifth Amendment whether the verdict was an acquittal or a conviction." [Emphasis Added].

That the objective of the subsequent Tax Court case was punishment is evident from the Tax Court's opinion.

3-2 Digests 55

Figure 3-1 cont.

Brief #2

IN THE UNITED STATES COURT OF APPEALS
FOR THE SIXTH CIRCUIT

———————

No. 88-1271
JAMES A. TRAFICANT, JR.,
                    Petitioner-Appellant
v.
COMMISSIONER OF INTERNAL REVENUE,
                    Respondent-Appellee

———————

ON APPEAL FROM THE DECISION OF THE
UNITED STATES TAX COURT

———————

BRIEF FOR THE APPELLEE

———————

STATEMENT OF THE ISSUES

1. Whether the Tax Court correctly found that taxpayer failed to report $108,000 on his 1980 income tax return and that the underpayment of tax was due to fraud within the meaning of Section 6653(b) of the Internal Revenue Code.

2. Whether the Tax Court abused its discretion in the following procedural rulings:

    A.   Refusing to permit taxpayer to act as a _pro se_ co-counsel with his attorney before the Tax Court.

    B.   Limiting the scope of taxpayer's cross-examination as a result of taxpayer's Fifth Amendment claim.

    C.   Admitting into evidence the audio tapes of taxpayer's conversation at the Carabbias' home.

    D.   Declining taxpayer's motions to have the Tax Court judge disqualified.

Figure 3-1 cont.

TABLE OF AUTHORITIES

Page

Cases:

Action Realty Co. v. Will, 427 F. 2d 843
(7th Cir. 1970) -------------------------- 44
Akland v. Commissioner, 767 F. 2d 618 (9th
Cir. 1985) ------------------------------- 22
American Trucking Associations, 310 U.S.
534 (1940) ------------------------------- 43
Anderson v. Bessemer City, 470 U.S. 564
(1985) ----------------------------------- 18,20,22
Anthracite Coal Antitrust Litigation, In re,
82 F.R.D. 364 (M.D. Pa. 1979) ----------- 37
Backos v. United States, 82 F.R.D. 743
(E.D. Mich. 1979) ----------------------- 37,38
Bahoric v. Commissioner, 363 F. 2d 151
(9th Cir. 1966) ------------------------- 23
Barksdale v. Emerick, 853 F. 2d 1359 (6th
Cir. 1988) ------------------------------ 44-46
Baxter v. Palmigiano, 425 U.S. 308 (1976) - 36
Beaver v. Commissioner, 55 T.C. 85 (1970) - 23
Biggs v. Commissioner, 440 F. 2d 1 (6th
Cir. 1971) ------------------------------ 21,22
Bradford v. Commissioner, 796 F. 2d 303
(9th Cir. 1971) ------------------------- 23
Browning v. Foltz, 837 F. 2d 276 (6th
Cir. 1988), cert. denied, 57 U.S.L.W.
3453 (Sup. Ct., Jan. 10, 1989) ---------- 45
By-Prod Corp. v. Armen-Berry Co., 668 F. 2d
956 (7th Cir. 1982) --------------------- 41
Cirillo v. Commissioner, 314 F. 2d 478 (3d
Cir. 1963) ------------------------------ 23
Cupp v. Commissioner, 65 T.C. 68 (1975),
aff'd without published opinion, 559 F.
2d 1207 (3d Cir. 1977) ------------------ 30
Daiflon v. Allied Chemical Corp., 534 F. 2d
221 (10th Cir. 1976), cert. denied, 429
U.S. 886 (1976) ------------------------- 43
Dellacroce v. Commissioner, 83 T.C. 269
(1984) ---------------------------------- 37
Factor v. Commissioner, 281 F. 2d at 100
(9th Cir. 1960) ------------------------- 23
Franklin v. Franklin, 283 S.W. 2d 483 (Mo.
1955) ----------------------------------- 37
Grudin v. Commissioner, 536 F. 2d 295 (9th
Cir. 1976) ------------------------------ 23
Habersham-Bey v. Commissioner, 78 T.C. 304
(1982) ---------------------------------- 23
Helvering v. Mitchell, 303 U.S. 391 (1938)- 21,26-28

Figure 3-1 cont.

> D. <u>The Tax Court properly declined taxpayer's motions to have the Tax Court judge disqualified</u>
>
> Taxpayer claims (Br. 41-50) that Judge B. John Williams, the Tax Court judge who heard this case, was required to recuse himself from this case pursuant to 28 U.S.C. Section 455,[27] because his statements during a pre-trial hearing and his prior employment by the Government reveal bias in favor of the United States. To prevail on appeal, taxpayer must show that Judge Williams abused his discretion in failing to disqualify himself. <u>Barksdale</u> v. <u>Emerick</u>, 853 F. 2d 1359, 1361 (6th Cir. 1988). Taxpayer fails to demonstrate any abuse of discretion because these allegations of partiality are unsupported by the facts in this case.
>
> It is well-established that a judge whose impartiality might reasonably be questioned must recuse himself from the trial. <u>Barksdale</u> v. <u>Emerick</u>, <u>supra</u>; <u>Roberts</u> v. <u>Bailar</u>, 625 F. 2d 125 (6th Cir. 1980). To be sufficient, a litigant's claims of judicial bias must contain specific facts and reasons; conclusory allegations and speculations are not sufficient. <u>Action Realty Co</u>. v. <u>Will</u>, 427 F. 2d 843 (7th Cir. 1970). The standard applied to those allegations is an objective one, <u>i.e.</u>, recusal is necessary if "a reasonable person with knowledge of all the facts would conclude that the judge's impartiality might reasonably be
>
> ---
>
> [27] It is not clear whether 28 U.S.C. Section 455 applies to Tax Court judges since they are not defined as "judges of the United States." Compare 28 U.S.C. Section 451 with Section 7443 of the Internal Revenue Code (26 U.S.C.) (judges of the United States Tax Court serve for a fifteen-year term (although they may be reappointed) rather than serve during "good behavior"); <u>cf</u>., <u>Sharon</u> v. <u>Commissioner</u>, 66 T.C. 515, 533-534 (1978), <u>aff'd</u> 591 F. 2d 1273 (9th Cir. 1978), cert. denied, 442 U.S. 941 (1948). But in any event, regardless of the specific applicable statute, taxpayer's claims of prejudice are unsupported by the record.

Because digests are essentially indexes, they are not themselves cited as authority. Because digest paragraphs are summaries, cases found with digests should always be read before they are cited as authority.

How a Digest Is Like an Index

To appreciate what a digest is, you should first understand how an ordinary index is created and how it is used.

Indexes help where the topics within a text are presented in a varied or sequential order, like chronological order. Since it is impractical for researchers to read an entire book just to find one piece of information or to determine that the one piece of information is not in the book, an index allows researchers to go directly to the information desired without reading the whole book, or to quickly determine that the book, or a portion of it, does not contain the information they desire.

To create an ordinary index, the text to be indexed is read by an editor and divided up into key concepts, words, and phrases. As the editor notes all the key concepts, words, and phrases in a word or a few words known as **entries,** indenting subordinate concepts under major ones where appropriate, the editor records their location in the text by the page numbers at which they appear, known as **references.** The major entries, and then the subordinate entries beneath them, are then arranged alphabetically (in the order of the alphabet from A to Z) carrying the page references with the entries. In final editing, references to other entries, known as **cross-references,** are noted, and the index is complete.

To use an ordinary index, the researcher makes an educated guess as to the editor's choice of words for the major entry for the concept, word, or phrase sought in the text, and then, if appropriate, for the subordinate entry. If and when an appropriate entry is found, the researcher notes the page reference. The researcher then turns to the appropriate page and reads or scans the page until the desired concept, word, or phrase is found.

Case law research is analogous to researching a particular concept, word, or phrase in a large book. (See Figure 3–2.) The cases are reported chronologically, but a legal researcher like you wants to find cases only like yours. It is obviously impractical for you to read every case in every reporter every time you want to find a case like yours or to discover that there has been no case like yours. A digest is a specialized index that allows you to go directly to the case like yours without reading every case, or to quickly determine that there has been no case like yours.

West's editors prepare their digests in the process of preparing case opinions for publication in the National Reporter System. Each case opinion received for publication is read by an editor, who notes major portions of the opinion, usually whole sentences and paragraphs, that appear to be legally significant, because they appear to describe the rules of law being laid down or followed as precedent. The editor summarizes these points of law into **headnotes,** notations to be placed ahead of the judges' opinion in the reporter (and generally falling at the top or "head" of a page), and makes similar, if not identical, summaries to be the entries in the digest, referred to as **digests** or **digest paragraphs.** With each digest paragraph, the editor records the location of its source in the reporter by legal citation reference: the volume, reporter, and page.

West's editors do not arrange the headnotes and the digest paragraphs alphabetically. Instead, they are keyed to an outline of the law originally developed by their company in the 1890s. Headnotes, after being keyed to the outline, are numbered sequentially and remain ahead of the opinion in the

Figure 3-2 Finding Tools

	Organization	Entry	Reference
Ordinary Index	A–Z	Word or Phrase	Page Number
Digest	Outline	Paragraph	Citation (Volume–Reporter–Page)

reporter for each case. The paragraph origin in the text of the opinion for each headnote is indicated in the text by the headnote number in brackets (e.g., [5]). The digest paragraphs reflecting the headnotes are classified to the digest according to the outline.

Modified over the years, West's outline has seven main divisions: Persons, Property, Contracts, Torts, Crimes, Remedies, and Government. Each main division is divided into subdivisions, and the subdivisions are divided into **Topics,** which are the central divisions in the outline. There are more than 400 Topics in the outline. (See Figure 3-3.) Each Topic is then separately outlined according to the nature of the Topic, and the lines in the Topic outline are numbered sequentially. (See Figure 3-4.)

The numerical designation of a line in a Topic outline is known as a **Key Number.** Since there are Key Numbers under each Topic, a Key Number has no significance in itself. A Topic with a Key Number has a significance. If you can determine the Topic and Key Number combination or combinations for cases like yours, the "Key Number" will "unlock" the entry to the digest paragraphs summarizing the cases like yours in the digest. (See Figure 3-5.)

Using a digest is analogous to using an ordinary index, but more is involved. Instead of (1) alphabetically searching entries to (2) find a short entry giving you (3) a page reference to (4) turn to and search the text to check if the information you want is there, as you would with an ordinary index, the digest method is (1) conceptually searching an outline of the law to determine the appropriate Topic and Key Number combinations to (2) find a long entry (i.e., a digest paragraph under the appropriate Topic and Key Number combinations in a digest) giving you (3) a citation reference (volume, reporter, and page) to (4) select the right reporter, turn to the right page, and search the text to check if the case is a case like yours.

A Digest Walk-Through

Let's walk through an example, examining the digest method in more detail. (See Figure 3-6.) Suppose you want to find a case that ruled whether or not a cemetery plot was an "interest in land" such that a contract for the transfer of one would have to be in writing.

The first step in the digest method is to determine the appropriate Topic and Key Number combinations to be searched. One obvious approach to doing this is to become thoroughly familiar with West's outline of the law. Set out in Figure 3-3, the outline can be found in the front of any of West's digest volumes and in West's legal research pamphlet *West's Law Finder*. Ideally, you would recognize that a cemetery plot is a type of property, and thus the appropriate

Figure 3-3 West's Outline of the Law

OUTLINE OF THE LAW

*Digest Topics arranged for your convenience by Seven Main Divisions of Law
For complete alphabetical list of Digest Topics, see Page XIII*

1. PERSONS
2. PROPERTY
3. CONTRACTS
4. TORTS
5. CRIMES
6. REMEDIES
7. GOVERNMENT

1. PERSONS

RELATING TO NATURAL PERSONS IN GENERAL

Civil Rights
Dead Bodies
Death
Domicile
Drugs and Narcotics
Food
Health and Environment
Holidays
Intoxicating Liquors
Names
Poisons
Seals
Signatures
Sunday
Time
Weapons

PARTICULAR CLASSES OF NATURAL PERSONS

Absentees
Aliens
Chemical Dependents
Children Out-of-Wedlock
Citizens
Convicts
Indians
Infants
Mental Health
Paupers
Slaves
Spendthrifts

PERSONAL RELATIONS

Adoption
Attorney and Client
Employers' Liability
Executors and Administrators
Guardian and Ward
Husband and Wife
Labor Relations
Marriage
Master and Servant
Parent and Child
Principal and Agent
Workers' Compensation

ASSOCIATED AND ARTIFICIAL PERSONS

Associations
Beneficial Associations
Building and Loan Associations
Clubs
Colleges and Universities
Corporations
Exchanges
Joint-Stock Companies and Business Trusts
Partnership
Religious Societies

PARTICULAR OCCUPATIONS

Accountants
Agriculture
Auctions and Auctioneers
Aviation
Banks and Banking
Bridges

2 West's Fed.Pr.Dig. 3d   VII   1—1

Figure 3-3 cont.

OUTLINE OF THE LAW

1. PERSONS—Cont'd

PARTICULAR OCCUPATIONS
—Cont'd

Brokers
Canals
Carriers
Commerce
Consumer Credit
Consumer Protection
Credit Reporting Agencies
Detectives
Electricity
Explosives
Factors
Ferries
Gas
Hawkers and Peddlers
Innkeepers
Insurance
Licenses
Manufactures
Monopolies
Physicians and Surgeons
Pilots
Railroads
Seamen
Shipping
Steam
Telecommunications
Theaters and Shows
Towage
Turnpikes and Toll Roads
Urban Railroads
Warehousemen
Wharves

2. PROPERTY

NATURE, SUBJECTS, AND INCIDENTS OF OWNERSHIP IN GENERAL

Abandoned and Lost Property
Accession
Adjoining Landowners
Confusion of Goods
Improvements
Property

PARTICULAR SUBJECTS AND INCIDENTS OF OWNERSHIP

Animals
Annuities
Automobiles
Boundaries
Cemeteries
Common Lands
Copyrights and Intellectual Property
Crops
Fences
Fish
Fixtures
Franchises
Game
Good Will
Logs and Logging
Mines and Minerals
Navigable Waters
Party Walls
Patents
Public Lands
Trade Regulation
Waters and Water Courses
Woods and Forests

PARTICULAR CLASSES OF ESTATES OR INTERESTS IN PROPERTY

Charities
Condominium
Dower and Curtesy
Easements
Estates in Property
Joint Tenancy
Landlord and Tenant
Life Estates
Perpetuities
Powers
Remainders
Reversions
Tenancy in Common
Trusts

PARTICULAR MODES OF ACQUIRING OR TRANS-FERRING PROPERTY

Abstracts of Title
Adverse Possession
Alteration of Instruments
Assignments
Chattel Mortgages
Conversion
Dedication
Deeds
Descent and Distribution
Escheat
Fraudulent Conveyances

VIII
1—2

62 Chapter 3 Case Finders

Figure 3-3 cont.

OUTLINE OF THE LAW

2. PROPERTY—Cont'd

PARTICULAR MODES OF ACQUIRING OR TRANSFERRING PROPERTY—Cont'd

Gifts
Lost Instruments
Mortgages
Pledges
Secured Transactions
Wills

3. CONTRACTS

NATURE, REQUISITES, AND INCIDENTS OF AGREEMENTS IN GENERAL

Contracts
Customs and Usages
Frauds, Statute of
Interest
Usury

PARTICULAR CLASSES OF AGREEMENTS

Bailment
Bills and Notes
Bonds
Breach of Marriage Promise
Champerty and Maintenance
Compromise and Settlement
Covenants
Deposits and Escrows
Exchange of Property
Gaming
Guaranty
Implied and Constructive Contracts
Indemnity
Joint Adventures
Lotteries
Principal and Surety
Rewards
Sales
Subscriptions
Vendor and Purchaser

PARTICULAR CLASSES OF IMPLIED OR CONSTRUCTIVE CONTRACTS OR QUASI CONTRACTS

Account Stated
Contribution

PARTICULAR MODES OF DISCHARGING CONTRACTS

Novation
Payment
Release
Subrogation
Tender

4. TORTS

Assault and Battery
Collision
Conspiracy
False Imprisonment
Forcible Entry and Detainer
Fraud
Libel and Slander
Malicious Prosecution
Negligence
Nuisance
Products Liability
Seduction
Torts
Trespass
Trover and Conversion
Waste

5. CRIMES

Abduction
Abortion and Birth Control
Adulteration
Adultery
Affray
Arson
Bigamy
Blasphemy
Breach of the Peace
Bribery
Burglary
Common Scold
Compounding Offenses
Counterfeiting
Criminal Law
Disorderly Conduct
Disorderly House
Disturbance of Public Assemblage
Dueling
Embezzlement
Embracery
Escape
Extortion and Threats
False Personation

IX   1—3

Figure 3-3 cont.

OUTLINE OF THE LAW

5. CRIMES—Cont'd

False Pretenses
Fires
Forgery
Fornication
Homicide
Incest
Insurrection and Sedition
Kidnapping
Larceny
Lewdness
Malicious Mischief
Mayhem
Miscegenation
Neutrality Laws
Obscenity
Obstructing Justice
Perjury
Piracy
Prize Fighting
Prostitution
Rape
Receiving Stolen Goods
Rescue
Riot
Robbery
Sodomy
Suicide
Treason
Unlawful Assembly
Vagrancy

6. REMEDIES

REMEDIES BY ACT OR AGREEMENT OF PARTIES

Accord and Satisfaction
Arbitration
Submission of Controversy

REMEDIES BY POSSESSION OR NOTICE

Liens
Lis Pendens
Maritime Liens
Mechanics' Liens
Notice
Salvage

MEANS AND METHODS OF PROOF

Acknowledgment
Affidavits
Estoppel
Evidence
Oath
Records
Witnesses

CIVIL ACTIONS IN GENERAL

Action
Declaratory Judgment
Election of Remedies
Limitation of Actions
Parties
Set-Off and Counterclaim
Venue

PARTICULAR PROCEEDINGS IN CIVIL ACTIONS

Abatement and Revival
Appearance
Costs
Damages
Execution
Exemptions
Homestead
Judgment
Jury
Motions
Pleading
Process
Reference
Stipulations
Trial

PARTICULAR REMEDIES INCIDENT TO CIVIL ACTIONS

Arrest
Assistance, Writ of
Attachment
Bail
Deposits in Court
Garnishment
Injunction
Judicial Sales
Ne Exeat
Pretrial Procedure
Receivers
Recognizances
Sequestration
Undertakings

x   1—4

Figure 3-3 cont.

OUTLINE OF THE LAW

6. REMEDIES—Cont'd

PARTICULAR MODES OF REVIEW IN CIVIL ACTIONS

Appeal and Error
Audita Querela
Certiorari
Exceptions, Bill of
New Trial
Review

ACTIONS TO ESTABLISH OWNERSHIP OR RECOVER POSSESSION OF SPECIFIC PROPERTY

Detinue
Ejectment
Entry, Writ of
Interpleader
Possessory Warrant
Quieting Title
Real Actions
Replevin
Trespass to Try Title

FORMS OF ACTIONS FOR DEBTS OR DAMAGES

Account, Action on
Action on the Case
Assumpsit, Action of
Covenant, Action of
Debt, Action of

ACTIONS FOR PARTICULAR FORMS OR SPECIAL RELIEF

Account
Cancellation of Instruments
Debtor and Creditor
Divorce
Partition
Reformation of Instruments
Specific Performance

CIVIL PROCEEDINGS OTHER THAN ACTIONS

Habeas Corpus
Mandamus
Prohibition
Quo Warranto
Scire Facias
Supersedeas

SPECIAL CIVIL JURISDICTIONS AND PROCEDURE THEREIN

Admiralty
Bankruptcy
Equity
Federal Civil Procedure

PROCEEDINGS PECULIAR TO CRIMINAL CASES

Extradition and Detainers
Fines
Forfeitures
Grand Jury
Indictment and Information
Pardon and Parole
Penalties
Searches and Seizures

7. GOVERNMENT

POLITICAL BODIES AND DIVISIONS

Counties
District of Columbia
Municipal Corporations
States
Territories
Towns
United States

SYSTEMS AND SOURCES OF LAW

Administrative Law and Procedure
Common Law
Constitutional Law
International Law
Parliamentary Law
Statutes
Treaties

LEGISLATIVE AND EXECUTIVE POWERS AND FUNCTIONS

Bounties
Census
Customs Duties
Drains
Eminent Domain
Highways
Inspection
Internal Revenue
Levees and Flood Control

XI   1—5

Figure 3–3 cont.

OUTLINE OF THE LAW

7. GOVERNMENT—Cont'd

LEGISLATIVE AND EXECUTIVE POWERS AND FUNCTIONS—Cont'd

Pensions
Post Office
Private Roads
Public Contracts
Public Utilities
Schools
Securities Regulation
Social Security and Public Welfare
Taxation
Weights and Measures
Zoning and Planning

JUDICIAL POWERS AND FUNCTIONS, AND COURTS AND THEIR OFFICERS

Amicus Curiae
Clerks of Courts
Contempt
Court Commissioners
Courts
Federal Courts
Judges
Justices of the Peace
Removal of Cases
Reports
United States Magistrates

CIVIL SERVICE, OFFICERS, AND INSTITUTIONS

Ambassadors and Consuls
Asylums
Attorney General
Coroners
District and Prosecuting Attorneys
Elections
Hospitals
Newspapers
Notaries
Officers and Public Employees
Prisons
Reformatories
Registers of Deeds
Sheriffs and Constables
United States Marshals

MILITARY AND NAVAL SERVICE AND WAR

Armed Services
Military Justice
Militia
War and National Emergency

Source: West's Federal Practice Digest 3d, vol. 2 (St. Paul, MN: West Publishing Company, 1984), pp. vii–xii. Reprinted permission.

Figure 3-4 Searches & Seizures Topic Outline

SEARCHES AND SEIZURES

SUBJECTS INCLUDED

Examination of persons or places for discovery of property stolen or otherwise unlawfully obtained or held, or of evidence of the commission of an offense

Taking into legal custody such property or proofs, or property forfeited for violation of law

Nature and scope of such remedies in general

Constitutional and statutory provisions relating to such searches and seizures

In what cases and to and against whom and in respect of what property they are allowed

Jurisdiction over and proceedings to obtain searches or seizures

Issuance, requisites and validity of search warrants and warrants for seizure, etc.

Execution of warrants, making searches and seizures, proceedings to enforce seizures, and disposition of property seized

Liabilities for wrongfully procuring or making searches or seizures

SUBJECTS EXCLUDED AND COVERED BY OTHER TOPICS

Arrest, searches incidental to, see ARREST

Evidence wrongfully obtained, see CRIMINAL LAW

Forfeiture for crime, grounds, see FORFEITURES and specific topics involving forfeitures

International law, operation as to seizures, see INTERNATIONAL LAW

Particular subjects, searches and seizures for enforcement of laws relating to, see CUSTOMS DUTIES, DRUGS AND NARCOTICS, GAMING, INTERNAL REVENUE, INTOXICATING LIQUORS, LOTTERIES

For detailed references to other topics, see Descriptive-Word Index

---

Analysis

   ⚖ 1. Nature and purpose of remedy.
      2. Constitutional and statutory provisions.
      3. Search warrants.
      3.1. —— In general.
      3.2. —— Necessity for warrant; opportunity to obtain.
      3.3. —— Search or seizure without warrant.
          (1). Circumstances justifying search or seizure.
          (2). —— Probable or reasonable cause in general.
          (3). —— Probable cause in particular cases.
          (4). —— Article in plain view or seized after valid entry.
          (5). —— Offenses in officer's presence; officer protecting himself.
          (6). Automobiles, search of.
          (7). —— Probable cause for search of automobile.

69 West's Fed.Pr.Dig.2d—1

Figure 3-4 cont.

SEARCHES & SEIZURES

69 F P D 2d—2

⚖︎3.3. —— Search or seizure without warrant.—Continued.
    (8). Conduct constituting illegal search; curing illegality.
    (9). Determination of right to search without warrant.
3.4. —— Requisites and validity of warrants in general.
3.5. —— Proceedings for issuance of warrants in general.
3.6. —— Factual showing required for issuance.
    (1). Affidavit or complaint in general.
    (2). Probable or reasonable cause.
    (3). Hearsay, beliefs, conclusions and competency.
    (4). Search of buildings, premises or vehicles.
    (5). Search for articles.
3.7. —— Description of places, persons or things in affidavits or warrants.
3.8. —— Execution and return of warrants.
    (1). In general.
    (2). Places, persons or things within scope of warrant.
3.9. —— Contesting, quashing or vacating proceedings.
4. Seizure proceedings against property forfeited.
5. Disposition of property seized.
7. Unreasonable searches and seizures.
    (1). Constitutional rights and violation thereof in general.
    (2). Application of federal Constitution to states or state officers.
    (3). Application of federal Constitution to territorial officers.
    (4). Application of Constitution to acts of private persons.
    (5). Search warrants.
    (6). —— Issuance and validity.
    (7). —— Affidavits and complaints.
    (8). —— Description.
    (9). —— Execution of warrants.
    (10). Persons, places, and possessions protected from searches and seizures without warrant.
    (11). —— Aliens and enemies.
    (12). —— Arrested persons.
    (13). —— Bankrupts.
    (14). —— Convicts.
    (15). —— Corporations, and corporate officers and records.
    (16). —— Disorderly house.
    (17). —— Game.
    (18). —— Income tax returns.
    (19). —— Intoxicating liquors.
    (20). —— Narcotics or poisons.
    (21). —— Railroad equipment.
    (22). —— Safe deposit boxes.
    (23). —— Stenographer's notes of testimony.
    (24). —— Weapons.
    (25). —— Witnesses and persons compelled to produce evidence.
    (26). Persons entitled to raise question of violation of constitutional rights.
    (27). —— Waiver or consent.
    (28). —— Voluntary character of consent.
    (29). Presumptions and burden of proof.
8. Actions for wrongful search or seizure.
9. Review.

For detailed references to other topics, see Descriptive-Word Index

Source: West's Federal Practice Digest 2d, vol. 69 (St. Paul, MN: West Publishing Company, 1978), pp. 1–2. Reprinted with permission.

Figure 3-5   Searches & Seizures Digest Paragraphs

69 F P D 2d—533   **SEARCHES & SEIZURES**   ⊶7(10)

For references to other topics, see Descriptive-Word Index

len articles therein were in plain view, and where plaintiff's wife consented to their seizure, search and seizure were not unreasonable, and defendants were not liable for damages. 42 U.S.C.A. § 1983; U.S.C.A.Const. Amend. 4.

    Robbins v. Bryant, 349 F.Supp. 94, affirmed 474 F.2d 1342.

⊶**7(10). Persons, places, and possessions protected from searches and seizures without warrant.**

U.S.Cal. 1976. Sanctity of private dwellings is ordinarily afforded the most stringent Fourth Amendment protection; one's expectation of privacy in automobile and of freedom in its operation is significantly different from traditional expectation of privacy and freedom in one's residence. U.S.C.A.Const. Amend. 4.

    U. S. v. Martinez-Fuerte, 96 S.Ct. 3074, 428 U.S. 543, 49 L.Ed.2d 1116, on remand 538 F.2d 858.

Decision of border patrol to locate checkpoint at San Clemente was reasonable in view of needs of law enforcement furthered by such location, high absolute number of apprehensions at such checkpoint, and fact that San Clemente was selected as location where San Diego-to-Los Angeles traffic was lightest, thereby minimizing interference with legitimate traffic. U.S.C.A.Const. Amend. 4.

    U. S. v. Martinez-Fuerte, 96 S.Ct. 3074, 428 U.S. 543, 49 L.Ed.2d 1116, on remand 538 F.2d 858.

Principal protection of Fourth Amendment rights at checkpoints lies in appropriate limitations on scope of stop. U.S.C.A.Const. Amend. 4.

    U. S. v. Martinez-Fuerte, 96 S.Ct. 3074, 428 U.S. 543, 49 L.Ed.2d 1116, on remand 538 F.2d 858.

U.S.Cal. 1974. Bank's keeping records of its customers pursuant to the Bank Secrecy Act does not constitute a "seizure," and inasmuch as access to the records is to be controlled by legal process, the record-keeping provisions did not give rise to an illegal search and seizure. U.S.C.A.Const. Amend. 4; 12 U.S.C.A. §§ 1730d, 1829b, 1951–1959.

    California Bankers Ass'n v. Shultz, 94 S.Ct. 1494, 416 U.S. 21, 39 L.Ed.2d 812.

Regulations of Secretary of Treasury implementing the domestic reporting requirements of the Bank Secrecy Act abridge no Fourth Amendment right of the bank itself inasmuch as bank is a party to the transaction, and requirements for reporting information with respect to abnormally large transactions in currency were not unreasonable. U.S.C.A.Const. Amend. 5; Currency and Foreign Transactions Reporting Act, §§ 206, 222, 31 U.S.C.A. §§ 1055, 1082.

    California Bankers Ass'n v. Shultz, 94 S.Ct. 1494, 416 U.S. 21, 39 L.Ed.2d 812.

see United States Code Annotated

U.S.Cal. 1967. What a person seeks to preserve as private, even in an area accessible to the public, may be constitutionally protected under Fourth Amendment. U.S.C.A.Const. Amend. 4.

    Katz v. U. S., 88 S.Ct. 507, 389 U.S. 347, 19 L.Ed.2d 576.

A person in a telephone booth may rely upon protection of Fourth Amendment, and is entitled to assume that words he utters into mouthpiece will not be broadcast to the world. U.S.C.A.Const. Amend. 4.

    Katz v. U. S., 88 S.Ct. 507, 389 U.S. 347, 19 L.Ed.2d 576.

Government's activities in electronically listening to and recording defendant's words spoken into telephone receiver in public telephone booth violated the privacy upon which defendant justifiably relied while using the telephone booth and thus constituted a "search and seizure" within Fourth Amendment, and fact that electronic device employed to achieve that end did not happen to penetrate the wall of the booth could have no constitutional significance. U.S.C.A.Const. Amend. 4.

    Katz v. U. S., 88 S.Ct. 507, 389 U.S. 347, 19 L.Ed.2d 576.

Search and seizure, without prior judicial sanction and attendant safeguards, conducted by electronic surveillance by way of an electronic listening and recording device attached to outside of public telephone booth from which defendant had placed calls did not comply with constitutional standards, although, accepting account of government's actions as accurate, magistrate could constitutionally have authorized with appropriate safeguards the very limited search and seizure that government asserted in fact took place and although it was apparent that agents had acted with restraint. U.S.C.A.Const. Amend. 4.

    Katz v. U. S., 88 S.Ct. 507, 389 U.S. 347, 19 L.Ed.2d 576.

U.S.Cal. 1967. Except in carefully defined classes of cases, search of private property without proper consent is unreasonable unless it has been authorized by valid search warrant. U.S.C.A.Const. Amend. 4.

    Camara v. Municipal Court of City and County of San Francisco, 87 S.Ct. 1727, 387 U.S. 523, 18 L.Ed.2d 930.

Lessee of ground floor of apartment building had constitutional right to insist that city housing inspector obtain warrant to search his premises and could not constitutionally be convicted of violating city housing code by refusing to consent to warrantless inspection. U.S.C.A.Const. Amend. 4.

    Camara v. Municipal Court of City and County of San Francisco, 87 S.Ct. 1727, 387 U.S. 523, 18 L.Ed.2d 930.

Source: West's Federal Practice Digest 2d, vol. 69 (St. Paul, MN: West Publishing Company, 1978), p. 533. Reprinted with permission.

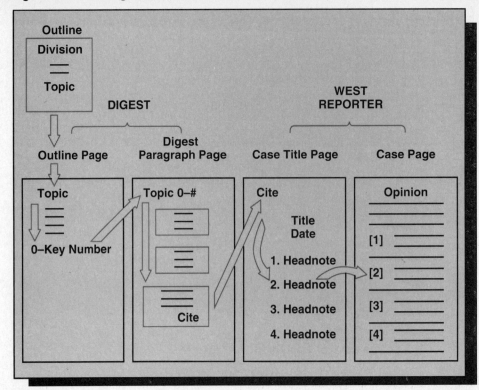

Figure 3-6 The Digest Method

major division of the outline to search is "Property." Under the major division "Property," you would go to the subdivision "Particular Subjects and Incidents of Ownership." Under that subdivision, "Cemeteries" is the relevant Topic.

To view the outline of the Topic, you would find the first few pages of the Topic in the appropriate digest volume in the appropriate digest set, each set being organized alphabetically by topic. You would scan the outline of the Topic—Cemeteries—for a line such as "Cemetery plots as interests in land," and pick up the line's Key Number.

Another approach to finding Topics and Key Numbers is to use West's "Descriptive-Word Index" volumes for the appropriate digest set. (See Figure 3-7.) The index contains a variety of catch words as entries, with references to Topic and Key Number combinations, intended to allow researchers to find the best combination or combinations that will enable them to find cases like theirs.

If you have already found one case like yours, another approach is to use West's tables of cases for the appropriate digest set. These tables list the Topic and Key Number combinations in which digest paragraphs have been made for each case. These Topic and Key Number combinations can also be picked up directly from the headnotes in the report of the case like yours in the National Reporter System. This leads to yet another approach, which is, generally, to get suggested Topic and Key Number combination cross-references from other West publications.

West publishes an array of books, discussed generally in West's legal research pamphlet *West's Law Finder,* and most are tied together by Topic and Key Number references.

West publishes the National Reporter System, discussed in Chapter 2. The federal and specialized courts are covered by specialized reporters, and the

Figure 3–7 Descriptive-Word Index

89 F P D 2d—263   **ELECTRONIC**

References are to Digest Topics and Key Numbers

ELECTRONIC EAVESDROPPING—Cont'd
TAPE recorded telephone conversations—
  Admissibility. Crim Law 394.3
  Consent—
    Induction coil, placing on extension. Crim Law 394.3
    Voluntariness, government's special employee giving. Crim Law 680(1)
  Interrogation without counsel. Crim Law 412.2(1)
  Order of proof, voluntariness of consent. Crim Law 680(1)
  Self-incrimination, compelling. Crim Law 393(1)
TAPE recordings—
  Copies, admissibility. Crim Law 398(2)
  Foreign language, playing to jury, interpreter translating. Crim Law 663
  Government agent's telephone conversation with defendant, admissibility with agent's consent. Crim Law 394.3
  Long distance telephone calls, placing without charge, investigating device for circumventing toll equipment. Crim Law 394.5(2)
  Taking without taxpayer's knowledge, interviews with treasury agents. Crim Law 438
  Transcripts for jury—
    Convenience. Crim Law 663
    Purpose, identification of speakers during deliberation. Crim Law 673(2)
TAX evasion case, transcripts containing attorney-client conversation, grand jury presentation warranting new trial. Crim Law 1189
TAX evasion prosecution, monitored conversations used in evidence. Crim Law 394.5(1)
TECHNICAL trespass—
  Violating federal eavesdropping rule. Tel 491
TELEPHONE booth. Const Law 266
  Conversation, violating privacy. Searches 7(10)
TELEPHONE company, monitoring own employees. Tel 495
TELEPHONE conversations—
  Magnetic pickup device, sender's consent to use. Tel 495
  Mother and daughter, separated husband recording. Tel 498
  Party's consent, admissibility. Crim Law 394.3
TELEPHONE service—
  Installation request not consent. Tel 495
TRANSMITTER planted on body of undercover agent, conversation between defendant and undercover agent—
  Crim Law 394.3
  Searches 7(10)
UNDERCOVER agent's conversation with illegal whiskey seller, admissibility. Crim Law 394.3
UNITED States courts—
  State laws prohibiting, affect. Crim Law 394
UNREASONABLE search or seizure. Searches 7(1)
VENTILATING shaft by sheriff. Searches 7(1)

ELECTRONIC EAVESDROPPING DEVICES
LIBEL, article caption that divorce litigant got assistant of spouse's employee to sell out. Libel 50½

ELECTRONIC EQUIPMENT
PRINTED circuits, patents. Pat 323
RAIL shipments—
  Character and value of goods, shipper's statement. Carr 110

ELECTRONIC FUNDS TRANSFER SYSTEMS
SAVINGS and loan association accounts, access of holders, status of systems as branch. B & L Assoc 24

ELECTRONIC LOCATION DEVICES
AIRCRAFT, attachment of device. Searches 1

ELECTRONIC MONITORING
HARMLESS error in admitting conversations overheard by. Crim Law 1169(1)

ELECTRONIC RECORDING DEVICES
DISCOVERY, make, model, and serial numbers. Crim Law 627.6(3)

ELECTRONIC SCANNED POSITIVES
SECONDARY boycott to persuade supplier to substitute photo-engraving method in printing industry, evidence. Labor 578

ELECTRONIC SURVEILLANCE
ACTING assistant attorney general, authorization of application before senate confirmation. Tel 496
AFFIDAVIT—
  Wiretap denial, effectiveness as denial of illegal use of pen register. Gr Jury 36
AGGRIEVED person's right to suppress content of wire or oral communication illegally intercepted. Crim Law 394.5(2)
ASSERTION of possible illegal surveillance, sufficiency to require government to reply. Tel 496
ASSISTANT attorney general designated ad hoc to authorize application, wiretap evidence suppressed—
  Crim Law 394.3
  Tel 496
ATTORNEY general, good faith, omnibus crime control. Tel 498
ATTORNEY General authorizing in interest of national security. Searches 7(1)
BAD faith, application not identifying person other than suspect—
  Crim Law 394.3
  Tel 496
BEEPERS, placement on vehicle. Searches 7(10)
BERGER decision, applicability to cases pending when Mapp case was decided. Courts 100(1)
BUSINESS premises, forcible entry to install wiretap—
  Searches 7(10)
  Tel 496
COMPELLING disclosure to defendants of records of. Crim Law 627.8(1)
CONTEMPT, grand jury witness, representation not discussed over tapped line—
  Crim Law 641.12(1)
  Gr Jury 36
CONTINUOUS listening for thirty days, validity of statute authorizing—
  Searches 7(1)
  Tel 492
CONTRABAND, monitor installed after lawful seizure. Searches 7(10)
CONVERSATIONS overheard as inadmissible against owner of premises whether present or not. Crim Law 394.3
CONVERSATIONS recorded illegally, examining government logs to determine relevancy. Crim Law 627.7(4), 627.8(4)
COURT not to assume that statute prohibiting would be disregarded. Crim Law 322
COURT order, person authorizing application, government not truthfully identifying—
  Crim Law 394.3
  Tel 496
DEFENSE counsel's conversation, bail pending appeal from civil contempt commitment. Contempt 56
DEPOSITIONS, F.B.I. agent supervising surveillance. Fed Civ Proc 1415
DISCLOSURE motion, search of files and affidavit denying request for surveillance. Crim Law 627.8(1)

Source: West's Federal Practice Digest 2d, vol. 89 (St. Paul, MN: West Publishing Company, 1978), p. 263. Reprinted with permission.

state courts are covered by regional reporters. Headnotes with Topic and Key Number take you back and forth between court opinions and West's digests.

As discussed in this chapter, West's American Digest System, and other West digests, index the reporters. Searches of reporters and digests, including Topics and Key Numbers, can be made electronically on West's computer-assisted legal research system, WESTLAW, to be discussed in Chapter 12.

West's annotated federal code, *United States Code Annotated* (U.S.C.A.), to be discussed in Chapter 5, and West's national encyclopedia, *Corpus Juris Secundum* (C.J.S.), to be discussed in Chapter 8, each contain Topic and Key Number research references.

West also publishes *Black's Law Dictionary*, to be discussed in Chapter 8, and a wide variety of form books and textbooks to be discussed in Chapter 9. The most recent editions of West's one-volume treatises for students, known as hornbooks, include digest references.

After determining the appropriate Topic and Key Number combinations to search, the next step in the digest method is to search the appropriate digest sets under the appropriate Topic and Key Number combinations. Under each Topic and Key Number, you will find all the digest paragraphs classified to that Topic and Key Number combination from all the cases. Under some Topic and Key Number combinations, there are only a few of these fine-print summaries, which you can quickly read and review. Under other Topic and Key Number combinations, however, there may be hundreds of these fine-print summaries, which may take you hours to read and review.

If you find a summary that appears to indicate a case like yours, the next step in the digest method is to use the citation (volume-reporter-page) to find the case in the National Reporter System.

The next step is to select the appropriate reporter, turn to the appropriate page, and search the text to check if the case is a case like yours. Sometimes this can be quickly done by finding the headnotes with your Topic and Key Number combinations and using the bracketed headnote numbers in the text to locate the part of the opinion discussing your topic. Because digest paragraphs are summaries, however, you may find upon reading the case you have been referred to that it is not really a case like yours.

In going through these steps, a legal researcher must also be aware that most digests are supplemented by cumulative annual pocket parts.

West's American Digest System

West Publishing Company began preparing digests in 1890. The digest sets indexing the case opinions in all the various units of the National Reporter System are known as the American Digest System.

In the same way that West reported federal cases before the National Reporter System started, in a special reporter, *Federal Cases*, West digested the cases before it made its Topic and Key Number outline of the law in a special digest. This special digest, the *Century Digest*, covers the years 1658–1896.

Since 1897, West has published a series of digests according to its Topic and Key Number outline of the law. Each major digest covers a 10-year period and is known as a decennial digest. Because of the tremendous growth in case law in the past few decades, West has started, with the Ninth Decennial, to issue the "decennials" in five-year parts. Until the next decennial part is published, the most recent coverage is collected in a series known as the General Digest. Thus, the American Digest System, which currently contains over 400 volumes, includes the following sets:

1658–1896 Century Digest	1946–1956 Sixth Decennial
1897–1906 First Decennial	1956–1966 Seventh Decennial
1907–1916 Second Decennial	1966–1976 Eighth Decennial
1916–1926 Third Decennial	1976–1981 Ninth Decennial, Part 1
1926–1936 Fourth Decennial	1981–1986 Ninth Decennial, Part 2
1936–1946 Fifth Decennial	1986–1991 General Digest (7th Series)

Thus, to thoroughly search a topic from the present back to 1658, it is necessary to search in each of 11 sets under the appropriate Topic and Key Number combination, and, because it used a different numbering system, in the Century Digest under the appropriate number found in the cross-reference *Table of Key Numbers Section for Century Digest* found in West's First and Second Decennials.

Other Digests

Because of the massive size of the American Digest System, many legal researchers ignore the entire system and use West's special digests, digests published by Lawyers Cooperative Publishing (LCP), and other publications.

West publishes the information contained in the American Digest System in special digests. Except for the states of Delaware, Nevada, and Utah, West publishes a digest for every state. The state digests are much more focused, and so they are easier to use than the decennials. To search for case law in a given state, including decisions in federal cases from that state, search the state's digest under the appropriate Topic and Key Number combinations.

West also publishes regional digests covering some of the regional reporters in the National Reporter System. The digest paragraphs are arranged alphabetically by the states in the region. The regional digests currently published include the *Atlantic Digest, Second Series*, the *North Western Digest, Second Series*, the *Pacific Digest, Third Series*, and the *South Eastern Digest, Second Series*.

For federal cases, West currently publishes *West's Federal Practice Digest, 4th*, covering cases since December 1975. Under each Topic and Key Number combination, the digest paragraphs are arranged chronologically by court level for the Supreme Court and the Courts of Appeals, then alphabetically through the District Courts. In addition, under the Topic "Patents," Key Number 328, there is a numerical list of all patents adjudicated since December 1975, and under the Topic "Trade Regulations," Key Number 736, there is an alphabetical list of the trademarks and trade names adjudicated since December 1975.

West's Federal Practice Digest, 4th, completely replaces *West's Federal Practice Digest, 3d*, which covered cases from December 1975 into 1983. Federal cases before December 1975 are digested in the following sets:

1961–Nov. 1975	West's Federal Practice Digest, 2d
1939–1960	Modern Federal Practice
1789–1938	Federal Digest

As might be expected, West publishes a digest covering only the opinions of the U.S. Supreme Court, the *U.S. Supreme Court Digest*.

LCP also publishes a U.S. Supreme Court digest, the *Digest of United States Supreme Court Reports*, more commonly known by the title on the spine: *U.S. Supreme Court Digest, Lawyers' Edition*. Of course, LCP cannot use West's Topic and Key Number system. LCP's editors create unique headnotes for the opinions in L. Ed and L. Ed. 2d and classify them to their L. Ed Digest according to nearly 400 digest Titles of their own, similar to the titles in LCP's national

West's Federal Practice Digest, 4th

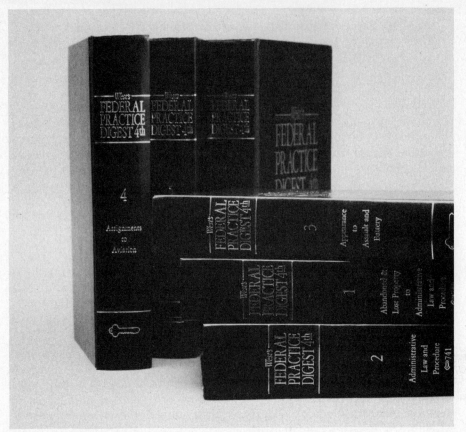

Source: © Doug Martin.

encyclopedia, *American Jurisprudence, Second Series*. (See Chapter 8.) Each digest Title is outlined according to the nature of the title, and each line is given a Section Number. (See Figure 3–8.)

The L. Ed. Digest also includes an extensive table of cases in several volumes, an index to L. Ed., L. Ed. 2d, and other annotations, and references to other parts of LCP's Total Client Service Library. (See Chapter 4.) LCP also publishes digests to cases and annotations in its various annotation series. (See Chapter 4.)

West also publishes digests for some of its specialized reporters, including *West's Bankruptcy Digest* and *West's Education Law Digest* along with the *Military Justice Digest* and the *U.S. Claims Court Digest*.

The Limitations of Digests

Digests have a number of limitations as case finders. In theory, you find the single West Topic and Key Number combination (or L. Ed. Title and Section Number combination), turn to the appropriate digest volume, and find all the cases like yours neatly summarized. In practice, there can be difficulties every step of the way.

It is not always a simple matter to find the appropriate Topic and Key Number (or Title and Section Number) combination. In the West digest search example used above, concerning cases that ruled whether or not a cemetery plot is an "interest in land" such that a contract for the transfer of one would have to be in writing, a researcher might just as logically try to search under the major

Figure 3–8 *U.S. Supreme Court Digest, Lawyers' Edition*

Accord and Satisfaction § 2

ACCORD AND SATISFACTION

Scope of Topic: This topic covers the general nature, requisites, and effect of agreements for the discharge of contracts, or settling a cause of action arising either from tort or contract, by substituting something else for such contract or cause of action.

Treated elsewhere are the compromise or settlement of disputed claims (see COMPROMISE AND SETTLEMENT); contracts whereby an old obligation is extinguished and a new one, between the same or different parties, substituted in its place (see NOVATION); and the relinquishment of rights or claims (see RELEASE). For matters as to procedure and proof, see such topics as APPEAL; EVIDENCE; PLEADING; etc.

[For fact-word approach see Word Index to this Digest]

§ 1 Generally.
§ 2 By part payment generally.
§ 3 —necessity and sufficiency of consideration.
§ 4 Unexecuted agreement.
§ 5 Effect of protest.

§ 1 Generally.

Research References

1 Am Jur 2d, Accord and Satisfaction §§ 1–4

ALR Digests: Accord and Satisfaction, § 1

Auto-Cite®—any case citation herein can be checked for form, parallel references, later history and annotation references through the Auto-Cite computer research system.

Where there is no unfairness, and all the facts are equally known to both sides, an adjustment by them is final and conclusive. Hager v Thompson, 1 Black 80,
17 L Ed 41

Courts will uphold adjustments of parties made in good faith and understanding. Brown v Spofford, 95 US 474,
24 L Ed 508

An accord and satisfaction requires the voluntary consent of the creditor. Wilmot v Mudge, 103 US 217,
26 L Ed 536

The common-law rule that actual payment of a debt of record cannot be pleaded in bar of an action to recover the debt has been changed by statute in both England and the United States and now an accord and satisfaction has the same effect. Bofinger v Tuyes, 120 US 198, 7 S Ct 529,
30 L Ed 649

A receipt in full, unless given in ignorance of its purport, or in circumstances constituting duress, is an acquittance in bar of any further demand. De Arnaud v United States, 151 US 483, 14 S Ct 374,
38 L Ed 244

An agreement that payment in United States currency should extinguish a larger amount due under a street-lighting contract estimated in Puerto Rican currency is binding where there was a bona fide dispute between the parties as to the medium of payment, the municipality insisting that it was Puerto Rican money, and the lighting company that it was current foreign money. San Juan v St. John's Gas Co. 195 US 510, 25 S Ct 108,
49 L Ed 299

§ 2 By part payment generally.

Research References

1 Am Jur 2d, Accord and Satisfaction §§ 6, 26, 33, 35

ALR Digests: Accord and Satisfaction, § 2

Cross References

Satisfaction of claim against government, see CLAIMS § 52.

Payment of a sum agreed upon in compromise of a decree appealed from constitutes an accord and satisfaction. Bofinger v Tuyes, 120 US 198, 7 S Ct 529,
30 L Ed 649

If there is a bona fide dispute as to the amount due from one person to another, or the amount is uncertain or unliquidated, a compromise and payment of a certain agreed sum as a satisfaction of the entire claim is

39

Source: U.S. Supreme Court Digest, Lawyers' Edition, vol. 1 (Rochester, NY: Lawyers Cooperative Publishing Co., 1984), p. 39. Reprinted with permission.

division "Contracts" instead of "Property," then under "Nature, Requisites, and Incidents of Agreements in General," and under the Topic "Frauds, Statute of," with a completely different Key Number. You may find that the cases like yours can be found under several different Topic and Key Number (or Title and Section Number) combinations.

In fact, as West Publishing Company founder John B. West discovered, his own editors sometimes disagreed about the "correct" classification of a case. Writing in the *Law Library Journal* West noted:

> The digester bound to a fixed classification soon finds himself sorely pressed to make certain cases "fit the classification." I remember three excellent digesters who spent an entire day in disagreeing as to whether seal fishery cases should be classified under the topic "Fish" or that of "Game" in the Digest Scheme. It is the old story of the camel's head in the tent. What seems at first a plausible pretext for forcing some novel case or new principle into a topic or subdivision to which it does not naturally belong, leads to hopeless confusion [West, *Multiplicity of Reports*, 2 LAW LIBR. J. 4 (1909)].

To keep up with changes in technology and the law, West has occasionally changed Topics and Key Numbers, including going to subdivided Key Numbers (e.g., a Key Number such as "37.15[2]"). This change can cause confusion, since a researcher going back in time must also trace the changes in the Topics and Key Numbers.

Again, once a legal researcher gets to a digest under a particular Topic and Key Number (or Title and Section Number), there may be hundreds of digest paragraphs to search. As to West's digests, the WESTLAW computer-assisted legal research system allows this search to be done electronically (see Chapter 12), but even electronic digest searches can be imperfect.

Finally, digest paragraphs, like headnotes, have been frequently called into question. An editor, in the rush to prepare headnotes for a reporter and digest paragraphs for a digest, may unavoidably miss significant points of law in the opinion, or misstate points, where the cases are read chronologically rather than topically. Moreover, headnotes and digest paragraphs, like the entries in an ordinary index, can be very superficial and give very little information or guidance.

Attorney Jesse Franklin Brumbaugh, as far back as his 1917 book *Legal Reasoning and Briefing* (Indianapolis: Bobbs-Merrill, 1917), noted these and other deficiencies in digests. He wrote:

> First the topical divisions may be so poorly chosen that the subject-matter is either not all covered, or there may result the most confusing overlapping. In such instances, unless the decisions are repeated, there may be all the way from one to a dozen places where good fishing may be had for the point desired. Furthermore, another blight of a peculiarly insidious type may follow from a careless classification of materials under the topics chosen. Presuming that excellent divisions into topics have been made, the entire field covered and the topics being mutually exclusive, still it does not follow that the material of the law will have been properly pigeonholed under the best topic. This will direct the searcher to cases that, while they may contain the point desired, were not decided upon this point and discuss it as merely incidental thereto, if not merely as dicta. The effect is to lead to false practice, the quoting of precedents not four-square to the proposition. It leads the hurried practitioner to use dictum for "The Law," and is all the more dangerous because so insidious an evil [p. 237].

Brumbaugh concluded that the worst feature of a digest is that it "involves such a tremendous waste of time on the part of the searcher in overcoming these logical discrepancies [p. 237]." He advised: "That set of books which supplies the lawyer with the case or cases which he desires in the simplest, quickest and most reliable manner is, other things being equal, the most valuable to him."

3–3 Other Case Finders

It is important to understand that there are many other case finders that are not discussed in detail in this chapter. The more you do legal research, the more you will come to realize that case citations are included in virtually every law book, and thus, *virtually every law book is a potential case finder*. Once you have a case cite, you have overcome the fundamental problem that cases are reported chronologically, but you want to find cases topically. The following sections briefly discuss other principal case finders and list the chapters in this book in which they are discussed in more detail.

A.L.R. Annotations

Partially in response to West's digest system, LCP developed a specialized series of collection case finders known as annotations. *American Law Reports* (A.L.R.) annotations will be discussed in Chapter 4.

Computer-Assisted Legal Research

Case reporters, case finders, and many other legal sources have been put on computer. Through word searching texts by computer, legal researchers can, in effect, make their own indexes of the source being searched. The two major computer-assisted legal research (CALR) systems, LEXIS and WESTLAW, will be discussed in Chapter 12.

Shepard's Citations

Shepard's Citations, a hybrid of case indexing and case collecting through tables of case cites, were developed to allow attorneys to check the status of cases as precedent, but they can also be used as imperfect case finders. *Shepard's Citations* will be discussed in Chapter 11.

Secondary Authority

Secondary authority includes everything that is not primary authority. Again, since case citations are included in virtually every law book, virtually every law book is a potential case finder. The principal secondary sources not otherwise discussed in this book will be discussed in Chapters 8 and 9.

SUMMARY

3-1

The fundamental problem in legal research is that cases are reported chronologically, but a legal researcher wants to find cases topically. The solution is to use a case finder; either an index or a collection. A case is customarily cited by its location in a reporter: volume-reporter-page. There are some obvious case finders that should not be ignored. Because of the Socratic, or "casebook," method, professors and scholars at leading law schools have, over the years, written hundreds of casebooks in almost every subject. Lawyers may astonish you with what they know "off the tops of their heads." In a well-run law firm, a memorandum of law, an in-house written discussion of a legal question, may already have been prepared. In the courthouse, you may find briefs, the formal written arguments filed with the court, in cases like yours.

3-2

West Publishing Company's solution to the fundamental legal research problem was to create a specialized index of the reported cases known as a digest. A digest allows you to go directly to the case like yours without reading every case or to quickly determine that there has been no case like yours. West prepares its digests in the process of preparing case opinions for publication in the National Reporter System. If you can determine the Topic and Key Number combination or combinations for cases like yours, the "Key Number" will "unlock" the entry to the digest paragraphs summarizing the cases like yours in the digest. West's digest sets indexing the case opinions in the various units of the National Reporter System are known as the American Digest System. Because of the massive size of the American Digest System, many legal researchers ignore the entire system and use special digests. West publishes a digest for almost every state, some regional digests, and federal digests, including the *U.S. Supreme Court Digest*. LCP publishes the *U.S. Supreme Court Digest, Lawyers' Edition*. Digests have a number of limitations as case finders, stemming from the difficulties inherent in classifying the law.

3-3

The more you do legal research, the more you will come to realize that case citations are included in virtually every law book. Thus, virtually every law book is a potential case finder. Besides casebooks, lawyers, memorandums, briefs, and digests, other case finders include annotations, computer-assisted legal research, *Shepard's Citations*, and other secondary sources.

REVIEW

Key Terms

Before proceeding, review the key terms listed below to be sure you understand each one. If necessary, read over the corresponding section of the chapter. When you are ready to test your understanding, answer the Review Questions.

brief
casebook
chronologically
citation
cite
cross-references
digest
digest paragraphs
digests
entries
headnotes
jump cite
Key Number
lawyer
memorandum of law

parallel citation
parallel cite
pinpoint cite
references
topically
Topics

Questions for Review and Discussion

1. What are the essential parts of a case citation?
2. What is a casebook?
3. Why is a memorandum of law prepared?
4. Why is a brief prepared?
5. How is a digest like an ordinary index?
6. Does a Key Number mean anything by itself?
7. What are the steps in the digest method?
8. Are state digests part of the American Digest System?
9. What are the limitations of digests as case finders?
10. What is true about almost every law book?

Activities

1. Go to a library that contains the entire American Digest System and examine some of its over 400 volumes. The entire set takes up many shelves or perhaps a whole wall. Realize that this is just the *index* to more than three million reported cases. Ponder just how much law is hidden, indeed, buried, in the cases.
2. Take some time to study West's outline of the law. Do you understand the divisions? Are they mutually exclusive? In particular, note the Topics. There's a good chance that you don't even know what some of the terms mean. Look them up in a law dictionary. (See Chapter 8.)
3. Examine LCP's digest Titles in the L. Ed. Digest. Compare them with West's Topics. As you perform legal research, as you learn more about the law, these Titles and Topics will become more familiar to you.

Review 79

CHAPTER 4 Annotations

OUTLINE

4–1 Annotations Generally
    Where Annotations Came From
    When to Use Annotations
4–2 A.L.R. Annotations
    Series
    Parts and Sections
    How an A.L.R. Annotation Is Prepared
4–3 A.L.R. Annotation Finders
    A.L.R. Indexes
    A.L.R. Digests
    A.L.R. Help Line
    Total Client Service Library
    Case & Comment Magazine
    Shepard's Citations
    Auto-Cite and LEXIS
4–4 A.L.R. Annotation Supplementation
    Blue Books
    Later Case Service
    Pocket Supplementation
    A.L.R. Latest Case Service
    Annotation History Table
4–5 The Limitations of A.L.R. Annotations

COMMENTARY

You find the county library and are greeted at the door by the librarian. You introduce yourself and your position with the City Law Department and ask where the federal digests are located. The librarian says they are shelved on the left wall across from the A.L.R. You think: "A.L.R.?" Thinking you're puzzled about the location of the digests, the librarian says, "Let me show you." The librarian takes you to the digests, you say, "Thank you," the librarian leaves, but all the time you're wondering, can I find cases on public religious displays in A.L.R.?

OBJECTIVES

In this chapter you will learn about a system for finding cases based on searching collections of cases, known as annotations. Emphasis is placed on the *American Law Reports* (A.L.R.) system published by Lawyers Cooperative Publishing (LCP). After reading this chapter, you should be able to:

1. Recognize the purpose and use of annotations.
2. Compare and contrast annotations and digests.

3. Identify and use the various annotation series.
4. Judge the quality of the various annotation series.
5. Identify and use the various parts of an A.L.R. annotation.
6. Find A.L.R. annotations using the digest method.
7. Find A.L.R. annotations using the index method.
8. Find A.L.R. annotations using miscellaneous methods.
9. Identify and use A.L.R. supplementation.
10. Understand the limitations of A.L.R. in legal research.

4–1 Annotations Generally

Unlike a digest, which is a method of finding cases in a specialized index of the law, an **annotation** is a method of finding cases in a specialized collection of the law.

The word *annotate* means to note. A common scholarship technique is to annotate—to note, or to mark up—a book or text. When a passage makes an important point, needs explanation, or deserves comment, a scholar often records related points, explanations, and comments right in the margin. Having all the related points, explanations, and comments collected in one spot, it is easy to study the subject in detail. A scholar can easily find what he or she wants to know about a particular point using these notes.

Annotation, in its ordinary sense, is especially useful in the law. Legal researchers are usually seeking to find all the cases, explanations, and comments available on a particular point of law. If someone has already read, analyzed, and synthesized the relevant law, and put it into note form for you, your research is virtually complete. All you have to do is read the notes.

Where Annotations Came From

To understand the nature of annotations, it's important to understand their origin. The annotation method of finding cases developed from a complex blend of scholarship, fate, and experience.

In 1856, bookseller Hubert Howe Bancroft started his own publishing house in San Francisco, California. Bancroft's, selling books of all kinds, soon became the largest publishing house west of the Mississippi. In 1871, recognizing the need of western lawyers for access to case reports, and the difficulty of having reporter sets shipped from the East Coast, Bancroft published a *selective* reporter, *American Reports*, in 60 volumes. Bancroft's editors selected cases of general value and authority from all the states, decided from 1868 to 1887, and published them with brief notes discussing other similar cases.

American Reports was a hit. In 1878, in response to customer requests, Bancroft began to publish another set, *American Decisions*, to selectively report cases from 1760 to 1868, with brief notes. The set was completed in 1888 with publication of the 100th volume. The two sets, *American Decisions* and *American Reports*, covering U.S. case law from 1760 to 1887, began the Annotated Reports System.

In 1886, Bancroft merged with another San Francisco law book publisher, Summer Whitney, to form the Bancroft-Whitney Company (BW). In 1888, BW started a third selective reporter, *American State Reports*, containing more extensive annotations. The 140-volume set, completed in 1911, along with *American Decisions* and *American Reports*, formed the Trinity Series.

Meanwhile, back on the East Coast, in Northport, New York, the Edward Thomson Company (ET), organized in 1887, also recognized the inherent value of a selective reporter with extensive annotations, and in 1906, began publishing a 53-volume set, completed in 1918, entitled *American and English Annotated Cases*.

Upstate, in Rochester, New York, the Lawyers Co-operative Publishing Company (LCP), was also publishing a selective annotated reporter, *Lawyers' Reports Annotated* (L.R.A.). Started in 1888, and completed in three parts (First Series, 70 volumes, covering 1888–1905; New Series, 52 volumes, covering 1905–1914; and Third Unit, 24 volumes, covering 1914–1918), L.R.A. featured **exhaustive annotations** of selected cases, collecting every case on the point annotated.

L.R.A. started as a secondary publication. LCP's principal case-finding publication was to be a special digest designed to compete with West's American Digest System.

The editors at LCP recognized an inherent weakness in West's American Digest System: the reality of change and conflict. To get the West reporters out in a timely fashion, the West editors had to prepare headnotes for a case and classify them to the digests long before the true significance of the case, if any, was known. On one hand, the case might be reversed, discredited, or overruled by statute, or, on the other hand, the case might become a leading or landmark case or become significant in an area of law other than that to which it was originally classified. No matter how skilled the West headnote editor was, he was limited insofar as he read cases chronologically, rather than topically. To make a better digest, LCP editors were assigned to read West's reported cases by topic, rather than chronologically, in order to prepare and collect more accurate and meaningful digest paragraphs.

In 1888, LCP began publishing its digest, the *General Digest*. In 1892, West countered by filing a copyright infringement suit, claiming that Volume VII of the *General Digest* was pirated from West's headnotes and digests. In 1897, a federal appeals court, ruling that there was sufficient evidence that some LCP editors had systematically borrowed from the West's headnotes in preparing the *General Digest*, enjoined its publication, in part. [*West Publishing Co. v. Lawyers Co-operative Publishing Co.*, 79 F. 756 (2d Cir. 1897)].

To avoid copyright infringement claims, LCP published the "New Series," *General Digest, American and English, Annotated*, in 22 volumes, from 1897 to 1907. As noted in the preface to Volume 3, the digest was **"annotated"** with "careful editorial compilation of the authorities on important points raised by the decisions."

After its 1897 court victory, however, West scored a major psychological victory by publishing in its advance sheets sweeping headlines stating: "GENERAL DIGEST PIRATICAL." [*Lawyers Co-operative Publishing Co. v. West Publishing Co.*, 52 N.Y.S. 1120 (App. Div. 1898)]. After a bitter advertising campaign, LCP withdrew the *General Digest*, because a more profitable opportunity had come along.

LCP rediscovered L.R.A. By 1906, L.R.A. had become LCP's leading publication, and its "New Series" was launched. L.R.A. became LCP's special case finder prepared by reading cases topically.

On April 18, 1906, BW was struck by the San Francisco earthquake and fire. BW's factory and books of account were destroyed. Although, remarkably, most of BW's lawyer-customers paid their debts despite the fact that BW's proof had been destroyed, BW struggled to get back on its feet. In a gesture of friendship, LCP sent BW $5,000 in gold. As a result of LCP's moral and financial support, in 1909, LCP was able to negotiate an option to purchase 51% of BW's stock after 10 years.

Two joint ventures then paved the way for a unification of all the annotated reporters in the country.

In 1912, BW entered into a joint venture with ET to merge *American State Reports* into *American and English Annotated Cases.* From 1912 to 1918, they co-published 32 volumes of a new and improved set, *American Annotated Cases,* with extensive annotations.

In 1919, LCP made its move. LCP executed its option to purchase 51% of BW's stock, and it made BW a subsidiary. LCP-BW then entered into a joint venture with ET to merge *American Annotated Cases* and *Lawyers' Reports Annotated,* and co-publish the super-annotated set *American Law Reports (A.L.R.).* (See Figure 4–1.)

A.L.R. was a hit. It started with "the largest subscription list of any set of reports ever published" and added 4,000 new subscriptions in its first year. [26#3 Case & Com., back cover (Mar.-Apr. 1920).]

A.L.R. had a number of features. It had annotations covering all areas of law and covering every U.S. court. Printed in a new typeface, with a single annotation-finding digest system and a single supplement, A.L.R. was prepared by a team of LCP-BW-ET editors who averaged 15 years of law writing experience.

Figure 4–1 The Birth of A.L.R.

Finally, in the 1930s, during the height of the Great Depression, LCP-BW bought out ET's interest in A.L.R., and BW became a wholly owned subsidiary of LCP. The following sections discuss LCP's management of A.L.R. since then. (In 1989, LCP was sold to International Thomson Organization Ltd., and on December 31, 1990, became the Lawyers Cooperative Publishing division of Thomson Legal Publishing Inc.)

When to Use Annotations

Annotations are best used early in the legal research process. They are designed to be a fast method for finding case law. If an annotation exists on the point you are researching and you can find it, you may be taken right to the heart of your issue. An annotation is similar to a memorandum of law.

A.L.R. is a shortcut in two significant ways. First, A.L.R. is LCP's answer to West's Digest System. When you use an A.L.R. annotation, the A.L.R. editor has already done the West digest search for you. Even in a simple annotation, the A.L.R. editor searches all the relevant West Topics and Key Numbers. For example, in an annotation such as "Mausoleum as Nuisance," 1 A.L.R. 546, the A.L.R. editor searches the West digests under both the subject (Cemeteries), and the cause of action (Nuisance). It is not uncommon for an A.L.R. editor to search through 20 or more West Key Numbers in preparing an A.L.R. annotation.

Second, the A.L.R. editor has read all of the cases relevant to the point annotated and is in a position to analyze them for you. The A.L.R. editor sifts through, chooses, compares, and weighs all the cases on the point annotated, summarizes them, organizes them by fact pattern or legal holding, and lists them pro and con. With a good annotation, you know the status of the common law on your point. In the words of a state supreme court justice, A.L.R. provides the service of "separating the wheat from the chaff." [26#5 Case & Com. 134 (Aug.-Sept.-Oct. 1920).]

4–2 A.L.R. Annotations

Over 500 volumes of A.L.R. have been published since 1919 in six different series. As discussed in Chapter 2, A.L.R.-style annotations also appear in LCP's Supreme Court reporter *United States Supreme Court Reports, Lawyers' Edition* (L. Ed. and L. Ed. 2d).

Early A.L.R. annotations contained few parts and sections. Modern A.L.R. annotations contain a number of parts and sections. A.L.R.'s style and content have also changed over the years.

Series

The A.L.R. system of annotations consists of six series (see Figure 4–2), plus L. Ed. and L. Ed. 2d.

The original A.L.R. (First Series) was published from 1919 to 1948 in 175 volumes. Before ET's interest was bought out in 1935, annotations were written at both LCP-BW and ET. After 1935, virtually all annotations were written at LCP. Starting in 1936, annotations were often written to support articles in LCP's encyclopedia, *American Jurisprudence*. (See below and Chapter 8.) Over

Volumes of A.L.R.

Source: © Doug Martin

15,000 annotations were collected in A.L.R. (First Series), and its reputation grew year after year.

A.L.R. Second Series (A.L.R.2d) was published from 1948 to 1965 in 100 volumes. The principal reason for the new series was to give LCP salesmen a "new" book to sell. Minor editorial changes included a section-numbered scheme (outline) and an index preceding each long annotation. In the late 1950s, A.L.R.-style annotations were included in L. Ed., and, in L. Ed. 2d, they became a permanent feature.

A.L.R.2d was the heyday of A.L.R. A small group of editors wrote most of the annotations, and few limitations were placed on their writing. Many viewed each annotation as a Ph.D. thesis. Within the company, LCP editors were viewed as "creative law writers," with some displaying "genius."

A.L.R. Third Series (A.L.R.3d) was published from 1965 to 1980 in 100

Figure 4–2 A.L.R. Series

A.L.R. (1st)	1919–1948	175 Volumes
A.L.R.2d	1948–1965	100 Volumes
A.L.R.3d	1965–1980	100 Volumes
A.L.R. Fed.	1969–Present	Over 100 Volumes
A.L.R.4th	1980–1992	90 Volumes
A.L.R.5th	1992–Present	Several Volumes

volumes. A.L.R.3d reflected the subtle but definite shift in writing style from "great book" to "product." In the 1960s, LCP management put every department, including editorial, on a strict budget. A.L.R.3d added new features, such as a larger typeface for "improved readability" (which also reduced the number of annotations per volume) and a box of Total Client Service Library references (that "billboarded" other LCP products). Annotations were written at both LCP and BW.

To capture the tremendous growth of federal law during the 1960s, and to sell another book, LCP, since 1969, has put federal law annotations in a separate series: A.L.R. Federal (A.L.R. Fed.).

By 1974, all A.L.R. editors were required to follow a strict style and content rulebook. A narrow interpretation of relevancy was imposed. Commentary was limited to "practice pointers." The idea that A.L.R. annotations were Ph.D. theses was discarded. Instead, each A.L.R. annotation became a narrow, carefully budgeted, slice of law.

A.L.R. Fourth Series (A.L.R.4th) was published from 1980 to 1992, and the strict rulebook style is evident. By 1987, LCP removed the phrase "creative law writing" from its editor recruiting materials, and no editor was considered a genius.

In 1992, LCP started A.L.R. Fifth Series (A.L.R.5th) with several cosmetic changes, including expanded research references, West digest references, and extensive jurisdiction tables. Reported cases are collected at the end of each volume.

LCP also publishes subject-specific A.L.R. sets, such as *A.L.R. Medical Malpractice*, containing medical malpractice annotations.

Parts and Sections

Prior to A.L.R.5th, the modern A.L.R. annotation contained the following parts and sections. (See Figure 4–3.)

Preceding the annotation is the reported case. The reported case is an example of the point annotated. A.L.R. editors attempt to collect "leading" cases wherein the point annotated is a "major feature" of the case. The case is summarized, and headnotes are made and classified to the A.L.R. Digests (see below). When available, the briefs of counsel on appeal are summarized just before the opinion of the court.

In A.L.R.4th the reported case is a state case. In A.L.R. Fed., the reported case is a Court of Appeals, District Court, or other lower federal court case. In L. Ed. 2d the reported case is a U.S. Supreme Court case.

The annotation begins with a short title and the name of the purported author. Keep in mind that an annotation is a cooperative effort. The purported author is usually the editor who read all the cases and prepared the first rough draft, but if that editor has left LCP, the purported author may be a revising editor. In any event, a revising editor will frequently make substantial changes in the first editor's content and emphasis. The reported case materials are prepared by a third editor, the indexing materials are prepared by clerical assistants, and the supplementary materials are prepared by still other editors and clerical assistants.

The next part of the annotation is the **TCSL Box.** Cross-references to other units of the LCP's Total Client Service Library are listed.

After the TCSL Box is a detailed logical section-numbered outline known as a **scheme.** After standardized §§ 1 and 2, the subject is outlined beginning with § 3. The analysis may be legal, factual, or both, depending on the subject annotated.

The next part is a legal word and fact index of the annotation, followed by the

Figure 4-3 Sample Annotation

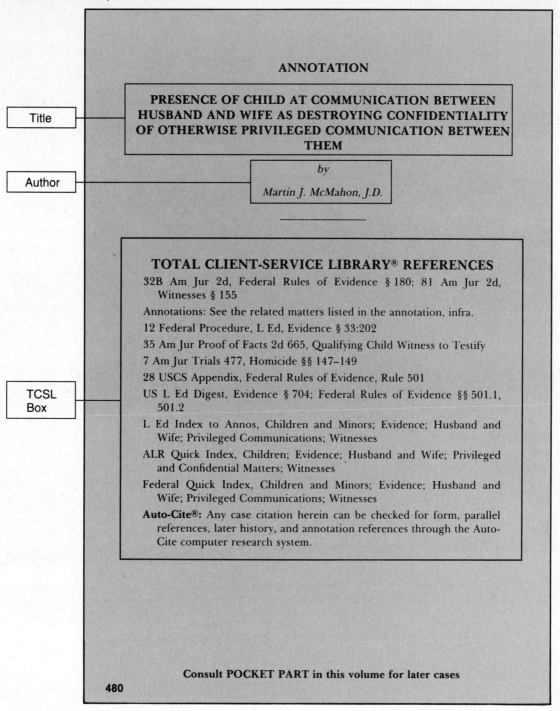

Figure 4–3 cont.

39 ALR4th   MARITAL PRIVILEGE—PRESENCE OF CHILD
39 ALR4th 480

Presence of child at communication between husband and wife as destroying confidentiality of otherwise privileged communication between them

[Scheme]

§ 1. Introduction:
    [a] Scope
    [b] Related matters

§ 2. Summary and comment:
    [a] Generally
    [b] Practice pointers

§ 3. Child 12 years or younger—where child did not participate in communication but paid attention to it

§ 4. —Where child was not shown to have paid attention to communication

§ 5. Child 13 years or older

§ 6. Child's age not specified—where child participated in communication

§ 7. —Where child did not participate in communication, generally

§ 8. —Where child was not shown to have paid attention to communication

INDEX

[Index]

Abduction, § 3
Abusive treatment, § 3
Address on letter, § 6
Administrator of estate, § 4
Age of child, §§ 3 et seq.
Anger, § 3
Arrest warrant, § 7
Arson, § 5
Assault, § 3
Attention of child to communication, §§ 4, 8
Baby's presence, § 4
Carnal knowledge, § 5
College, arson at, § 5
Comment, § 2
Conveyance of property, § 8
Co-ownership of real property, § 5
Corporation's action, § 8
Cruel and abusive treatment, § 3
Crying child, § 3
Custody suit, § 4
Debauchery, § 5
Decedent's estate, § 4
Deed, § 5
Divorce, §§ 3-7
Enforcement or execution of trust, §§ 4, 5
False pretenses, money obtained under, § 7
Fire, setting of, § 5
First-degree murder, § 6
Fraud, §§ 7, 8
Grand larceny, § 7
Homicide, §§ 5-7
Incest, §§ 5-7
Introduction, § 1
Investments, § 4
Kidnapping, § 3
Larceny, §§ 5-7
Letter communication, § 6
Microphone, § 7
Murder, §§ 5-7
Newspaper, tax sale notice, § 7
Participation of child in communication, §§ 3, 6
Partition of property, § 5
Practice pointers, § 2[b]
Rape, §§ 3, 5
Real estate matters, §§ 5, 8
Recorded conversation, §§ 4, 7
Related matters, § 1[b]
Robbery, §§ 5, 6
School, arson at, § 5
Scope of annotation, § 1[a]
Second-degree murder, § 7
Segregated property, § 6
Sex offenses, §§ 3, 5-7
Statutory rape, § 5
Summary, § 2

481

Figure 4-3 cont.

§ 1[a] MARITAL PRIVILEGE—PRESENCE OF CHILD 39 ALR4th
39 ALR4th 480

Support and maintenance action, § 4
Tape recording, §§ 4, 7
Tax sale, § 7
Tender age of child, §§ 3 et seq.
Theft, §§ 5-7
Threat, § 5
Title to property, §§ 5, 7
Trusts, §§ 4, 5
University, arson at, § 5
Warrant for arrest, § 7
Written communication, § 6

TABLE OF JURISDICTIONS REPRESENTED
Consult POCKET PART in this volume for later cases

US: §§ 5, 7
Ill: §§ 2[b], 5
Ind: §§ 5, 7
Kan: §§ 6
Ky: §§ 6
Me: §§ 3, 4
Md: §§ 2[b], 7
Mass: §§ 2[b], 3-5, 8
Mo: §§ 4, 6

NY: §§ 5, 7
NC: §§ 2[b], 4
Pa: §§ 2[b], 7
RI: §§ 7
Tenn: §§ 5
Tex: §§ 6
Wash: §§ 7
W Va: §§ 5
Wyo: §§ 5

§ 1. Introduction

[a] Scope

This annotation collects and analyzes the state and federal cases in which the courts have discussed or decided whether, or under what circumstances, the presence of a child during a communication, verbal or nonverbal, between husband and wife vitiates the privilege against a spouse's testimony in opposition to the other spouse, on the ground that the child's presence destroys the otherwise confidential nature of the communication.

Since relevant statutes are included only to the extent that they are reflected in the reported cases within the scope of this annotation, the reader is advised to consult the latest enactments of pertinent jurisdictions.

[b] Related matters

Instructions to jury as to credibility of child's testimony in criminal case. 32 ALR4th 1196.

Applicability of marital privilege to written communication between spouses inadvertently obtained by third person. 32 ALR4th 1177.

Existence of spousal privilege where marriage was entered into for purpose of barring testimony. 13 ALR4th 1305.

Testimonial privilege for confidential communications between relatives other than husband and wife—state cases. 6 ALR4th 544.

Communication between unmarried couple living together as privileged. 4 ALR4th 422.

Spouse's betrayal or connivance as extending marital communications privilege to testimony of third person. 3 ALR4th 1104.

Effect, on competency to testify against spouse or on marital communication privilege, of separation or other marital instability short of absolute divorce. 98 ALR3d 1285.

Competency of one spouse to testify against other in prosecution for

482

Figure 4-3 cont.

39 ALR4th   MARITAL PRIVILEGE—PRESENCE OF CHILD   § 2[a]
39 ALR4th 480

offense against child of both or either. 93 ALR3d 1018.

Competency of one spouse to testify against other in prosecution for offense against third party as affected by fact that offense against spouse was involved in same transaction. 36 ALR3d 820.

Husband or wife as competent witness for or against co-offender with spouse. 90 ALR2d 648.

Calling or offering accused's spouse as witness for prosecution as prejudicial misconduct. 76 ALR2d 920.

Effect of divorce or annulment on competency of one former spouse as witness against other in criminal prosecution. 38 ALR2d 570.

Crimes against spouse within exception permitting testimony by one spouse against other in criminal prosecution. 11 ALR2d 646.

"Communications" within testimonial privilege of confidential communications between husband and wife as including knowledge derived from observation by one spouse of acts of other spouse. 10 ALR2d 1389.

Conversations between husband and wife relating to property or business as within rule excluding private communications between them. 4 ALR2d 835.

Marital privilege under Rule 501 of Federal Rules of Evidence. 46 ALR Fed 735.

Competency of one spouse to testify in federal criminal prosecution of other. 3 L Ed 2d 1607.

§ 2. Summary and comment

[a] Generally

Ordinarily, the fact that a conversation between husband and wife is overheard and understood by anyone, even a member of their family, vitiates the privilege against one spouse's testimony against the other (81 Am Jur 2d, Witnesses § 155).

The courts have generally held that the presence of a child, who was shown to have paid attention to the communication, destroyed the confidentiality of an otherwise privileged communication between husband and wife (§§ 3, 5, 7, infra). The presence of a child at such communication, the courts have held, did not destroy the spouses' confidentiality, however, where the child was not paying attention at the time of the communication (§§ 4, 8, infra).

In cases in which the children in question were 13 years of age or older, the courts have usually held that the presence of the children destroyed any spousal confidentiality, even though the children did not participate in the communication between their parents (§ 5, infra). However, it has been held that the presence of a teenaged child, who testified to her remembering the conversation between her parents, would not destroy the confidentiality of that conversation (§ 5, infra).

In cases involving the presence of children who were in their preteen years, the determination of whether confidentiality has been destroyed has depended largely on whether the children appeared to have been paying attention to the communications in question (§§ 3, 4, infra).

Without regard to the ages of the children who were present during spousal communications, the courts have generally held that confidentiality was destroyed where the child actually participated in the communications (§ 6, infra). In cases in which children did not participate in conversations between their parents, courts have usually held that, regardless of the children's ages, confidentiality was destroyed (§ 7, infra). The failure of such children to pay attention,

Figure 4-3 cont.

§ 2[a]   MARITAL PRIVILEGE—PRESENCE OF CHILD   39 ALR4th
39 ALR4th 480

however, has been a ground for holding that the confidentiality of the parents' communication was not destroyed (§ 8, infra).

There appears to be a tendency of the courts, in early cases from the 19th century, to hold that the confidentiality of communications between husbands and wives was not destroyed by the presence of their children of ages in the 11- to 14-year-old category (§§ 4, 5, 7, infra), while in more recent cases, beginning in the 1920s, the courts have held that confidentiality was destroyed with respect to children in the same general age group (§§ 3, 5, infra).

[b] Practice pointers

Counsel is reminded that an objection to the admission of a conversation between husband and wife may be overruled on the ground of evidence that a child overheard and understood the communication.[1] Counsel is advised that it is generally a question of fact for the trial judge to determine whether the child in question was of sufficient intelligence to pay attention and to understand what was being said between the parents.[2]

In challenging the admission into evidence of a spousal communication, counsel is reminded that the challenging party has the burden of rebutting the presumption that statements between spouses are confidential.[3]

Even if there has been error in the admission of testimony by a spouse as to a privileged communication with the other spouse, counsel is advised that the error might not be held to be prejudicial where other witnesses testified to the same communication.[4]

Counsel who represents the spouses jointly, in seeking to introduce testimony as to conversations between the spouses, should try to establish separately the facts and circumstances from which the trier of fact may determine whether the presence of children rendered the spouses' communication admissible; counsel should not rely only on the phrasing of counsel's question to a witness spouse, asking whether there were any conversations between the spouses in the presence of their children.[5]

1. See, for example, Linnell v Linnell (1924) 249 **Mass** 51, 143 NE 813, where the court found that the daughter heard the conversation in question, in view of the fact that when she came into the room in which the husband and wife were conversing angrily, the daughter was crying.

2. See, for example, Freeman v Freeman (1921) 238 **Mass** 150, 130 NE 220, in which the trial judge admitted a conversation between husband and wife in the presence of their daughters, the eldest being 9 years old.

3. See People v Sanders (1982) 111 **Ill** App 3d 1, 66 Ill Dec 761, 443 NE2d 687, revd on other grounds 99 Ill 2d 262, 75 Ill Dec 682, 457 NE2d 1241, 39 ALR4th 471, on remand 127 Ill App 3d 471, 82 Ill Dec 753, 469 NE2d 287, in which the court stated that the presumption can be rebutted by the presence of children who are old enough to understand what is being said and who could possibly testify as to what they heard, or who participated in the marital communication itself.

4. See, for example, Master v Master (1960) 223 **Md** 618, 166 A2d 251, where the court held that any error in the admission of the wife's testimony by the trial court could hardly be held prejudicial after her two daughters testified to the same conversation.

5. See, for example, Amer Realty Co. v Spack (1932) 280 **Mass** 96, 181 NE 753, in which the court held that evidence of an alleged conversation between the defendant spouses was rightly excluded by the trial judge absent any testimony to

484

Figure 4-3 cont.

39 ALR4th   MARITAL PRIVILEGE—PRESENCE OF CHILD   § 3
39 ALR4th 480

Counsel is advised that, in addition to the rule that a spouse may not testify directly as a witness to a privileged communication, the reading of recorded conversations into the record has been held to constitute testimony of privileged communications, since the courts have refused to allow a spouse to utilize mechanical means of repeating the other spouse's words, thus accomplishing indirectly what the spouse could not do directly by disclosing the confidential communication.[6]

In the event that a child witness is to be used to testify to a conversation between the parents, counsel is advised that the question of whether a child witness is competent to testify can depend on such information as the child's age, grades in school, ability to differentiate between right and wrong, sense of moral obligation to speak the truth, and recollection of other events that took place at about the same time as the communication to which the child will testify.[7]

§ 3. Child 12 years or younger—where child did not participate in communication but paid attention to it

[Introductory Paragraph] In the following cases, the confidentiality of otherwise privileged communications between husband and wife was held destroyed by the presence of children at the communications where the children, who were 12 years old or younger, were found to have paid attention to and to have understood the spousal communication, although they did not participate in it.

[Setout] Affirming a decree of divorce in favor of a husband who brought an action against his wife on the grounds of cruel and abusive treatment, the court, in Linnell v Linnell (1924) 249 **Mass** 51, 143 NE 813, overruled the wife's exceptions to the admission of a conversation between her husband and herself where the husband had testified that his 10-year-old daughter was in the next room and that the door was open, the distance from one room to the other being 10 or 12 feet, "just across the hall." In view of the husband's further testimony that his wife's voice was extremely angry and excited, that afterwards the daughter came into the room in which the husband and wife were conversing, and that the daughter was crying, the court held that this evidence, if believed, warranted a finding that the daughter heard the conversation, which made it admissible.

Overruling the husband's exceptions to the trial court's rulings relating to evidence in a wife's action for divorce in which she charged her husband with cruel and abusive treatment, the court, in Freeman v Freeman (1921) 238 **Mass** 150, 130 NE 220, held that the trial court's admission of a conversation between the husband and wife in the presence of

establish the ages of the children who were alleged to have been present during the conversation, or other circumstances from which it could be determined whether any of the children possessed sufficient intelligence to pay attention to the conversation, if, in fact, any of them heard it.

6. For example, see Hicks v Hicks (1967) 271 **NC** 204, 155 SE2d 799 (wife did not know that her conversation with husband, in presence of their 8-year-old daughter, was being tape recorded); and Hunter v Hunter (1951) 169 **Pa** Super 498, 83 A2d 401 (husband's son by former marriage recorded conversations with wife pursuant to prearrangement between husband and son).

7. See 35 Am Jur Proof of Facts 2d 665, Qualifying Child Witness to Testify.

485

Source: American Law Reports, Fourth Series, vol. 39 (Rochester, NY: Lawyers Cooperative Publishing Co., 1985), pp. 480–485. Reprinted with permission.

"Table of Jurisdictions Represented." The **jur table** is useful in determining if the annotation cites any cases from a given state or federal circuit.

The most important part of the annotation is § 1[a] **Scope.** It states, with some specificity, the purported contents of the annotation. The scope statement may indicate that the annotation contains less than the title of the annotation might imply. To keep annotations artificially short, A.L.R. editors are usually prohibited from making reference to cases in the annotation that are not literally within the scope of the annotation as perceived by the revising editor, even though the revising editor may not have read all the cases. Moreover, doubts about problem cases are usually resolved in favor of exclusion, rather than inclusion.

Section 1[b], **Related matters,** is a list of similar, related annotations, along with a token sample of law articles and treatises on the point annotated. The quality of the related matters section indicates the quality of the coverage of the annotation system in your area of interest. If a statute or court rule is particularly relevant to the point annotated, a copy is included in a § 1[c].

Section 2, "Summary and comment," is a summary of the law found in the preparation of the annotation, but not a free commentary by the editor who read all the cases. Each statement is required to be supported by a citation to another part of the annotation or another outside source. Section 2[b], **Practice pointers,** contains "useful hints" on how to handle a case involving the point annotated.

Beginning with § 3, the cases are collected according to the scheme. Each section, or part of a section, begins with an introductory paragraph defining the type of cases to follow. Each case is then set out—sketched—in a paragraph known as a **setout.** If there are numerous repetitive cases, the case cites are merely listed with sample setouts. Since a setout is but a sketch of a case, it may not reflect the true nature of the case. Thus, cases found in A.L.R. should be read in full before being cited in a brief.

If an annotation contains only a few cases, it will not have a scheme, index, jurisdiction table, or numbered sections.

How an A.L.R. Annotation Is Prepared

Just as it's important to understand how a digest is prepared to begin to understand its limitations, it's important to understand how an annotation is prepared to begin to understand its limitations.

An A.L.R. annotation begins with topic selection. Selectors read current cases looking for emerging legal issues of interest to the average lawyer. The goal is to find an interesting case to lead a "hot" topic. If the expense of making an annotation on a given topic can be justified to LCP management, a selection memo is prepared for an editor.

The editor begins by making an exhaustive search of the subject, including secondary sources of all kinds. Rather than maintaining a massive law database, LCP has its editors separately research each annotation. The editor collects and reads all the relevant cases in, on, and around the point being annotated. While actual techniques vary, editors are instructed to read each case once, decide if it is explicitly on point, prepare setouts, then organize the setouts within a scheme. The rough draft is then edited by a revising editor to keep each annotation within the strict "rulebook" style. True commentary and creativity are thus kept to a minimum.

Again, an important part of the process is the A.L.R. editor's search of the West Digest System. West Topics and Key Numbers searched for each annotation are kept on file, along with other key sources searched, and the

Topics and Key Numbers are used as the basis for supplementing each annotation in the future.

4–3 A.L.R. Annotation Finders

While annotations are essentially finding tools, there are so many of them that there are finding tools to find annotations. There are several ways to find an A.L.R. annotation.

A.L.R. Indexes

Over the years, LCP published a complex series of "Word" and "Quick" indexes for A.L.R. annotations. Finally, in 1986, LCP simplified the matter somewhat with the publication of *Index to Annotations*. (See Figure 4–4.) *Index to Annotations*, a five-volume set, indexes all the annotations in A.L.R.2d, A.L.R.3d, A.L.R.4th, A.L.R. Fed., and L. Ed. 2d. To cut costs, A.L.R. (First Series) was not covered. A.L.R. (First Series) annotations are still indexed with the *A.L.R. First Series Quick Index*.

The A.L.R. indexes are known as "word-fact" indexes. To search for law relating to an automobile accident, for example, one can search traditional legal words like *negligence* and *due care*, along with fact words like *automobile* and *highway*. Under each entry are the appropriate annotation titles and their cites. (See Figure 4–5.)

The last (S–Z) volume of *Index to Annotations*, at page 757, also contains useful tables that show "where federal statutes, regulations, and court rules, uniform and model acts, restatements of law, and professional codes of ethics, are cited in annotations" in A.L.R.3d, A.L.R.4th, A.L.R. Fed., and L. Ed. 2d.

Each modern volume of A.L.R. also contains a "Subjects Annotated" volume index and a table of cases reported in the volume. Recent volumes also contain a table of contents.

Figure 4–4 A.L.R. "Quick" Indexes

Figure 4-5 Index to Annotations

INDEX TO ANNOTATIONS

VICTIMS—Cont'd

Sex crime victims—Cont'd

- res gestae: time element as affecting admissibility of statement or complaint made by victim of sex crime as res gestae, spontaneous exclamation, or excited utterance, 89 ALR3d 102

Similarity of occupation between proposed juror and alleged victim of crime as affecting juror's competency, 71 ALR3d 974

Spectators at trial, see group Trial spectators in this topic

Suppression or withholding of evidence by prosecution in criminal case as vitiating conviction, 34 ALR3d 16, § 24

Time element as affecting admissibility of statement or complaint made by victim of sex crime as res gestae, spontaneous exclamation, or excited utterance, 89 ALR3d 102

Trial spectators

- disruptive conduct of spectators in presence of jury during criminal trial as basis for reversal, new trial, or mistrial, 29 ALR4th 659, § 4
- emotional manifestations by victim or family of victim during criminal trial as ground for reversal, new trial, or mistrial, 31 ALR4th 229
- seating at trial, propriety and prejudicial effect of permitting nonparty to be seated at counsel table, 87 ALR3d 238, §§ 10, 11

Venue change, pretrial publicity in criminal case as ground for change of venue, 33 ALR3d 17, §§ 27, 39

Verdicts, inconsistency of criminal verdict with verdict on another indictment or information tried at same time, 16 ALR3d 866, §§ 6, 9

Vouching for witness, propriety, and prejudicial effect, of comments by counsel vouching for credibility of witness—federal cases, 78 ALR Fed 23, § 9

VIDEO CASSETTE RECORDERS

Motion pictures and videotapes, applicability of sales or use taxes to, 10 ALR4th 1209

VIDEO GAMES

Commercial video game enterprises, statute or ordinance regulating, 38 ALR4th 930

Copyrightability of video games, 66 ALR Fed 490

Trademarks, application of functionality doctrine under § 43(a) of Lanham Act (15 USCS § 1125(a), 78 ALR Fed 712, §§ 3[a], 7[c]

VIDEOTAPES

Copyright infringement, Supreme Court's views as to what constitutes, 78 L Ed 2d 957, §§ 3, 4, 6

Depositions, use of videotape to take deposition for presentation at civil trial in state court, 66 ALR3d 637

Evidence

- civil trial, generally, 66 ALR3d 637
- criminal trial, generally, 60 ALR3d 333
- depositions, use of videotape to take deposition for presentation at civil trial in state court, 66 ALR3d 637
- event or matter giving rise to litigation or prosecution, 41 ALR4th 812
- event or matter other than that giving rise to litigation or prosecution, 41 ALR4th 877

Obscenity, processor's right to refuse to process or return film or videotape of obscene subject, 18 ALR4th 1326

Sales or use tax: applicability of sales or use taxes to motion pictures and video tapes, 10 ALR4th 1209

VIETNAM WAR

Flag desecration, what constitutes violation of flag desecration statutes, 41 ALR3d 502, § 4

Schools

- demonstrations, participation of student in demonstration on or near campus as warranting expulsion or suspension from school or college, 32 ALR3d 864, §§ 7[b], 8
- forbidding unauthorized persons to enter upon or remain in school building or premises, 50 ALR3d 340, §§ 12[a], 16[b]

VIEW

Arbitrator's viewing or visiting premises or property alone as misconduct justifying vacation of award, 27 ALR2d 1160

Automobiles

- audible signal before passing, 22 ALR3d 325
- drunken driving, what amounts to violation of drunken driving statute in officer's "presence" or "view" so as to permit warrantless arrest, 74 ALR3d 1138
- smoke, vehicle operator's liability for accident occurring while driving with vision obscured by smoke or steam, 32 ALR4th 933

Billboards (this index)

Confrontation of witnesses, constitutional right, Supreme Court cases, 23 L Ed 2d 853, § 5[c]

604   Consult POCKET PART for Later Annotations

Source: Index to Annotations, vol. S–Z (Rochester, NY: Lawyers Cooperative Publishing Co., 1986), p. 604. Reprinted with permission.

A.L.R. Digests

LCP publishes a digest for A.L.R. (First Series), a digest for A.L.R.2d, and a digest for A.L.R.3d, A.L.R.4th, and A.L.R. Fed. combined. (See Figure 4–6.) The law is classified under a few hundred topics. Under each topic are annotation titles and their cites, along with digest paragraphs prepared for the reported cases and their cites.

A.L.R. Help Line

LCP operates a toll-free number, 1-800-543-2068, which you may call to receive editorial assistance in locating annotations.

Total Client Service Library

Although L. Ed. was the first set of books published by LCP, the company's defining set, its backbone, is A.L.R. Just as each A.L.R. annotation is researched and written individually, without reference to a master outline, so each LCP publication is researched and written individually, without reference to a master outline. Just as LCP struggled to develop organizational tools—digests and indexes—for A.L.R. the company also struggled to develop a system of organization for its array of books.

A partial solution came in the mid-1930s. After preparing A.L.R. annotations for several years, some A.L.R. editors were sitting around at lunch one day discussing their work. One remarked that so many A.L.R. annotations had been written that an encyclopedia could be made out of them. The editor-in-chief overheard him and said, "Let's do it." As a result, in 1936, *American Jurisprudence* (Am. Jur.)—and later, *American Jurisprudence 2d* (Am. Jur. 2d)—was born. (See Chapter 8.)

Whereas A.L.R. provided a point-by-point treatment of the law, Am. Jur. provided an overview of the law, built on, and citing, among other things, A.L.R. annotations and the cases within A.L.R. annotations. As it turned out, some annotations had to be written to fill in gaps in coverage for the new encyclopedia, but the close relationship indicates why Am. Jur. 2d is an excellent tool for finding A.L.R. annotations.

From 1953 to 1964, LCP created a series of national form books, which will be discussed in Chapter 9. Each picked up the "Am Jur" moniker: *Am Jur Legal Forms* (1953) [and *Am Jur Legal Forms 2d* (1971)], *Am Jur Pleading and Practice Forms*

Figure 4–6 A.L.R. Digests

A.L.R. (1st), A.L.R.2d, A.L.R.3d, A.L.R.4th, A.L.R. Fed.

→ A.L.R. (First) Digest
→ A.L.R. Second Digest
→ A.L.R. 3d, 4th & Federal Digests

(1956) [now *Am Jur Pleading and Practice Forms, Revised* (1967)], *Am Jur Proof of Facts* (1959) [and *Am Jur Proof of Facts 2d* (1974)], and *Am Jur Trials* (1964).

Finding that lawyers liked buying "coordinated" books, in 1961 LCP's marketing department devised a slogan for LCP's national sets: the **Total Client Service Library** (TCSL). Every new national set LCP created was then made part of the TCSL, including among others, *A.L.R. Federal* (1969), *United States Code Service* (U.S.C.S.) (1972) (to be discussed in Chapter 5), *Federal Procedural Forms, Lawyers' Edition* (1975) (to be discussed in Chapter 9), *Bankruptcy Service, Lawyers' Edition* (1979), and *Federal Procedure, Lawyers' Edition* (1981) (to be discussed in Chapter 9). Auto-Cite (to be discussed in Chapter 11) was added in 1982.

LCP's editorial department supported the TCSL "coordination" claim by thoroughly cross-referencing each set in the TCSL with each other set in the TCSL, and in particular, with A.L.R. It is important to remember, however, that each is independently researched and written, and thus, as with A.L.R. itself, some law may fall through the cracks.

In 1986, LCP's indexing department took a step toward editorially coordinating LCP's books with the development of the *Thesaurus of Legal Fact Words and Concepts*. The thesaurus provides a "general model for an index." To the extent LCP indexers have followed it, there is now editorial coordination in the indexing of LCP books, including the A.L.R. *Index to Annotations*.

Case & Comment Magazine

In 1894, LCP started *Case & Comment*, "The Lawyers Magazine," to advertise L.R.A., and, in 1919, continued the idea by advertising A.L.R. *Case & Comment* contains practical articles for practicing lawyers, along with summaries of A.L.R.'s reported cases. At the end of each summary is the announcement "ALR . . . covers the point" and a citation to A.L.R.

Shepard's Citations

Shepard's Citations, which will be discussed in Chapter 11, includes cites to A.L.R. annotations.

Auto-Cite and LEXIS

To be discussed in Chapters 11 and 12, A.L.R. annotations can be found by Auto-Cite, and word-searched directly, using the LEXIS computer-assisted legal research system (ALR;ANNO file).

4–4 A.L.R. Annotation Supplementation

Cases are frequently decided after an A.L.R. annotation on the point has already been published. A.L.R. annotations are kept up to date by supplementary material that collects these "later cases." The method of supplementation has changed frequently over the years. (See Figure 4–7.)

Figure 4-7 A.L.R. Supplementation

Blue Books

To supplement A.L.R. (First Series) annotations, LCP started publishing the *A.L.R. Blue Book of Supplemental Decisions.* The volumes in this set simply list cites to later cases on each annotation topic.

Later Case Service

To supplement A.L.R.2d annotations, LCP started publishing the *A.L.R. 2d Later Case Service.* Instead of simply listing cites to later cases on each annotation topic, each case is keyed to the appropriate section of the annotation supplemented.

Pocket Supplementation

To supplement A.L.R.3d, A.L.R.4th, and A.L.R. Fed., LCP now publishes annual cumulative pocket parts for each volume. Again, each case is keyed to the appropriate section of the annotation supplemented.

A.L.R. Latest Case Service

LCP operates a toll-free number, 1-800-225-7488, which you may call to get references to cases decided since the last A.L.R. supplement was published.

Annotation History Table

Another method used to keep annotations up to date is to issue superseding or supplementing annotations. If the subject matter of an annotation, or a part of it, has changed significantly, a **superseding annotation** may be prepared. The subject will be rewritten as if there were no annotation on the point. If there have been a lot of cases on an annotated point, but no fundamental changes, a **supplementing annotation** may be prepared. The new cases are discussed with reference to the original annotation.

To check if a particular annotation, or a part of it, has been superseded or supplemented, refer to the supplemental service for that series of annotations or to the Annotation History Table in the last (S–Z) volume of the *Index to*

Annotations. (See Figure 4-8.) To check if a particular annotation supersedes or supplements another annotation, refer to the scope section of the annotation.

4-5 The Limitations of A.L.R. Annotations

During the heyday of A.L.R., some A.L.R. editors saw themselves as the keepers of the common law. Marketing slogans like "All the case law on your point" were developed. Today, A.L.R. is simply an unusual case finder.

If your point is annotated, you may find more cases and quicker with an A.L.R. annotation than with West's digests. But, relatively speaking, less and less of U.S. case law is being annotated. A.L.R. annotations collect (and West's digests index) reported cases, but more and more of U.S. case law is going unreported. When there is no A.L.R. annotation on your point, you must turn to other sources. Moreover, even if there is an annotation on your point, it merely collects "in point" cases, without real commentary.

Figure 4-8   Annotation History Table

ANNOTATION HISTORY TABLE

This table lists annotations in all series of American Law Reports (ALR) and United States Supreme Court Reports, Lawyers Edition (L Ed) which have been superseded or supplemented by later annotations. Consult the pocket part in this volume for later history.

ALR (First Series)

1 ALR 148–149 Superseded 74 ALR2d 828	**1 ALR 1688–1691** Superseded 99 ALR2d 7	**2 ALR 1576–1579** Superseded 77 ALR2d 1182
1 ALR 222–264 Subdiv VIII superseded 71 ALR2d 1140	**2 ALR 6–36** Supplemented 49 ALR2d 982	**3 ALR 242** Superseded 72 ALR2d 342
1 ALR 329–331 Superseded 36 ALR2d 861	**2 ALR 61–67** Superseded 14 ALR3d 783	**3 ALR 312–323** Superseded 24 ALR2d 194
1 ALR 343–349 Superseded 51 ALR2d 1404	**2 ALR 225–236** Supplemented 41 ALR2d 1263	**3 ALR 610–612** Superseded 12 ALR2d 611
1 ALR 383–392 Superseded 13 ALR4th 1153	**2 ALR 287–293** Superseded 11 ALR4th 345	**3 ALR 824–829** Superseded 13 ALR3d 848
1 ALR 449–450 Superseded 28 ALR2d 662	**2 ALR 345–347** Superseded 44 ALR2d 1242	**3 ALR 833–844** Superseded 22 ALR3d 1346
1 ALR 546–547 Superseded 50 ALR2d 1324	**2 ALR 545–551** Superseded 54 ALR3d 9	**3 ALR 902–928** Superseded 57 ALR3d 1083
1 ALR 834 Superseded 91 ALR2d 1344	**2 ALR 579–582** Superseded 50 ALR2d 1161	**3 ALR 1003–1021** Superseded 98 ALR3d 605
1 ALR 861–878 Superseded 41 ALR2d 1213	**2 ALR 592–593** Superseded 12 ALR3d 933	**3 ALR 1096** Superseded 89 ALR3d 551
1 ALR 884–892 Superseded, as to private easements, 25 ALR2d 1265	**2 ALR 867–879** Superseded 25 ALR3d 941	**3 ALR 1104** Superseded 8 ALR4th 886
1 ALR 1163–1172 Superseded 28 ALR4th 482	**2 ALR 1008–1014** Superseded 90 ALR2d 1210	**3 ALR 1109** Superseded 92 ALR2d 1009
1 ALR 1267–1277 Superseded 87 ALR2d 271	**2 ALR 1068** Superseded 6 ALR3d 1457	**3 ALR 1130–1145** Supplemented 41 ALR2d 739
1 ALR 1368–1374 Superseded 46 ALR2d 1140	**2 ALR 1368–1371** Superseded 56 ALR3d 1182	**3 ALR 1279–1282** Subdiv II superseded 100 ALR2d 227
1 ALR 1528–1532 Superseded 13 ALR3d 42	**2 ALR 1376** Superseded 45 ALR2d 1296	**3 ALR 1304–1306** Superseded 82 ALR2d 611
1 ALR 1632–1634 Superseded 53 ALR2d 572	**2 ALR 1389–1390** Superseded 28 ALR3d 1344	**3 ALR 1385–1393** Superseded 92 ALR3d 623
	2 ALR 1522–1526 Superseded 157 ALR 1359	

Consult POCKET PART for Later Entries   1079

Source: Index to Annotations, vol. S–Z (Rochester, NY: Lawyers Cooperative Publishing Co., 1986), p. 1079. Reprinted with permission.

SUMMARY

4-1

The annotation method of finding cases is based on finding cases in a specialized collection of law. If someone has already read, analyzed, and synthesized the relevant law for you, and put it into note form, your research is virtually complete. *American Law Reports* (A.L.R.) is the super-annotated set; LCP's special case finder is prepared by reading cases topically.

4-2

There are six series of A.L.R. annotations: A.L.R. (First Series), A.L.R.2d, A.L.R.3d, A.L.R.4th, A.L.R.5th, and A.L.R. Fed. L. Ed. and L. Ed. 2d also contain A.L.R.-style annotations. The reported cases serve as examples of the points annotated. Large annotations have a detailed logical section-numbered outline known as a *scheme*. When using a modern annotation, be aware of its scope statement and the fact that commentary and creativity have been artificially limited.

4-3

Annotations can be found with the *Index to Annotations* and the A.L.R. digests. References to annotations are also found in Total Client Service Library volumes (such as *American Jurisprudence*), in *Case & Comment* magazine, and in other sources.

4-4

Modern annotations are supplemented by pocket supplementation. To check if an annotation has been supplemented or superseded, consult the Annotation History Table in the last volume of the *Index to Annotations*.

4-5

A.L.R. is an unusual case finder. If your point is annotated, you may find more cases and quicker with an A.L.R. annotation than with West's digests.

REVIEW

Key Terms

Before proceeding, review the key terms listed below to be sure you understand each one. If necessary, read over the corresponding section of the chapter. When you are ready to test your understanding, answer the Review Questions.

American Law Reports (A.L.R.)
annotate
annotated
annotation
exhaustive annotations
jur table
Practice pointers
Related matters
scheme
Scope
setout
superseding annotation
supplementing annotation
TCSL Box
Total Client Service Library (TCSL)

Questions for Review and Discussion

1. What is the purpose and use of an annotation?
2. What are the differences between an annotation and a digest?
3. What are the current annotation series?
4. What series of A.L.R. was written by a small group of creative law writers, without rule books or artificial limitations of any kind?
5. What are the parts and sections of a modern A.L.R. annotation and what do they do?

6. What is the index for modern A.L.R. annotations?
7. What is the digest for modern A.L.R. annotations?
8. In what other ways can you find an A.L.R. annotation?
9. How are modern A.L.R. annotations supplemented?
10. Why might an A.L.R. annotation not contain "All the case law on your point," as advertised?

Activities

1. Read through several modern-schemed A.L.R. annotations, noting the structure of the annotation. Make sure you understand each part and section. Note how well the scheme outlines the topic. Find out if, and where, the A.L.R. editor has collected cases on opposite sides of the same issue.
2. Look up the word *annotate* in an ordinary dictionary. Decide how much an A.L.R. editor, in writing an A.L.R. annotation, annotates, in the ordinary sense of the word.
3. After completing this book, select a modern A.L.R. annotation and research the titled topic, on your own, without using the annotation. Compare your results with the annotation. Did you miss relevant cases found (or included) by the A.L.R. editor? Did you find relevant cases missed (or excluded) by the A.L.R. editor? Reread the title and scope of the annotation. Did the A.L.R. annotation contain what you expected to find, based on its title and scope?

CHAPTER 5 Statutory Law

OUTLINE

5–1 Legislation
      Legislative History
      After a Bill Becomes Law
5–2 Federal Codes
      United States Code (U.S.C.)
      Annotated Codes
      United States Code Annotated (U.S.C.A.)
      United States Code Service (U.S.C.S.)
      The Limitations of Codes
5–3 State Codes
5–4 Local Codes

COMMENTARY

On your way back to the office after researching public religious displays, you learn that a train carrying hazardous materials has derailed near the center of the city. Tank cars are on fire, spewing poisonous smoke and gas, and several thousand residents have been forced to evacuate. When you get back to the office, you find the law director and everybody else watching the mayor's press conference on TV. The mayor is asked why trains carrying such hazardous cargo were allowed to pass through the city. The mayor says he doesn't know, but he's going to ask the law director to find out what the city can do about it. The law director tells you to put the public religious display project on hold. Instead, your assignment is to find out what federal laws apply to the transportation of hazardous materials and if they preempt (i.e., prohibit) any state or local law.

OBJECTIVES

In this chapter you will learn about the books that track the law made by the legislative branch. Emphasis is placed on federal legislation and its publication. After reading this chapter, you should be able to:

1. Define basic legislative terminology.
2. Understand the nature of legislative history.
3. Identify the official chronological source of federal legislation.
4. Explain how federal legislation is found topically.
5. Identify the official code of federal legislation.
6. Describe the benefits of an "annotated" code.
7. Recognize the indexes available for annotated codes.
8. Compare and contrast West's annotated code with LCP's annotated code.
9. Recognize the limitations of annotated codes.
10. Describe the usual features of state and local codes.

5-1 Legislation

The legislative branch of government makes the law. Unlike judges, who must be confronted with an actual legal controversy and interpret the law to make precedent, legislators simply "dream up" the law. The legislative branch makes **statutes,** and law from the legislative branch is known as **statutory law.** (See Figure 5-1.) The legislative process resulting in the making of a statute is known as **enactment.** Because the federal legislative process is illustrative of the legislative processes in the states, the federal legislative process is discussed in detail in this chapter.

Federal law is made in the sense of being "dreamed up" by Congress. Congress meets in two-year periods, each known as a **Congress,** with 1789-1790 as the 1st Congress and 1991-1992 as the 102nd Congress. The Twentieth Amendment, Section 2, of the Constitution of the United States, requires Congress to "assemble at least once in every year, and such meeting shall begin at noon on the 3d day of January, unless they shall by law appoint a different day." Accordingly, each Congress consists of a first and a second **session,** each approximately one year in length.

A proposed permanent law introduced in the House of Representatives or in the Senate is known as a **bill** (introduced with the words "Be it enacted"). Bills introduced in the House of Representatives during a Congress are numbered sequentially beginning with H.R. 1. Bills introduced in the Senate during a Congress are numbered sequentially beginning with S. 1.

In each house, bills are studied by committees. Public hearings may be held, after which the committees report their recommendations to the full house. Placed on the calendar, bills come up for debate, possible amendment, and a vote. Bills considered and passed by one house (each an **act;** each corrected, final, officially signed copy known as an **engrossed bill**) are sent to the other house for consideration and passage. Substantial differences between versions

Figure 5-1 The Legislative Branch

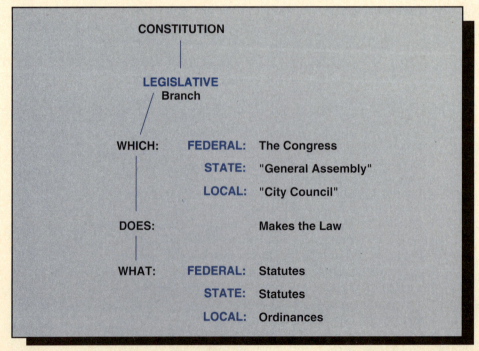

may be ironed out by a joint conference committee, followed by a vote in each house.

As specified by Article 1, Section 7, of the Constitution of the United States, bills that pass both houses (each corrected, final, officially signed copy on parchment known as an **enrolled bill**) are presented to the President for signature (approval), return without a signature **(veto),** timely nonreturn (abstention), or untimely nonreturn **(pocket veto).** A bill becomes law if the President signs it, if the President returns it within 10 days (Sunday excepted) and the veto is overridden by a two-thirds vote in each house, or if the President does not return it within 10 days (Sunday excepted) and the houses of Congress have not adjourned.

Bills not passed during a Congress must be reintroduced to be considered again for passage. Bills should be compared and contrasted with joint resolutions, concurrent resolutions, and simple resolutions.

A **joint resolution** (designated H.J. RES. or S.J. RES.) is a proposed temporary (time-oriented) law (introduced with the words "Be it resolved"), such as an extension of a law about to expire or a one-time expenditure. Joint resolutions are passed like bills, except that a proposed constitutional amendment must be passed by a two-thirds vote of each house and need not be presented to the President. (See Figure 5–2.)

A **concurrent resolution** (designated H. CON. RES. or S. CON. RES.) is a proposed *administrative* (not legislative) statement of Congress, such as an expression of congressional opinion or the creation of a joint committee, which must be passed by each house to become effective, but is not a law commanding all. Similarly, a **simple resolution** (designated H. RES. or S. RES.) is a proposed *administrative* (not legislative) statement of one house, such as an expression of the house's opinion or the creation of a committee, which must be passed to become effective, but is not a law commanding all.

Legislative History

The laws enacted by the legislature are subject to interpretation by the courts. While it is true that in interpreting a statute a court may consider **legislative history,** the committee reports, floor debates, and other information considered by the legislature in enacting a bill or joint resolution, this is ordinarily done only when the statute has never been interpreted by a court before. Most legal research texts bury this fact in a blizzard of information about the sources of legislative history.

If a statute has never been interpreted by a court before, a court may seek to determine the intent of the legislature in passing the law and apply the law in a manner consistent with that intent. But a court is not bound by legislative intent. A court is bound only by the wording of the statute if the statute is constitutional. More importantly, once a statute has been interpreted by a court, that interpretation becomes a precedent that does have persuasive, if not mandatory, authority. A court can be bound by another court's interpretation of a statute.

As a practical matter, then, the only time a legal researcher need research legislative history is if a court is deciding a case of first impression as to interpreting a statute. If the statute has already been interpreted, legislative history is usually discussed and determined, if at all, in the first few case opinions under the statute.

A detailed discussion of legislative history is beyond the scope of this book. In summary, legislative intent can be inferred from amendments, committee reports, debates, and hearings.

Figure 5–2 Sample Joint Resolution

Sixty-sixth Congress of the United States of America;

At the First Session,

Begun and held at the City of Washington on Monday, the nineteenth day of May, one thousand nine hundred and nineteen.

JOINT RESOLUTION

Proposing an amendment to the Constitution extending the right of suffrage to women.

Resolved by the Senate and House of Representatives of the United States of America in Congress assembled (two-thirds of each House concurring therein), That the following article is proposed as an amendment to the Constitution, which shall be valid to all intents and purposes as part of the Constitution when ratified by the legislatures of three-fourths of the several States.

"ARTICLE ―――――.

"The right of citizens of the United States to vote shall not be denied or abridged by the United States or by any State on account of sex.

"Congress shall have power to enforce this article by appropriate legislation."

Speaker of the House of Representatives.

Vice President of the United States and
President of the Senate.

Legislative intent may be inferred by comparing the original version of a bill or joint resolution with any amendments and whether or not those amendments were enacted. The original version of a bill and its amendments can be found by working with the official record of Congress, the *Congressional Record*, and by checking the bill number in the *History of Bills and Resolutions* part of the *Congressional Record Index* for the appropriate session of Congress.

If passage of a bill or joint resolution is recommended by a committee, the committee usually writes a report explaining its recommendation. Legislative intent may be inferred from a committee report. West Publishing Company (West)'s *United States Code Congressional and Administrative News* (U.S. Code Cong. & Admin. News) publishes selected committee reports for significant enacted legislation.

A significant bill or joint resolution may be debated on the floor in each house of Congress. Legislative intent may be inferred from the debate, especially from statements by a sponsoring legislator about the scope of the legislation. Such statements can be found in the *Congressional Record* (Cong. Rec.).

The shortcut to all of this is to find a legislative history that has already been compiled. Sources that may help include *Sources of Compiled Legislative Histories*, Commerce Clearing House, Inc. (CCH)'s *Public Laws—Legislative Histories Microfiche*, and the Congressional Information Service, Inc. (CIS)'s *Legislative History Service*.

The most widely used indexes of legislative history are the *Congressional Information Service/Index* ("CIS Index") and the *CCH Congressional Index*.

Some legislative history materials have been put on the LEXIS and WEST-LAW computer-assisted legal research systems, which will be discussed in Chapter 12.

Because of the nature of legislative history research, it is appropriate to obtain the assistance of a librarian familiar with the resources available in a given library. Similarly, "legislative history" on a current bill or joint resolution may be found by contacting the local office of your congressman or congresswoman, or one of your senators, and asking for assistance.

The only major difference between federal legislation and state legislation is the availability of legislative history. While state legislative history theoretically exists, sources of state legislative history are usually nonexistent. State committee reports and floor debates are rarely published. At best, a state legislative bureau (e.g., Ohio's Legislative Service Commission) may be able to provide summaries of proposed legislation. Legislative history may be limited to a drafting committee's commentary collected in the state's annotated code (discussed in section 5–3 below).

After a Bill Becomes Law

A bill or joint resolution that has become law during a particular session of the legislature is known as a **session law.** (See Figure 5–3.) Most laws apply to everyone, and each is known as a **public law.** During each Congress, public session laws are numbered sequentially beginning with Public Law No. 1 (Pub. L. No. 1). Some laws apply only to an individual or a few individuals, and each is known as a **private law.** During each Congress, private session laws are numbered sequentially beginning with Private Law No. 1 (Priv. L. No. 1).

A copy of a particular law passed during a session of the legislature is known as a **slip law.** Slip laws are collected and officially published in numerical order by the U.S. Government Printing Office in the *United States Statutes at Large*

Figure 5-3 Enactment of a Bill

(Stat.). Slip laws are also published by West in U.S. Code Cong. & Admin. News (see Figure 5-4) and by Lawyers Cooperative Publishing (LCP) in its advance sheets to the *United States Code Service* (U.S.C.S.) (discussed in section 5-2 below).

The Stat. includes enacted bills, joint resolutions, and concurrent resolutions. Simple resolutions are included in the *Congressional Record*.

5-2 Federal Codes

The *United States Statutes at Large* (Stat.), published by the U.S. Government Printing Office, is the official chronological source of federal legislation. Legal researchers, however, want to find the law on a given topic. If statutes come out chronologically, how do you find them topically? The solution is to use a specialized collection. Since the number of pages of statutes issued each year is much less than the number of pages of case opinions, and legislation often expires, is repealed, or is later superseded, legislatures have undertaken to have all their permanent public statutes in force organized topically. Such a topical collection of statues is known as a **code.** The process of collecting permanent public statutes topically, adding amendments, and deleting expired, repealed, or superseded statutes, is known as **codification.**

The statutes of the U.S. government were first codified by commissioners in the *Revised Statutes of 1875*. The *Revised Statutes of 1875* was introduced as a bill, which also repealed the public laws then in *Statutes at Large*. With the bill's passage, the codification became **positive law,** the law "actually enacted."

However, this first codification, known as the first edition, was later discovered to contain errors and improper additions, and a second edition was authorized by Congress in 1878, but never enacted into positive law. The second codification was only *prima facie* (accepted on its face, but not irrebuttably) evidence of the law as actually enacted. The one official source again became *Statutes at Large*. Congress did not codify its statutes again until 1926.

108 Chapter 5 *Statutory Law*

Figure 5-4 Slip Law Published in *U.S. Code Congressional and Administrative News*

PUBLIC LAW 99-280 [S. 1282]; April 24, 1986

HEALTH SERVICES AMENDMENTS ACT OF 1986

For Legislative History of Act see Report for P.L. 99-280 in Legislative History Section, post.

An Act to amend the Public Health Service Act to revise and extend the programs of assistance for primary health care.

Be it enacted by the Senate and House of Representatives of the United States of America in Congress assembled, | Health Services Amendments Act of 1986.

SECTION 1. SHORT TITLE: REFERENCE TO ACT.

(a) SHORT TITLE.—This Act may be cited as the "Health Services Amendments Act of 1986". | 42 USC 201 note.

(b) REFERENCE TO ACT.—Whenever in this Act an amendment or repeal is expressed in terms of an amendment to, or a repeal of, a section or other provision, the reference shall be considered to be made to a section or other provision of the Public Health Service Act. | 42 USC 201 note.

SEC. 2. MEDICALLY UNDERSERVED POPULATIONS.

Section 330(b) (42 U.S.C. 254c(b)) is amended—
(1) by striking out the second, third, fourth, and fifth sentences of paragraph (3); and
(2) by adding at the end thereof the following:

"(4) In carrying out paragraph (3), the Secretary shall by regulation prescribe criteria for determining the specific shortages of personal health services of an area or population group. Such criteria shall— | Regulations.

"(A) take into account comments received by the Secretary from the chief executive officer of a State and local officials in a State; and | State and local governments.

"(B) include infant mortality in an area or population group, other factors indicative of the health status of a population group or residents of an area, the ability of the residents of an area or of a population group to pay for health services and their accessibility to them, and the availability of health professionals to residents of an area or to a population group. | Children and youth.

"(5) The Secretary may not designate a medically underserved population in a State or terminate the designation of such a population unless, prior to such designation or termination, the Secretary provides reasonable notice and opportunity for comment and consults with— | Prohibition. State and local governments.

"(A) the chief executive officer of such State;
"(B) local officials in such State; and
"(C) the State organization, if any, which represents a majority of community health centers in such State.

"(6) The Secretary may designate a medically underserved population that does not meet the criteria established under paragraph (4) if the chief executive officer of the State in which such population is located and local officials of such State recommend the designation of such population based on unusual local conditions which are a barrier to access to or the availability of personal health services.". | State and local governments.

100 STAT. 399

Source: United States Code Congressional and Administrative News, vol. 4 (St. Paul: West Publishing Company, 1986), p. 1286. Reprinted with permission.

United States Code (U.S.C.)

In 1926, committees of the House and Senate collected the current laws in the *Revised Statutes of 1875* and the current laws in *Statutes at Large* since 1873, and created the *United States Code* (U.S.C.), published by the Government Printing Office. Since 1926, a new edition of U.S.C. has been issued every six years. Since 1932, cumulative supplements have been issued each intervening year. U.S.C. has a general index.

The U.S.C. officially collects federal statutes topically in 50 **titles.** In 1982, the Office of Law Revision Counsel was created to collect, restate, and revise the federal statutes one title at a time for enactment into positive law. The titles of U.S.C. and their status are as follows:

1. General Provisions [positive law]
2. The Congress
3. The President [positive law]
4. Flag and Seal, Seat of Government and the States [positive law]
5. Government Organization and Employees [positive law]
6. [Surety bonds] [superseded by Title 31]
7. Agriculture
8. Aliens and Nationality
9. Arbitration [positive law]
10. Armed Forces [positive law]
11. Bankruptcy [positive law]
12. Banks and Banking
13. Census [positive law]
14. Coast Guard [positive law]
15. Commerce and Trade
16. Conservation
17. Copyrights [positive law]
18. Crimes and Criminal Procedure [positive law]
19. Customs Duties
20. Education
21. Food and Drugs
22. Foreign Relations and Intercourse
23. Highways [positive law]
24. Hospitals and Asylums
25. Indians
26. Internal Revenue Code
27. Intoxicating Liquors
28. Judiciary and Judicial Procedure [positive law]
29. Labor
30. Mineral Lands and Mining
31. Money and Finance [positive law]
32. National Guard [positive law]
33. Navigation and Navigable Waters
34. [Navy] [superseded by Title 10]
35. Patents [positive law]
36. Patriotic Societies and Observations
37. Pay and Allowances of the Uniformed Services [positive law]
38. Veterans' Benefits [positive law]
39. Postal Service [positive law]
40. Public Buildings
41. Public Contracts
42. The Public Health and Welfare
43. Public Lands
44. Public Printing and Documents [positive law]
45. Railroads
46. Shipping [Subtitle II is positive law]
47. Telegraphs, Telephones, and Radiotelegraphs
48. Territories and Insular Possessions
49. Transportation [Subtitles I, II, and IV are positive law]
50. War and National Defense; and Appendix.

U.S.C. titles may be divided into subtitles. Titles or subtitles may be divided into chapters, which may be divided into subchapters. Chapters or subchapters may be divided into parts, which may be divided into subparts. Under each title, statutes are organized in **sections.** Sections (which may have letter additions) may be divided into subsections. Sections or subsections may be further divided into paragraphs, subparagraphs, sentences, and words.

For example, the word *business* in the tax statute that defines a "Subchapter S" corporation (i.e., a corporation that may be taxed like a partnership) is the nineteenth word in the only sentence in the first paragraph of the first subsection of § 1361, which falls in part I of Subchapter S of Chapter 1 of Subtitle A of Title 26 of the U.S.C. Going back:

1. Title 26: Internal Revenue Code of 1986 as amended.
2. Subtitle A: Income Taxes.
3. Chapter 1. Normal Taxes and Surtaxes.
4. Subchapter S. Tax Treatment of S Corporations and Their Shareholders.
5. Part I. In General.
6. Section 1361. S Corporation defined.
7. Subsection (a). S Corporation defined.
8. Paragraph 1. In general.
9. Only sentence.
10. Nineteenth word.

Statutes are cited by title number, code abbreviation, and section number. For example, the statute that makes it a federal crime to assassinate the President of the United States, Section 1751 of Title 18 of the U.S.C., is cited 18 U.S.C. § 1751. The "Subchapter S" definition discussed above would be cited 26 U.S.C. § 1361 (a)(1).

The concept of positive law is discussed in the U.S.C. at 1 U.S.C. § 204(a). It is important to note, however, that the courts have uniformly held that if there is a conflict in wording between the chronological Stat. and the topical U.S.C., the chronological version, the Stat., controls.

Annotated Codes

The official U.S.C., published by the U.S. Government Printing Office, lacks a few basic features of importance to legal researchers.

First, as a government publication, the U.S.C. is not always published in a timely manner. A statute may be enacted and not appear in the U.S.C. or in a U.S.C. supplement for several months.

Second, the U.S. Government Printing Office does not publish an array of law books on par with West or LCP. As a result, the U.S.C. does not provide useful cross-references to other law books.

Third, as discussed above, the laws enacted by the legislature are subject to interpretation by the courts. The U.S.C. does not include summaries of court opinions that have interpreted particular statutes.

Filling the void, West and LCP publish their own versions of the U.S.C., using the same title and section numbering system.

West publishes the *United States Code Annotated* (U.S.C.A.) and LCP publishes the *United States Code Service* (U.S.C.S.). (See Figure 5–5.) Each is an **annotated code,** containing case summaries of how the courts have interpreted each statute. Each federal annotated code is a multivolume set, with each title of the U.S.C. contained in one or more volumes of the set. Each statute is set out, followed by history notes, research references, and case summaries. The history notes usually include references to Public Law numbers and the Stat. Each federal annotated code is kept current by cumulative annual pocket parts and replacement volumes, as well as by a current service.

Unless a legal researcher already has a reference to a particular code section,

Figure 5–5 Federal Codes

Publisher	Title	Features
U.S. Government Printing Office	U.S.C.	Official; unannotated
West	U.S.C.A.	Unofficial; annotated
LCP	U.S.C.S.	Unofficial; annotated

NOTE: These federal codes all have same title and section numbering system.

the most common method of entry into a federal annotated code is through an index. Each federal annotated code has a general index for the set and a "volume index" (i.e., an index of just one title, found in the last volume of the set containing statutes from that title). Since the volume indexes are usually much more detailed than the general index, you should generally use the volume index if you know the title in which the statute you are looking for will be found.

It is interesting to note that the general index for the U.S.C. was prepared under contract by West and that the indexers at LCP used that public domain index in preparing LCP's general index of the federal code.

Examples of Volume Indexes

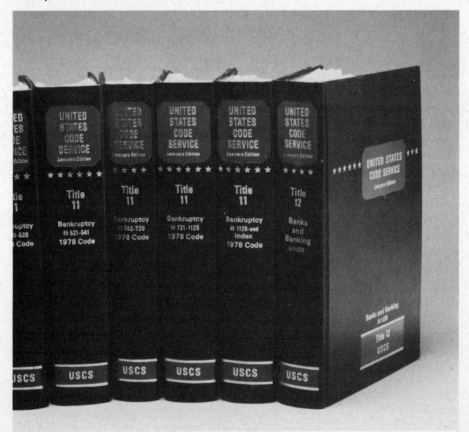

Source: © Doug Martin.

112 Chapter 5 *Statutory Law*

The next most common method of entry into a federal annotated code is to work with the tables of contents in the front of each volume and at the front of each chapter of a title.

As will be discussed in Chapter 12, the U.S.C. and both federal annotated codes may be searched by computer.

The U.S.C. and both federal annotated codes also contain tables showing where statutes in the Stat. may be found in the U.S.C., where a section can be found in a revised title, and other similar tables. Both federal annotated codes also contain tables of acts by popular names.

United States Code Annotated (U.S.C.A.)

Since 1927, West has published the *United States Code Annotated* (U.S.C.A.). The U.S.C.A. follows the format and language of the U.S.C., which, as discussed above, is only *prima facie* evidence of the law, unless the relevant title has been enacted into positive law.

The U.S.C.A., as a major West publication, lists Topic and Key Number research references for a statute, references to other West publications, and references to specific sections of the *Code of Federal Regulations* (C.F.R.) (to be discussed in Chapter 7). Following West's philosophy of comprehensive publishing, the set includes extensive case summaries, apparently drawn from

A Set of United States Code Annotated (U.S.C.A.)

Source: © Doug Martin.

headnotes in the National Reporter System and/or digest paragraphs from West's digests. The case summary section is entitled "Notes of Decisions." (See Figure 5–6.)

As will be discussed in Chapter 6, the U.S.C.A. also includes volumes covering the Constitution of the United States and federal court rules.

The U.S.C.A. can also be searched on the WESTLAW (USCA database) computer-assisted legal research system, to be discussed in Chapter 12.

United States Code Service (U.S.C.S.)

Since 1972, LCP has published the *United States Code Service* (U.S.C.S.). The U.S.C.S. follows the format of the U.S.C., but its text follows the language in the Stat., which, as discussed above, controls when there is a conflict with the U.S.C. The titles of the U.S.C. are conveniently listed on the inside front cover of each volume. The U.S.C.S. also includes advance sheets with cumulative tables and slip laws.

The U.S.C.S., as part of LCP's Total Client Service Library, lists research references to other LCP publications (especially A.L.R. annotations), references to law review articles (to be discussed in Chapter 9), and references to the *Code of Federal Regulations* (C.F.R.) (to be discussed in Chapter 7). Following a philosophy of selective publishing, LCP's editors prepare case summaries for the U.S.C.S., known as **casenotes,** only when a case appears to add something new to the law. LCP also frequently prepares casenotes for administrative decisions. The casenote section is entitled "Interpretive Notes and Decisions." (See Figure 5–7.)

As will be discussed in Chapter 6, the U.S.C.S. also includes volumes covering the Constitution of the United States and federal court rules.

The U.S.C.S. can also be searched on the LEXIS (GENFED;USCS file) computer-assisted legal research system, to be discussed in Chapter 12.

The Limitations of Codes

A legal researcher should bear in mind that like headnotes, digest paragraphs, and A.L.R. setouts, U.S.C.A. case summaries and U.S.C.S. casenotes are finding aids that do not always accurately reflect the detail of a case opinion. They are written in a competitive environment and usually give only the holding of a court without its reasoning.

Moreover, the recent flood of court decisions has affected casenoting. In 1986, to limit the number of casenotes being drawn for the U.S.C.S., LCP directed its casenoters to avoid casenoting U.S. District Court opinions.

5–3 State Codes

Just as the legislative process of the federal government is illustrative of the legislative processes in the states, the books covering the legislative branch of the federal government are illustrative of the books covering the legislative branches of the states.

In general, state legislatures meet in sessions. The session laws are published separately as slip laws and in official chronological collections similar to the Stat. (e.g., *Laws of Washington*). Again, since legal researchers need to find legislation

Figure 5-6 Excerpt From the U.S.C.A.

21 § 880
Note 10

FOOD AND DRUGS

Ch. 13

10. Suppression of evidence

Where inspection of defendant's premises was conducted following issuance of inspection warrant under this section, inspection was limited to administrative inspection and was conducted in accordance with this section, any matters revealed by such inspection were not subject to suppression in criminal proceeding. U. S. v. Prendergast, D.C.Pa.1977, 436 F.Supp. 931, affirmed 585 F.2d 69.

Where subsequent statements made by defendant were directly related to information gathered by Drug Enforcement Agency compliance officers as result of illegal search of defendant's pharmacy, defendant was entitled to suppression of such statements. U. S. v. Enserro, D.C. N.Y.1975, 401 F.Supp. 460.

§ 881. Forfeitures

Property subject

(a) The following shall be subject to forfeiture to the United States and no property right shall exist in them:

(1) All controlled substances which have been manufactured, distributed, dispensed, or acquired in violation of this subchapter.

(2) All raw materials, products, and equipment of any kind which are used, or intended for use, in manufacturing, compounding, processing, delivering, importing, or exporting any controlled substance in violation of this subchapter.

(3) All property which is used, or intended for use, as a container for property described in paragraph (1) or (2).

(4) All conveyances, including aircraft, vehicles, or vessels, which are used, or are intended for use, to transport, or in any manner to facilitate the transportation, sale, receipt, possession, or concealment of property described in paragraph (1) or (2), except that—

(A) no conveyance used by any person as a common carrier in the transaction of business as a common carrier shall be forfeited under the provisions of this section unless it shall appear that the owner or other person in charge of such conveyance was a consenting party or privy to a violation of this subchapter or subchapter II of this chapter; and

(B) no conveyance shall be forfeited under the provisions of this section by reason of any act or omission established by the owner thereof to have been committed or omitted by any person other than such owner while such conveyance was unlawfully in the possession of a person other than the owner in violation of the criminal laws of the United States, or of any State.

(5) All books, records, and research, including formulas, microfilm, tapes, and data which are used, or intended for use, in violation of this subchapter.

(6) All moneys, negotiable instruments, securities, or other things of value furnished or intended to be furnished by any

624

Figure 5-6 cont.

Ch. 13   DRUG ABUSE PREVENTION   **21 § 881**

person in exchange for a controlled substance in violation of this subchapter, all proceeds traceable to such an exchange, and all moneys, negotiable instruments, and securities used or intended to be used to facilitate any violation of this subchapter, except that no property shall be forfeited under this paragraph, to the extent of the interest of an owner, by reason of any act or omission established by that owner to have been committed or omitted without the knowledge or consent of that owner.

Seizure pursuant to Supplemental Rules for Certain Admiralty and Maritime Claims

(b) Any property subject to forfeiture to the United States under this subchapter may be seized by the Attorney General upon process issued pursuant to the Supplemental Rules for Certain Admiralty and Maritime Claims by any district court of the United States having jurisdiction over the property, except that seizure without such process may be made when—

    (1) the seizure is incident to an arrest or a search under a search warrant or an inspection under an administrative inspection warrant;

    (2) the property subject to seizure has been the subject of a prior judgment in favor of the United States in a criminal injunction or forfeiture proceeding under this subchapter;

    (3) the Attorney General has probable cause to believe that the property is directly or indirectly dangerous to health or safety; or

    (4) the Attorney General has probable cause to believe that the property has been used or is intended to be used in violation of this subchapter.

In the event of seizure pursuant to paragraph (3) or (4) of this subsection, proceedings under subsection (d) of this section shall be instituted promptly.

Custody of Attorney General

(c) Property taken or detained under this section shall not be repleviable, but shall be deemed to be in the custody of the Attorney General, subject only to the orders and decrees of the court or the official having jurisdiction thereof. Whenever property is seized under the provisions of this subchapter, the Attorney General may—

    (1) place the property under seal;

    (2) remove the property to a place designated by him; or

    (3) require that the General Services Administration take custody of the property and remove it to an appropriate location for disposition in accordance with law.

Other laws and proceedings applicable

(d) The provisions of law relating to the seizure, summary and judicial forfeiture, and condemnation of property for violation of

Figure 5-6 cont.

21 § 881   FOOD AND DRUGS   Ch. 13

the customs laws; the disposition of such property or the proceeds from the sale thereof; the remission or mitigation of such forfeitures; and the compromise of claims shall apply to seizures and forfeitures incurred, or alleged to have been incurred, under the provisions of this subchapter, insofar as applicable and not inconsistent with the provisions hereof; except that such duties as are imposed upon the customs officer or any other person with respect to the seizure and forfeiture of property under the customs laws shall be performed with respect to seizures and forfeitures of property under this subchapter by such officers, agents, or other persons as may be authorized or designated for that purpose by the Attorney General, except to the extent that such duties arise from seizures and forfeitures effected by any customs officer.

Disposition of forfeited property

(e) Whenever property is forfeited under this subchapter the Attorney General may—

    (1) retain the property for official use;

    (2) sell any forfeited property which is not required to be destroyed by law and which is not harmful to the public;

    (3) require that the General Services Administration take custody of the property and remove it for disposition in accordance with law; or

    (4) forward it to the Drug Enforcement Administration for disposition (including delivery for medical or scientific use to any Federal or State agency under regulations of the Attorney General).

The proceeds from any sale under paragraph (2) and any moneys forfeited under this subchapter shall be used to pay all proper expenses of the proceedings for forfeiture and sale including expenses of seizure, maintenance of custody, advertising, and court costs. The Attorney General shall forward to the Treasurer of the United States for deposit in the general fund of the United States Treasury any amounts of such moneys and proceeds remaining after payment of such expenses.

Forfeiture of schedule I substances

(f) All controlled substances in schedule I that are possessed, transferred, sold, or offered for sale in violation of the provisions of this subchapter shall be deemed contraband and seized and summarily forfeited to the United States. Similarly, all substances in schedule I, which are seized or come into the possession of the United States, the owners of which are unknown, shall be deemed contraband and summarily forfeited to the United States.

Plants

(g)(1) All species of plants from which controlled substances in schedules I and II may be derived which have been planted or cultivated in violation of this subchapter, or of which the owners or cul-

626

Figure 5-6 cont.

Ch. 13   DRUG ABUSE PREVENTION   21 § 881

tivators are unknown, or which are wild growths, may be seized and summarily forfeited to the United States.

(2) The failure, upon demand by the Attorney General or his duly authorized agent, of the person in occupancy or in control of land or premises upon which such species of plants are growing or being stored, to produce an appropriate registration, or proof that he is the holder thereof, shall constitute authority for the seizure and forfeiture.

(3) The Attorney General, or his duly authorized agent, shall have authority to enter upon any lands, or into any dwelling pursuant to a search warrant, to cut, harvest, carry off, or destroy such plants.

Pub.L. 91–513, Title II, § 511, Oct. 27, 1970, 84 Stat. 1276; Pub.L. 95–633, Title III, § 301(a), Nov. 10, 1978, 92 Stat. 3777; Pub.L. 96–132, § 14, Nov. 30, 1979, 93 Stat. 1048.

Historical Note

References in Text. "This subchapter", referred to in text, was in the original "this title" which is Title II of Pub.L. 91–513, Oct. 27, 1970, 84 Stat. 1242, and is popularly known as the "Controlled Substances Act". For complete classification of Title II to the Code, see Short Title note set out under section 801 of this title and Tables volume.

"Subchapter II of this chapter", referred to in subsec. (a)(4)(A), was in the original "title III", meaning Title III of Pub.L. 91–513, Oct. 27, 1970, 84 Stat. 1285. Part A of Title III comprises subchapter II of this chapter. For classification of Part B, consisting of sections 1101 to 1105 of Title III, see Tables volume.

The criminal laws of the United States, referred to in subsec. (a)(4)(B), are classified generally to Title 18, Crimes and Criminal Procedure.

The Supplemental Rules for Certain Admiralty and Maritime Claims, referred to in subsec. (b), are set out in Title 28, Judiciary and Judicial Procedure.

The customs laws, referred to in subsec. (d), are classified generally to Title 19, Customs Duties.

Schedules I and II, referred to in subsecs. (f) and (g)(1), are set out in section 812(c) of this title.

Codification. "Drug Enforcement Administration" was substituted for "Bureau of Narcotics and Dangerous Drugs" in subsec. (e)(4) to conform to congressional intent manifest in amendment of section 802(4) of this title by Pub.L. 96–132, § 16(a), Nov. 30, 1979, 93 Stat. 1049, now defining term "Drug Enforcement Administration" as used in this subchapter.

1979 Amendment. Subsec. (d). Pub.L. 96–132 substituted "The provisions" for "All provisions", and struck out "and the award of compensation to informers in respect of such forfeitures" following "compromise of claims".

1978 Amendment. Subsec. (a)(6). Pub.L. 95–633, § 301(1), added par. (6).

Subsec. (e). Pub.L. 95–633, § 301(a)(2), (3), struck out of cl. (2) provisions relating to use of proceeds of sale and added provision relating to the forwarding by the Attorney General of money and proceeds remaining after payment of expenses.

Effective Date. Section effective Oct. 27, 1970, see section 704(b) of Pub.L. 91–513, set out as an Effective Date note under section 801 of this title.

Legislative History. For legislative history and purpose of Pub.L. 91–513, see 1970 U.S.Code Cong. and Adm. News, p. 4566. See, also, Pub.L. 95–633, 1978 U.S. Code Cong. and Adm.News, p. 9496; Pub.L. 96–132, 1979 U.S.Code Cong and Adm. News, p. 2003.

Cross References

Contraband articles, including narcotic drugs, seizure and forfeiture of carriers transporting, see section 781 et seq. of Title 49, Transportation.
Narcotic drug defined, see section 787 of Title 49.

Figure 5-6 cont.

21 § 881
Note 1

FOOD AND DRUGS

Ch. 13

Library References

Drugs and Narcotics ⊆⇒191.   C.J.S. Drugs and Narcotics § 141.

West's Federal Forms

Forfeiture proceedings, see § 5891 et seq.
Judgment of condemnation, forfeiture and destruction, see § 4543.
Process in admiralty, see § 11271 et seq.

Code of Federal Regulations

Administrative policies, practices, and procedures, see 21 CFR 1316.01 et seq.
Inspection, search, and seizure, see 19 CFR 162.0 et seq.

Notes of Decisions

Acquittal or dismissal of charges, effect of 18
Admissibility of evidence 40
Authority of enforcement agents 14
Burden of proof
    Generally 38
    Shifting of burden 39
Civil nature of proceedings 25
Common carriers 8
Completed transactions 21
Concealment as grounds for forfeiture 6
Conditional sales 22
Constitutionality 1
Construction
    Generally 2
    With other laws 3
Custody of Attorney General 9
Defenses
    Generally 32
    Double jeopardy 33
    Innocent ownership 34
    Laches 35
Delay in institution of proceedings 27
Destruction of seized articles 12
Discretion of court 30
Disfavoring of forfeitures 13
Dismissal 36
Disposition or sale of forfeited property 11
Double jeopardy, defenses 33
Effect of acquittal or dismissal of charges 18
Evidence, admissibility 40
Facilitation of prohibited activities 7
Innocent ownership, defenses 34
In rem nature of proceedings 26
Intent 17
Inventory search 23
Issues in proceedings 31
Jurisdiction 29
Knowledge or intent 17
Jury trial 37
Laches, defenses 35
Mitigation of forfeitures 10
Objections to forfeiture 19
Probable cause
    Generally 15
    Particular cases 16
Property subject to forfeiture 5
Purpose 4
Remission or mitigation of forfeitures 10

Sale of forfeited property 11
Scope of review 41
Shifting of burden of proof 39
Standing to challenge forfeiture 28
Tax liens 24
Time of forfeiture 20
Transportation, concealment, etc. as grounds for forfeiture 6
Trial by jury 37

---

1. Constitutionality

This section, section 1595a of Title 19, and section 781 of Title 49 are not unconstitutional in failing to provide a prior hearing before seizure of the property. U. S. v. One 1973 Volvo, D.C.Tex.1974, 377 F.Supp. 810.

2. Construction

Provisions of subsec. (d) of this section relating to remission of forfeited vehicles should be liberally construed to effectuate remission. U. S. v. One 1976 Buick Skylark, 2-Door Coupe, Vehicle Identification No. 4W27C6K148647, D.C.Colo.1978, 453 F.Supp. 639.

This section authorizing seizure of derivative contraband articles, which are not intrinsically illegal in character, but derive their contraband status only from their association with criminal activity, must be strictly construed. U. S. v. One 1972 Datsun, Vehicle Identification No. LB1100355950, D.C.N.H.1974, 378 F.Supp. 1200.

3. Construction with other laws

Warrant requirement of this section would not be read into section 1595a of Title 19. U. S. v. One 1972 Chevrolet Nova, C.A.Mass.1977, 560 F.2d 464.

Forfeiture proceedings arising out of drug offenses are governed by same provisions as apply to customs forfeitures under section 1595 et seq. of Title 19. U. S. v. One Motor Yacht Named Mercury, C.A.R.I.1975, 527 F.2d 1112.

628

Source: United States Code Annotated, vol. 21 (St. Paul, MN: West Publishing Company, 1981), pp. 624–628. Reprinted with permission.

A Set of United States Code Service (U.S.C.S.)

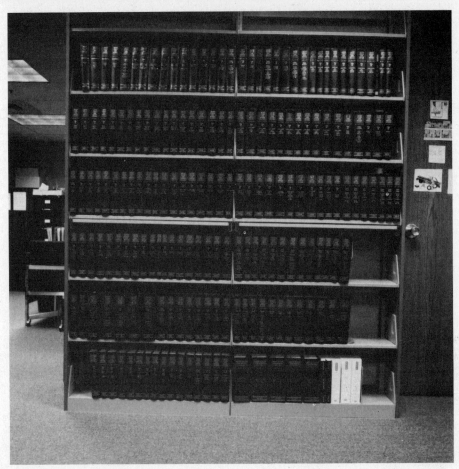

Source: © Doug Martin.

topically, an official topical code is authorized in each state (e.g., *Revised Code of Washington*), which may or may not be positive law. The code is usually available in an annotated form (e.g., *Revised Code of Washington Annotated*). (See Appendix III.)

Again, unless a legal researcher already has a reference to a particular code section, the most common method of entry into a state annotated code is through an index. For example, in Ohio, each state annotated code has a general index for the set and more-detailed volume indexes for each title.

The codes set out each statute, followed by history notes, research references, and case summaries. Tables usually correlate earlier and later versions of the code. State codes also generally include some type of legislative service as a source of recent legislation.

To be discussed in Chapter 6, state codes generally also include volumes covering the state constitution and court rules.

Interestingly, there is no one book that collects the statutes of all the states. Some looseleaf services, which will be discussed in Chapter 7, contain comparative charts, and the *Martindale-Hubbell Law Directory*, which will be discussed in Chapter 8, includes a "law digests" volume comparing various state laws; but no one book collects the text of the law from each state. However, all statutes databases can be searched on the LEXIS and WESTLAW computer-assisted legal research systems, to be discussed in Chapter 12.

Under Article I, Section 10, Clause 3, of the Constitution of the United States,

Figure 5-7 Excerpt From the U.S.C.S.

ENFORCEMENT OF VOTING RIGHTS 42 USCS § 1973e

CROSS REFERENCES

This section is referred to in 42 USCS §§ 1973a, 1973b, 1973i, 1973k.

RESEARCH GUIDE

Federal Procedure L Ed:
Elections and Elective Franchise, Fed Proc, L Ed §§ 28:81, 83, 109.

Am Jur:
16A Am Jur 2d, Constitutional Law § 655.
25 Am Jur 2d, Elections § 57.

INTERPRETIVE NOTES AND DECISIONS

42 USCS § 1973d(b) is constitutional, as it does not exceed authority granted to Congress by § 2 of Fifteenth Amendment; moreover, assignment of federal examiners does not violate Due Process Clause in precluding judicial review of administrative findings because right to due process applies only to persons and not to states. South Carolina v Katzenbach (1966) 383 US 301, 15 L Ed 2d 769, 86 S Ct 803.

§ 1973e. Examination of applicants for registration

(a) Form of application; requisite allegation of nonregistration. The examiners for each political subdivision shall, at such places as the Civil Service Commission [Director of the Office of Personnel Management] shall by regulation designate, examine applicants concerning their qualifications for voting. An application to an examiner shall be in such form as the Commission [Director] may require and shall contain allegations that the applicant is not otherwise registered to vote.

(b) Placement of eligible voters on official lists; transmittal of lists. Any person whom the examiner finds, in accordance with instructions received under section 9(b) [42 USCS § 1973g(b)], to have the qualifications prescribed by State law not inconsistent with the Constitution and laws of the United States shall promptly be placed on a list of eligible voters. A challenge to such listing may be made in accordance with section 9(a) [42 USCS § 1973g(a)] and shall not be the basis for a prosecution under section 12 of this Act [42 USCS § 1973j]. The examiner shall certify and transmit such list, and any supplements as appropriate, at least once a month, to the offices of the appropriate election officials, with copies to the Attorney General and the attorney general of the State, and any such lists and supplements thereto transmitted during the month shall be available for public inspection on the last business day of the month and in any event not later than the forty-fifth day prior to any election. The appropriate State or local election official shall place such names on the official voting list. Any person whose name appears on the examiner's list shall be entitled and allowed to vote in the election district of his residence unless and until the appropriate election officials shall have been notified that such person has been removed from such list in accordance with subsection

213

Figure 5–7 cont.

42 USCS § 1973e   ELECTIVE FRANCHISE

(d): Provided, That no person shall be entitled to vote in any election by virtue of this Act unless his name shall have been certified and transmitted on such a list to the offices of the appropriate election officials at least forty-five days prior to such election.

(c) Certificate of eligibility. The examiner shall issue to each person whose name appears on such a list a certificate evidencing his eligibility to vote.

(d) Removal of names from list by examiners. A person whose name appears on such a list shall be removed therefrom by an examiner if (1) such person has been successfully challenged in accordance with the procedure prescribed in section 9 [42 USCS § 1973g], or (2) he has been determined by an examiner to have lost his eligibility to vote under State law not inconsistent with the Constitution and the laws of the United States.

(Aug. 6, 1965, P. L. 89-110, Title I, § 7, 79 Stat. 440; June 22, 1970, P. L. 91-285, § 2, 84 Stat. 314.)

HISTORY; ANCILLARY LAWS AND DIRECTIVES

References in text:
"This Act", referred to in this section, is Act Aug. 6, 1965, P. L. 89-110, 79 Stat. 437, which appears generally as 42 USCS §§ 1973a et seq. For full classification of such Act, consult USCS Tables volumes.

Explanatory notes:
The bracketed words "Director of the Office of Personnel Management" and "Director" are inserted in subsec. (a) of this section on the authority of Reorg. Plan No. 2 of 1978, 43 Fed. Reg. 36037, 92 Stat. 3784, which appears as 5 USCS § 1101 note, which transferred all functions vested by statute in the Civil Service Commission, except as otherwise specified, to the Director of the Office of Personnel Management effective Jan. 1, 1979, as provided by Ex. Or. No. 12107 of Dec. 28, 1978, § 1-102, 44 Fed. Reg. 1055, which appears as 5 USCS § 1101 note.

Redesignation:
This section, formerly part of Act Aug. 6, 1965, P. L. 89-110 was redesignated as part of Title I of such Act by Act June 22, 1970, P. L. 91-285, § 2, 84 Stat. 314.

CODE OF FEDERAL REGULATIONS

Office of Personnel Management, Voting Rights Program, 45 CFR Part 801.

CROSS REFERENCES

This section is referred to in 42 USCS § 1973j.

RESEARCH GUIDE

Federal Procedure L Ed:
Elections and Elective Franchise, Fed Proc, L Ed §§ 28:70, 82, 84, 87, 103.

Figure 5-7 cont.

ENFORCEMENT OF VOTING RIGHTS 42 USCS § 1973f

Am Jur:
16A Am Jur 2d, Constitutional Law § 655.
25 Am Jur 2d, Elections § 115.

Annotations:
Diluting effect of minorities' votes by adoption of particular election plan, or gerrymandering of election district, as violation of equal protection clause of Federal Constitution. 27 ALR Fed 29.

INTERPRETIVE NOTES AND DECISIONS

42 USCS § 1973e is constitutional, as it does not exceed authority granted to Congress by § 2 of Fifteenth Amendment. South Carolina v Katzenbach (1966) 383 US 301, 15 L Ed 2d 769, 86 S Ct 803.

Fact that Congress directs—in 42 USCS § 1973e—that voting examiners follow state law gives state court jurisdiction to enjoin examiners from acting contrary to state law, and administrative remedy provided in 42 USCS § 1973g applies only to questions of individual applicants' compliance with qualifications required and not to questions of what qualifications should be. Perez v Rhiddlehoover (1965, ED La) 247 F Supp 65.

Holder of federal certificate of eligibility to vote is not required to go to Mississippi registrar's office and sign oath in registration book, because eligibility to vote is determined as of the time of application to be registered, and this Act is self-executing once the applicant is listed and the certificate of eligibility is issued. United States v Mississippi (1966, SD Miss) 256 F Supp 344.

§ 1973f. Observers at elections; assignment; duties; reports

Whenever an examiner is serving under this Act in any political subdivision, the Civil Service Commission [Director of the Office of Personnel Management] may assign, at the request of the Attorney General, one or more persons, who may be officers of the United States, (1) to enter and attend at any place for holding an election in such subdivision for the purpose of observing whether persons who are entitled to vote are being permitted to vote, and (2) to enter and attend at any place for tabulating the votes cast at any election held in such subdivision for the purpose of observing whether votes cast by persons entitled to vote are being properly tabulated. Such persons so assigned shall report to an examiner appointed for such political subdivision, to the Attorney General, and if the appointment of examiners has been authorized pursuant to section 3(a) [42 USCS § 1973a(a)], to the court.
(Aug. 6, 1965, P. L. 89-110, Title I, § 8, 79 Stat. 441; June 22, 1970, P. L. 91-285, § 2, 84 Stat. 314.)

HISTORY; ANCILLARY LAWS AND DIRECTIVES

References in text:
"This Act", referred to in this section, is Act Aug. 6, 1965, P. L. 89-110, 79 Stat. 437, which appears generally as 42 USCS §§ 1973a et seq. For full classification of such Act, consult USCS Tables volumes.

Explanatory notes:
The bracketed words "Director of the Office of Personnel Management" are inserted in this section on the authority of Reorg. Plan No. 2 of 1978, 43 Fed. Reg. 36037, 92 Stat. 3784, which appears as 5 USCS

215

Source: *United States Code Service*, Title 42, Sections 1861–1982 (Rochester, NY: Lawyers Cooperative Publishing Co., 1986), pp. 213–215. Reprinted with permission.

states may enter into interstate compacts (e.g., to resolve boundary disputes or to create a port authority) with the consent of Congress. The text of an interstate compact can be located in the session laws of the respective sovereigns (congressional consent in the *United States Statutes at Large*). The text may also be located in the annotated codes of the respective states. Cases interpreting interstate compacts are digested under *States* Key Number 6 in West digests and under *States* Section Number 22 in the L. Ed. Digest.

5–4 Local Codes

Local governments exist only after the appropriate sovereign's legislature passes an **enabling act** allowing or creating the local government. The enabling act, along with the sovereign's constitution, gives the local government its power. When a local governmental body, such as a city council, legislates, it makes an **ordinance.** Ordinances may be collected topically in a code.

The codified ordinances of a local government are usually published by small private publishers. It can be difficult, if not impossible, to locate a copy of a local government's code outside the territory of the local government. If a copy is not available at the local law or public library, a legal researcher may have no choice but to review the code in the local government's offices.

Local codes are rarely annotated. However, local codes, especially local traffic laws, often mimic the state's statutes. When this is so, the state's annotated code may be consulted for case authority interpreting the statute/ordinance.

If the desired ordinance cannot be located in the local code by working the table of contents, you may find that the local code has a general index you can search.

SUMMARY

5–1

The legislative branch of government makes statutes. Federal law is made in the sense of being "dreamed up" by Congress. A proposed permanent law introduced in the House of Representatives or in the Senate is known as a bill. A bill that passes both houses is presented to the President and becomes law if the President signs it, if the President returns it within 10 days (Sunday excepted) and the veto is overridden by a two-thirds vote in each house, or if the President does not return it within 10 days (Sunday excepted) and the houses of Congress have not adjourned. Bills should be compared and contrasted with joint resolutions, concurrent resolutions, and simple resolutions. The laws enacted by the legislature are subject to interpretation by the courts. As a practical matter, the only time a legal researcher need research legislative history is if a court is deciding a case of first impression as to interpreting a statute. Legislative intent can be inferred from amendments, committee reports, debates, and hearings. While state legislative history theoretically exists, sources of state legislative history are usually nonexistent. Slip laws are collected and officially published in chronological order by the U.S. Government Printing Office in the *United States Statutes at Large* (Stat.).

5–2

Statutes come out chronologically, but they may be found topically with a specialized collection known as a code. The process of collecting permanent public statutes topically, adding amendments, and deleting expired, repealed, or superseded statutes is known as codification. The *United States Code* (U.S.C.) officially collects federal statutes topically in 50 titles. Titles may be divided into subtitles, chapters, subchapters, parts, and subparts. Under each title, statutes are organized into sections. Sections may be divided into subsections, paragraphs, subparagraphs, sentences, and words. Statutes are cited by title number, code abbreviation, and section number. The U.S.C. does not provide useful cross-references to other law books, and it does not include summaries of court opinions that have interpreted particular statutes. West and LCP each publish a federal annotated code. Each is a multivolume set, with each title of the U.S.C. contained in one or more volumes of the set. Each statute is set out, followed by history notes, research references, and case summaries. Each federal annotated code is kept current by cumulative annual pocket parts and replacement volumes, as well as a current service. Each has a general index and volume indexes for each title. West publishes the *United States Code Annotated* (U.S.C.A.), which lists Topic and Key Number research references for a statute, along with other references to West publications. LCP publishes the *United States Code Service* (U.S.C.S.), which lists research references to A.L.R. annotations and other LCP publications. A legal researcher should bear in mind that like headnotes, digest paragraphs, and A.L.R. setouts, casenotes are finding aids that do not always accurately reflect the detail of a case opinion or even refer you to every case.

5–3

Like the federal legislature, state legislatures meet in sessions. The session laws are published separately as slip laws, in official chronological collections, and in official topical codes, usually in annotated form. The most common method of entry into a state annotated code is through an index. The codes set out each statute, followed by history notes, research references, and case summaries. There is no one book that collects the statutes of all the states.

5–4

Local governments exist only after the legislature of the appropriate sovereign passes an enabling act allowing or creating the local government. When a local governmental body, such as a city council, legislates, it makes an ordinance. Ordinances may be collected topically in a code. The codified ordinances of a local government are usually published by small private publishers. A legal researcher often has no choice but to review the code in the local government's offices.

REVIEW

Key Terms

Before proceeding, review the key terms listed below to be sure you understand each one. If necessary, read over the corresponding section of the chapter. When you are ready to test your understanding, answer the Review Questions.

act
annotated code
bill
casenotes
code
codification
concurrent resolution
Congress
enabling act
enactment
engrossed bill
enrolled bill
joint resolution
legislative history
ordinance
pocket veto
positive law
prima facie
private law
public law
sections
session
session law
simple resolution
slip law
statutes
statutory law
titles
veto

Questions for Review and Discussion

1. What is the difference between a bill, a joint resolution, a concurrent resolution, and a simple resolution?
2. When do you need to research legislative history?
3. What is the official chronological source of federal legislation?
4. What is codification?
5. What is the official code of federal legislation?
6. What are the benefits of an annotated code?
7. How are the federal annotated codes indexed?
8. What research references does the U.S.C.A. have that the U.S.C.S. doesn't have? What research references does the U.S.C.S. have that the U.S.C.A. doesn't have?
9. Why shouldn't you cite a casenote in a brief?
10. Is there an annotated code for your state?

Activities

1. Go to a library that contains West's *United States Code Congressional and Administrative News* (U.S. Code Cong. & Admin. News). Pick out a recent volume. Examine some of the laws that have passed Congress. Develop a sense of the magnitude of man's quest for order under law.
2. Review a statute in LCP's *United States Code Service* (U.S.C.S.). Read the material printed just after the statute. "P.L." is referring you to "Public Law" whatever. "Stat." is referring you to *United States Statutes at Large*. Read through the history of the statute. If you feel like you understand some of it, you're on the right track.
3. If you can, visit Capitol Hill in Washington, D.C., or your state capitol. Visit the chambers of each house, and the offices of your local representatives. If you can't go to Washington, D.C., visit the local office of your congressional representative. Understand that you have a voice in the federal legislature and in your state legislature. Recognize the importance of exercising your right to vote.

CHAPTER 6 Constitutional Law, Court Rules, and Other Promulgations

OUTLINE

6–1 Constitutional Law
    Federal Constitution
    Annotated Constitutions
    State and Local Constitutions
6–2 Court Rules
    Annotated Court Rules
6–3 Treaties

COMMENTARY

In your research of the federal laws that apply to the transportation of hazardous materials and the issue of preemption, you see references to the supremacy clause of the Constitution of the United States. Your mind is full of questions. Where is the supremacy clause in the Constitution? What exactly does it state? How have the courts interpreted it in other kinds of cases? Is preemption in your case typical or atypical?

OBJECTIVES

In this chapter you will learn about the sources of law under the Constitution and under the legislative, executive, and judicial branches of government, other than case law, statutory law, and administrative law. After reading this chapter, you should be able to:

1. Recognize the nature of constitutional law.
2. Identify sources of the text of the Constitution.
3. Identify the official version of the Constitution.
4. Identify the annotated sources of the Constitution.
5. Find the text of state constitutions.
6. Understand the nature of court rules.
7. List the different kinds of court rules.
8. Identify the annotated sources of the federal court rules.
9. Find state court rules.
10. Find treaties and executive orders.

6-1 Constitutional Law

The documents that form a government are known as that government's **charter.** In a loose sense, documents such as the Declaration of Independence and the Federalist Papers are part of the charter of the United States of America. In a strict sense, the charter of the United States of America is its written fundamental law, its **constitution,** the Constitution of the United States. Law directly derived from this fundamental document is known as **constitutional law.** (See Figure 6-1.)

Federal Constitution

Law is the command of a sovereign, and in the United States of America the people are sovereign. As the **preamble**—the introductory statement of legal intent—states, the people "to form a more perfect Union, establish Justice, insure domestic Tranquillity, provide for the common defence, promote the general Welfare, and secure the Blessings of Liberty" have exercised their power through the Constitution of the United States. As Article VI, Clause 2, of the Constitution provides, the Constitution, federal laws made pursuant to it, and treaties made under it, are the supreme law of the land. The Constitution returns some powers to the people, including the power to amend the Constitution and the power to vote.

The Constitution was drafted at the Constitutional Convention held in Philadelphia in the summer of 1787. Signed by 39 delegates on September 17, 1787, the Constitution became effective, by its terms, when it was ratified by the ninth state, which was New Hampshire, on June 21, 1788. The federal government began operating under the Constitution on April 30, 1789.

The Constitution is organized into articles, sections, and clauses. Articles I, II, and III cover the branches of the federal government. Article I covers the legislative branch; Article II covers the executive branch; and Article III covers the judicial branch. Article IV covers the states. Article V covers the amendment process. Articles VI and VII cover miscellaneous matters.

Figure 6-1 Constitutional Law

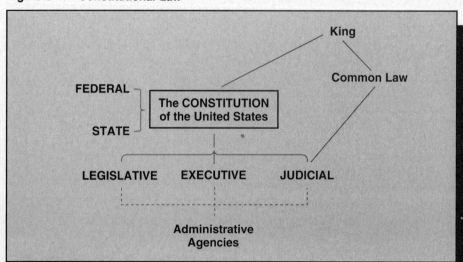

128 Chapter 6 Constitutional Law, Court Rules, and Other Promulgations

There have been 27 amendments (technically, additional articles) to the Constitution. The first 10 amendments, ratified by three-fourths of the states on December 15, 1791, are known as the **Bill of Rights.** The twenty-seventh was certified on May 18, 1992.

The Constitution is the most widely available law in the United States. The text is routinely reproduced in almanacs, encyclopedias, and dictionaries, especially law dictionaries. The text is also found in law, history, and political science texts, and in patriotic pamphlets and prints. Ironically, few people have ever read the Constitution from beginning to end. This fundamental document, important to legal researchers because it explains the structure of the government and the sources of law, is reproduced in Appendix I.

What is the official version of the Constitution of the United States? The answer is *the* Constitution of the United States, on parchment, under glass, bathed in helium, and lowered nightly into a vault below the floor of the Exhibition Hall Rotunda of the National Archives on Constitution Avenue in Washington, D.C.

Annotated Constitutions

Under the doctrine of **judicial review,** the clauses of the Constitution, like statutes, are subject to interpretation by the courts, particularly by the U.S. Supreme Court. In fact, since the Constitution was designed to be a flexible general guide for the government, it is subject to more interpretation than a

The Constitution of the United States at the National Archives

Source: © Paul Conklin.

statute, which, by design, is usually quite specific. Legal researchers usually need to refer to an **annotated constitution,** a version of the Constitution containing case summaries of how the courts have interpreted the Constitution.

Three annotated constitutions are preferred by most legal researchers for researching constitutional law. The most readily available annotated constitutions are the *United States Code Annotated* (U.S.C.A.) and the *United States Code Service* (U.S.C.S.); both were discussed with regard to statutes in Chapter 5. Both sets have volumes in which each clause of the Constitution is set out, followed by the usual code treatment: history notes, research references, and case summaries. The U.S.C.A., published by West Publishing Company (West), gives digest Topic and Key Number references. The U.S.C.S., published by Lawyers Cooperative Publishing (LCP), gives *American Law Reports* (A.L.R.) annotation references. Both sets may be entered by a volume index, and both sets are kept current by cumulative annual pocket parts and a current service.

The third source, much less widely available, is a one-volume annotated constitution entitled *The Constitution of the United States of America*. Published pursuant to a congressional resolution (see 2 U.S.C. § 168), it is prepared by the Congressional Research Service of the Library of Congress. Significant cases are weaved into the analysis following each clause.

Other sources of case authority and interpretation concerning the Constitution can be found in a variety of publications. As discussed in Chapter 3, both West and LCP publish digests covering the Supreme Court. As discussed in Chapter 4, LCP publishes annotations, particularly in *United States Supreme Court Reports, Second Lawyers' Edition* (L. Ed. 2d), that cover points ruled on by the Supreme Court. As discussed in Chapter 9, there are numerous treatises and periodicals covering legal issues of all kinds, including constitutional law.

State and Local Constitutions

As the people as a whole have for the federal government, the people of each state, as sovereign, have **promulgated** (made official and public) a constitution to be the fundamental law for their state. Just as the federal constitution can be found with a federal annotated code, state constitutions are usually found with their state annotated code, either as a separate volume or in an appendix. For example, Anderson Publishing Company publishes the Ohio Constitution, annotated, in an appendix volume to its *Page's Ohio Revised Code Annotated*. Again, an annotated version includes case summaries of how the courts have interpreted the constitution. Often cross-references are provided to similar constitutional provisions in other states and in the federal constitution, so a legal researcher can research case interpretations in other states as persuasive authority. Like codes, entry into an annotated state constitution may be made through a general or a volume index.

Another source of state constitutions is a three-volume set, *Constitutions of the United States: National and State,* prepared by the Columbia University Legislative Drafting Research Fund.

The fundamental law of a local government agency is usually known as its **charter.** Like local ordinances, a legal researcher may have no choice but to review the local charter in the local government's offices.

6–2 Court Rules

As discussed in Chapter 2, the courts have the power to decide real cases. Insofar as the sovereign's constitution and statutes (not unconstitutional) empower and direct the judicial process, the courts are bound to follow them. However, if no constitutional clauses or statutes direct the judicial process, the judicial branch has inherent power to promulgate its own rules governing its own activities in deciding cases. It is common for high-level courts to govern the lower courts and to establish uniform procedures through a system of court rules. (See Figure 6–2.)

For example, suppose your local county courthouse opens at 8:30 a.m. Why is it 8:30 a.m. instead of, say, 9:00 a.m.? The Constitution of the United States does not provide when state courts must open for the day. The state constitution probably does not provide when the state's courts must open for the day. The state statutes probably do not provide when the state's courts must open for the day. Since the court must open sometime to decide cases, and the relevant constitutions and statutes don't provide a time, the state courts then have inherent authority to set the opening time by rule. If the high or supreme court does not set the time, then an intermediate court might set the time. If not, the matter will be left to the discretion of the local trial judges. If they enter a rule on the public journal of the court, that's the time. If they don't, the matter will be left to the discretion of the individual judge.

Who makes the rules governing the filing of a civil lawsuit in a U.S. District Court? The U.S. Supreme Court does, but not because of inherent power. The Constitution provides twice, in Article I, Section 8, and in Article III, Section 1, that Congress has the power to create the lower federal courts. This is the legislative branch's check on the power of the judicial branch provided by the framers of the Constitution. Under Title 28 of the *United States Code* (U.S.C.), Congress has created the lower federal courts, but, under 28 U.S.C. § 2072, Congress has delegated to the Supreme Court the authority to make rules of procedure for the District Courts. Who makes the rules of procedure for cases before the Supreme Court? The Supreme Court. Since the Constitution is silent on the matter, the Supreme Court has inherent power and authority to make its own rules.

There are rules covering virtually every procedural act possible in the judicial branch. There are rules of civil procedure, criminal procedure, evidence (trial procedure), and appellate procedure and practice. There are rules of juvenile procedure, traffic court, claims court, and bankruptcy. There are rules governing

Figure 6–2 Court Rules

attorneys, judges, admission to the bar, grievances, and discipline. There are "codes" of rules regarding ethics and judicial conduct. The rules may be local, or, most often, rules of superintendence (general applicability).

Major publishers often publish court rules in pamphlet form. West, for example, publishes the rules of most states, including the federal courts in the state, in pamphlets titled by the state, "Rules of Court," year, and volume (e.g., *Michigan Rules of Court—1992—Federal*).

Publishers also publish pamphlets covering specific areas of law, which include the relevant statutes and court rules. West, for example, publishes the *Federal Criminal Code and Rules,* covering the relevant portions Titles 18, 21, 28, and 46 of the U.S.C., and the Federal Rules of Criminal Procedure, Rules Governing Section 2254 Cases, Rules of Procedure for the Trial of Misdemeanors Before United States Magistrates, Federal Rules of Evidence, Federal Rules of Appellate Procedure, and Rules of the Supreme Court.

Annotated Court Rules

Like constitutional clauses, court rules are subject to interpretation by the courts, and in particular, by the court that promulgated them. Thus, a legal researcher may need to refer to an annotated version of the court rules, a version of the court rules containing case summaries of how the courts have interpreted the court rules.

Just as an annotated constitution can be found with a federal annotated code, annotated federal court rules are found with a federal code, either in a separate volume or at the end of the volume of the relevant title. The principal federal annotated codes—the U.S.C.A. and the U.S.C.S.—were discussed with regard to statutes in Chapter 5. The U.S.C.S. covers federal rules in special "Court Rules" volumes.

The U.S.C.A. follows the relevant title method, locating, for example, the Federal Rules of Criminal Procedure at the end of Title 18, and the Federal Rules of Civil Procedure at the end of Title 28. In both sets, each rule is followed by the usual code treatment: history notes, research references, and case summaries. The U.S.C.A., published by West, gives digest Topic and Key Number references. The U.S.C.S., published by LCP, gives A.L.R. annotation references. Again, both sets may be entered by a volume index, and both sets are kept current by cumulative annual pocket parts and a current service.

Just as annotated federal court rules can be found with a federal annotated code, annotated state court rules are usually found with their state annotated code, either in a separate volume or at the end of the volume of the relevant title.

Other sources of case authority and interpretation concerning court rules can be found in a variety of publications. As discussed in Chapter 2, West publishes *Federal Rules Decisions* (F.R.D.) as part of its National Reporter System. As discussed in Chapter 3, LCP's *United States Supreme Court Digest, Lawyers' Edition* contains court rules volumes. LCP also publishes *Federal Rules Service*. As discussed in Chapter 4, LCP publishes annotations that cover points ruled on by the courts, including court rules. To be discussed in Chapter 9, there are numerous treatises and form books covering legal matters of all kinds, including those arising under court rules.

6–3 Treaties

As mentioned in Chapter 1, a nation-binding agreement with a foreign country is known as a **treaty.** Treaties are part of the rules governing sovereign countries by their consent, the law of nations, known as **international law.** Article II,

Court Rules Volumes of the U.S.C.S.

Source: © Doug Martin.

Section 2, Clause 2, of the Constitution of the United States provides that the President "shall have Power, by and with the Advice and Consent of the Senate, to make Treaties; provided two-thirds of the Senators present concur." If the President makes an agreement with a foreign country, but does not seek the advice and consent of the Senate, it is known as an **executive agreement.** The President may abide by an executive agreement, but his successor may ignore it, since it is, by definition, not nation-binding.

Article VI, Clause 2, of the Constitution of the United States provides that along with the Constitution and the laws made pursuant to it, "all Treaties made, or which shall be made, under the Authority of the United States, shall be the supreme Law of the Land; and the Judges in every State shall be bound thereby, any Thing in the Constitution or laws of any State to the Contrary notwithstanding." As the supreme law of the land, treaties affect everyone.

Treaties have been published in a variety of publications. Currently, all treaties and executive agreements in which the United States is a party are published as pamphlets in the *Treaties and Other International Acts Series* (T.I.A.S.), bound in volumes as *United States Treaties and Other International Agreements* (U.S.T.), each published pursuant to 1 U.S.C. § 112a by the U.S. Department of State. They are indexed by the *United States Treaties and Other International Agreements Cumulative Index*. Treaties and executive agreements are also published in *United States Statutes at Large* (Stat.) by the U.S. Government Printing Office.

Treaties in Force is an annual publication of the U.S. Department of State. It can be used, along with the monthly *Department of State Bulletin* and its monthly and annual indexes, to determine the current status of a treaty or executive agreement. *Treaties in Force* lists all currently effective treaties and executive agreements by country and by subject.

Some treaty publications cover particular subjects. Commerce Clearing House Inc. (CCH) publishes *Commerce Clearing House, Tax Treaties,* which covers treaties involving tax law. C. Kappler's *Indian Affairs, Laws and Treaties* covers treaties involving Indian tribes.

Like constitutional clauses and court rules, treaties are subject to interpretation by the courts. Thus, a legal researcher may need to refer to an annotated version of a treaty. LCP's annotated code, U.S.C.S., includes volumes of treaties by year of ratification, with casenotes.

SUMMARY

6-1

The charter of the United States of America is its written fundamental law, the Constitution of the United States. In the United States the people are sovereign, and they exercise their power through the Constitution. The Constitution, organized into articles, sections, and clauses, now includes 26 amendments. The clauses of the Constitution are subject to interpretation by the courts. The most readily available annotated constitutions are the constitutional volumes of the *United States Code Annotated* (U.S.C.A.) and the *United States Code Service* (U.S.C.S.). Both set out each clause of the Constitution, followed by history notes, research references, and case summaries. Both sets may be entered by a volume index. Just as the federal constitution can be found with a federal annotated code, state constitutions are usually found with their state annotated code.

6-2

If no constitutional clauses or statutes direct the judicial process, the judicial branch has inherent power to promulgate its own rules governing its own activities in deciding cases. It is common for high-level courts to govern the lower courts and to establish uniform procedures through a system of court rules. There are rules covering virtually every procedural act possible in the judicial branch. Major publishers often publish court rules in pamphlet form. Court rules are subject to interpretation by the courts, and so a legal researcher may need to refer to an annotated version. Annotated federal court rules are found with the annotated federal codes, either in a separate volume or at the end of the volume of the relevant title. Annotated state court rules are usually found with their annotated state code.

6-3

A nation-binding agreement with a foreign country is known as a treaty. If the President makes an agreement with a foreign country, but does not seek the advice and consent of the Senate, it is known as an executive agreement. Treaties have been published in a variety of publications. Currently, all treaties and executive agreements in which the United States is a party are published in *Treaties and Other International Acts Series* (T.I.A.S.) and in *United States Statutes at Large* (Stat.). *Treaties in Force* can be used, along with the *Department of State Bulletin*, to determine the current status of a treaty or an executive agreement. Treaties are subject to interpretation by the courts. *United States Code Service* (U.S.C.S.) includes volumes of treaties with casenotes.

REVIEW

Key Terms

Before proceeding, review the key terms listed below to be sure you understand each one. If necessary, read over the corresponding section of the chapter. When you are ready to test your understanding, answer the Review Questions.

annotated constitution
Bill of Rights
charter
constitution
constitutional law
executive agreement
international law
judicial review
preamble
promulgated
treaty

Questions for Review and Discussion

1. What is the fundamental law?
2. Do you have a source of the text of

the Constitution of the United States at home?
3. Where is the original Constitution of the United States?
4. Why would you use an annotated federal code to study a clause of the Constitution?
5. Where would you expect to find the text of your state constitution?
6. Where do the courts get the power to make court rules?
7. Name some of the different kinds of court rules.
8. Why would you use an annotated federal code to study a federal court rule?
9. Where would you expect to find your state's rules of civil procedure?
10. What book would you use to find out if a treaty is still in force?

Activities

1. Despite its fundamental importance, few people have ever read the Constitution of the United States from beginning to end. If you haven't, do so now. Turn to Appendix I for a copy of the complete text.
2. Find and read your state constitution. What are your constitutional rights under state law?
3. Find and read the two most-cited rules of court, the Federal Rules of Civil Procedure and the Federal Rules of Evidence. Note, however, that the most important rules of all may be the various appellate court rules. Appellate courts will throw out your appeal if you don't strictly comply with their rules. Before you appeal, *always* read, study, and follow the appropriate appellate court rules.

CHAPTER 7 Administrative Law

OUTLINE

7–1 Administrative Agencies and Executive Departments
      Administrative Regulations
      Administrative Codes
      Administrative Orders and Executive Orders
      Administrative Decisions
      Attorney General Opinions
7–2 Looseleaf Services
      Tax Services

COMMENTARY

In your research of the federal laws that apply to the transportation of hazardous materials and the issue of preemption, you see references to the *Federal Register*, for example, 47 Fed. Reg. 51991 (1982), and to the *Code of Federal Regulations*, for example, 49 C.F.R. § 171 (1985). You are intrigued. To what extent does the U.S. Department of Transportation regulate the transportation of hazardous materials?

OBJECTIVES

In this chapter you will learn about sources of law subordinate to, but important as, law from the legislative, executive, or judicial branches. Emphasis is placed on the federal executive departments and independent agencies. After reading this chapter, you should be able to:

1. Understand why administrative agencies were created.
2. Compare and contrast administrative agencies and executive departments.
3. Understand basic administrative rulemaking.
4. Find regulations chronologically.
5. Find regulations topically.
6. Compare and contrast administrative and executive orders.
7. Recognize administrative decisions.
8. Recognize the nature and use of looseleaf services.
9. Identify the basic features of looseleaf services.
10. Identify the major federal tax services.

7–1 Administrative Agencies and Executive Departments

As a practical matter, as technology advances and society grows more complex, a sovereign's legislative, executive, and judicial branches become increasingly unable to manage all the details of government. The gaps are filled and the details are managed by the branches of government creating specialized governmental entities, known in the broad sense as **administrative agencies**.

For example, when the transmission and reception of electromagnetic radiation, radio, were developed in the early 1900s, few, if any, of the federal government's legislators, executives, or judges had sufficient expertise in electronics or physics to be able to govern its development. When the nation's first commercial radio station, KDKA in Pittsburgh, Pennsylvania, went "on the air" in 1920, the average legislator, executive, or judge did not foresee that someday there would be hundreds of radio stations across the country and countless radio-wave transmitting devices (e.g., automatic garage door openers) with potentially conflicting signals, causing "interference" with each other. When the need to govern the details of radio became apparent, such as the need to assign stations to particular frequencies of amplitude modulation (AM) or frequency modulation (FM), the legislature acted by creating a body of experts to manage the problem.

Under its constitutional authority to regulate interstate commerce, Congress, with the Federal Communications Act of 1934, created an independent agency, the Federal Communications Commission (FCC), to manage radio communications. The FCC grants radio station licenses, assigns frequencies, and is responsible for tracking down and stopping unauthorized radio broadcasts. One requirement of the FCC is familiar to almost everyone. Licensed broadcast stations must identify themselves on the air at least once every hour ("station identification").

In the narrow sense, an **administrative agency** is an "independent agency," a governmental entity distinct from the three branches of government, created to independently govern a limited specialized area of the law. (See Figure 7–1.) Since an administrative agency is distinct from the three branches of government, it has to answer only to the three branches of government in a formal way. For example, if the National Labor Relations Board (NLRB) wants to order a particular company committing an unfair labor practice against a union to reinstate a particular employee with back pay, it need not ask for specific permission from any of the three branches of government to do so. The legislature has already granted general authority to do so in the National Labor

Figure 7–1 Administrative Agencies

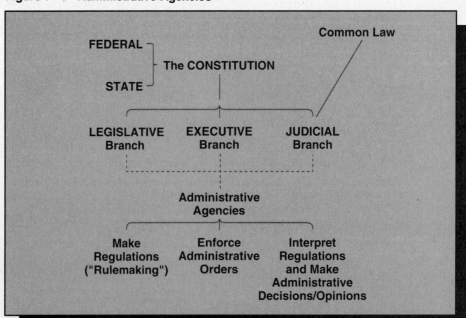

Relations Act, the executive has already appointed members to the NLRB with the power to do so, and the judiciary will enforce the orders of the NLRB to do so that the judiciary interprets to be within the mandate of the act.

Under the executive branch of government, groups of specialists may be organized to assist the executive in carrying out the functions of the executive branch. Among administrative agencies in the broad sense, these organizations are known as **executive departments.** (See Figure 7–2.) The heads of executive departments do not run entities distinct from the executive branch, and so they must answer to the executive both formally and informally. For example, if the Secretary of the Department of Defense wants to eliminate a major weapon system, it must be with the approval of the executive, the President, who is the commander in chief. Similar "executive departments" may also be created under the legislative branch (e.g., the General Accounting Office and the Library of Congress) and are known as **legislative departments.**

The technical distinction between administrative agencies and executive departments has been blurred in two ways. First, administrative agencies and executive departments are generally required by the sovereign to follow similar operating procedures. In the federal government, for example, each must follow the Administrative Procedure Act, which requires them to notify the public of proposed rule changes, hold public hearings, and the like. Second, the names given to the various administrative agencies and executive departments are often confusingly similar, yet widely varied.

An administrative agency, or a part of it, may be called, among other things, an administration, agency, authority, board, bureau, commission, corporation, department, division, foundation, office, or service. For example, local weather reports, watches, and warnings originate from offices of the National Weather Service (NWS), which is part of the National Oceanographic and Atmospheric Administration (NOAA), which is part of the U.S. Department of Commerce, which is, of course, an executive department of the President.

Usually the best way to sort out "who's who" is to consult an almanac, encyclopedia, directory, or manual. For the federal government, an extremely

Figure 7–2 The Executive Branch

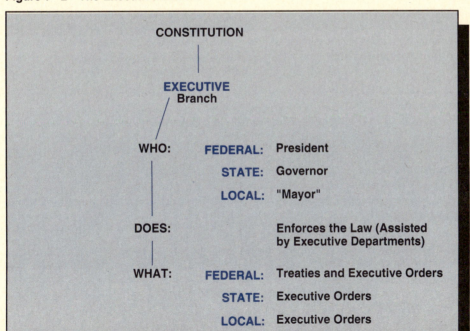

useful text is the *U.S. Government Manual* prepared annually by the National Archives. The *U.S. Government Manual* is a "road map" to the federal government. Each entity in the federal government is covered, with emphasis on the executive departments and independent agencies. Each entity and its function are described in a concise narrative, usually with citations to its statutory source of authority. The names and functions of the major officials are also listed. (See Figure 7–3.)

The *U.S. Government Manual* includes several useful indexes and tables. Appendix A lists agencies that have been abolished, or whose powers have been transferred and to where they have been transferred (e.g., the powers of the former Materials Transportation Bureau [MTB] of the Department of Transportation [DOT] are now exercised by the Office of Hazardous Materials Transportation [OHMT]). Appendix B is the famous "alphabet soup" table listing the acronyms for all the governmental agencies (e.g., CIA, FAA, FBI, NRC) and what they stand for (i.e., Central Intelligence Agency, Federal Aviation Administration, Federal Bureau of Investigation, Nuclear Regulatory Commission, respectively). (See Figure 7–4.) Appendix C contains governmental organizational charts.

Monitor Publishing Co. publishes several "Yellow Book" directories for the federal government. The *Federal Yellow Book*, for example, is described by the company as the "who's who in federal departments and agencies."

There are now hundreds of administrative agencies in the federal and state governments. Insofar as the number of administrative agencies is an accurate reflection of the complexity of society and its technological advances, it is evident that we live in a very complex, technologically advanced society.

Administrative Regulations

Like the sovereign's legislature, administrative agencies may "dream up" laws, so long as they are within the scope of the authority, the specialized area of law, given to the administrative agency by the legislature. To reflect the difference between the broad powers of the legislative branch and the limited powers of an administrative agency, however, the terminology is different. Whereas a legislature enacts statutes, an administrative agency issues **regulations.** Whereas a legislature legislates, an administrative agency **regulates.** Whereas statutes are made as the result of a legislature's enactment, regulations are made as the result of an administrative agency's **rulemaking.**

Until 1936, there was no official source for federal regulations. Ignorance of federal regulations and the resulting confusion were rampant. The situation came to a head in the infamous Supreme Court case *Panama Refining Co. v. Ryan* [293 U.S. 388 (1935)]. The Panama Refining Company was prosecuted for violating an administrative regulation, and the case reached the Supreme Court on appeal before it was discovered that the regulation in question had been revoked before the prosecution had begun.

To clear up some of the ignorance and confusion, in 1936, Congress passed the Federal Register Act [49 Stat. 500, 44 U.S.C. § 1504 et seq.]. The National Archives was given the duty of preparing and publishing (through the Government Printing Office) the *Federal Register* (Fed. Reg.). Published daily, except on Saturdays, Sundays, or legal holidays and the day following, the *Federal Register* is the official chronological source of federal regulations. For any federal administrative regulation or ruling to have legal effect, it must be published in the *Federal Register*.

Each daily *Federal Register* is about the size of a magazine, and bound volumes of the set are truly massive. The pages of the set are numbered consecutively

Figure 7-3 Excerpt From the *U.S. Government Manual*

POSTAL RATE COMMISSION
1333 H Street NW., Washington, DC 20268-0001
Phone, 202-789-6800

Chairman	Janet D. Steiger
Special Assistant	Maureen Drummy
Legal Adviser to the Chairman	Gerald E. Cerasale
Vice Chairman	Patti Birge Tyson
Special Assistant	W. Lawrence Graves
Commissioner	Henry R. Folsom
Special Assistant	(vacancy)
Commissioner	John W. Crutcher
Special Assistant	Leonard Merewitz
Commissioner	W.H. Trey LeBlanc III
Special Assistant	Jennafer W. Moreland
Chief Administrative Officer and Secretary	Charles L. Clapp
General Counsel	David F. Stover
Assistant General Counsel	Stephen L. Sharfman
Director, Office of Technical Analysis and Planning	Robert Cohen
Assistant Director, Office of Technical Analysis and Planning	Charles C. McBride
Director, Office of the Consumer Advocate	Stephen A. Gold
Personnel Officer	Cyril J. Pittack

[For the Postal Rate Commission statement of organization, see the *Code of Federal Regulations*, Title 39, Part 3002]

The major responsibility of the Postal Rate Commission is to submit recommended decisions to the United States Postal Service on postage rates and fees and mail classifications. In addition, the Commission may issue advisory opinions to the Postal Service on proposed nationwide changes in postal services; initiate studies and submit recommendations for changes in the mail classification schedule; and receive, study, and issue recommended decisions or public reports to the Postal Service on complaints received from the mailing public as to postage rates, postal classifications, postal services on a substantially nationwide basis, and the closing or consolidation of small post offices.

The Postal Rate Commission is an independent agency created by the Postal Reorganization Act (39 U.S.C. 3601–3604), as amended.

The Postal Rate Commission promulgates rules and regulations and establishes procedures and takes other actions necessary to carry out its functions and obligations. Acting upon requests from the United States Postal Service, or on its own initiative, the Commission recommends to the Board of Governors of the United States Postal Service changes in rates or fees in each class of mail or type of service. It submits recommended decisions on establishing or changing the mail classification schedule, and holds such hearings on the record as are required by law and are necessary to arrive at sound and fair recommendations. The Commission has appellate jurisdiction to review Postal Service determinations to close or consolidate small post offices.

Sources of Information

Employment The Commission's programs require attorneys, economists, statisticians, accountants, industrial engineers, marketing specialists, and administrative and clerical personnel. Requests for employment information should be directed to the Personnel Officer.

Reading Room Facilities for inspection and copying of records that are available to the public are located in Suite 300, 1333 H Street NW., Washington, DC. The room is open from 8 a.m. to 4:30 p.m., Monday through Friday, except legal holidays.

Rules of Practice and Procedure The Postal Rate Commission's Rules of Practice and Procedure governing the conduct of proceedings before the Commission may be found in part 3001 of title 39 of the *Code of Federal Regulations*.

For further information, contact the Secretary, Postal Rate Commission, 1333 H Street NW., Washington, DC 20268-0001. Phone, 202-789-6840.

Source: United States Government Manual, 1988–1989 ed. (Washington, DC: United States Government Printing Office), pp. 666–667.

Figure 7-4 Excerpt From the *U.S. Government Manual*, Appendix B

APPENDIX B: Commonly Used Abbreviations and Acronyms

ABMC	American Battle Monuments Commission	AID	Agency for International Development
ACDA	United States Arms Control and Disarmament Agency	AMS	Agricultural Marketing Service
ACUS	Administrative Conference of the United States	Amtrak	National Railroad Passenger Corporation
		ANA	Administration for Native Americans
ACYF	Administration for Children, Youth, and Families	AOA	Administration on Aging
		APHIS	Animal and Plant Health Inspection Service
ADAMHA	Alcohol, Drug Abuse, and Mental Health Administration	ARC	Appalachian Regional Commission
ADB	Asian Development Bank	ARS	Agricultural Research Service
ADD	Administration on Developmental Disabilities	ASCS	Agricultural Stabilization and Conservation Service
ADEA	Age Discrimination in Employment Act	ATSDR	Agency for Toxic Substances and Disease Registry
AEDS	Atomic Energy Detection System	BEA	Bureau of Economic Analysis
AFBCMR	Air Force Review Board for Correction of Military Records	BIA	Bureau of Indian Affairs
		BIB	Board for International Broadcasting
AFCARA	Air Force Civilian Appellate Review Agency	BJA	Bureau of Justice Assistance
AFDB	African Development Bank	BJS	Bureau of Justice Statistics
AFDC	Aid to Families with Dependent Children	BLM	Bureau of Land Management
AFDF	African Development Fund	BLMRCP	Bureau of Labor-Management Relations and Cooperative Programs
AFIS	American Forces Information Service		
AFPC	Armed Forces Policy Council	BLS	Bureau of Labor Statistics
		BPA	Bonneville Power Administration
AFPPS	American Forces Press and Publications Service	BSC's	Business Service Centers
AFRRI	Armed Forces Radiobiology Research Institute	CBO	Congressional Budget Office
		CCC	Commodity Credit Corporation
AFRTS	Armed Forces Radio and Television Service	CCEA	Cabinet Council on Economic Affairs
AFSC	Armed Forces Staff College	CCR	Commission on Civil Rights
AGRICOLA	Agricultural OnLine Access		

Source: *United States Government Manual*, 1988–1989 ed. (Washington, DC: United States Government Printing Office), p. 785.

throughout the year and run into five figures. (See Figure 7–5.) Weekly, quarterly, and annual indexes are issued, but they are not cumulative. Seizing the publishing opportunity, the Congressional Information Service publishes the *CIS Federal Register Index*, which is cumulative.

The text of the *Federal Register* since July 1, 1980, is also available on the LEXIS (GENFED;FEDREG file) and WESTLAW (FR database) computer-assisted legal research systems, which will be discussed in Chapter 12.

State administrative regulations are rarely published chronologically.

Sample Issues of the *Federal Register* (Fed. Reg.)

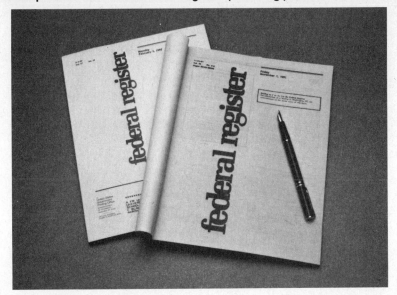

Source: © Doug Martin.

Administrative Codes

Just as statutes made by legislatures are collected topically in books called codes, regulations made by administrative agencies are also collected topically in books also called codes, or more specifically, **administrative codes.** As with the codification of statutes, the codification of regulations adds amending regulations to regulations currently in force and removes expired, repealed, or superseded regulations.

The official administrative code of the federal government, the topical collection of federal regulations, is the *Code of Federal Regulations* (C.F.R.), prepared and published (through the Government Printing Office) by the National Archives under the Federal Register Act. The C.F.R. is published in pamphlets in 50 titles generally parallel to the 50 titles of the *United States Code* (U.S.C.). The covers of the pamphlets are white and another color. To keep the code up to date, approximately one-quarter of the pamphlets are replaced each calendar quarter. The covers of the new year's pamphlets are white and a color contrasting from the previous year's color (e.g., 1990 was blue; 1991 was maroon).

To bring a pamphlet of C.F.R. up to date, one must consult the *Federal Register*. A monthly pamphlet, *LSA: List of CFR Sections Affected*, lists regulatory changes made since a particular title pamphlet was last published. The *Federal Register* also has a list "CFR Parts Affected" cumulated on the last day of each month, and cumulated daily back to the last day of the previous month.

The C.F.R. includes an annual index volume. Its entries are coordinated with the Office of the Federal Register's *Thesaurus of Indexing Terms* developed in 1980 (see 45 Fed. Reg. 2998, Jan. 15, 1980). The index also includes tables in a "Finding Aids" section.

The text of the C.F.R. is also available on the LEXIS (GENFED;CFR file) and WESTLAW (CFR database) computer-assisted legal research systems, to be discussed in Chapter 12.

If there is a conflict in language between the *Federal Register* and C.F.R., the *Federal Register* version controls.

Figure 7-5 Excerpt From the *Federal Register* (Fed. Reg.)

27872 Federal Register / Vol. 56, No. 116 / Monday, June 17, 1991 / Rules and Regulations

DEPARTMENT OF TRANSPORTATION

Research and Special Programs Administration

49 CFR Parts 107, 173, 178, and 180

[Docket No. HM-183, 183A; Amdt. Nos. 107-20, 173-212, 178-89, 180-2]

RIN 2137-AA42

Requirements for Cargo Tanks; Corrections

AGENCY: Research and Special Programs Administration (RSPA), DOT.

ACTION: Final rule; corrections and revisions.

SUMMARY: This amendment makes corrections and clarifying revisions to certain requirements pertaining to cargo tank motor vehicles in the Hazardous Materials Regulations (HMR, 49 CFR parts 171–180). These requirements were adopted in a final rule issued under Docket Nos. HM-183/183A (June 12, 1989, 54 FR 24982; May 22, 1990, 55 FR 21035; September 7, 1990, 55 FR 37028). The changes contained in this amendment will impose no new requirements on persons subject to the HMR.

EFFECTIVE DATE: June 17, 1991.

FOR FURTHER INFORMATION CONTACT:

Charles Hochman, telephone (202) 366-4545, Office of Hazardous Materials Technology, or Hattie Mitchell, telephone (202) 366-4488, Office of Hazardous Materials Standards, Research and Special Programs Administration, U.S. Department of Transportation, 400 Seventh Street SW., Washington, DC 20590-0001;

or

Richard Singer, telephone (202) 366-2994, Office of Motor Carriers, Federal Highway Administration, U.S. Department of Transportation, 400 Seventh Street SW., Washington, DC 20590-0001.

SUPPLEMENTARY INFORMATION: This document corrects typographical errors, omissions, and discrepancies to requirements in the HMR pertaining to cargo tank motor vehicles. Additionally, in response to inquiries received by RSPA concerning the clarity of particular requirements, changes are made which should reduce uncertainties. These changes impose no new requirements on persons subject to the HMR.

Because the amendments adopted herein clarify and correct certain provisions in the HMR, relieve certain restrictions in those regulations, and impose no new regulatory burden on any person, notice and public procedure are unnecessary. For these same reasons, these amendments are being made effective without the usual 30-day delay following publication.

The following is a section-by-section review of the amendments.

Section 107.504

The second sentence of § 172.504(c) implies that only those persons registered under the provisions of § 172.502(f) are eligible to renew their registrations. This error is corrected by changing "§ 172.502(f)" to "§ 172.502".

Section 173.33

RSPA has received several requests for clarification of the requirements contained in § 173.33(a)(2). The intent of this section is to prevent the transportation of two or more materials in the same cargo tank motor vehicle which, if mixed, would cause a vehicle fire, tank rupture or the release of acutely toxic vapors. An example of materials which would be prohibited are nitric acid and fuel oil. It was not intended to prevent the shipment of materials which if mixed would produce a moderate exothermic reaction that would not start a fire, rupture the tank or release acutely toxic vapors.

For hazardous materials offered for transportation in a cargo tank motor vehicle supplied by the motor carrier, § 173.22(a)(2) was revised in the September 7, 1990 amendment to clarify that shippers' responsibilities extend to the requirements in part 173 but not to the continuing requalification requirements contained in part 180. Section 173.33(a)(3) contains a requirement that, when the prescribed periodic retest or reinspection under subpart E of part 180 is past due, a specification cargo tank motor vehicle may not be filled and offered for transportation until the retest or reinspection has been successfully completed. Hazardous materials are often loaded at bulk loading facilities in cargo tank motor vehicles supplied by the motor carrier without the offeror in attendance. In these instances, verification of a carrier's compliance with part 180 is not possible. To alleviate this discrepancy, paragraph (a)(3) is revised to reflect that this requirement does not apply to an offeror in situations where the cargo tank is supplied by the motor carrier.

Paragraphs (c)(4) and (d)(1) contain criteria for the continued use of certain cargo tanks manufactured prior to December 31, 1990. Included are cargo tanks marked with a design pressure rather than a Maximum Allowable Working Pressure (MAWP), and cargo tanks fitted with non-reclosing pressure relief devices. The December 31, 1990 date should have been adjusted to coincide with the last date on which a cargo tank may be marked or certified to the MC specifications in effect on December 30, 1990. Accordingly in paragraphs (c)(4) and (d)(1), the date "December 31, 1990" is revised to read "August 31, 1993". In paragraph (c)(2), the December 31, 1990 date for requiring a cargo tank to be marked or remarked with an MAWP or design pressure in accordance with § 180.405(k) remains unchanged.

Many hazardous material liquids transported in cargo tanks are required to be completely blanketed with an inert gas, (e.g., see §§ 173.190 and 173.247a). To clarify the intent of the requirements of paragraph (d)(2), the wording "in its gaseous state" is revised to read "with a gas pad".

Formerly, § 173.33 contained various provisions pertaining to commodities, cargo tank design, qualification, maintenance and use of cargo tanks. Under HM-183/183A, these provisions were placed elsewhere in parts 173, 178 and 180, as appropriate. It has been brought to RSPA's attention that several provisions placed in the MC 331 specification, i.e. in §§ 178.337–1(e), 178.337–9 (b) and (d), and 178.337–15, also apply to existing MC 330 cargo tanks, and that Parts 173 and 180 contain no references to apply those requirements to MC 330 cargo tanks. RSPA plans to address reinstating these provisions for MC 330 cargo tanks in a rulemaking proposal in the near future.

Sections 173.245–17.374

In § 173.245, authorization for the use of DOT 406 cargo tanks was inadvertently omitted in the introductory text to paragraph (a)(29). This omission is corrected.

Also in the September amendment, §§ 172.101 and 173.154 were amended by increasing the concentration cut-off point for ammonium nitrate solution from "containing not less than 15% water" to "containing 35% or less water". RSPA stated in the preamble discussion that the entry for "Ammonium nitrate solution" was being revised to reflect that ammonium nitrate solutions with "35% or less water" do not meet the definition of an oxidizer. This statement should have read that such solutions with "over 35% water" do not meet the definition of an oxidizer. Also, in Docket HM-181 (December 21, 1990; 55 FR 52584), § 172.101 Hazardous Materials Table, special provision B5 to the entry "Ammonium nitrate, liquid (hot concentrated solution)" refers to

144 Chapter 7 Administrative Law

Code of Federal Regulations (C.F.R.)

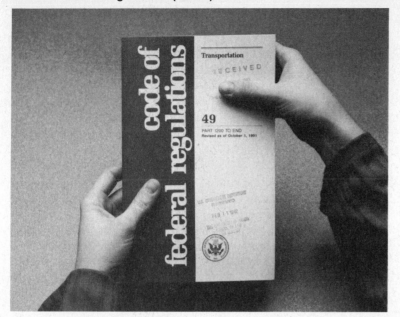

Source: © Doug Martin.

State administrative regulations are often published topically in state administrative codes. (See Appendix III.) Often a free copy of current codified regulations can be obtained simply by calling or writing the relevant agency.

Administrative Orders and Executive Orders

When the administrator of an administrative agency formally exercises discretionary "executive" power, the administrator makes an **administrative order.** When the executive of the executive branch formally exercises discretionary executive power, the executive makes an **executive order.** For example, Congress has given the President the discretion to suspend trade with a foreign country for 30 days without congressional consent. If the President wants to exercise the discretion to suspend trade with a foreign country for 30 days, the President does so by issuing an executive order. By custom, executive orders having no continuing legal effect, such as declaring a certain day to be "National Whatever Day," are known as **proclamations.** Presidential documents can be found in a variety of sources. The Office of Federal Register sources include the *Federal Register*, Title 3 of the C.F.R., the *Codification of Presidential Proclamations and Executive Orders,* and the *Weekly Compilation of Presidential Documents,* the latter including lists of laws approved, nominations, and other material released by the White House. Proclamations and executive orders are also found in *United States Code Congressional and Administrative News* (U.S. Code Cong. & Admin. News) and in advance pamphlets to the *United States Code Service* (U.S.C.S.). Proclamations also appear in *United States Statutes at Large* (Stat.).

State administrative and executive orders are rarely published, but they are in some states (e.g., Michigan).

7–1 Administrative Agencies and Executive Departments

Administrative Decisions

Since there may be a continuing need to interpret administrative regulations, many administrative agencies exercise judicial-like functions. For example, the Office of Hearings and Appeals of the Social Security Administration hears disputes concerning whether a person is disabled enough to be entitled to Social Security disability benefits. The "judge" in an administrative hearing is known as an **administrative law judge**. The administrative law judge's decision may be explained in an **administrative decision**.

Administrative decisions may or may not be appealed to the courts, depending on the subject matter involved. For example, decisions of the federal government's Employees' Compensation Appeals Board are not appealable to the courts because the board interprets a voluntary compensation act, the Federal Employee's Compensation Act, and not a liability act, such as the Federal Employers' Liability Act.

Like judicial opinions, administrative decisions are published in reports. The Government Printing Office publishes federal administrative decisions of various agencies in a variety of specialized reporters. These Government Printing Office publications are usually available at major federal depository libraries. Decisions of major federal administrative agencies are also published, usually in looseleaf form, by private publishers. State administrative decisions, except in the areas of tax law and workers' compensation, are rarely published.

Attorney General Opinions

An **attorney general** is the chief lawyer for a sovereign. The attorney general gives legal advice to officials in the executive branch, especially about the proper operation of governmental entities and agencies. When an executive official asks the attorney general for advice, it is a common practice, especially in the various states, for the attorney general to answer with a formal written opinion: an official memorandum of law.

Although the opinion of an attorney general is official, it is essentially advice and so is not considered primary authority. However, the opinions of attorneys general are ordinarily followed by governmental officials, and so they are considered very persuasive authority.

The opinions of the attorneys general are usually published by the appropriate sovereign. Many are also available on the LEXIS (e.g., GENFED;USAG file) and WESTLAW (e.g., USAG database) computer-assisted legal research systems, which will be discussed in Chapter 12. They are usually annotated in the sovereign's annotated codes. Citations to opinions of attorneys general are also cited in *Shepard's Citations*, to be discussed in Chapter 11.

7–2 Looseleaf Services

A **looseleaf service** is a law publication, usually a set of books, issued in notebook form.

Until recently, the law was published in notebook form only where the law was so complex and changed so rapidly that it was impractical to publish it in the permanent bound volumes or in permanent bound volumes with pocket supplements. The advantage of a looseleaf service, that the publisher could keep the service up to date simply by periodically issuing new or replacement

Looseleaf Services

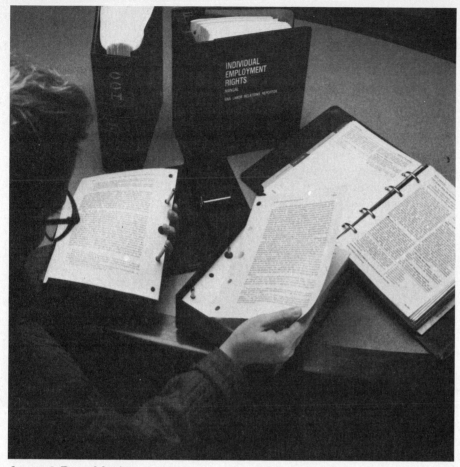

Source: © Doug Martin.

pages to be inserted into the set, was compatible with the need to keep up with the complex nature of, and rapid changes in, the law.

Recently, however, some publishers have shifted to publishing in notebook form simply because it is cheaper for them to do so. In 1986, for example, the Lawyers Co-operative Publishing Company (LCP) started several publications as looseleaf services, rather than as a set of bound volumes, in part because it had acquired the ability to make notebooks at its own manufacturing plant. Moreover, some publishers simply prefer to offer their supplementation in looseleaf form. Sometimes, instead of issuing individual replacement pages, publishers issue whole replacement sections, thereby making the updating of the looseleaf service quicker, simpler, and more convenient.

Understand that in the age of computer databases, the value of the permanent bound volume has declined. Information in a computer database, properly backed up, is almost as permanent as the information in a bound volume. When information is in a computer database it can be searched electronically, and it doesn't take up nearly as much shelf space as information in a book. Today, the importance of printed material is more in its readability than in its permanency, and in terms of readability, a looseleaf service is just as readable as a bound volume.

Still, most looseleaf services are published for complex and rapidly changing areas of the law, and the law that is most complex (involving specialized areas of the law), and changes most rapidly, is administrative law. In addition, most looseleaf services tend to cover areas of the law dealing with money, where the practitioners of the law tend to be those who can afford to pay for an up-to-date notebook service. As a result, most looseleaf services cover tax and business law.

Most of the major national looseleaf services are published by one of four major private publishers: Bureau of National Affairs, Inc. (BNA); Commerce Clearing House, Inc. (CCH); Prentice-Hall Information Services (P-H), a division of Simon & Schuster, Inc.; and Research Institute of America (RIA). There are looseleaf services available in almost every conceivable tax and business-related area of the law, including income tax, estate tax, pensions, securities, labor law, employment discrimination law, and the like. Looseleaf services can usually be located in law libraries according to the Library of Congress Classification system discussed in Appendix IV.

Almost every major looseleaf service begins with a section explaining how to use the set, including summaries of the contents, indexes, tables, and other available finding aids. Most looseleaf services are organized according to sections or paragraph numbers, which are relatively permanent, rather than by page number. There are page numbers, but they are there only to keep track of the pages in the set. Pages may be added to the set, but they are kept under a particular section or paragraph number by adding letters after page numbers (e.g., a page 12A to be added after page 12 but before page 13).

One excellent feature of a looseleaf service is the ease in which the publisher can bring together in one place all the sources of law, primary and secondary, on a particular subject, even while the law is changing. Instead of a researcher having to look in one book for a statute, another for a regulation, another for a textbook discussion, and another for a case opinion, a looseleaf service can be designed to bring all of this information together on a particular topic in consecutive pages of the notebook. Whether there are major or minor changes, a replacement page can be sent to the customer.

Looseleaf services ordinarily contain the text of the statutes, legislative history, and regulations concerning a particular topic, along with a text discussion, tables, and indexes. Sometimes there is a "current developments" section that includes the most recent material available that the publisher has not had sufficient time to edit into the main text and provide the replacement pages.

Tax Services

The complexity of tax law is well known, as is its political nature, making it subject to frequent changes and revisions. Thus, tax law is ideally suited to treatment in looseleaf services. Accordingly, the three major federal tax looseleaf services deserve special mention.

CCH publishes the *Standard Federal Tax Reporter*. It is organized in the format of the Internal Revenue Code (26 U.S.C.). After each code section, relevant regulations are presented, followed by a text discussion of the topic of the code section, followed by case summaries. CCH supports its commitment to tax law by publishing a general tax case reporter, *United States Tax Cases* (U.S.T.C.), and a reporter of U.S. Tax Court memorandum opinions, *Tax Court Memorandum Decisions* (T.C.M.). CCH also publishes a tax handbook, *U.S. Master Tax Guide*, keyed to the *Standard Federal Tax Reporter*.

RIA publishes the 35-volume *Federal Tax Coordinator 2d*. Rather than following the Internal Revenue Code section by section, RIA has broken down the law by topic. Major topic headings are lettered from A to V, with each federal code section and regulation reprinted by topic in the appropriate volume. The text is broken down into paragraphs cited by letter heading and paragraph number (e.g., V-2118). There are multiple finding aids for the set, including a topical index, and finding tables from the Internal Revenue Code, regulations, rulings, and cases. A companion set, *Tax Action Coordinator*, includes a tax analysis of legal forms and a complete set of tax forms. RIA also publishes a two-volume streamlined set, *Tax Guide*, and a tax handbook, the *Master Federal Tax Manual*, keyed to the *Federal Tax Coordinator 2d*. The entire RIA editorial staff consists of tax attorneys and accountants, who seek to write RIA services in "clear business English."

P-H publishes *Federal Taxes 2d*. Whereas P-H's first tax service was organized around the Internal Revenue Code (26 U.S.C.), like CCH's *Standard Federal Tax Reporter*, *Federal Taxes 2d* is broken down by topic, similar to RIA's *Federal Tax Coordinator 2d*. P-H supports its commitment to tax law by publishing a general tax case reporter, the *American Federal Tax Reports 2d* (A.F.T.R.2d) and a reporter of U.S. Tax Court memorandum opinions, *Memorandum Decisions of the Tax Court* (T.C.M.).

SUMMARY

7–1

The details of government are increasingly being managed by specialized governmental entities known as administrative agencies. Technically, an administrative agency is an "independent agency," a governmental entity distinct from the three branches of government, created to independently govern a limited specialized area of the law, which only has to answer to the three branches of government in a formal way. Executive departments are groups of specialists organized to assist the executive in carrying out the functions of the executive branch. The heads of executive departments must answer to the executive both formally and informally. An administrative agency, or a part of it, may be called, among other things, an administration, agency, authority, board, bureau, commission, corporation, department, division, foundation, office, or service. Usually the best way to sort out "who's who" is to consult an almanac, encyclopedia, or government directory or manual. For the federal government, a useful text is the *U.S. Government Manual*, which includes several useful indexes and tables. Appendix B is the famous "alphabet soup" table listing the acronyms for all the governmental agencies and what they stand for. An administrative agency issues regulations. The *Federal Register* (Fed. Reg.) is the official chronological source of federal regulations. Regulations made by administrative agencies are collected topically in books known as codes. The official topical collection of federal regulations is the *Code of Federal Regulations* (C.F.R.). When the executive of the executive branch formally exercises discretionary executive power, the executive makes an executive order. Executive orders having no continuing legal effect are known as proclamations. Presidential documents can be found in a variety of sources. Many administrative agencies exercise judicial-like functions. An administrative law judge's decision may be explained in an administrative decision. Administrative decisions may or may not be appealed to the courts, depending on the subject matter involved. Administrative decisions are published in reports.

7–2

A looseleaf service is a law publication, usually a set of books, issued in notebook form. Until recently, the law was published in notebook form only where the law was so complex and changed so rapidly that it was impractical to publish it in the permanent bound volumes or in permanent bound volumes with pocket supplements. Recently, however, some publishers have shifted to publishing in notebook form simply because it is cheaper for them to do so. Most looseleaf services are published for complex and rapidly changing areas of the law, and the law that is most complex (involving specialized areas of the law), and changes most rapidly, is administrative law. Most looseleaf services cover tax and business law. There are looseleaf services available in almost every conceivable tax and business-related area of the law. Most looseleaf services are organized according to sections or paragraph numbers, which are relatively permanent, rather than by page number. There are page numbers, but they are there only to keep track of the pages in the set. One feature of a looseleaf service is that it brings together in one place all the sources of law, primary and secondary, on a particular subject, even while the law is changing. Looseleaf services ordinarily contain the text of the statutes, legislative history, and regulations concerning a particular topic, along with a text discussion, tables, and indexes. Tax law is ideally suited to treatment in looseleaf services. The three major federal tax looseleaf services are CCH's *Standard Federal Tax Reporter*, RIA's *Federal Tax Coordinator 2d*, and Prentice-Hall's *Federal Taxes 2d*.

REVIEW

Key Terms

Before proceeding, review the key terms listed below to be sure you understand each one. If necessary, read over the corresponding section of the chapter. When you are ready to test your understanding, answer the Review Questions.

administrative agencies
administrative agency
administrative codes
administrative decision
administrative law judge
administrative order
attorney general
executive departments
executive order
legislative departments
looseleaf service
proclamations
regulates
regulations
rulemaking

Questions for Review and Discussion

1. Why are administrative agencies created?
2. How is an independent administrative agency different from an executive department?
3. What is the process called of making a regulation?
4. What is the official chronological source of federal regulations?
5. What is the official topical source of federal regulations?
6. How is a proclamation different from other executive orders?
7. What is an administrative law judge's written reasons for his or her decision called?
8. What, essentially, is a looseleaf service?
9. Why is a looseleaf better than a statutory code, an administrative code, a textbook, and a case reporter?
10. What are the major federal tax services?

Activities

1. Select a volume of U.S.C.A. or U.S.C.S., look up a statute, and find a cross-reference to C.F.R. Find the appropriate C.F.R. pamphlet and look up the C.F.R. reference. Notice how the regulations in C.F.R. are much more detailed than the statutes on the same topic.
2. Browse the aisles of your local law library and look for looseleaf services. How many does the library have? Is there an assortment, on a variety of topics? Do you feel that the collection is adequate and appropriate for your needs?
3. Thoroughly examine a major tax service, such as RIA's *Federal Tax Coordinator 2d*. Read the instructions on the use of the set. Do you understand each part, index, and table? Do you agree that basic tax research is not as difficult as it first appears?

PART THREE

RESEARCHING SECONDARY AUTHORITY

Chapter 8
General Works

Chapter 9
Specialized Works

CHAPTER 8 General Works

OUTLINE

8–1 Encyclopedias
Guide to American Law
Corpus Juris Secundum
American Jurisprudence 2d
State Encyclopedias
Law Outlines

8–2 Dictionaries
Black's Law Dictionary
Ballentine's Law Dictionary
Gifis' Law Dictionary
Other Dictionaries

8–3 Directories
Martindale-Hubbell Law Directory
Other National Directories
State, Local, and Specialized Directories

COMMENTARY

After completing your research of the federal laws that apply to the transportation of hazardous materials and the issue of preemption, you return to your preparation of a memorandum on public religious displays. But first, you want to get more background information on First Amendment law because you find the subject fascinating. What books can you turn to for an overview? Are there any books that explain words like *sedition* and phrases like "clear and present danger"?

OBJECTIVES

In this chapter you will learn about the general secondary sources of the law. These reference books are often used as a starting point for research in an unfamiliar area of the law, as a tool for legal self-study, or as a source of information about a particular lawyer or law firm. After reading this chapter, you should be able to:

1. Begin legal research in an unfamiliar area of the law.
2. Use *Corpus Juris Secundum* (C.J.S.).
3. Use *American Jurisprudence 2d* (Am. Jur. 2d).
4. Identify any legal encyclopedia for your state.
5. Understand the status of commercial law outlines.
6. Understand the poor quality of law dictionaries.
7. Recognize the benefits of *Black's Law Dictionary*.

8. Recognize the benefits of *Ballentine's Law Dictionary*.
9. Recognize the benefits of Gifis' *Law Dictionary*.
10. Use national and state legal directories.

8–1 Encyclopedias

An **encyclopedia** is a comprehensive work that covers all of the subjects within a particular branch of knowledge (or all branches of knowledge). While an encyclopedia covers all of a branch of knowledge and includes some detail, it is essentially a summary that does not include everything. An encyclopedia does not replace all other books on a given subject, it just ties them together.

A famous saying about the law, variously attributed, is that "the law is a seamless web." This is true in two senses. First, the law of property overlaps the law of contracts, which overlaps the law of torts, which overlaps criminal law, and so on. Second, the various forms of sovereign commands (from case opinions, to statutes, and back to court rules) mesh with each other to form "the" law. It has always been the dream of legal researchers to be able to read one text statement of the law bringing it all together. West Publishing Company (West) and Lawyers Cooperative Publishing (LCP) publish three national encyclopedias covering all of U.S. law: *Guide to American Law*, *Corpus Juris Secundum* (C.J.S.), and *American Jurisprudence 2d* (Am. Jur. 2d).

Guide to American Law, C.J.S., and Am. Jur. 2d

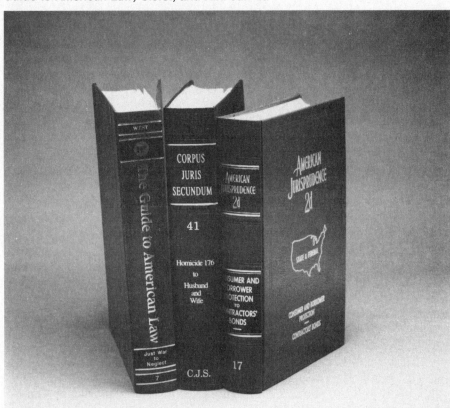

Source: © Doug Martin.

Guide to American Law

West publishes the "World Book" A-to-Z encyclopedia of the law, *Guide to American Law*. Written for lawyers and nonlawyers alike, the 12-volume set covers each legal subject in an easy-to-read style, but with formal legal citations. Unique among legal encyclopedias, *Guide to American Law* contains biographies of famous persons in the law, articles about famous cases and movements, and articles about governmental bodies and other legal organizations. (See Figure 8–1.) If, for example, you want to find out when the American Bar Association was founded, you could find the answer in *Guide to American Law*. If you have no idea where to start when researching a new topic, use this underrated general legal encyclopedia.

Corpus Juris Secundum

West's original encyclopedia for lawyers and legal researchers was *Corpus Juris* (C.J.), first published in 1936. Famous because a volume of the set sat on Perry Mason's desk in the opening of the classic television program, the title means "the body of the law."

In the late 1950s, West began publishing a modern version of the set, *Corpus Juris Secundum* (C.J.S.), the title meaning "the body of the law, second." Containing over 100 thick bound volumes, C.J.S. attempts to cover "the body" of U.S. law from its inception. The coverage includes federal law and, insofar as it can be stated generally, state law. Following West's philosophy of comprehensive law publishing, the text is supported by footnotes that purportedly include citations to every reported case on the point covered. (See Figure 8–2.) However, since 1961, C.J.S. has also included cross-references to West Topic and Key Numbers for each encyclopedia topic, so additional cases can be found using the West digests. C.J.S. is supplemented by replacement volumes as needed and annual cumulative pocket parts.

As an A-to-Z encyclopedia, C.J.S. can be entered by finding the volume with the appropriate topic, reviewing the topic outline at the beginning of the topic, then locating the desired section by its section number. The most common method of entry into C.J.S., however, is through an index. There are both a general index for the set and "volume" indexes for each topic, which are found in the last volume of the set containing that topic. Since the volume indexes are usually much more detailed than the general index, you should generally use the volume index if you know the topic you want to search.

American Jurisprudence 2d

LCP's original encyclopedia for lawyers and legal researchers was *Ruling Case Law*, started in 1914. In 1936, using *American Law Reports* (A.L.R.) annotations as a major resource, LCP began *American Jurisprudence* (Am. Jur.), the title meaning "all the law of America." Described as "[a] thoroughly modern statement of the American law in concise quotable text" [22 A.B.A. J. 363 (1936)], Am. Jur. was conceived as LCP's analytical source to the law in breadth, complementing A.L.R., its analytical source to the law in depth.

A bit of legal research humor was immortalized when volume 16 of Am. Jur. was shipped in November 1938. Indicating the topics covered in the volume, the spine proclaimed "Death to Diplomatic Officers." A whimsical advertisement in

156 Chapter 8 General Works

Figure 8-1 Excerpt From *Guide to American Law*

NATIONAL FOUNDATION ON THE ARTS AND THE HUMANITIES

The 1964 amendments also provided financing for the construction of the Capitol Page school in Washington, D.C.

The National Defense Education Act program is administered by the Department of Education.

NATIONAL DISTRICT ATTORNEYS ASSOCIATION The National District Attorneys Association was established in 1950, according to the association, "in direct response to the growth of organized crime and the increasing difficulty in monitoring interstate crime. Simply stated, its objective was to stem these undesirable elements through nation-wide exertion of prosecutional influence." Toward that end, the association sponsors regional institutes for prosecutors and enforcement officers; carries out educational and economic surveys of members; operates a placement service; and disseminates information on developments in criminal justice and civil liberties. Other activities include the awarding of scholarships, the preparation of amicus curiae briefs, and semiannual meetings. The members of the association include prosecutors and assistant prosecutors. The association maintains the following committees: Civil Function of a Prosecuting Attorney; Judicial Interpretation; Legislative Liaison; Planning and Research; and Prosecution Management. The association publishes *The Prosecutor* (bimonthly), a directory (annually), manuals, pamphlets, briefs of criminal and civil cases, and other materials.

NATIONAL ECONOMIC DEVELOPMENT LAW CENTER The National Economic Development Law Center was formed in 1969 to assist legal services attorneys working in economic development law, Community Economic Development Corporations (CDCs) funded by the Community Services Administration, and other organizations concerned with economic development. The center provides planning, training, research, and education services to concerned organizations in the hopes of promoting a uniform and comprehensive approach to community economic development policy. In addition to services provided directly, the center serves as a liaison with local, state, and Federal policy workers, recommending administrative, legal, and legislative proposals in response to community development needs. The center provides counseling and representation to development organizations in connection with funding, business transactions, tax exemptions, security offerings, and comprehensive planning. Other services include seminars and workshops on legal and tax issues. The center publishes *Economic Development Law Center Report* (bimonthly).

NATIONAL EMPLOYMENT LAW PROJECT The National Employment Law Project was initiated in 1969 to stimulate legal reform in areas relating to employment problems of the poor, such as employment discrimination, employment for the handicapped, public works programs, the Comprehensive Employment Training Act (CETA) (29 U.S.C.A. § 801 et seq.), compulsory welfare work requirements, unemployment insurance, and pension rights. In addition to the promotion of employment law reform through legal, legislative, and administrative advocacy, the project sponsors specialized seminars and maintains a library. Its publications include *Employment Law News* (quarterly), *Manual for Title VII Litigation*, *Legal Services Guide to Federal Unemployment*, and other materials related to employment law.

NATIONAL ENVIRONMENTAL POLICY ACT ☐ Federal legislation (42 U.S.C.A. § 4331 et seq.) that proclaimed a nationwide policy directed toward the protection and preservation of the environment. ☐

Among its provisions, the National Environmental Policy Act (NEPA) requires that every Federal agency submit an environmental impact statement with every legislative recommendation or program proposing major projects that will most likely affect the quality of the surrounding environment. If the Environmental Protection Agency, created pursuant to NEPA's mandate to safeguard the environment, determines that the intended project would adversely affect the environment, it can refuse to approve the project until steps are taken to minimize its effects. See also, entry on Environmental Law and Joseph L. Sax's essay on Environmental Law.

NATIONAL FOUNDATION ON THE ARTS AND THE HUMANITIES The general purpose of the National Foundation on the Arts and Humanities is to encourage and support national progress in the humanities and the arts.

The earth we abuse and the living things we kill will, in the end, take their revenge; for in exploiting their presence we are diminishing our future.

MARYA MANNES

Source: *Guide to American Law*, vol. 7 (St. Paul: West Publishing Company, 1984), p. 417. Reprinted with permission.

Figure 8–2 Excerpt From *Corpus Juris Secundum* (C.J.S.)

§§ 141–142 NEGLIGENCE   65A C.J.S.

jury, but is merely of dull mind, is chargeable with the same degree of care for his personal safety as one of brighter intellect.[5]

§ 142. Persons under Physical Disability

A person under any physical disability is required to exercise ordinary care to avoid injury, and if he fails to do so, and such failure contributes proximately to the injury, he is guilty of contributory negligence.

Library References
Negligence ⬤=86.

A person laboring under any physical disability increasing his liability to injury must nevertheless exercise ordinary care to avoid injury;[6] and if he fails to exercise that degree of care, and such failure contributes proximately to cause his injury, he is guilty of contributory negligence.[7] Such a person is not required to exercise a higher degree of care to that end than is required of a person under no disability;[8] ordinary care is all that is required.[9]

However, in determining whether such a person exercised ordinary care for his own safety, his disability is a circumstance to be considered.[10] Thus, while it has been said that ordinary care is such care as an ordinarily prudent person with the same disability would exercise under the same or similar circumstances,[11] it has also been held that it may be incumbent on one with a physical disability to put forth a greater degree of effort than would otherwise be necessary in order to attain that standard of care which is required of everyone.[12]

Blind persons and persons with defective vision. The fact that a person is wholly or partially blind does not relieve him of the duty to exercise ordinary care for his own safety;[13] and if he fails to exercise such care, and his failure to do so contributes proximately to cause his injury, he is guilty of contributory negligence.[14] It is not negligence as a matter of law for a blind person to be present in a public place[15] or to walk unattended on a public street.[16] In the absence of knowledge to the contrary, actual or imputed, such a person may assume that he is not exposed to, or threatened by, injury which can come to him only from a breach of the duty which others owe to avoid injury to him.[17]

---

5. Ala.—Worthington v. Mencer, 11 So. 72, 96 Ala. 310, 17 L.R.A. 407.
45 C.J. p 995 note 54.
6. Iowa.—**Corpus Juris Secundum cited in** Tisserat v. Peters, 99 N.W. 2d 924, 926, 251 Iowa 250.
Mass.—Keith v. Worcester, etc., R. Co., 82 N.E. 680, 196 Mass. 478, 14 L.R.A.,N.S., 648.
N.J.—Berger v. Shapiro, 152 A.2d 20, 30 N.J 89.
Karmazin v. Pennsylvania R. Co., 196 A.2d 803, 82 N.J.Super. 123, rehearing denied 198 A.2d 97, 82 N.J. Super. 435.
45 C.J. p 995 note 56.
Care required to avoid injury to person under physical disability see supra § 12.
Knowledge of danger
(1) Old woman of frail and slight physique suing for injuries resulting from fall sustained when salesman in provision, fruit, and vegetable market slightly brushed woman's elbow or arm must be charged with knowledge of her physical condition and of the risk she incurred in stationing herself so near to salesman that an ordinary movement on his part might jeopardize her safety.
Cal.—Ury v. Fredkin's Markets, 79 P.2d 749, 26 C.A.2d 501.
(2) Person whose faculties of observation are temporarily suspended as regards a dangerous condition is virtually in the same mental position as one who has never acquired knowledge of such condition.
Kan.—Cox v. City of Coffeyville, 110 P.2d 772, 153 Kan. 392.

7. Tenn.—Felton v. Horner, 37 S.W. 696, 97 Tenn. 579.
45 C.J. p 995 note 57.
Failure of passengers on trains to have an attendant as contributory negligence see Carriers § 776 a.
8. Cal.—Jones v. Bayley, 122 P.2d 293, 49 C.A.2d 647.
Me.—McCullough v. Lalumiere, 166 A.2d 702, 156 Me. 479.
S.C.—**Corpus Juris Secundum cited in** Conner v. Farmers and Merchants Bank, 132 S.E.2d 385, 392, 243 S.C. 132.
45 C.J. p 996 note 58.
9. Cal.—Jones v. Bayley, 122 P.2d 293, 49 C.A.2d 647.
S.C.—Conner v. Farmers and Merchants Bank, 132 S.E.2d 385, 243 S.C. 132.
45 C.J. p 996 note 59.
10. Conn.—Goodman v. Norwalk Jewish Center, Inc., 139 A.2d 812, 145 Conn. 146.
Mass.—Keith v. Worcester, etc., R. Co., 82 N.E. 680, 196 Mass. 478, 14 L.R.A.,N.S., 648.
45 C.J. p 996 note 60.
11. Cal.—Conjorsky v. Murray, 287 P.2d 505, 135 C.A.2d 478—Jones v. Bayley, 122 P.2d 293, 49 C.A.2d 647.
Conn.—Goodman v. Norwalk Jewish Center, Inc., 139 A.2d 812, 145 Conn. 146.
Me.—Ham v. Lewiston, 47 A. 548, 94 Me. 265.
S.C.—**Corpus Juris Secundum cited in** Conner v. Farmers and Merchants Bank, 132 S.E.2d 385, 392, 243 S.C. 132.

12. U.S.—Darter v. Greenville Community Hotel Corp., C.A.S.C., **301** F.2d 70.
Cal.—Jones v. Bayley, 122 P.2d 293, 49 C.A.2d 647—Armstrong v. Day, 284 P. 1083, 103 C.A. 465.
Me.—McCullough v. Lalumiere, **166** A.2d 702, 156 Me. 479.
Neb.—Trumbley v. Moore, 39 N.W.2d 613, 151 Neb. 780.
45 C.J. p 996 note 62.
Requirement stated in terms of degree of care
In some cases the text requirement has been stated in terms of a commensurately greater degree of care.
U.S.—Darter v. Greenville Community Hotel Corporation, C.A.S.C., 301 F.2d 70.
13. Cal.—**Corpus Juris Secundum cited in** Krause v. Apodaca, 186 C. A.2d 413, 9 Cal.Rptr. 10, 12.
Iowa.—Balcom v. Independence, 160 N.W. 305, 178 Iowa 685, L.R.A.1917C 120.
Pa.—Davis v. Feinstein, 88 A.2d 695, 370 Pa. 449.
45 C.J. p 996 note 64.
Care required to avoid injury to blind person see supra § 12.
14. Pa.—Karl v. Juniata County, **56** A. 78, 206 Pa. 633.
45 C.J. p 996 note 65.
15. N.Y.—Harris v. Uebelhoer, 75 N. Y. 169.
16. Or.—Weinstein v. Wheeler, 271 P. 733, 127 Or. 406, 62 A.L.R. 574.
17. Tenn.—**Corpus Juris cited in** East Tennessee Light & Power Co.

172

Source: Corpus Juris Secundum, vol. 65A (St. Paul: West Publishing Company, 1966), p. 172. Reprinted with permission.

the *American Bar Association Journal* mused: "Were we thinking of Munich? No—Only of every-day law." [25 A.B.A. J. 263 (1939).]

Planned by LCP editor Alfred W. Gans, who had worked on Am. Jur. from its inception, the modern *American Jurisprudence 2d* (Am. Jur. 2d) was begun in 1962. Containing over 80 volumes, Am. Jur. 2d, like C.J.S., covers federal law and, insofar as it can be stated generally, state law. However, following LCP's philosophy of selective law publishing, the text is supported by footnotes that purportedly include citations to only selected leading or landmark cases on the point covered. (See Figure 8–3.) Footnotes are also made to statutory sources and to A.L.R. annotations. Topics also begin with cross-references to other units of the Total Client Service Library. Am. Jur. 2d, like C.J.S., is supplemented by replacement volumes as needed and annual cumulative pocket parts, except for the federal tax volumes, which are prepared annually by the Research Institute of America (RIA).

As an A-to-Z encyclopedia, Am. Jur. 2d can be entered by finding the volume with the appropriate topic, reviewing the topic outline at the beginning of that topic, then locating the desired section by its section number. The most common method of entry into Am. Jur. 2d, however, is through an index. There are both a general index for the set and "volume" indexes for each topic, which are found in the last volume of the set containing that topic. Again, since the volume indexes are usually much more detailed than the general index, you should generally use the volume index if you know the topic you want to search.

Am. Jur. 2d includes a separate volume entitled *Table of Statutes and Rules Cited*, which allows a researcher of a federal statute or rule to find the Am. Jur. 2d topic and section number, if any, in which it is cited. The Am. Jur. 2d *New Topic Service*, as its name implies, contains new topics not yet incorporated into the main volumes. The one-volume Am. Jur. 2d *Desk Book*, created as a marketing tool, is a general legal almanac. Other than a list of Am. Jur. 2d topics, the *Desk Book* contains an odd collection of information, including historical documents, ethical codes, bar admission standards, uniform laws, financial tables, reporter abbreviations, and Latin phrases.

LCP also sells a separate student textbook, *Summary of American Law*, which is keyed to and summarizes Am. Jur. 2d. The first edition was prepared in 1947 (for Am. Jur.) by LCP editor Robert T. Kimbrough, with later editions by George L. Clark (1974) and Martin Weinstein (1988).

In the mid-1980s, LCP set out to modernize Am. Jur. 2d and its state encyclopedias. The editors of new and revised topics were encouraged to cite more modern cases in the supporting footnotes. However, to cut costs, LCP instructed some of its editors *not* to take the time to update material used from earlier versions. Thus, even in new and revised topics, some footnotes cite old cases.

Another aspect of LCP's modernization can be gleaned from an October 1987 advertising mailer:

> The contemporary topics in Ohio Jur 3d are grouped together under "problem areas." This eliminates searching through several volumes for one answer. For example, "Creditors' Rights and Remedies" gathers information from the areas of attachments, garnishment, civil arrest, fraudulent conveyances, and insolvency. And related matters are brought to your attention . . . automatically. It's an approach designed for the practitioner and not the professor.

State Encyclopedias

In states with a sufficient customer base to make publication of an encyclopedia feasible, there are state encyclopedias. West publishes encyclopedia sets in the

Figure 8–3 Excerpt From *American Jurisprudence 2d* (Am. Jur. 2d)

49 Am Jur 2d   LANDLORD AND TENANT   § 761

XXI. DUTIES AND LIABILITIES OF LANDLORD AS TO CONDITION, USE, REPAIR, AND IMPROVEMENT

A. In General

§ 761. Generally; effect of want of title.

With respect to the duties and liabilities of the landlord as to condition, use, repair, and improvement, it is important to distinguish between his responsibility to the tenant and persons on the premises in the right of the tenant[19] and his responsibility to other third persons such as trespassers,[20] persons on the demised premises[1] or other premises with the consent of the landlord,[2] or persons on adjoining or nearby premises[3] and persons on the highway or street.[4] It is also important to distinguish between the landlord's responsibility as to the demised premises,[5] his responsibility as to other premises owned and possessed by him,[6] and his responsibility as to other premises owned, but not possessed, by him.[7] Another important consideration is whether he has made any special express or implied agreement as to condition, use, repair, or improvement.[8]

The general rule that one who assumes to be the owner of real property and, as such, assumes to control and manage it, cannot escape liability for injuries resulting from its defective condition, by showing want of title in himself,[9] has been applied to one who acts as landlord.[10] Accordingly, one in possession and control of real estate may be liable for injury to a tenant through failure to make repairs, although he does not have the legal title.[11] Thus, if an alleged landlord, by his conduct in dealing with the property and by his knowledge and transactions in reference to it, so acted that it could be fairly said that he assumed the duties and responsibilities of a landlord, it could be found that he was in fact the landlord with a landlord's usual liabilities, although he did not have legal title to the property

19. §§ 767 et seq., infra.

20. § 762, infra.

1. § 763, infra.

2. §§ 799 et seq., infra.

3. §§ 898 et seq., infra.

4. See 39 Am Jur 2d, Highway, Streets, and Bridges §§ 369, 370, 499, 502, 521, 522, 537, 544.

5. §§ 767 et seq., infra.

6. §§ 799 et seq., 803, infra.

7. § 804, infra.

8. §§ 828 et seq., infra.

9. See Negligence (1st ed § 95).

10. Ziulkowski v Kolodziej, 119 **Conn** 230, 175 A 780, 96 ALR 1065; Skolnick v East Boston Sav. Bank, 307 **Mass** 1, 29 NE2d 585, 130 ALR 1519; Lindsey v Leighton, 150 **Mass** 285, 22 NE 901; Bannigan v Woodbury, 158 **Mich** 206, 122 NW 531 (in which it was held that an administrator lawfully in possession and control of a building belonging to the estate was personally liable for injuries sustained by a pedestrian on the adjoining sidewalk as a result of being struck by glass falling from a window negligently permitted to become unsafe).

Annotation: 96 ALR 1068, s. 130 ALR 1525.

11. Ziulkowski v Kolodziej, 119 **Conn** 230, 175 A 780, 96 ALR 1065, wherein it appeared that an intestate's widow, on the death of her husband, assumed possession and control for herself and her children of a three-family house owned by the intestate, collecting rents and making some repairs; and that while she was so in control and before her appointment as administratrix, one of the tenants was injured by falling on a common stairway because of its defective condition, and the court held that the widow was liable for the tenant's injuries although she was not in control as administratrix.

In Lindsey v Leighton, 150 **Mass** 285, 22 NE 901, it was held that one who assumed to be the owner of real estate the title to which was in his wife, and leased it as owner, could not escape liability for injuries sustained by the tenant by reason of the defective condition of the property, by showing want of title in himself.

68

Source: American Jurisprudence 2d, vol. 49 (Rochester, NY: Lawyers Co-operative Publishing Co., 1970), p. 68. Reprinted with permission.

style of C.J.S. for Illinois, Maryland, and Michigan. LCP publishes encyclopedia sets in the style of Am. Jur. 2d for California, Florida, New York, Ohio, and Texas. Although a state encyclopedia can be quite specific as to the law of a given topic, you should remember that as an encyclopedia, it is a summary secondary source of the law. As such, it should never be cited as if it were a primary authority.

Law Outlines

While an encyclopedia is a narrative summary, an **outline** is a summary showing the pattern of subordination of one thought to another. As discussed in Chapter 3, most law schools use the casebook method. Under this method, law students read cases and are encouraged to prepare for exams by outlining what they have learned. Commercially prepared law outlines are frowned upon and carry about as much weight as Cliff's Notes do with the typical high school English teacher. Because of this attitude, you should never cite a commercial law outline as either primary or secondary authority.

Nevertheless, commercial law outlines, like legal encyclopedias, summarize the law and cite cases and other legal materials in support. Many law students find through the grapevine that they can learn the fundamentals of the law effectively by reading and studying commercial law outlines. They're the books that everyone knows about, buys, and uses, but nobody talks about.

One publisher of a complete series of law outlines is Emanuel Law Outlines, Inc., founded by a *cum laude* graduate of Harvard Law School, Steven L. Emanuel. Emanuel law outlines feature an easy, read-like-a-book writing style, concise summaries of significant cases, and numerous examples, all set in large, easy-to-read type. In the 1988–1989 academic year, Emanuel sold nearly 100,000 law outlines. Emanuel also sells the Smith's Review Series, formerly published by West.

There are many other sets of commercial law outlines. They include Gilbert Law Summaries, Legalines, Ryan Law Capsules, Sum & Substance, and West's Black Letter Series. There are also guides to law school casebooks known as **canned briefs,** since each major case is preanalyzed ("canned") for the reader. The major canned-brief series are Casenote Legal Briefs and Cambridge Law Study Aids.

Law outlines and canned briefs are often sold in law school bookstores and are generally available by mail from the Chicago Law Book Company of Chicago, Illinois, The Law Annex at Harvard Book Stores, Inc., of Cambridge, Massachusetts, and the Law Distributors of Gardena, California.

8–2 Dictionaries

A **dictionary** is a book containing an alphabetical list of words, along with information about each word, usually including its spelling, pronunciation, **etymology** (word origin), **definitions** (meanings), forms, and uses. A **law dictionary** is a book containing a list of words unique to the legal profession, words often used by the legal profession (e.g., Latin phrases), and ordinary words with a legal meaning.

The two leading law dictionaries are published by the two largest law publishers: *Black's Law Dictionary* by West and *Ballentine's Law Dictionary* by LCP. Both dictionaries were originally prepared over 75 years ago: *Black's* in 1891, and *Ballentine's* in 1916.

Black's Law Dictionary and Ballentine's Law Dictionary

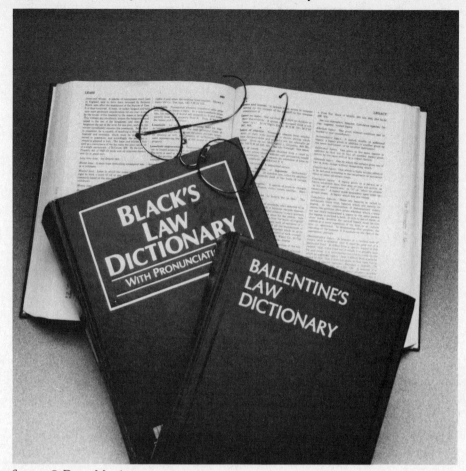

Source: © Doug Martin.

Because of their age and dated word lists, *Black's* and *Ballentine's* have become the objects of increasing derision within the legal profession. In 1985, Robert D. White took aim at *Black's Law Dictionary* with a satirical book entitled *White's Law Dictionary* (NY: Warner Books, Inc., 1985). The cover of *White's Law Dictionary* defines *Black's Law Dictionary* as "an overlarge medieval legal lexicon. Preeminent in the field, until superseded by this book." As White explains:

> Lawyers say words are their stock in trade. If so, they are burdened by an excess of inventory. Consider a volume which by default has held primacy among legal lexicons since its original publication in 1891: *Black's Law Dictionary*.
>
> The preface to *Black's* states that the latest edition includes 10,000 entries. Let's examine some of those 10,000.
>
> A random perusal turns up *zemindar*. You think, "Wow, I really didn't know that one. Good thing I have *Black's*." Its definition? "In Hindu Law, Landkeeper." You sigh a breath of relief; thank God your ignorance of zemindars didn't come up in public.
>
> Flipping back to the beginning, you see:
>
>> *A* The first letter in the English and most other alphabets derived from the Roman or Latin alphabet, which was one of several ancient Italian alphabets derived from the Greek, which was an adaptation of the Phoenician.
>
> Amazing. Just the other day you were wondering if that wasn't adapted from the Phoenician.

Come on, Mr. Black, what gives?

Do we really need a sixty-seven-word definition of "wrongful act," including a citation to a decision of the Illinois Court of Appeals? You couldn't leave it at "something one shouldn't do?"

How about "*Apt* Fit; suitable; appropriate"? Do I see a little padding to get the total up to 10,000?

And "*Cerebellum* Lower portion of brain below back of cerebrum concerned with muscular coordination and body equilibrium"—aren't we poaching a wee bit on another profession's turf? [p. viii–ix.]

White could have just as easily attacked *Ballentine's Law Dictionary*. Among its 30,000 terms is *zingara*, meaning "[a]ny female in a band of gypsies." It also defines the letter *A*, gives a 350-word definition for *accident*, and defines words such as *weather* and *umbilical cord*.

The problem with both *Black's* and *Ballentine's*, and virtually all other law dictionaries, is that they are not citation-based. A **citation-based** dictionary, the standard among general dictionaries, is created by collecting a fair sample of actual uses of each word in context **(citations),** allowing the editor of the dictionary to authoritatively determine whether the word is current or archaic and its "correct" spelling, etymology, meaning, and usage. The current law dictionaries simply do not include etymologies or citation-based authoritative definitions, and archaic words are rarely identified or eliminated.

Law dictionaries are substandard because of economics. The legal market has not been deemed large enough for a private publisher to profitably commit the resources necessary to create a citation-based law dictionary, although both West and LCP have the resources to do so. In 1989, the University of Texas School of Law and the Oxford University Press announced their plan to produce a citation-based law dictionary entitled the *Oxford Law Dictionary*, but the project has been abandoned.

Black's Law Dictionary

Despite its limitations, *Black's Law Dictionary* remains the most cited, most respected, and best-selling dictionary for the legal profession. It was originally prepared in 1891 (as *A Dictionary of the Law*) by Henry Campbell Black, the author of an obscure series of law treatises. Since then, *Black's* has been published in seven editions, dated 1910, 1933, 1951, 1957, 1968, 1979, and 1990. After Black's death, revisions were made by the publisher's editorial staff.

The major features of *Black's* include pronunciations for selected entries, selected citations to cases, a table of abbreviations, the Constitution of the United States, a time chart of the U.S. Supreme Court, an organizational chart of the U.S. government, and a table of British regnal years.

Black's is available in its standard edition (the basic hard-cover version), a deluxe edition (a more expensive version with a fancy cover and thumb-hole tabs), and an abridged edition (a shorter, cheaper soft-cover version). *Black's* is also available on the WESTLAW (DI database) computer-assisted legal research system, to be discussed in Chapter 12.

West also publishes a set of word-books combining elements of the National Reporter System and West's digest system: *Words and Phrases*. When a case opinion appears to judicially define a word or phrase, a headnote is drawn from the definition. These headnotes are collected in the manner of a digest, under the appropriate words and phrases listed from A to Z. *Words and Phrases* allows you to look up a word or phrase and to read digest paragraphs summarizing judicial definitions of that word or phrase. (See Figure 8–4.) The set is supplemented by annual cumulative pocket parts. Modern volumes of the

Figure 8-4 Excerpt From West's *Words and Phrases*

RES IPSA LOQUITUR

Injuries from breaking or explosion of bottle—Cont'd

v. Garrett, Tex.Civ.App., 143 S.W.2d 1020, 1022, 1023.

In action for injuries sustained by plaintiff, who was engaged in cold drink business, when bottled soft drink exploded and piece of glass bottle struck plaintiff, even if "res ipsa loquitur doctrine" was applicable, plaintiff was not entitled to judgment simply because jury found that plaintiff suffered damages in a given sum, where defendant's evidence was sufficient to make jury question of defendant's negligence, since the finding of extent of plaintiff's injuries was not a finding of negligence by defendant. Alagood v. Coca Cola Bottling Co., Tex.Civ.App., 135 S.W.2d 1056, 1060, 1061.

Where plaintiff, who operated a restaurant, was injured when a bottle of carbonated beverage manufactured and bottled by defendant exploded while plaintiff was putting bottle in an icebox after a case of beverage had been brought to restaurant by defendant's employee, the doctrine of "res ipsa loquitur" was applicable, and doctrine of "unavoidable accident" did not apply to relieve defendant from liability for injuries, notwithstanding that bottle was in plaintiff's possession and control at time of explosion. Bradley v. Conway Springs Bottling Co., 118 P.2d 601, 603, 605, 154 Kan. 282.

Where plaintiff in action for injuries against manufacturer of bottled beverages proved that plaintiff was taking a bottle of beverage from an ice box furnished plaintiff by manufacturer and had pulled bottle a few inches above top of water in box when bottle exploded causing fragments of glass to strike plaintiff and that bottle was purchased from manufacturer on day preceding explosion and was not frozen or knocked against other bottles or sides of box as it was being pulled from water before explosion, the doctrine of "res ipsa loquitur" was applicable, and plaintiff established a "prima facie case" of negligence against manufacturer. Lanza v. De Ridder Coca Cola Bottling Co., La.App., 3 So.2d 217, 218.

Where doctrine of "res ipsa loquitur" was otherwise applicable in action against manufacturer of beverages for injuries sustained when a bottle of beverage exploded, application of doctrine was not excluded or limited because plaintiff failed to produce bottle for examination by manufacturer, especially where bottle had burst into fragments and there was no evidence that plain-

Injuries from breaking or explosion of bottle—Cont'd

tiff willfully failed to preserve and produce remains thereof. Lanza v. De Ridder Coca Cola Bottling Co., La.App., 3 So.2d 217, 218.

Injuries from consumption of beverage, food or candy, etc.

"Res ipsa loquitur" doctrine was not applicable to sustain recovery against manufacturer and bottler for injuries sustained in explosion of bottle of beer which was not within bottler's exclusive control for several days preceding explosion, in absence of evidence of reasonably discoverable defect in bottle, where proof of any such defect by means of fragments of bottle in his possession was available to person injured. Curley v. Ruppert, 71 N.Y.S.2d 578, 580.

In action against bottler for injuries caused by explosion of bottle of carbonated water, evidence not showing that bottle between time it left possession of bottler and when it came into possession of plaintiff who bought it in a store, that it was not subjected to any condition that would tend to bring about the explosion was insufficient to warrant verdict for plaintiff under "res ipsa loquitur doctrine". Kees v. Canada Dry Ginger Ale, 199 S.W.2d 76, 77, 79, 239 Mo.App. 1080.

Doctrine applicable where abnormal condition of soft drink was due to fermentation, caused by defective sealing of bottle. White v. Coca-Cola Bottling Co., La.App., 16 So.2d 579, 582.

In action against dairy company for injuries allegedly sustained from paint in milk, doctrine of "res ipsa loquitur" was applicable. Welter v. Bowman Dairy Co., 47 N.E.2d 739, 762, 318 Ill.App. 305.

In an action for damages for personal injuries resulting from consumption of a bottled beverage, the plaintiff may not rely on doctrine of "res ipsa loquitur." Tickle v. Hobgood, 4 S.E.2d 444, 445, 216 N.C. 221.

In action against a bottling company to recover for damages allegedly resulting from drinking bottled beverage containing noxious substance, the doctrine of "res ipsa loquitur" is inapplicable. Evans v. Charlotte Pepsi-Cola Bottling Co., 6 S.E.2d 510, 511, 216 N.C. 716.

In action by consumer against manufacturer for injuries allegedly caused by a fish

555

Source: Words and Phrases, vol. 37 (St. Paul: West Publishing Company, 1965), p. 555. Reprinted with permission.

National Reporter System also include a "Words and Phrases" section derived from the cases in those volumes.

Ballentine's Law Dictionary

Despite its limitations, *Ballentine's Law Dictionary* continues to be a major dictionary for the legal profession. Originally prepared in 1916 by James A. Ballentine, Assistant Professor of Law at the University of California and Dean of the San Francisco Law School, *Ballentine's* has had five printings and three editions: 1916 and 1923—first edition, 1930 and 1948–second edition, and 1969—third edition. The third edition was edited by LCP editor William S. Anderson.

The major features of *Ballentine's* include pronunciations for selected entries, selected citations to cases, and selected citations to *United States Supreme Court Reports, Lawyers' Edition* (L. Ed.), A.L.R., and Am. Jur.

Gifis' *Law Dictionary*

The most practical, readable, and useful law dictionary currently published is Gifis' *Law Dictionary*, published by Barron's Educational Series, Inc. Originally prepared in 1975 by Steven H. Gifis, Associate Professor of Law at the Rutgers School of Law, Gifis' *Law Dictionary* is now in its second edition, published in 1984.

The major feature of this law dictionary is Gifis' careful selection of entries to include modern legal words and ancient legal words still in use, and to exclude archaic legal words. (See Figure 8–5.) Other features include the cross-references of entries with their use in other definitions, pronunciations for selected entries, selected citations to cases, the Constitution of the United States, the ABA Model Code of Professional Responsibility, and the ABA Model Rules of Professional Conduct. Perhaps most important, this law dictionary is reasonably priced.

Other Dictionaries

Many other law dictionaries have been published. They include West's *Bouvier's Law Dictionary* (1914); Datinder S. Sodhi's *The Attorney's Pocket Dictionary* (1981), published by Law and Business Publications Inc.; William Statsky's *Legal Thesaurus/Dictionary* (1985), published by West; and Wesley Gilmer, Jr.'s *The Law Dictionary* (1986), published by Anderson Publishing Co.

There are also legal **thesauri** (books of words and their synonyms and near synonyms). These include *Cochran's Law Lexicon* (1973), Burton's *Legal Thesaurus* (1980), and Statsky's *Legal Thesaurus/Dictionary* (1985).

8–3 Directories

A **directory** is a list of names and certain other information, such as addresses, telephone numbers, and the like. A **legal directory** is a guide to lawyers, law firms, and/or governmental agencies.

Legal directories are often used to find and select lawyers admitted to practice in another state or in another jurisdiction. This is necessary because no

Figure 8-5 Excerpt From Gifis' *Law Dictionary*

SEDITION   431   SEGREGATION

ests that arise by operation of law.

The clearest examples of security interests are the **mortgage**, the **pledge** and the **conditional sale**. The mortgage involves the situation wherein the mortgagor gives the mortgagee a security interest in a specific asset, which is usually real property. The pledge deals with the situation wherein the creditor takes possession of the property. The conditional sale involves the situation wherein the seller gives credit and takes a security interest. The Uniform Commercial Code ignores differences of form and treats all secured interests in personal property simply as "security interests." See U.C.C. §9-102. Compare **security deposit**.

PURCHASE-MONEY SECURITY INTEREST one "taken or retained by the seller of the **collateral** to secure all or part of its price; or is one taken by a person who, by making advances or incurring an obligation, gives value in order to enable the debtor to acquire rights in or the use of collateral if such value is in fact so used." U.C.C. §9-107.

SEDITION illegal action tending to cause the disruption and overthrow of the government. The United States had enacted an Alien and Sedition Act as early as 1798. Sedition acts were also enacted during World War I, prohibiting types of communication advocating the overthrow of the government. In 1919, the Supreme Court held that seditious communications could be punished consistent with the First Amendment, if they presented a **clear and present danger** of bringing about an evil (violence) which the government had a right to prevent. See 249 U.S. 47.

The state governments also have the power to prevent harmful sedition. See 254 U.S. 325. However, the states cannot punish sedition against the United States where Congress has already **preempted** legislation in this area by "occupying the field" with legislation of its own. See 350 U.S. 497. See **treason**.

SEDITIOUS LIBEL in English law a misdemeanor involving the publishing of any words or document, with a seditious intention. "A seditious intention means an intention to bring into contempt or excite disaffection against the government or to promote feelings of ill will between the classes. If the seditious statement is published, the publisher is guilty of a seditious libel." Black, Constitutional Law 543 (2d ed. 1897). The law of seditious libel is now severely circumscribed in **the United States** by the **First Amendment** to the Constitution. See **freedom** [FREEDOM OF PRESS]; [FREEDOM OF SPEECH].

SEDUCTION "[i]nducing a chaste, unmarried woman, by means of temptation, deception, acts, flattery, or a promise of marriage, to engage in sexual intercourse." 151 So. 2d 752, 757. A woman may also entice a man to commit sexual intercourse. 138 So. 2. Force is not an **element** of "seduction." At common law, seduction merely created a **civil** liability and in some states the woman could recover **damages** for her seduction. In states where seduction is now a criminal offense, the chastity or reputation of chastity of the victim prior to seduction may be essential for conviction. See 18 U.S.C. §2198; Model Penal Code §213.3. Other states have barred actions for seduction. See N.Y. Civ. Rights L. §80a. Perkins & Boyce, Criminal Law 462 (3d ed. 1982). See **fornication**. Compare **rape**.

SEGREGATION to set apart; the separation of some persons or things from others. 170 S.E. 189, 191. For instance, a contract may require a party to keep certain funds segregated so that they will

Source: Steven H. Gifis, *Law Dictionary*, 2nd ed. (New York: Barron's Educational Series, Inc., 1984), p. 431. Reprinted with permission.

lawyer is admitted to practice in every state, or can in every jurisdiction, and clients may have legal problems that extend into other states and jurisdictions. Legal directories are also used to find correct addresses for, and certain information about, other lawyers. Moreover, legal directories are effective job-hunting tools, particularly if you are seeking a position in another state.

Martindale-Hubbell Law Directory

The long-established leading national law directory is the *Martindale-Hubbell Law Directory*, published annually by the Martindale-Hubbell division of Reed Publishing (USA) Inc. The directory is a multivolume set, arranged in alphabetical order by state. Since 1990, *Martindale-Hubbell* is also available for purchase on CD-ROM. It is also available on the LEXIS computer-assisted legal research system, to be discussed in Chapter 12.

Each volume of *Martindale-Hubbell* contains two parts. The first part, containing relatively few pages, purports to list all the lawyers in a given state, arranged alphabetically by city of practice, then by last name and first name. The information provided in this part includes birth date, bar admission date, college attended, and law school attended. Where Martindale-Hubbell has received confidential recommendations, a lawyer may be given a rating, the highest being *av*, meaning *a*, very high legal ability; and *v*, very high faithful adherence to ethical standards. Lawyers are listed in the first part at no cost.

The second part, containing most of the pages, consists of paid advertisements. Arranged by city of practice, then by sole practitioner or law firm, the information provided in this part includes addresses, telephone and fax numbers, areas of practice, biographies, and representative clients.

Martindale-Hubbell also includes, in separate volumes, "Law Digests" that summarize the laws of the various states, the laws of many foreign countries (including Canada and Canadian provinces), and other useful information (e.g., summaries of U.S. copyright, patent, and trademark laws). The state law digests, written by law firms in the respective states, are excellent starting points for researching the law in each state.

Martindale-Hubbell Law Directory

Source: © Doug Martin.

Other National Directories

There are several other national directories of lawyers, and two have unique formats.

Marquis Who's Who, Macmillan Directory Division, publishes *Who's Who in American Law*. The sixth edition was published in 1989. As its preface states, *Who's Who in American Law* "provides biographical information on approximately 27,600 lawyers and professions in law-related areas, including, among others, judges, legal educators, law librarians, legal historians, and social scientists."

West is developing, and has on-line, *West's Legal Directory*. Part of the WESTLAW computer-assisted legal research system, which will be discussed in Chapter 12, *West's Legal Directory* is an on-line database (WLD). For each attorney, there is a basic attorney profile (including address and telephone number, bar admissions, and areas of practice) and a professional profile (including birth date, education, representative clients, and foreign language ability).

State, Local, and Specialized Directories

Legal directories for several states and regions are published by the Legal Directories Publishing Company, Inc., of Dallas, Texas. The directories include alphabetical lists of attorneys statewide, an alphabetical list of law firms statewide, and an attorney list by county and city.

Local legal directories are also published by local bar associations and other publishers. In Ohio, for example, Anderson Publishing Company publishes the multivolume *Profiles of Ohio Lawyers*.

There are countless specialized directories, ranging from the *Congressional Directory* to the Association of American Law Schools' *Directory of Law Teachers* (for law school teachers). Some are available on the LEXIS and WESTLAW computer-assisted legal research systems, to be discussed in Chapter 12.

SUMMARY

8-1

It has always been the dream of legal researchers to be able to read one text statement of the law bringing it all together. Written for both lawyers and nonlawyers alike, West publishes the easy-to-read A-to-Z encyclopedia of the law, *Guide to American Law*. West's current encyclopedia for lawyers and legal researchers is *Corpus Juris Secundum* (C.J.S.), the title meaning "the body of the law, second." Following West's philosophy of "comprehensive" law publishing, the text in C.J.S. is supported by footnotes that purportedly include citations to every reported case on the point covered. C.J.S. also includes cross-references to West Topic and Key Numbers. The most common entry into C.J.S. is through the general index or a volume index. LCP's current encyclopedia for lawyers and legal researchers is *American Jurisprudence 2d* (Am. Jur. 2d), the title meaning "all the law of America, second." Am. Jur. 2d, like C.J.S., covers federal law and, insofar as it can be stated generally, state law. Following LCP's philosophy of "selective" law publishing, the Am. Jur. 2d text is supported by footnotes that purportedly include citations to only selected leading or landmark cases on the point covered and to A.L.R. annotations. The most common entry into Am. Jur. 2d is through the general index or a volume index. Am. Jur. 2d includes *Table of Statutes and Rules Cited*, *New Topic Service*, and a desk book. LCP also sells a separate student textbook, *Summary of American Law*, which is keyed to and summarizes Am. Jur. 2d. Some states have a state encyclopedia. Although they should never be cited as either primary or secondary authority, many law students find that they can effectively learn the fundamentals of the law by reading and studying commercial law outlines, including Emanuel law outlines, Gilbert Law Summaries, Legalines, Ryan Law Capsules, Sum & Substance, and West's Black Letter Series.

8-2

The two leading law dictionaries are *Black's Law Dictionary* and *Ballentine's Law Dictionary*. Because of their dated word lists, both are being increasingly derided within the legal profession. The problem with both *Black's* and *Ballentine's*, and virtually all other law dictionaries, is that they are not citation-based. Despite its limitations, *Black's* remains the most cited, most respected, and best-selling dictionary for the legal profession. West's *Words and Phrases* allows you to read digest paragraphs summarizing judicial definitions of particular words or phrases. Despite its limitations, *Ballentine's Law Dictionary* continues to be a major dictionary for the legal profession. The most practical, readable, and useful law dictionary currently published is the *Law Dictionary* (second edition) by Steven H. Gifis. It excludes archaic legal words and is reasonably priced.

8-3

Legal directories are often used to find and select lawyers admitted to practice in another state or in another jurisdiction, and to find correct addresses for, and certain information about, other lawyers. They are also effective job-hunting tools. The long-established leading national law directory is *Martindale-Hubbell Law Directory*. Lawyers are listed in the first part at no cost, whereas the second part contains paid advertisements. Marquis Who's Who publishes *Who's Who in American Law*. West is developing, and has on-line, *West's Legal Directory*, an on-line database. Legal directories for several states and regions are published by the Legal Directories Publishing Company, Inc.

REVIEW

Key Terms

Before proceeding, review the key terms listed below to be sure you understand each one. If necessary, read over the corresponding section of the chapter. When you are ready to test your understanding, answer the Review Questions.

canned briefs
citation-based
citations
definitions
dictionary
directory
encyclopedia
etymology
law dictionary
legal directory
outline
thesauri

Questions for Review and Discussion

1. Where would you begin research about a legal topic if you had no idea what it was about (e.g., Admiralty)?
2. What is West's national encyclopedia?
3. What is LCP's national encyclopedia?
4. Is there a legal encyclopedia for your state?
5. Why should you never cite a commercial law outline?
6. What quality do virtually all law dictionaries lack?
7. Why would you cite a definition from *Black's Law Dictionary* in a brief?
8. Why would you cite a definition from *Ballentine's Law Dictionary* in a brief?
9. Why would a student want to buy Gifis' *Law Dictionary?*
10. What is the leading long-established national legal directory?

Activities

1. Find the list of Am. Jur. 2d topics in the Am. Jur. 2d *Desk Book.* Select a topic and find it in the main set. Read a few pages and examine the footnotes. Find the volume index for the topic and compare it with the general index for the set. Are you confident that you can find and read about almost anything in the law in just a few minutes?
2. Compare Gifis' *Law Dictionary* with *Black's* or *Ballentine's.* Do you agree that Gifis' is a better value, or do you prefer *Black's* or *Ballentine's?* Compare your favorite with a good general "college" dictionary, such as the *Ninth New Collegiate Dictionary* by Merriam-Webster Inc. Do you think someone could publish a better law dictionary than those currently on the market?
3. Find the name of a lawyer you know in *Martindale-Hubbell Law Directory.* Can you find it in both the general listing and the advertising section? Why or why not?

CHAPTER 9 Specialized Works

OUTLINE

9-1 Textbooks and Treatises
      Hornbooks and Nutshells
      Restatements
      Uniform Laws
9-2 Form Books
      Legal Forms
      Pleading and Practice Forms
      Trial and Practice Books
9-3 Periodicals
      Law Reviews
      Law Journals
      Newsletters
      Newspapers
      Periodical Indexes

COMMENTARY

As you continue to research public religious displays, and First Amendment law generally, you continue to find the subject fascinating. It occurs to you that others may have found the subject fascinating as well. You wonder if any scholars have ever written a book on constitutional law. You wonder if a scholarly article has ever been written on public religious displays. What specialized sources can you find?

OBJECTIVES

In this chapter you will learn about most of the specialized secondary sources of the law. Emphasis is placed on textbooks, form books, and periodicals. After reading this chapter, you should be able to:

1. Compare and contrast textbooks and treatises.
2. Explain what a "hornbook" is.
3. Define "restatement."
4. Compare and contrast legal forms, and pleading and practice forms.
5. Identify and use national legal form sets.
6. Identify and use national pleading and practice form sets.
7. Recognize trial and practice books.
8. Explain what a "law review" is.
9. Recognize national legal magazines.
10. Identify national legal newspapers.

9-1 Textbooks and Treatises

A **textbook** contains the principles of a given subject, thus it is useful in the study of that subject. Most nonfiction books contain at least some of the principles of a given subject, and so may be loosely termed textbooks.

A **treatise** is a systematic scholarly discussion, or "treatment," of the principles of a given subject; thus it is especially useful in the study of that subject. Since most legal textbooks are written in a systematic form by legal professionals for legal professionals, they are generally known as treatises. Legal treatises contain references to case opinions, statutes, and other primary and secondary sources of the law. They may be critical (suggesting what the law should be), interpretative (explaining the law as it is), or expository (enumerating the sources of the law), or a combination of each type.

There are thousands of legal textbooks and treatises, and they cover virtually every legal subject. They may be published in either single volumes or multivolume sets. They may be published either in bound volumes or as a looseleaf service. (See Chapter 7.) Textbooks and treatises usually include the features of an ordinary book, such as a table of contents, the main body in chapters, and an index. Textbooks and treatises also usually include "legal" features, such as a table of cases cited, organization by section number, and pocket parts or other supplementation. Textbooks and treatises usually cover a

Treatises

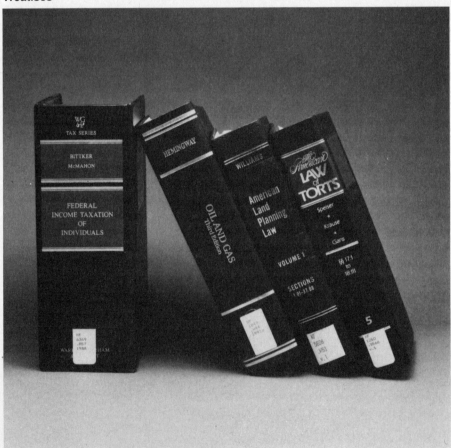

Source: © Doug Martin.

172 Chapter 9 Specialized Works

subject in more detail than an encyclopedia, outline, periodical, or other secondary source.

In most law libraries, textbooks and treatises are shelved together according to the Library of Congress Classification. (See Figure 9–1 and Appendix IV.) Since there are so many different textbooks and treatises, you have to check what is available in your local law library.

Although there is no formal classification of textbooks and treatises beyond the Library of Congress Classification system, textbooks and treatises may be grouped by their purpose for publication.

Many textbooks and treatises are written for practicing lawyers and paralegals. Examples include *The American Law of Torts* (Rochester, NY: LCP, 1983–1987), by Stuart M. Speiser, Charles F. Krause, and Alfred W. Gans; *Nimmer on Copyright* (New York: Matthew Bender, 1963), by Melville B. Nimmer; *The Paralegal Resource Manual* (Cincinnati: Anderson Publishing Co., 1989), by Charles P. Nemeth; *Pattern Deposition Checklists*, 2nd ed. (Rochester, NY: LCP, 1984), by Douglas Danner; and *Trademarks and Unfair Competition*, 2nd ed. (Rochester, NY: LCP, 1984), by J. Thomas McCarthy.

Some textbooks and treatises are written for scholarly purposes, such as *Jurisprudence: The Philosophy and Method of the Law* (Cambridge, MA: Harvard University Press, 1962), by Edgar Bodenheimer; and *The Language of the Law* (Boston: Little, Brown and Co., 1963), by David Mellinkoff.

Most textbooks and treatises, however, are written for educational purposes. Along with casebooks, discussed in Chapter 3, and continuing legal education seminar outlines, examples include *Business Law: With UCC Applications*, 7th ed. (Westerville, OH: the Glencoe Division of Macmillan/McGraw-Hill School

Figure 9–1 Example of a Treatise Shelf Directory

Publishing Co., 1989), by Gordon W. Brown, Edward E. Byers, and Mary Ann Lawlor; *Fundamentals of Criminal Advocacy* (Rochester, NY: LCP, 1974), by F. Lee Bailey and Henry B. Rothblatt; and *Real Estate and the Law* (Westerville, OH: the Glencoe Division of Macmillan/McGraw-Hill School Publishing Co., 1982), by Robert N. Corley, Peter J. Shedd, and Charles F. Floyd.

Hornbooks and Nutshells

Named after teaching tablets with handles used from the late 1400s to the middle 1700s (i.e., a sheet of paper protected by a sheet of translucent horn), **hornbooks** are today a series of one-volume, student-oriented treatises published by the West Publishing Company (West). Hornbooks generally cover basic legal subjects, such as criminal law, evidence, and property. (See Figure 9–2.) The authors are generally law professors renowned as experts in their field.

Among hornbooks, the most famous and influential was probably William L. Prosser's *Handbook of the Law of Torts* 4th ed. (1971). Often cited in briefs and court opinions, Prosser's text trained a generation of lawyers in the law of torts, to the point that a lawyer's "innate" ability to find a legal theory under which to sue is a national stereotype. Charles T. McCormick's *Law of Evidence,* 2nd ed. (1972) was another leading hornbook. *Corbin on Contracts* (1952) also deserves special mention. Many people believe that the character Professor Kingsfield in the movie and television series *The Paper Chase* was based on its author, Yale Law School professor Arthur Linton Corbin.

West's hornbooks are true treatises, and expensive. Realizing that there is a market for a wider range of less expensive textbooks than the hornbook series, West also publishes an "accurate, brief, convenient" series of paperback textbooks "priced for student budgets" known as **nutshells.** Named after the student's perpetual dream of putting an entire subject "in a nutshell" (like one's cranium), a nutshell, focusing on essentials and citing less law, costs about half of what a hornbook costs. Nutshells cover both basic subjects (e.g., criminal law, evidence, and property) and esoteric subjects (e.g., injunctions, insurance, and military law).

A list of West hornbooks and nutshells is printed on the pages preceding the title page of any nutshell.

Restatements

In 1923, a group of judges, lawyers, and law professors founded the American Law Institute (ALI), an organization dedicated to the simplification of the common law. This was to be achieved by preparing a clear and systematic exposition of the common law as if it were a codified statutory code, known as a **restatement,** prepared by expert "reporters." From 1923 to 1944, restatements were adopted and published for the laws of agency, contracts, property, torts, and several other subjects, but they never became authorities on a par with the decisions of the courts as originally intended. They have been frequently cited as persuasive authority, however, and since 1952, a second series of restatements has been adopted and published.

The current set of restatements may be determined from the latest ALI *Annual Report*. Each restatement has an index, and the First Series has its own index. In the Second Series, the "Reporter's Notes" after each section contains case citations. There may also be references to West's digest system and annotations

Figure 9–2 Excerpt From a Hornbook

§ 116 TRUTH AND OTHER DEFENSES 839

ing. The mere fact that the publication was not privileged because it was inaccurately and negligently made does not mean of course that under present law the plaintiff would recover. The plaintiff, as a public official, or public figure, or private person, would have to establish the kind of fault on the part of the defendant with respect to the truth or falsity of the alleged defamatory imputation made about the plaintiff in the proceeding as is constitutionally required.

WESTLAW REFERENCES

digest(qualified /5 privilege* immunity /s defam! slander! libel!)

qualified /5 privilege* immunity /p defam! slander! libel! /p constitution! unconstitution!

Interest of Publisher

topic(237) /p selfdefense selfprotection
237k46

Interest of Others

restatement /s torts +5 603

libel! slander! defam! /p limited qualified /5 privilege /s profession**

restatement /s torts /5 595 596

Common Interest

digest(defam! libel! slander! /p "common interest*")
237k51(4)

Communications of One Who May Act in the Public Interest

libel! slander! defam! /p "public interest" /s qualified /s immunity privilege
237k51(5)

digest(libel! slander! defam! /p public /p "fair comment")

Abuse of Qualified Privilege Regarding Private Publication of Private Matters

opinion(abus! misus! /s qualified conditional /s privilege immunity)

"private defamation"

Burden of Proof—Court and Jury

digest(defam! slander! libel! /p "burden of proof")

defam! slander! libel! /p burden /4 proof proving /s defense privilege* immunity

Report of Public Proceedings—A Special Type of Privilege

defam! slander! libel! /p public legislative executive council committee /7 proceeding* meeting* /s report!

fair** accurate** correct** /s report! /s public legislative executive council committee /s proceeding* meeting* /p libel! slander! defam!

The Constitution Privilege

negligen! /s publish! publication! /p defam! libel! slander! /p constitution! unconstitution!

§ 116. Truth and Other Defenses

Truth or Justification

To create liability for defamation, there must be publication of matter that is both defamatory and false.[1] The well-settled common law rule prior to decisions by the United States Supreme Court related to the constitutional privilege to defame was that truth is an affirmative defense which the defendant must plead and prove. Thus, under the common law rule, the defamatory statement is regarded as false unless the defendant proves truth. It has been said that meeting the constitutional requirements regarding the necessity for proof of at least negligence with respect to the truth or falsity of a defamatory statement makes it necessary for the plaintiff to allege and prove the falsity of the communication.[2] The basis for this position is that the Supreme Court of the United States, in holding that the plaintiff must establish some kind of fault with respect to the issue of truth or falsity, has by implication allocated the issue of falsity to the plaintiff. But there can be two answers to this. In the first place, the constitutional privilege to defame may not extend to defamatory utterances privately made about private persons.[3] In the second place, there is no inconsistency in assuming falsity until defendant publisher proves otherwise and requiring the plaintiff to prove negligence or recklessness with respect to the truth or falsity of the imputation. There is, in other words, nothing inconsistent about requiring the defendant to prove truth if absolute protection is to be provided for a

§ 116

1. Second Restatement of Torts, § 581A, Comment a.

2. See, Second Restatement of Torts, § 613, Comment j; Eldredge, The Law of Defamation, 1978, Sec. 63; Morris on Torts, Second edition, 1980, p. 350.

3. See § 113.

Figure 9–2 cont.

842   DEFAMATION   Ch. 19

the defense of truth, and formerly these rules were carried to ridiculous extremes,[28] but it is now generally agreed that it is not necessary to prove the literal truth of the accusation in every detail, and that it is sufficient to show that the imputation is substantially true,[29] or, as it is often put, to justify the "gist," the "sting," or the "substantial truth" of the defamation.[30] Thus an accusation that the mayor of a town has wasted $80,000 of the taxpayers' money has been held to be justified by proof that he wasted $17,500, since there is no more opprobrium attached to the greater amount.[31] If, however, the defendant adds to the facts stated an opinion or comment of his own, the comment must be justified as a proper one in the light of the facts proved.[32]

The defense of truth frequently is a hazardous venture for the defendant, since if he fails to sustain it the jury may be permitted to find that he has reiterated the defamation, and to consider the fact in aggravation of the damages.[33] The modern cases, however, have tended quite properly to recognize that the defendant is entitled to present an honest defense without being penalized, and have limited such aggravation to cases where it appears that the defense was entered in bad faith, without evidence to support it.[34]

WESTLAW REFERENCES

Truth or Justification
digest(defam! libel! slander! /s truth /s defense)
defam! libel! slander! /p commonlaw /p burden /5 proof proving

Truth
justification /s libel! slander! defam!
truth /s justification /s libel! slander! defam!

§ 116A. Damages and Matters in Mitigation

Damages which may be recovered in an action for defamation are: (1) compensatory or actual, which may be either (a) general or (b) special; (2) punitive or exemplary; and (3) nominal.[1]

Downs v. Hawley, 1873, 112 Mass. 237; Sun Printing & Publishing Association v. Schenck, 2d Cir. 1900, 98 F. 925; Kilian v. Doubleday & Co., 1951, 367 Pa. 117, 79 A.2d 657.

27. Gardner v. Self, 1852, 15 Mo. 480; Buckner v. Spaulding, 1891, 127 Ind. 229, 26 N.E. 792; Pallet v. Sargent, 1858, 36 N.H. 496; Haddock v. Naughton, 1893, 74 Hun 390, 26 N.Y.S. 455. Cf. Stewart v. Enterprise Co., Tex.Civ.App.1965, 393 S.W.2d 372, refused n.r.e., appeal after remand 439 S.W.2d 674, refused n.r.e. (two accusations, truth of only one proved).

28. See for example Swann v. Rary, Ind.1833, 3 Blackf. 298 (two hogs and one); Sharpe v. Stephenson, 1851, 34 N.C. (12 Ired.) 348 (time and place); cf. Coffin v. Brown, 1901, 94 Md. 190, 50 A. 567 (time and place). See Courtney, Absurdities of the Law of Slander and Libel, 1902, 36 Am.L.Rev. 552, 561–564.

29. Alexander v. North Eastern R. Co., 1865, 6 B. & S. 340, 122 Eng.Rep. 1221; Zoll v. Allen, S.D.N.Y.1950, 93 F.Supp. 95; Florida Publishing Co. v. Lee, 1918, 76 Fla. 405, 80 So. 245; McGuire v. Vaughan, 1896, 106 Mich. 280, 64 N.W. 44; Skrocki v. Stahl, 1910, 14 Cal. App. 1, 110 P. 957.

30. Edwards v. Bell, 1824, 1 Bing. 403, 130 Eng. Rep. 162; Bell Publishing Co. v. Garrett Engineering Co., Tex.Civ.App.1941, 154 S.W.2d 885, affirmed 141 Tex. 51, 170 S.W.2d 197.

31. Fort Worth Press Co. v. Davis, Tex.Civ.App. 1936, 96 S.W.2d 416. Cf. Smith v. Byrd, 1955, 225 Miss. 331, 83 So.2d 172 (statement that sheriff shot a man justified by proof that sheriff was acting in concert with deputy who shot him).

32. Cooper v. Lawson, 1838, 8 Ad. & El. 746, 112 Eng.Rep. 1020; Commercial Publishing Co. v. Smith, 6th Cir. 1907, 149 F. 704; cf. Morrison v. Harmer, 1837, 3 Bing.N.C. 759, 132 Eng.Rep. 603.

33. Will v. Press Publishing Co., 1932, 309 Pa. 539, 164 A. 621; Coffin v. Brown, 1901, 94 Md. 190, 50 A. 567; Krulic v. Petcoff, 1913, 122 Minn. 517, 142 N.W. 897; Hall v. Edwards, 1942, 138 Me. 231, 23 A.2d 889 (with other evidence of malice). See Note, 1958, 56 Mich.L.Rev. 659.

In Domchick v. Greenbelt Consumer Services, 1952, 200 Md. 36, 87 A.2d 831, it was held that pleading truth makes a prima facie case as to malice. In Shumate v. Johnson Publishing Co., 1956, 139 Cal.App.2d 121, 293 P.2d 531, a publisher who verified a pleading of truth was held subject to punitive damages, although he was out of the state and took no other part.

34. Webb v. Gray, 1913, 181 Ala. 408, 62 So. 194; Fodor v. Fuchs, 1910, 79 N.J.L. 529, 76 A. 1081; Willard v. Press Publishing Co., 1900, 52 App.Div. 448, 65 N.Y.S. 73; Las Vegas Sun, Inc. v. Franklin, 1958, 74 Nev. 282, 329 P.2d 867; Snyder v. Fatherly, 1930, 153 Va. 762, 151 S.E. 149.

§ 116A

1. See, Stidham v. Wachtel, Del.1941, 2 Terry 327, 21 A.2d 282; Dobbs, Remedies, 1973, Sec. 7.2, pp. 513–523.

216

Source: Prosser & Keeton, *Torts*, 5th ed. (St. Paul: West Publishing Company, 1984), p. 839. Reprinted with permission.

Sample of West Hornbooks and Nutshells

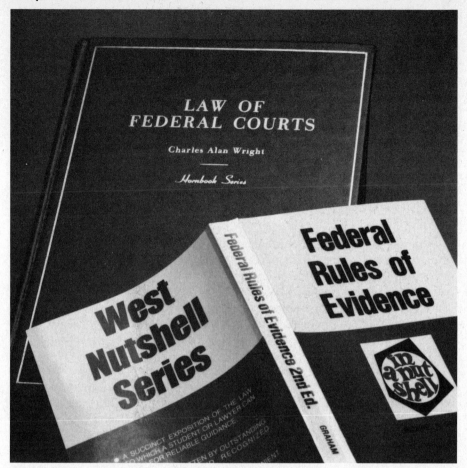

Source: © Doug Martin.

to the *American Law Reports* (A.L.R.). The *Restatement in the Courts* collects summaries of cases citing a restatement.

Uniform Laws

Some uniformity has been achieved in state statutory law through the work of the National Conference of Commissioners on Uniform State Laws, created in 1912. Following up on a recommendation by the American Bar Association, each state and the District of Columbia have appointed commissioners who meet once a year to review drafts of proposed uniform laws. If the commissioners find a proposed uniform law is desirable and practical, they promote its passage by their state legislature. Approved uniform laws are published in the commissioners' annual handbook and in West's *Uniform Laws Annotated, Master Edition*.

For example, ALI worked with the National Conference of Commissioners on Uniform State Laws to draft and promote the most pervasive uniform law to be substantially enacted in all 50 states and the District of Columbia: the Uniform Commercial Code (U.C.C.). As a result, the state laws of sales, negotiable instruments, and secured transactions are almost identical throughout the country.

9-2 Form Books

Lawyers and paralegals use **form books,** collections of sample legal documents used by other lawyers and paralegals to help them prepare documents for clients. Most form books also include checklists, and case, statute, and other cross-references, which are very helpful in preparing legal documents. However, while form books are excellent sources of ideas for how to handle a legal matter, you should *never* blindly follow a form. The law must always be individualized for the client. Most legal professionals agree with the statement: "I never saw a form that didn't need to be fixed."

Legal Forms

Samples of legally effective documents—such as contracts, deeds, and wills—are known as **legal forms.** There are several legal form books, some devoted to legal forms in general and others devoted to a single subject or jurisdiction.

One leading general legal form set is *American Jurisprudence Legal Forms 2d*, published by Lawyers Cooperative Publishing (LCP). Covering over 100 topics, the set is a collection of forms actually used in practice. (See Figure 9-3.) Cross-referenced with LCP's Total Client Service Library, the appropriate form can be found using the set's index volumes.

West also publishes an excellent general legal form set: *West's Legal Forms, 2d*. The set is divided into 11 topical units authored by experienced experts. In a guide to the set, West lists the following features: "expert authors; summary of contents for each volume; detailed table of contents; general background information; text analysis of subject matter; forms for information gathering; drafting checklists; basic and comprehensive forms; alternative provisions; comments to specific forms; tax considerations; federal laws; references to model acts and uniform laws; library references (including Key Numbers and C.J.S.); automation of form drafting; 'plain language' forms; indexes and tables; and updating."

Matthew Bender & Company, Inc. (MB), also publishes an excellent general legal form set: *Current Legal Forms With Tax Analysis*, originally prepared by Jacob Rabkin and Mark H. Johnson. The major feature of "Rabkin and Johnson" is its emphasis on the tax aspects of legal transactions represented by the legal forms involved.

Along with other national legal form books, there are also legal form books covering particular states. MB is the leader, publishing a "Transaction Guide" for each of several different states and regions.

The competition in form books can be intense. In Ohio, for example, there are four general legal form sets to choose from: Anderson Publishing Company's *Couse's Ohio Form Book*; Banks-Baldwin Law Publishing Company's *Baldwin's Ohio Legal Forms*; MB's *Ohio Transaction Guide—Legal Forms*; and LCP's *Ohio Forms: Legal and Business*.

Pleading and Practice Forms

Samples of documents used in actually litigating a case—such as complaints, answers, replies, interrogatories, motions, and judgments—are known as **pleading and practice forms.** Again, there are several pleading and practice form books; some are devoted to pleading and practice forms in general and others are devoted to a single subject or jurisdiction.

Figure 9–3 Excerpt From *American Jurisprudence Legal Forms 2d*

ASSIGNMENT FOR CREDITORS   § 26:113

C. RELEASE OF ASSIGNOR

§ 26:111 Scope of division

The forms collected in this division consist of various clauses pertaining to releases by creditors that can be considered in connection with an assignment for the benefit of creditors. Included are federal tax references and text references for use in drafting such forms.

§ 26:112 Acceptance by creditors as release

Acceptance under this assignment by the creditors of ___1___ *[debtor]* shall be taken and deemed as a complete payment by and release of ___2___ *[debtor]* from the payment of any further sums to any existing creditor, except such part thereof as may be realized out of the net proceeds of the sale of the properties herein conveyed and of the money coming into assignee's hands by virtue of this assignment.

☑ **Notes on Use:**

Text reference: For discussion of provision according priority of payment to releasing creditors, see 6 AM JUR 2d, Assignments for Benefit of Creditors § 52.

§ 26:113 Creditor's release

Agreement made ___1___, 19_2_, between ___3___, of ___4___ *[address]*, City of ___5___, County of ___6___, State of ___7___, herein referred to as creditor, and ___8___, of ___9___ *[address]*, City of ___10___, County of ___11___, State of ___12___, herein referred to as assignor.

Inasmuch as assignor, by a certain assignment, dated ___13___, 19_14_, conveyed, assigned, transferred, and set over to ___15___, of ___16___ *[address]*, City of ___17___, County of ___18___, State of ___19___, as assignee, all property and effects of every kind and description, real, personal, and mixed, of assignor (except as was exempt from levy and sale under execution) for the benefit of the creditors of assignor; and

The trust imposed by the assignment has been duly executed according to law by the assignee therein appointed, and the proceeds of the property, estate and effects mentioned in that assignment duly applied to the payment of the claims of the creditors of assignor, according to law, and creditor received ___20___ *[number]* respective ___21___ *[share or shares]* of the proceeds of that estate, according to the amount of ___22___ *[number]* respective claims against assignor; and assignee has duly accounted,

The parties agree as follows:

In consideration of the premises, and in consideration of ___23___ Dollars ($___), in hand paid by assignor, the receipt of which is acknowledged, creditor releases and discharges assignor from all further liability to or on

(For Tax Notes and Notes on Use of form, see end of form)

2 Am Jur Legal Forms 2d   607

Figure 9–3 cont.

§ 26:121　　ASSIGNMENT FOR CREDITORS

account of any and all claims and demands whatsoever that the creditor had against assignor at the time of the making of the assignment, as aforesaid.

Creditor, for himself and his heirs, executors and administrators, agrees that from the date of this release, he will have and claim no further right, benefit, or interest in, to, or in respect of any and all claims or demands of whatever kind that he may have had against assignor at the time of the making of the assignment.

In witness whereof, I have executed this release at ___24___ *[designate place of execution]* the day and year first above written.

[Signature]

[Acknowledgment]

☑ **Tax Note:**

For discussion of tax consequences of an agreement in cancellation of a bad debt, see FEDERAL TAX GUIDE TO LEGAL FORMS, Cancellation of Indebtedness ¶ 1505.

☑ **Notes on Use:**

Text reference: For discussion of relinquishment of release provision as validating assignment, see 6 AM JUR 2d, Assignments for Benefit of Creditors § 54.

Cross reference: For forms of acknowledgments, see ACKNOWLEDGMENTS (Ch 7).

V. ADMINISTRATION OF ESTATE

§ 26:121　Scope of division

The material in this division consists of forms pertaining to the administration of the assignor's estate, together with federal tax references, text references, and annotations for use in drafting the instruments.

§ 26:122　Notice to assignee of preferred claim—For labor

State of ___1___
County of ___2___
To: ___3___, assignee of ___4___ *[debtor]*, and to whom it may concern.

I, ___5___, the undersigned, being first duly sworn, say:

1. ___6___ *[Debtor]*, who on ___7___, 19_8_, executed a general assignment for the benefit of creditors to ___9___ *[assignee]* now is, and was at

(For Tax Notes and Notes on Use of form, see end of form)

608　　　　　　　　　　　　　　　　　　　　　　　2 Am Jur Legal Forms 2d

Source: Am Jur Legal Forms 2d, vol. 2 (Rochester, NY: Lawyers Co-operative Publishing Co., 1971), p. 607. Reprinted with permission.

One leading set of general pleading and practice forms is LCP's *American Jurisprudence Pleading and Practice Forms Revised*. LCP also publishes an excellent pair of guides to federal pleading and practice (including practice before federal administrative agencies): a textbook set, *Federal Procedure, Lawyers' Edition*, and a form book set, *Federal Procedural Forms, Lawyers' Edition*. The pair anchor what LCP advertised in 1991 as its federal "family," including *United States Supreme Court Reports, Lawyers' Edition, Second Series* (L. Ed. 2d), A.L.R. Fed., *United States Code Service* (U.S.C.S.), and several other federal law publications. These sets can be entered through the general index for each set.

There are several other guides to federal procedure. West publishes *West's Federal Practice Manual* and *West's Federal Forms*. MB publishes *Moore's Federal Practice* and *Bender's Federal Practice Forms*. MB also publishes *Bender's Forms of Discovery* and several state pleading and practice form books.

Again, the competition in form books can be intense. In Ohio, for example, there are three general pleading and practice form sets to choose from: Anderson Publishing Company's *Anderson's Ohio Civil Practice With Forms*, Banks-Baldwin Law Publishing Company's *Baldwin's Ohio Civil Practice*, and MB's *Ohio Forms of Pleading and Practice*.

Trial and Practice Books

Books that guide a lawyer or a paralegal through the proof of contentions at trial, often with samples of litigation aids and trial testimony, are known as **trial and practice books.** LCP publishes two unique trial and practice sets: *American*

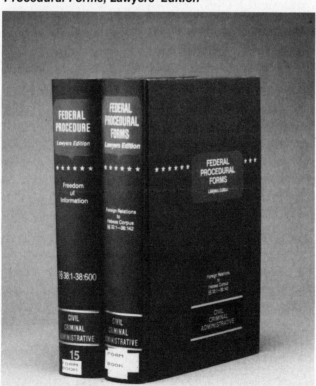

LCP's *Federal Procedure, Lawyers' Edition*, and *Federal Procedural Forms, Lawyers' Edition*

Source: © Doug Martin.

Jurisprudence Proof of Facts 2d and *American Jurisprudence Trials*. *American Jurisprudence Proof of Facts 2d* includes checklists for the proof of crucial facts in depositions and trials, and sample questions and answers to use in doing so. (See Figure 9–4.) *American Jurisprudence Trials*, after six volumes of general trial practice advice, is a collection of advice on how to try over 200 different kinds of cases, from airplane crashes to exploding gas tanks, from lawyers who have taken such cases to court. Each of these trial and practice guides has a general index for the set.

Trial and practice books blur into textbooks and treatises. There are several excellent guides to trial practice. For example, MB publishes the *Art of Advocacy* series, including *Preparation of the Case, Discovery, Settlement, Jury Selection, Opening Statement, Documentary Evidence, Direct Examination, Cross-Examination of Medical Experts, Cross-Examination of Non-Medical Experts, Summation,* and *Appeals*. LCP publishes the *Federal Trial Handbook 2d*, by Robert S. Hunter, and a series of state trial handbooks. An excellent state trial handbook, *Trial Handbook for Ohio Lawyers, Second Edition*, was put together for LCP by former Judge Richard M. Markus.

9–3 Periodicals

A **periodical** is a work that is published at regular intervals. Whereas reporters (discussed in Chapter 2) are published at regular intervals because cases occur chronologically, periodicals are published at regular intervals by the publisher's design. A.L.R. (discussed in Chapter 4) qualifies as a periodical, since the reported cases are not always reported in chronological order.

In the same way that ordinary periodicals are excellent sources of market information, recent scholarship, and current events, legal periodicals are excellent sources of information about the legal market, legal scholarship, and legal events. Specialty periodicals are also available to help keep the specialists up to date in their areas of specialty. Periodicals are also useful for historical research—to find out what people knew and what people were thinking at any given time.

Most of the periodicals in the following discussion are available on either or both the LEXIS and WESTLAW computer-assisted legal research systems, to be discussed in Chapter 12.

Law Reviews

A scholarly periodical published by a law school is known as a **law review.** Law reviews generally contain articles written by law professors, prominent practitioners, or outstanding students (known as **comments**), and short book, case, or subject reviews (known as **notes**).

A quality law review article, as an excellent critical commentary, may be treated by a court as persuasive authority. Because it may lead to the development of a new field of law or turn an established field of law in a new direction, it may have a significant and substantial effect on the law. Some lawyers, however, believe that most law review articles are nothing but academic drivel.

Virtually every law school publishes a law review. Most cover the law in general, but some stress the law of the state where the school is located.

Some law schools publish more than one review. One covers the law

Figure 9-4 Excerpt From *American Jurisprudence Proof of Facts 2d*

SUITABILITY OF WORK 1-613
§ 16

III. PROOF THAT WAGE AND SKILL LEVELS ARE INADEQUATE

A. Elements of Proof

§ 15. Guide and checklist

The following facts and circumstances, among others, tend to establish that the offer of employment that the claimant refused was unsuitable for him because it failed to utilize his existing skills and because the offered wage was inadequate:

- ☐ Claimant's existing skill and wage levels [§ 16]
- ☐ Circumstances of unemployment [§ 17]
  —Claimant unemployed through no fault of his own [§ 17]
- ☐ Duration of unemployment [§ 17]
- ☐ Offer of employment to claimant [§ 18]
- ☐ Investigation of offer [§ 18]
  —Comparison with existing skill and wage levels [§ 18]
- ☐ Refusal of offer because below existing skill and wage levels [§ 19]
- ☐ Availability for work at customary skill and wage levels [§ 20]
- ☐ Reasonable prospects of obtaining local work at customary skill and wage levels [§ 21]

B. Testimony of Claimant

§ 16. Existing skill level and earnings record

Q. Please state your name and address.
A. My name is _____. I live at _____.
Q. What is your occupation?
A. I an a tool and die maker.
Q. Are you working now?
A. No, I'm unemployed.
Q. Where were you last employed as a tool and die maker?
A. At _____.
Q. Could you describe what you did there?
A. I worked in the machine shop, on construction and maintenance of tools, and calibrating them, also making dies that they use in their forging and stamping operations. Sometimes I had

1 POF 2d 635

Figure 9–4 cont.

1-613 **SUITABILITY OF WORK**
§ 16

to do layout work and assembly work, fitting machines together.

Q. Was this considered skilled labor?
A. Yes, it's considered highly skilled work.
Q. How long did you work there?
A. For _____ years.
Q. Were you a tool and die maker all that time?
A. Yes.
Q. How much were you making?
A. At the time I was laid off, $2.90 an hour.
Q. Was that the most you ever made?
A. No, for a while before that I made $3.15 an hour.

☐ **Note: Suitability of pay cut.** In determining the suitability of offered employment involving a pay cut, both the relative amount of the reduction and the absolute amount of the offered wage may be relevant. For example, a cut of 20 percent may be unsuitable for a person whose original wage was barely above subsistence level, but acceptable for someone whose previous wage was much higher. Therefore, to provide a clear illustration of a wage reduction that was deemed unsuitable under the circumstances presented, figures from an actual case have been used. See Re Troutman 264 **NC** 289, 141 SE2d 613. The claimant in that case became unemployed in 1964.

Q. What happened to cause a reduction?
A. The company shut down for a while back in 19___, because there wasn't any work, and when they reopened they had to lower the wage levels.
Q. Were you rehired at $2.90 an hour?
A. No, I was rehired at $2.60, then worked my way up.
Q. How long were you working at $2.90 an hour before you became unemployed?
A. _____ months.

§ 17. Circumstances of unemployment

Q. What happened to make you unemployed this time?
A. The company cut back its operations and laid off a lot of people, including me.

636 **1 POF 2d**

Source: Am Jur Proof of Facts 2d, Vol. 1 (Rochester, NY: Lawyers Co-operative Publishing Co., 1974), p. 635. Reprinted with permission.

Sample Law Reviews

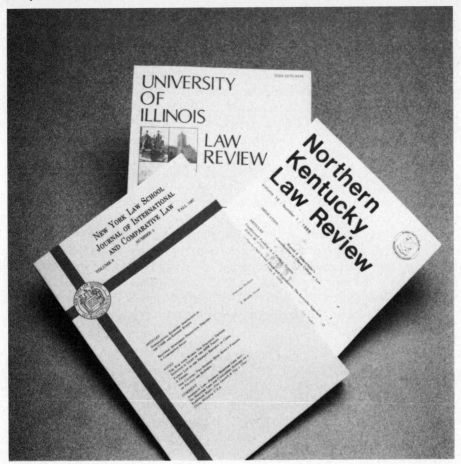

Source: © Doug Martin.

in general and the rest cover a specialized subject, such as environmental law or international law.

Law reviews are usually edited by law students as an academic exercise. Students research topics and check the work of outside authors and each other. Because the students invited to work on a law review usually have high grade point averages or demonstrated writing ability, serving on a law review is usually considered an honor. However, "law review" does not always mean "excellence." The author is aware of an incident in which a law student declined an invitation to join the law review at his school because the student editors could not articulate any purpose or goal for the law review other than the self-adulation of its members.

Law Journals

A **law journal** is a legal periodical emphasizing current events; if published by a bar association, it is usually known as a **bar journal.** They are legal magazines, supported in part by advertising that gives the readers market information. These journals keep legal professionals informed about current legal events and trends.

The leading national legal magazine is the American Bar Association's *ABA Journal* (A.B.A. J.). Self-described as "the lawyer's magazine" and "an independent, thoughtful and inquiring observer of the law and the legal profession," A.B.A. J. is a monthly "edited for members of the American Bar Association." Along with the feature articles, A.B.A. J. regularly includes a message from the ABA president, letters, news, the Supreme Court Report, trends in the law, books, classified advertising, and legal "war" stories. (See Figure 9–5.)

Specialty sections of the American Bar Association also publish journals. For example, the section on Business Law publishes *The Business Lawyer* quarterly and *The Business Lawyer Update* bi-monthly; the section on General Practice publishes *The Compleat Lawyer* quarterly; and the section on Law Practice Management publishes *Legal Economics* eight times a year.

Most state bar associations also publish journals. The Ohio State Bar Association, for example, publishes the weekly *Ohio State Bar Association Report* containing legislative reports, classified advertising, court rule changes, and official advance sheets. It also publishes *Ohio Lawyer*, a monthly journal with articles.

Many large county and city bar associations also publish journals. Local journals usually emphasize local activities, court decisions, and current events.

There are hundreds of journals covering specialized subjects, published by a variety of organizations. Examples include the *Catholic Lawyer*, the *Practical Lawyer*, and the *Practical Tax Lawyer*. Two journals cover the subject of legal research: *Law Library Journal* and *Legal Reference Services Quarterly*.

Newsletters

As they come down in scale and scope, legal journals blur into newsletters. Some formal governmental publications are published in newsletter form. The Internal Revenue Service (IRS), for example, publishes a weekly *Internal Revenue Bulletin* (I.R.B.), cumulated yearly in a *Cumulative Bulletin* (C.B.). The IRS's district directors publish *Tax Practitioner Newsletter*, which is distributed to tax practitioners in their districts. State newsletters are also published, such as *The Ohio State Tax Report*, published by the Ohio Department of Taxation, and the *State Public Defender Report*, published by the Ohio Public Defender.

Countless newsletters are published by private publishers. For example, Boardroom Reports, Inc., publishes the monthly *Tax HOTline*, featuring inside information from tax lawyers, accountants, and former IRS agents.

Newspapers

The national weekly legal newspapers are the *National Law Journal* and the *Legal Times* (formerly the *Legal Times of Washington*). *The American Lawyer* is a national monthly newspaper.

In major metropolitan areas, there are local legal newspapers. Examples include the *Los Angeles Daily Journal* and the *New York Law Journal*.

Periodical Indexes

The only practical way to find an article in a periodical that is no longer current is through an index. There are two principal general legal periodical indexes.

For many years, H. W. Wilson Company has been known for its general *Index to Periodicals*. In 1961, H. W. Wilson Company purchased the *Index to Legal Periodicals* from the American Association of Law Libraries. Covering the period

Figure 9–5   Excerpt From the American Bar Association *ABA Journal*

Attorney Discipline

Do we need an ethical rule restricting sexual relations with clients?

Simultaneously bedding and representing clients, Arnie Becker of "L.A. Law" has popularized an image of lawyers that many in the profession find disturbing. In response to increasing lawsuits, members of the Illinois and California bars have attempted to specifically prohibit attorneys from coercing and demanding sex of clients, while the American Academy of Matrimonial Lawyers has adopted an advisory standard.

The issue of regulating this activity is a complex one, says Susan Michmerhuizen of the American Bar Association's Center for Professional Responsibility: "Horror stories abound, and yet it's a difficult situation to reach under existing ethical rules."

Chicago lawyer Cornelia Honchar Tuite argues that a separate rule regulating sexual relations with clients is necessary to set clear standards for behavior. She believes that it could be reasonably tailored to distinguish romantic liaisons from dangerous ones.

Her colleague, Chicago trial lawyer Philip Corboy, believes that existing rules offer adequate protection. He doubts that yet another rule will deter the truly unethical attorney.

Yes: Put It in Writing

BY CORNELIA HONCHAR TUITE

Among the goals of the Model Rules of Professional Conduct is the comprehensive delineation of lawyers' fiduciary duties to clients—duties of trust, confidence and fair dealing.

Common sense says we should not gouge our clients, use confidentially obtained information for financial or professional gain, or counsel clients in any future criminal conduct.

Yet, the Model Rules specifically prohibit such conduct for several reasons: 1) to make a lawyer's duties clear, establishing a profession-wide baseline of proper behavior, below which no lawyer can fall with impunity; 2) to determine who may practice law, since it is a privilege, not a right; and 3) to inform the public of its rights and expectations.

The Rules function as much as a policy statement about the values of the American justice system as a disciplinary framework. In this context, should sexual relations with clients be ethically regulated? Yes.

A failure to regulate this sensitive aspect of a trusting relationship would mean we hold a client's money (given to us as fiduciaries) more valuable than the intangible, but far more precious, emotional trust our clients give us in trying times of their lives.

What we choose or decline to regulate is the litmus test of our values. What is wrong with recognizing the worth of emotional trust or with imposing the same fiduciary duties on intangible as well as tangible client valuables? Certainly, misappropriation of a $100 check pales in significance with charges that lawyers demand sex in return for representation.

Can anyone who values individual dignity honestly argue that a lawyer who sexually exploits a client meets a baseline standard of a profession resting on the same terrain of special public trust with the ministry and medicine?

We do not condone sexual exploitation by ministers or doctors; how can we, as lawyers, fail to say we, too, reject it?

I find no currency in arguments that common sense and general principles of misconduct, fitness to practice or bans on attorney-client conflict of interest provide a sufficient disciplinary mechanism to sanction those lawyers who sexually abuse their clients.

The Case for Specificity

Model Rule 1.8(d) bars lawyers from negotiating book contracts with clients before the representation's conclusion. About 99 percent of American lawyers never face this prospect, yet the potential conflict of interest prompted this rule's adoption. If we specifically regulate book contracts, how can we refuse to prohibit specifically the sexual exploitation of clients? What logic says regulate one, but not the other?

Similarly, under Rule 1.8(a) lawyers cannot enter business transactions with clients without written, full disclosure; the existence of fair, reasonable terms; and giving the client an opportunity to seek independent advice. Again, the inherent problems of conflicts of interest, impairment of the lawyer's judgment by self-interest, and potential breach of trust underlie this specific prohibition.

A carefully tailored, reasonable rule prohibiting client sexual exploitation during a representation would define the prohibited conduct so disciplinary agencies would have an established burden of proof and protect lawyers from spurious claims.

Currently, most lawyers are disciplined under general misconduct provisions, raising the potential for uneven application of the Rules, and the decided cases generally offer little guidance.

Most importantly, a rule articulates the profession's values, its abhorrence of sexual exploitation, its commitment to fiduciary duty in emotional as well as in business transactions, book contracts and safe-keeping of tangible assets. We must clearly state that sexual exploitation breaches client trust. The absence of a rule implies we do not believe it.

The law's primary goals are the protection of human worth and dignity. The law governing lawyers should echo those same goals. ∎

Source: ABA Journal, Oct. 1970 (Chicago: American Bar Association), p. 46. Reprinted with permission.

from 1908 to the present, the *Index to Legal Periodicals* is published monthly (except September) and includes articles in over 500 periodicals deemed to have permanent reference value. The index is primarily by subject, with secondary indexing by author. The *Index to Legal Periodicals* is also available in many law libraries on the Wilsondisc CD-ROM system, and on the LEXIS (LAWREF; LGLIND and LEXREF;LGLIND files) and WESTLAW (LRI database) computer-assisted legal research systems, to be discussed in Chapter 12.

In 1980, the Information Access Corporation began to put out two indexes published with the assistance of an Advisory Committee of the American Association of Law Libraries: *Current Law Index* and *Legal Resource Index*. The *Current Law Index* indexes over 700 permanent legal periodicals by author, title, and other indexes. The *Legal Resource Index* is the computerized and microfilmed version of the *Current Law Index.* In addition to the coverage of the *Current Law Index*, the *Legal Resource Index* covers legal newspapers and other similar sources. The *Legal Resource Index* is also available in many law libraries as the LegalTrac database on the InfoTrac CD-ROM system, and on the LEXIS (LAWREF; LGLIND and LEXREF;LGLIND files), WESTLAW (LRI database), and DIALOG computer-assisted legal research systems, to be discussed in Chapter 12.

There are numerous specialized legal periodical indexes. Check with your local law library to see what is available there.

SUMMARY

9-1

The principles of a given legal subject can be found in a textbook or a treatise. There are thousands of legal textbooks and treatises, and they cover virtually every legal subject. They may be published in either single volumes or multivolume sets. Textbooks and treatises usually include the features of an ordinary book (e.g., a table of contents, the main body in chapters, and an index) and legal features (e.g., a table of cases cited, organization by section number, and pocket parts or other supplementation). In most law libraries, textbooks and treatises are shelved together according to the Library of Congress Classification system. Hornbooks are a series of one-volume, student-oriented treatises. Nutshells focus on essentials and cite less law. Restatements restate the common law as if it were a statutory code.

9-2

Lawyers and paralegals use form books—collections of sample legal documents used by other lawyers and paralegals—to help them prepare documents for clients. Most form books also include checklists, and case, statute, and other cross-references that are very helpful in preparation of legal documents. Samples of legally effective documents, such as contracts, deeds, and wills, are known as legal forms. There are several legal form books, some devoted to legal forms in general, and others devoted to a single subject or jurisdiction. National general legal form sets include *American Jurisprudence Legal Forms 2d* and *West's Legal Forms, 2d*. Samples of documents used in actually litigating a case—such as complaints, answers, replies, interrogatories, motions, and judgments—are known as pleading and practice forms. There are several guides to federal procedure. Books that guide a lawyer or paralegal through the proof of contentions at trial, often with samples of litigation aids and trial testimony, are known as trial and practice books.

9-3

A periodical is a work published at regular intervals. Legal periodicals are excellent sources of information about the legal market, legal scholarship, and legal events. A scholarly periodical published by a law school is known as a law review. A quality law review article may be treated by a court as persuasive authority. Virtually every law school publishes a law review. A law journal is a legal periodical emphasizing current events; if published by a bar association, it is usually known as a bar journal. The leading national legal magazine is the American Bar Association's *ABA Journal* (A.B.A. J.). Specialty sections of the American Bar Association also publish journals, as do most state bar associations. Some formal governmental publications are published in newsletter form. Countless newsletters are published by private publishers. The national legal weekly newspapers are the *National Law Journal* and the *Legal Times*. The only practical way to find an article in a periodical that is no longer current is through an index. There are two principal general legal periodical indexes: the *Index to Legal Periodicals*, published by the H. W. Wilson Company, which is also available on the Wilsondisc CD-ROM system; and the *Current Law Index/Legal Resource Index*, published by the Information Access Corporation, which is also available as the LegalTrac database on the InfoTrac CD-ROM system.

REVIEW

Key Terms

Before proceeding, review the key terms listed below to be sure you understand each one. If necessary, read over the corresponding section of the chapter. When you are ready to test your understanding, answer the Review Questions.

bar journal
comments
form books
hornbooks
law journal
law review
legal forms
notes
nutshells
periodical
pleading and practice forms
restatement
textbook
treatise
trial and practice books

Questions for Review and Discussion

1. When does a textbook become a treatise?
2. What is a hornbook?
3. What is a restatement?
4. What is the difference between a legal form and a pleading and practice form?
5. Where can you find legal forms?
6. Where can you find pleading and practice forms?
7. Who uses *American Jurisprudence Trials*?
8. How important are law reviews?
9. What is the leading national legal magazine?
10. What is the *National Law Journal*?

Activities

1. Read through a chapter of a West hornbook. Was the subject of the chapter explained to your satisfaction? Would you ever use a hornbook as a case finder?
2. Imagine that you are drafting the articles of incorporation for a nonprofit corporation, and use the form books available to you. Which form books were most helpful? Would your answer be different if you were drafting a purchase agreement for the sale of a business?
3. Examine the law review of the law school closest to your home. How practical are the articles? Read through an article. Did you learn anything you couldn't have found out yourself?

PART FOUR

CITING

THE LAW

Chapter 10
A Uniform System of Citation

Chapter 11
Shepard's Citations and Other Citators

CHAPTER 10 A Uniform System of Citation

OUTLINE

10-1 Citation Style
    The Bluebook: A Uniform System of Citation
    Other Systems of Citation
10-2 Technical Rules
    Citing Cases
    Citing Statutes
    Citing Other Primary Sources
    Citing Secondary Sources
    Computer-Assisted Citation Style
10-3 Citation Requirements

COMMENTARY

The law director, impressed with the breadth and depth of your research into public religious displays, reminds you that you must put your research down in writing by the end of next week. As you start to write your memorandum, you realize that you must cite authority for all the legal propositions you make. And as a professional, you want your work to be in the proper form and style. You remember seeing a copy of *The Bluebook: A Uniform System of Citation* on the law director's desk.

OBJECTIVES

In this chapter you will learn about the conventions for citing legal materials. Emphasis is placed on *The Bluebook: A Uniform System of Citation*. After reading this chapter, you should be able to:

1. Understand the importance of *The Bluebook: A Uniform System of Citation*.
2. Identify and use *The Bluebook: A Uniform System of Citation*.
3. Identify other systems of citation.
4. Properly cite case names.
5. Properly cite case reporters.
6. Properly cite deciding courts.
7. Properly cite decision dates.
8. Properly cite statutes.
9. Properly cite constitutions, court rules, and administrative regulations.
10. Properly cite books and periodicals.

10-1 Citation Style

No matter how well you perform legal research, if you can't communicate your results to others, most of your time and effort will be wasted. It's not enough that you've found cases like yours (or other law) where the person like you won. You must be able to communicate that fact to the decision maker involved. In court, the judge will want you to prove your case, if only to make it easy for the judge to decide in your favor. The judge will expect you to **cite,** to point out the location of legal authority for, the law that supports your case. With your cites (i.e., your references to legal authority) in hand, the judge can compare the originals of what you've found with what, if anything, your opponent has found, and then make a decision.

As a matter of style, however, if you always cite legal materials in full (e.g., the annotation "Standing to sue for copyright infringement under 17 U.S.C.S. § 501(b)," by Edward A. Nolfi, J.D., found at page 509 of volume 82 of *American Law Reports, Federal,* published by the Lawyers Co-operative Publishing Company of Rochester, New York, in 1987), your reader would soon become overwhelmed by the citations, and the law for which you cite the legal materials will be obscured. For brevity and clarity, it is much more efficient to cite legal materials in an abbreviated form (e.g., Edward A. Nolfi, Annotation, *Standing to sue for copyright infringement under 17 U.S.C.S. § 501(b),* 82 A.L.R. Fed. 509 (1987) or simply 82 ALR Fed. 509), and that is the custom.

The only question is **citation style:** how legal materials should be abbreviated to avoid reader confusion. Without a uniform system of citation style, there might be confusion if the same or different abbreviations are used for the same or different publications covering the same or different law. For example, "M.C.A." might indicate the Annotated Code of Maryland, Mississippi, or Montana.

The question of citation style has never been answered comprehensively and authoritatively by the command of a sovereign, probably because of the complexity of the task. For the most part, there is no citation style required by law. Instead, there is a widely followed system developed by the editors of the East Coast Ivy League law school law reviews, and other systems developed by major law publishers.

The Bluebook: A Uniform System of Citation

The leading system of citation style is *The Bluebook: A Uniform System of Citation,* 15th ed. (1991), compiled by the editors of the *Columbia Law Review,* the *Harvard Law Review,* the *University of Pennsylvania Law Review,* and *The Yale Law Journal,* and published by the Harvard Law Review Association, 1511 Massachusetts Avenue, Cambridge, MA 02138. A spiral-bound book with a blue cover, *The Bluebook: A Uniform System of Citation* is often referred to as ***The Bluebook,*** and the citation style it suggests is often referred to as **Bluebook style.** Some people incorrectly refer to the book as the "Harvard Blue Book" or the "Harvard Citator" but, as the editors explain on page vii, the book is titled the *Bluebook* and subtitled *A Uniform System of Citation.*

The Bluebook expresses an appropriate citation style for law review articles and other legal writing, including appellate briefs. As the back cover indicates, *The Bluebook* consists of an introduction, practitioners' notes, general rules of citation style, specialized rules, tables and abbreviations, and an index. For the most part, *The Bluebook* is a reference book, not a textbook.

The Bluebook: A Uniform System of Citation

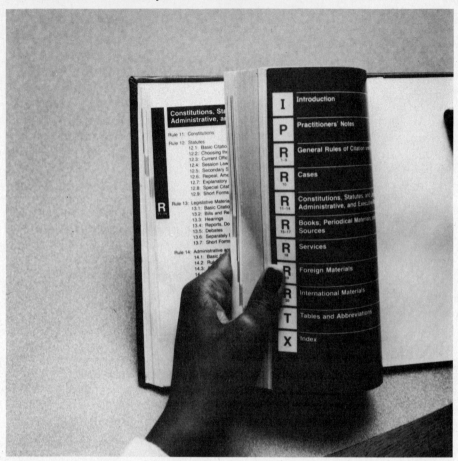

Source: © Doug Martin.

    The Bluebook rules, full of exceptions and inexplicable conventions, display some favoritism toward particular publishers and publications. These rules have long been criticized as being complex, complicated, confusing, and vague, but they do reflect the tremendous variety of legal sources available in the United States and around the world. Other books have been published to explain Bluebook style, including C. Edward Good, *Citing & Typing the Law: A Guide to Legal Citation & Style* (Charlottesville: Legal Education Ltd., 1987); Elaine C. Maier, *How to Prepare a Legal Citation* (Woodbury, NY: Barron's Educational Series, Inc., 1986); and Alan L. Dworsky, *User's Guide to A Uniform System of Citation: The Cure for the Bluebook Blues* (Littleton, CO: Fred B. Rothman & Co., 1988); but some find these books to be as complicated, confusing, or vague as *The Bluebook* they seek to explain.

    For the most part, there is no law requiring Bluebook style. In fact, as we shall see in the final section of this chapter, there are some laws that direct you not to follow Bluebook style. While Bluebook style is the customary standard for briefs, law review articles, and other legal writings, if there is no requirement to the contrary (e.g., an instructor's requirement or a court rule) and you're not preparing the final draft of a legal writing, it is not absolutely necessary to use Bluebook style. Nevertheless, it is good practice, both literally and figuratively, to use Bluebook style whenever possible.

Other Systems of Citation

Many people wonder why all law books do not use the same citation style. Since there is no comprehensive citation style required by law, major law publishers have been able to adopt their own citation styles for competitive reasons.

At West Publishing Company (West), for example, National Reporter System volumes suggest a citation style for the reported cases in the running head. But these cites do not give parallel cites to non-West reporters. Moreover, citations in *Corpus Juris Secundum* (C.J.S.), usually to West reporters, do not include dates, so to formally cite a case found in C.J.S. you must refer to the West reporter for the date of the case.

Lawyers Cooperative Publishing (LCP) also leaves dates out of its encyclopedia *American Jurisprudence 2d*, which frequently cites *American Law Reports* (A.L.R.). LCP claims this is done to save space, even though its cites often contain long strings of parallel citations. LCP's modern citation style (e.g., Miller v Robinson (1966) 241 Md 335, 216 A2d 743, 17 ALR3d 1425) minimizes the number of periods and spaces in the citation in order to save memory space in the company's computers, and thereby save money. Underscoring and italics are avoided to save production costs.

To be discussed in Chapter 11, Shepard's/McGraw-Hill, Inc., has developed and maintained its own system of citation and symbols in order to pack into each column and each page of its *Shepard's Citations* as much information as possible.

Unfortunately, under the circumstances, many legal researchers follow the citation style of the material they happen to be using and attempt to convert it into Bluebook style when they prepare their final draft.

10–2 Technical Rules

While Bluebook style is, for the most part, not required by law, it is the style that a legal researcher must know. Most courts do not explicitly require it, but most judges expect a legal professional's briefs and other legal writings to substantially conform to Bluebook style. It's a badge of competence. The judge will be impressed if, based on the style used in the brief, the author was once a member of a law review, or could have been.

This "badge-of-competence" attitude is pervasive in the legal profession. Most legal research and writing instructors require Bluebook style to be followed in all academic work. That is appropriate and commendable. But some have taken this attitude too far: they *define* sound legal research by its legal citation style. Sound research is proved by citing sound authority. If you cite poor authority properly, all you prove is that you can properly cite unsound research.

The following discussion covers the basic elements of Bluebook style for the simplest and most common citations. It is designed to be easily recalled so that in a pinch, you can quickly and confidently prepare briefs that substantially conform to Bluebook style. To strictly follow Bluebook style, however, carefully study *The Bluebook* or a *Bluebook* guide.

Citing Cases

Cases are usually cited by an underscored abbreviated case title, volume-reporter-page citations, court identification (if necessary), and year of decision. (See Figure 10–1 and *Bluebook* Rule 10.)

Figure 10-1 Citing a Case

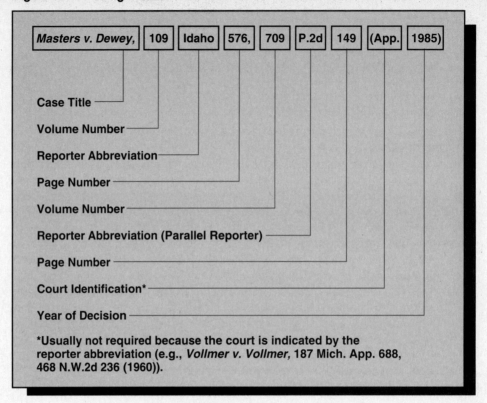

Case titles are abbreviated versions of the full name of the case, usually the last name of the first named plaintiff, followed by a space, the letter *v* and a period, a space, then the last name of the first named defendant, all underscored. Thus, Robert Smith suing John Doe, Jane Doe, and Richard Roe, comes out "Smith v. Doe." Use appropriate abbreviations (see *Bluebook* Table T.6), but spell out all essential terms of a name or title (e.g., "Red Lion Broadcasting Co. v. FCC") and eliminate redundant abbreviations (e.g., omit *Inc.* from *ABC Co., Inc.*). *State, People,* or *Commonwealth* is sufficient to identify a state in a case from that state's state courts. For the federal government, use *United States*. If the cite is used in a formally printed publication, put the case title in italics instead of underscoring it.

Separate the case title from the reporter citations with a comma and a space. What follows is the volume number of the official reporter (if any), a space, the proper abbreviation of the official reporter, a space, and the page number of the first page of the case report in the official reporter (e.g., *New York Times Co. v. Sullivan*, 376 U.S. 254). If the volume number or page number is currently unknown, insert an underscore blank in place of the unknown number (e.g., _____ U.S. _____).

Except when citing an officially reported U.S. Supreme Court case in a formal brief (strict Bluebook style requires you to cite only to U.S., but a researcher may appreciate having the parallel cites), follow the official cite of the case (if any) with the appropriate unofficial cite(s) (if any). That is, follow the official cite (if any) with a comma, a space, the volume number of the unofficial reporter, a space, the proper abbreviation of the unofficial reporter, a space, and the page number of the first page in the unofficial reporter, continuing likewise until all unofficial cites are listed (e.g., *New York Times Co. v. Sullivan*, 376 U.S. 254, 84 S. Ct. 710, 11 L. Ed. 2d 686) (strict Bluebook style: *New York Times Co. v. Sullivan*, 376 U.S. 254).

After the last reporter citation, put a space, then the year of decision in parentheses (e.g., *New York Times Co. v. Sullivan*, 376 U.S. 254, 84 S. Ct. 710, 11 L. Ed. 2d 686 (1964)) (strict Bluebook style: *New York Times Co. v. Sullivan*, 376 U.S. 254 (1964)). If the citation is to a reporter that covers only one court, or if the particular court can be identified or presumed from the reporters cited (e.g., *Ricketts v. Scothorn*, 59 Neb. 51, 77 N.W. 365 (1898)), the case citation is complete.

However, if the citation is to a reporter that covers more than one court (such as a regional or intermediate appellate court reporter), you should indicate in an appropriate abbreviated form, within the parentheses and before the date, the particular court being cited (e.g., *Mitchell v. C.C. Sanitation Co.*, 430 S.W.2d 933 (Tex. Civ. App. 1968) or *McCormick & Co. v. Childers*, 468 F.2d 757 (4th Cir. 1972)).

With regard to the use of spaces in case names, reporter abbreviations, and court identification, note that single-letter abbreviations (and "2d"-like abbreviations) are not spaced (e.g., N.E.2d), except next to multiletter abbreviations (e.g., F. Supp.), which have a space before and after the multiletter abbreviation (e.g., Cir. Ct. App.).

Citing Statutes

Statutes are usually cited by title number, code abbreviation, section number, and year of publication (See Figure 10–2 and *Bluebook* Rule 12.) Statutes may also be cited by a "statutes at large" reference.

Statutes may be cited to either official or unofficial codes. A proper citation to a federal statute can be as simple as "42 U.S.C. § 1983 (1982)." The essential cite consists of the title number, space, code abbreviation, space, section symbol (i.e., §) or "sec.," space, and section number. After a space, the year of publication is added in parentheses to identify the proper version of the statute. If the statute is in a supplement, that should be indicated within the parentheses and before the date (e.g., 5 U.S.C.A. § 654 (West Supp. 1979)). If desired, the popular name of the statute can be given before the code reference (e.g., National Environmental Policy Act of 1969, § 102, 42 U.S.C. § 4332 (1982)). If necessary, a federal statute may also be cited to the session law (e.g., National Environmental Policy Act of 1969, Pub. L. No. 91–190, 83 Stat. 852 (1970)).

State statutes are usually cited to state codes, beginning with the state code

Figure 10–2 Citing a Statute

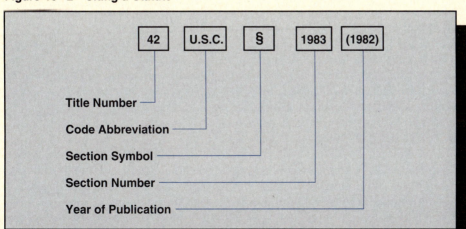

abbreviation, the combination title and section number, and year of publication (e.g., Colo. Rev. Stat. § 24-3-204 (1973)). (See Appendix III.)

Citing Other Primary Sources

Constitutions are cited by sovereign abbreviation, space, "Const." and space, followed by the subdivision cited (e.g., U.S. Const. art. I, sec. 7, para. 2, cl. IV). Use "amend." to cite an amendment (e.g., U.S. Const. amend. IV). (See *Bluebook* Rule 11.)

Court rules are cited by the proper abbreviation for the rules, space, and rule number (e.g., Fed. R. Civ. P. 60(b)). (See *Bluebook* Rule 12.8.3.)

Administrative regulations are usually cited like a statute to the appropriate administrative code (e.g., 45 C.F.R. § 405 (1978)). If a federal administrative regulation is not in C.F.R., cite to the *Federal Register* (e.g., 48 Fed. Reg. 760 (1983)). A federal executive order is cited by "Exec. Order No." and space, order number, comma, space, and a cite to its location in C.F.R., or else in the *Federal Register* (e.g., Exec. Order No. 13,902, 3 C.F.R. 205 (1979)). (See *Bluebook* Rule 14.)

Citing Secondary Sources

Although primary authority is preferred over secondary authority, secondary authority may be cited.

Annotations in *American Law Reports* (A.L.R.) are cited by the author's full name, comma, space, "Annotation" and comma, space, the title of the annotation (underscored or in italics), comma, space, volume number, space, proper annotation series abbreviation, space, page number (of the annotation, not the reported case), space, and year of publication in parentheses (e.g., Colleen R. Courtade, Annotation, *Application of Functionality Doctrine Under § 43(a) of Lanham Act (15 U.S.C.S. § 1125(a)*, 78 A.L.R. Fed. 712 (1986)). (See *Bluebook* Rule 16.5.5.)

Legal encyclopedias are cited by volume number, space, proper abbreviation, space, topic title (underscored or in italics), space, section symbol and section number, space, and year of publication in parentheses (e.g., 21 Am. Jur. 2d *Bailments* § 3 (1975)). (See *Bluebook* Rule 15.7.)

Textbooks, treatises, and other nonfiction books are cited by volume number (if more than one), author, comma, space, title of the book (underscored or in italics), space, section and/or page (or paragraph) number (if necessary), space, and in parentheses the edition (if more than one; "2d" or whatever, space, "ed." and space) and year of publication (e.g., William L. Prosser, *Law of Torts* § 122 (4th ed. 1972)). (See *Bluebook* Rule 15.) A reasonable alternative (not Bluebook style) to emphasize the publisher is generally accepted citation style: author, comma, title, edition, and, in parentheses, city of publication, colon, publisher, space, and year of publication, followed by any page references (e.g., Legal citation is also discussed in Frank S. Gordon, Thomas M. S. Hemnes, and Charles E. Weinstein, *The Legal Word Book,* 2nd ed. (Boston: Houghton Mifflin Co., 1982), pp. 149-168).

Consecutively paginated legal periodicals are cited author, comma, space, title of the article (underscored or in italics), comma, space, volume number (or if none, year of publication), space, proper periodical abbreviation, space, first page number of the issue, comma, space, page numbers of the cited material, space, and in parentheses the year of publication (unless used as volume number) (e.g., Patricia J. Williams, *Alchemical Notes: Reconstructed Ideals From*

Deconstructed Rights, 22 Harv. C.R.-C.L. Rev. 401, 407 (1987)). (See *Bluebook* Rule 16.2.)

Nonconsecutively paginated legal periodicals are cited author, comma, space, title of the article (underscored or in italics), comma, space, proper periodical abbreviation, comma, space, date of issue, comma, space, "at" and space, first page number of the issue, comma, space, page numbers of the cited material (e.g., Barbara Ward, *Progress for a Small Planet*, Harv. Bus. Rev., Sept.-Oct. 1979, at 89, 90). (See *Bluebook* Rule 16.3.)

Computer-Assisted Citation Style

Jurisoft, a division of Mead Data Central, Inc., sells *CheckRite* software, which checks citations in word-processing documents for proper Bluebook style. Paralegals are frequently delegated the task of shepardizing case citations in briefs and checking them for proper Bluebook style. (See Chapter 11.)

10–3 Citation Requirements

Before citing material in a brief, you should check the applicable court rules and statutes for any matters of citation style required by law. As *The Bluebook* advises: "The practitioner should also be aware that many courts have their own rules of citation that may differ in some respects from *The Bluebook* (p. 11)."

For example, a lawyer or paralegal preparing a brief for the Ohio Court of Appeals for the First Judicial District (Hamilton County, including Cincinnati), should refer to Local Rule 6, which addresses the "Form and Content of Appellate Briefs." Part D(1) provides:

> a. All citations to reported Ohio cases in briefs or memoranda shall recite the date, volume and page of the official Ohio report and the parallel citation, where the same exists, to the Northeastern Reporter, e.g., W.T. Grant Co. v. Lindley (1977), 50 Ohio St.2d 7, 361 N.E.2d 454; State v. Durham (1976), 49 Ohio App.2d 231, 360 N.E.2d 743; State v. Gastown, Inc. (1975), 40 Ohio Misc. 29, 360 N.E.2d 970.
> b. All citations to the United States Supreme Court cases in briefs or memoranda shall cite the date, volume and page of the official report and parallel citation to the Supreme Court Reporter, e.g. Jones v. United States (1960), 362 U.S. 257, 80 S.Ct. 725.

Citing the date first and giving a citation to an unofficial U.S. Supreme Court reporter are not Bluebook style, but they are part of the style required in briefs filed with the Ohio Court of Appeals for the First Judicial District.

The Ohio Supreme Court also follows the "date-up-front" convention, since its court rule examples follow that style, but there is no rule that explicitly requires this. The Ohio Supreme Court also prefers the "R.C." abbreviation for citations to the Ohio Revised Code, as explicitly permitted by the Ohio General Assembly in R.C. 1.01.

In the state of Michigan, the *Michigan Uniform System of Citation* "provides a comprehensive scheme for citation of authority in documents filed with or issued by Michigan courts."

Again, check the applicable court rules and statutes for special citation requirements, if any, before you submit your brief.

SUMMARY

10-1

In court, the judge expects you to cite the law that supports your case. For brevity and clarity, legal materials are cited in an abbreviated form. The leading system of citation style is *The Bluebook: A Uniform System of Citation*, 15th edition (1991). It is also known as *The Bluebook*, and the citation style it suggests is known as Bluebook style. For the most part, no law requires Bluebook style. Nevertheless, it is good practice to use Bluebook style unless there is a requirement to the contrary. Since there is no comprehensive citation style required by law, major law publishers have adopted their own style for competitive reasons.

10-2

Although most courts do not explicitly require it, most judges and most legal research and writing instructors expect a legal professional's briefs and other writings to substantially conform to Bluebook style. Cases are usually cited by an underscored abbreviated case title, volume-reporter-page citations, court identification (if necessary), and year of decision. If the cite is being used in a formally printed publication, put the case title in italics instead of underscoring it. Statutes are usually cited by title number, code abbreviation, section number, and year of publication. Constitutions are cited by sovereign abbreviation, space, "Const." and space, followed by the subdivision cited. Court rules are cited by the proper abbreviation for the rules, space, and rule number. Administrative regulations are usually cited like a statute to the appropriate administrative code. A.L.R. annotations are cited by the author's full name, comma, space, "Annotation" and comma, space, the title of the annotation (underscored or in italics), comma, space, volume number, space, proper annotation series abbreviation, space, page number (of the annotation, not reported case), space, and year of publication in parentheses. Legal encyclopedias are cited by volume number, space, proper abbreviation, space, topic title (underscored or in italics), space, section symbol and section number, space, and year of publication in parentheses. Textbooks, treatises, and other nonfiction books are cited by volume number (if more than one), author, comma, space, title of the book (underscored or in italics), space, section and/or page (or paragraph) number (if necessary), space, and in parentheses the edition (if more than one; "2d" or whatever, space, "ed." and space) and year of publication. Consecutively paginated legal periodicals are cited author, comma, space, title of the article (underscored or in italics), comma, space, volume number (or if none, year of publication), space, proper periodical abbreviation, space, first page number of the issue, comma, space, page numbers of the cited material, space, and in parentheses the year of publication (unless used as volume number). Nonconsecutively paginated legal periodicals are cited author, comma, space, title of the article (underscored or in italics), comma, space, proper periodical abbreviation, comma, space, date of issue, comma, space, "at" and space, first page number of the issue, comma, space, page numbers of the cited material.

10-3

Before citing any material in a brief, you should check the applicable court rules and statutes for any matters of citation style required by law.

REVIEW

Key Terms

Before proceeding, review the key terms listed below to be sure you understand each one. If necessary, read over the corresponding section of the chapter. When you are ready to test your understanding, answer the Review Questions.

The Bluebook
Bluebook style
citation style
cite

Questions for Review and Discussion

1. Why does the legal profession need a uniform system of citation style?
2. Why is it incorrect to speak of the "Harvard Citator"?
3. Why do legal publishers use different citation styles?
4. If there is more than one plaintiff or defendant, how do you abbreviate the case name?
5. Why do you need to know which reporters are official and which are unofficial?
6. In a case citation, what is put in the parentheses before the year of decision?
7. Is it true that if the year in a case citation is the year of decision, then the year in a statute citation is the year of enactment?
8. How are federal statutes and state statutes cited?
9. How are constitutions, court rules, and administrative regulations cited?
10. What information do you need to cite a law treatise?

Activities

1. Examine the citation style used in a modern A.L.R. annotation. Is it easier to follow than Bluebook style? Is it more efficient? Which style do you prefer?
2. Study the tables in part T of *The Bluebook*. Part T is an excellent checklist of the primary sources of U.S. law.
3. Check the applicable court rules and statutes in your state for matters of citation style required by law.

CHAPTER 11 Shepard's Citations and Other Citators

OUTLINE

11–1   *Shepard's Citations*
       Using *Shepard's* as a Case Reviewer
       Using *Shepard's* as a Case Finder
       Shepard's on LEXIS or WESTLAW
11–2   Other Citators
       Parallel Cites
       Auto-Cite
       Insta-Cite
       LEXIS or WESTLAW as a Citator

COMMENTARY

As you near completion of your memorandum on public religious displays, focusing on *Lynch v. Donnelly*, 465 U.S. 668 (1984), you discover another case dealing with public religious displays, *Allegheny County v. ACLU*, 492 U.S. 573 (1989), in a constitutional law treatise. The fact that you almost missed this important case, decided after *Lynch*, shocks you. You think how embarrassing it would have been if you had made such an error and it was exposed. Is there a way to avoid such an embarrassment?

OBJECTIVES

In this chapter you will learn about systems for checking the validity of case precedents and finding parallel citations. Emphasis is placed on *Shepard's Citations* published by Shepard's/McGraw-Hill, Inc. After reading this chapter, you should be able to:

1. Resist being deceived by human nature while performing legal research.
2. Resist being deceived by time while performing legal research.
3. Identify the greatest embarrassment in advocacy and legal research.
4. Find parallel citations using *Shepard's Citations*.
5. Find the appropriate volumes and pamphlets of *Shepard's Citations* for a particular search.
6. Use *Shepard's Citations* as a case reviewer.
7. Use *Shepard's Citations* as a case finder.
8. Find parallel citations using cross-reference books.
9. Identify the origins and use of Auto-Cite.
10. Identify the origins and use of Insta-Cite.

11-1 Shepard's Citations

As discussed in Chapter 1, the purpose of legal research is to find a case like yours where the person like you won. Finding cases is discussed in Chapters 2, 3, and 4. Of course, your best "case" could turn out to be a statute, regulation, or other primary law, or a secondary source, as discussed in Chapters 5 to 9. Cite your "case" to the judge in the style discussed in Chapter 10, argue simple justice ("persons in like circumstances should be treated alike"), and you can't lose. Or can you?

It is important to realize that there are two powerful forces that are always at work: human nature and time. Acting alone or in concert, these forces can deceive any legal researcher, no matter how experienced.

As discussed in Chapter 1, there is no perfect law book. It is human nature to seize on the first thing that meets one's expectations, even though it may not be the truth. It takes a lot of mental work to be objective, much more than most people imagine. A lot of people are "checkmated" while they dream of checkmating their opponent.

A law book editor, working in a competitive environment under time pressure and other stresses, may unwittingly cut corners. The law book editor may seize on and write, or be instructed to seize on and write, something not 100% accurate. A legal researcher, also working in a competitive environment under time pressure and other stresses, may also unwittingly cut corners. The legal researcher, eager to find a case like his where the person like him won, may seize on and cite the inaccurate statement without checking it out. As a result, the legal researcher can lose the case to a more careful and objective opponent.

Even if the law book editor and the legal researcher have been careful, honest, humble, and objective, the case can still be lost because of the march of time. As discussed in Chapter 1, the law is always changing. Using a recently published law book, the legal researcher finds a case like the legal researcher's, where the person like the legal researcher won, and argues it to the court. His opponent rises and agrees that the case cited is like the case at bar, but notes that the legal researcher's case was reversed on appeal, and so the person like the opponent ultimately won. The court agrees, and finds for the opponent. The legal researcher has experienced the greatest embarrassment in advocacy: *unwittingly arguing the opponent's case.*

A legal researcher can lose by unwittingly citing and arguing **bad law:** overruled (or otherwise discredited) precedent. Bad law is precedent without authority. Precedent can lose its value in a number of ways. A precedent may be overruled by a higher court (or by a statute). A court may overrule its own precedent. Or a precedent may be left alone to die, whether distinguished away by other courts, overwhelmed by contrary precedent, or simply forgotten. Courts have the power to declare precedents out of date, and they frequently do. It is the insidious power of the march of time.

In 1873, an Illinois law book salesman, Frank Shepard, gave some thought to the nature of law books and precedent, and how the value of a precedent is altered over time by later case precedent. Although he was not a lawyer, Shepard observed that some lawyers made notes in the margins of their law books when they became aware of later cases that altered the precedential value of a reported case. Shepard realized that the idea was sound, but that no practicing lawyer would have the time to keep such a system up to date. There were thousands of cases published each year in a variety of reporters and keeping up with it all would be a full-time job. Shepard decided that he would provide the service, and he founded his own company to do so.

Shepard started small. He began to read all the reports of the Illinois courts.

He carefully noted every time an earlier case was cited by a later case. He printed his notes for each case on gummed slips and sold them to lawyers, instructing them to paste them in the margins of their reports at the cited case. It was a hit. Shepard expanded into other states, hired several assistants, and changed the format of the service to book form. *Shepard's Citations* quickly became a standard legal research tool.

After Shepard died in 1900, his business was incorporated and transferred to New York City. In 1947, the company was moved to Colorado Springs, Colorado, and, in 1966, it was acquired by and became a division of McGraw-Hill, Inc. *Shepard's* current publisher is thus Shepard's/McGraw-Hill, Inc.

Shepard's leads a group of books and other media that list citations, which are known as **citators**. In listing parallel cites, citators list cites to a target case, known as the **cited case**. In listing cites of cases that make reference to a target case, citators list referring cases, known as **citing cases**.

Shepard's is a book of tables uniquely listing all the citing cases for a cited case. Under each cited case (volume number and reporter noted in the running head; page number noted in boldface between dashes in the tables), the cites of the citing cases are listed by volume number, Shepard's reporter abbreviation, and page number. (See Figures 11–1 and 11–2.) In the first listing for the cited case, parallel citations are listed in parentheses immediately following the page number heading. Note that *Shepard's* cryptic reporter abbreviations are not Bluebook style, and so they should not be used in formal legal writing.

When legal researchers **shepardize** a case, they review all the citing cases for a cited case to make sure the cited case is not bad law or to help find other cases like the cited case. When legal researchers shepardize a brief or other legal writing, they review all the cases cited in the brief or other legal writing to make

Shepard's Citations

Source: © Doug Martin.

Figure 11–1 Example of a *Shepard's Citations* Page

Source: Shepard's *United States Citations, Case Edition,* vol. 6 (Colorado Springs, CO: Shepard's/McGraw-Hill, Inc., 1984), p. 241. Reprinted with permission.

Figure 11–2   Excerpt of *Shepard's* Reporter Abbreviations

ABBREVIATIONS—REPORTS

AA–Antitrust Adviser, Third Edition (Shepard's, 1987)
AABA–Atwood & Brewster, Antitrust and American Business Abroad (Shepard's, 1981)
A2d–Atlantic Reporter, Second Series
Ab–Abstracts
AB–American Bankruptcy Reports
ABA–American Bar Association Journal
ABA(2)–American Bar Association Journal, Part 2
AbD–Abbott's Court of Appeals Decisions (N.Y.)
AbN–Abstracts, New Series
ABn–American Bankruptcy Reports, New Series
AbP–Abbott's Practice Reports (N.Y.)
AbPn–Abbott's Practice Reports, New Series (N.Y.)
AC–American Annotated Cases
AD–American Decisions
ADC–Appeal Cases, District of Columbia Reports
Add–Addison's Reports (Pa.)
Advo–Givens, Advocacy (Shepard's, 1985)
AE(2)–Acret, Architects and Engineers, Second Edition (Shepard's, 1984)
AE(2s)–Acret, Architects and Engineers, Second Edition, Supplement (Shepard's, 1984)
AEn–Buck, Alternative Energy (Shepard's, 1982)
AFW–Newberg, Attorney Fee Awards (Shepard's, 1987)
AgD–Eglit, Age Discrimination (Shepard's, 1982)
AgL–Davidson, Agricultural Law (Shepard's, 1981)
AGSS–Laritz, Attorney Guide to Social Security Disability Claims (Shepard's, 1986)
Aik–Aiken's Reports (Vt.)
AL–Turley, Aviation Litigation (Shepard's, 1986)
Æ2–American Law Reports, Second Series
Æ3–American Law Reports, Third Series
Æ4–American Law Reports, Fourth Series
Ala–Alabama Supreme Court Reports
AlA–Alabama Appellate Court Reports
Alk–Alaska Reports
Allen–Allen's Reports (Mass.)
ÆR–American Law Reports

ÆRF–American Law Reports, Federal
AMP–Bauernfeind, Income Taxation: Accounting Methods and Periods (Shepard's, 1983)
AN–Abbott's New Cases (N.Y.)
AntNP–Anthon's Nisi Prius Cases (N.Y.)
AOA–Anderson's Ohio Appellate Unreported Decisions
AR–American Reports
ARAP–Analytical Review: A Guide to Analytical Procedures (Shepard's, 1988)
ARD–Application for Review Decisions
Ark–Arkansas Reports
ARm–O'Reilly, Administrative Rulemaking (Shepard's, 1983)
AS–American State Reports
At–Atlantic Reporter
AtSN–Attorney Sanctions Newsletter (Shepard's)
Az–Arizona Reports
AzA–Arizona Court of Appeals Reports
Bar–Barbour's Supreme Court Reports (N.Y.)
BCh–Barbour's Chancery Reports (N.Y.)
Binn–Binney's Reports (Pa.)
Blackf–Blackford's Reports (Ind.)
Bland–Bland's Chancery Reports (Md.)
Bos–Bosworth's Reports (N.Y.)
Boy–Boyce's Reports (Del.)
BP–Drake & Mullins, Bankruptcy Practice (Shepard's, 1980)
BP(2)–Drake, Bankruptcy Practice, Second Edition (Shepard's, 1990)
Bradb–Bradbury's Pleading & Practice Reports (N.Y.)
Bradf–Bradford's Surrogate's Court Reports (N.Y.)
Bray–Brayton's Reports (Vt.)
Breese–Breese's Reports (Ill.)
BRW–Bankruptcy Reporter (West)
BTA–United States Board of Tax Appeals Reports
BTCL–Givens, Business Torts and Competitor Litigation (Shepard's, 1989)
Bur–Burnett's Reports (Wis.)
C2d–California Supreme Court Reports, Second Series
C3d–California Supreme Court Reports, Third Series

viii

Source: Shepard's United States Citations, Statute Edition, vol. 4 (Colorado Springs, CO: Shepard's/McGraw-Hill, Inc., 1986), p. viii. Reprinted with permission.

sure the brief or other legal writing does not cite bad law or to help find other cases like the case cited to use in a reply or a revision.

There are *Shepard's* sets covering virtually every set of court reports published in the United States, including every major unit of the National Reporter System. Note, however, that a *Shepard's* covering a particular state's reporters lists only citing cases from that state or cases originating in the federal courts in that state.

For the U.S. Supreme Court, for example, Shepard's/McGraw-Hill, Inc., publishes the *Shepard's United States Citations* (Case Edition) set. There are tables for the three major Supreme Court reporters—one for cites to *United States Reports* (U.S.), one for cites to *United States Supreme Court Reports, Lawyers' Edition* (L. Ed.), and *Lawyers' Edition, Second Series* (L. Ed. 2d), and one for cites to *Supreme Court Reporter* (S. Ct.)—running through several bound volumes and pamphlets covering different periods of time.

Suppose in June 1991, for example, you wanted to see the complete list of cites made to 450 U.S. 24. To limit the number of volumes and pamphlets you have to look through to make the complete list of cites for a cited case, Shepard's/McGraw-Hill, Inc., periodically publishes comprehensive bound volumes and pamphlets. However, in June 1991, the complete list of cites for 450 U.S. 24 happens to be in the maximum number of bound volumes (3) and pamphlets (3).

As of June 1991, the last major comprehensive bound volume covering 450 U.S. was published in 1984, covering cites to 409–458 U.S. (and parallel cites) from the date of the cited case to 1984. The next comprehensive volume covering 450 U.S., a "Supplement," was published in 1986, covering cites to 404–467 U.S. from 1984–1986. The next comprehensive volume covering 450 U.S., another "Supplement," was published in 1988, covering cites to 438–463 U.S. from 1986–1988.

To cover the six-month periods after major comprehensive bound volumes and "Supplements," Shepard's/McGraw-Hill, Inc., publishes yellow comprehensive pamphlets in January and July. To cover three-month periods after yellow comprehensive pamphlets (or after the latest bound volume but before the first yellow pamphlet), Shepard's/McGraw-Hill, Inc., publishes red comprehensive pamphlets in May and November. To cover periods after red comprehensive pamphlets (or after the latest yellow pamphlet or bound volume but before the first red pamphlet), Shepard's/McGraw-Hill, Inc., also publishes white "Advance Sheet" pamphlets.

In June 1991, the pamphlets covering 450 U.S. 24 included a yellow pamphlet published in January 1991, a red pamphlet published in May 1991, and a white "Advance Sheet" pamphlet published in June 1991.

Because some people find the comprehensive volume and pamphlet system confusing, and because the volumes and pamphlets can be easily misshelved by the uninformed, Shepard's/McGraw-Hill, Inc., publishes a list entitled "What Your Library Should Contain" on the cover of each pamphlet. (See Figure 11–3.) It is a good practice to consult this list, as necessary, before you begin to shepardize a case.

Although *Shepard's* was originally designed to list all the citing cases for a cited case, Shepard's/McGraw-Hill, Inc., has added to the concept. As the title page of each *Shepard's* volume indicates for the cited cases in the volume, *Shepard's* may also list other citing legal materials, such as A.L.R. annotations and law reviews, for a cited case. A **statute edition** lists all the citing cases for a particular statute or ordinance. *Shepard's United States Citations* (Statute Edition), for example, lists all the citing cases for a particular section of the *United States Code*. Constitutions, treatises, court rules, selected administrative decisions, and patents listed by patent number, copyrights listed by title of the copyrighted work, and trademarks listed alphabetically can also be shepardized.

Figure 11-3 Example of "What Your Library Should Contain"

Shepard's United States Citations

SEMIANNUAL SUPPLEMENT (IN TWO PARTS)
CASES PART 1A

IMPORTANT NOTICE
   A 1990-1991 Hardbound Supplement for Shepard's United States Citations, Cases will be published in December, 1991 and delivered by January 31, 1992.

WHAT YOUR LIBRARY SHOULD CONTAIN
PART 1, CASES
BEFORE YOU RECEIVE THE 1990-1991 HARDBOUND SUPPLEMENT, RETAIN THE FOLLOWING:
1988 Bound Volumes (Vols. 1A, 1B, 1C, 2A, 2B, 2C)*
1984 Bound Volumes (Vols. 3, 4, 5, 6)*
1984-1986 Bound Supplement (Vols. 7A and 7B)*
1986-1988 Bound Supplement (Vols. 8, 9, 10, 11, 12)*
1988-1990 Bound Supplement (Vols. 13, 14, 15, 16, 17)*
Supplemented with:
   –July, 1991 Semiannual Cumulative Supplement Vol. 90 No. 2 (Parts 1A and 1B)
   –Sept., 1991 Cumulative Supplement Vol. 90 No. 4 (Part 1)
   –Nov., 1991 Cumulative Supplement Vol. 90 No. 6 (Part 1)
   –Jan., 1992 Semiannual Cumulative Supplement Vol. 90 No. 8 (Parts 1A and 1B)

AFTER YOU RECEIVE THE 1990-1991 HARDBOUND SUPPLEMENT, RETAIN THE FOLLOWING:
Bound Volumes and Bound Supplements same as above
1990-1991 Bound Supplement (Vols. 18 and 19)*
Supplemented with:
   –Jan., 1992 Semiannual Cumulative Supplement Vol. 90 No. 8 (Parts 1A and 1B)

PART 2, STATUTES
   Please refer to the current supplement cover for Part 2, Statutes.

Source: Shepard's United States Citations, Semiannual Supplement July (1991), Cases Part 1A, vol. 90., No 2 (Colorado Springs, CO: Shepard's/McGraw-Hill, Inc., 1991), front cover. Reprinted with permission.

Shepard's/McGraw-Hill, Inc., also publishes other publications and subject-specific *Shepard's*. Publication examples include *Code of Federal Regulations* (Citations), *Law Review Citations, Professional Responsibility Citations* (covering the American Bar Association *Code of Professional Responsibility* and *Code of Judicial Conduct*), and *Restatement Citations*. Subject examples include *Bankruptcy Citations, Federal Labor Law Citations, Federal Tax Citations, Military Justice Citations,* and *Uniform Commercial Code Citations.*

Using *Shepard's* as a Case Reviewer

Frank Shepard conceived of his book as a case reviewer. He listed all the citing cases for a cited case, so a legal researcher could make sure the cited case was not bad law (i.e., make sure it was "still" **good law** and to what extent). Over time, Shepard and his successors developed a system of analysis abbreviations, listed in the front of each volume, to add to the bare list of citing cases, to help the legal researcher quickly review the cited case, and to do so in a refined way. (See Figure 11–4.)

Shepard and his successors noted that there are two general types of citing cases. Often the "citing" case is really a later history of the cited case itself; the same case on appeal or remand. "History of Case" abbreviations—such as *a* for "same case affirmed on appeal," *m* for "same case modified on appeal," and *r* for "same case reversed on appeal"—have been added as appropriate to the citing references for the cited case.

Most often the citing case is a true citing case; that is, another case citing the cited case, perhaps as precedent. "Treatment of Case" abbreviations—such as *c* for the "decision or reasoning in cited case criticized," *d* for the citing case that "distinguished" itself from the cited case, and *f* for the citing case that "followed" the cited case as "controlling"—have been added as appropriate to the citing references for the cited case.

Although the analysis abbreviations help you to quickly review a cited case, remember they are not perfect, and can't be, because there is no perfect law book. Analysis abbreviations are generally added only when they are supported by the express language of the citing case. If a citing case implicitly criticizes the cited case, no analysis abbreviation appears to indicate that. Since the analysis is a literal one-time judgment expressed in summary form, you should always read the relevant cases. Moreover, *Shepard's* cannot be used in any direct way to determine if a case precedent has been overruled by statute.

One weakness inherent in *Shepard's* results from the fact that the cited case may deal with several points of law. It is not always clear for what point of law (if any) in the cited case the citing case referred to the cited case. Thus, it is not always clear for which point of law (if any) in the cited case the analysis abbreviation applies. To address this problem, modern *Shepard's* citing references include, to the extent possible, a superior figure (an "exponent") to the left of the page number. The superior figure indicates the headnote or syllabus paragraph of the *cited case* that states the point of law about which the *citing case* referred to the cited case.

In reviewing a case with *Shepard's,* remember that *Shepard's* lists only all citing cases for a cited case. Two case opinions can discuss the same point of law, but nothing requires the judge drafting the later opinion to cite the earlier case. The judge may not even be aware of the earlier case. Moreover, a case precedent can be "followed" or "overruled"—indirectly—by a nonciting case.

You should also realize that a statute edition of *Shepard's* cannot be used directly as a case reviewer because a "statute edition" collects all the citing cases

Figure 11-4 Example of *Shepard's* Abbreviations

ABBREVIATIONS—ANALYSIS

History of Case

a	(affirmed)	Same case affirmed on rehearing.
cc	(connected case)	Different case from case cited but arising out of same subject matter or intimately connected therewith.
m	(modified)	Same case modified on rehearing.
r	(reversed)	Same case reversed on rehearing.
s	(same case)	Same case as case cited.
S	(superseded)	Substitution for former opinion.
v	(vacated)	Same case vacated.
US	cert den	Certiorari denied by U.S. Supreme Court.
US	cert dis	Certiorari dismissed by U.S. Supreme Court.
US	reh den	Rehearing denied by U.S. Supreme Court.
US	reh dis	Rehearing dismissed by U.S. Supreme Court.
US	app pndg	Appeal pending before the U.S. Supreme Court.

Treatment of Case

c	(criticised)	Soundness of decision or reasoning in cited case criticised for reasons given.
d	(distinguished)	Case at bar different either in law or fact from case cited for reasons given.
e	(explained)	Statement of import of decision in cited case. Not merely a restatement of the facts.
f	(followed)	Cited as controlling.
h	(harmonized)	Apparent inconsistency explained and shown not to exist.
j	(dissenting opinion)	Citation in dissenting opinion.
L	(limited)	Refusal to extend decision of cited case beyond precise issues involved.
o	(overruled)	Ruling in cited case expressly overruled.
p	(parallel)	Citing case substantially alike or on all fours with cited case in its law or facts.
q	(questioned)	Soundness of decision or reasoning in cited case questioned.

ABBREVIATIONS—COURTS

Cir. Fed.–U.S. Court of Appeals, Federal Circuit
Cir (number)–U.S. Court of Appeals Circuit (number)
CIT–United States Court of International Trade
CCPA–Court of Customs and Patent Appeals
Cl Ct–Claims Court (U.S.)
Ct Cl–Court of Claims Reports (U.S.)
Cu Ct–Customs Court Decisions
DC–District of Columbia
EC or ECA–Temporary Emergency Court of Appeals
ML–Judicial Panel on Multidistrict Litigation
RRR–Special Court Regional Rail Reorganization Act of 1973

Source: Shepard's United States Citations, Case Edition, vol. 6 (Colorado Springs, CO: Shepard's/McGraw-Hill, Inc., 1984), pp. xix. Reprinted with permission.

for a statute or ordinance, and not for a case. Statute editions of *Shepard's* are excellent case finders, however, as discussed in the next part.

Using *Shepard's* as a Case Finder

Although *Shepard's* was designed as a case reviewer, it is frequently used as an imperfect case finder to help find other cases like the cited case. *Shepard's* lists all the citing cases for a case. There may be hundreds of cases that have cited a given cited case. Note, however, that the court deciding the citing case may cite the cited case for a number of reasons. Sometimes there's a legal significance; sometimes it's a coincidence. *Shepard's* perpetuates all citations of legal authority: the great, the good, the bad, and the ugly.

You can assume that 50% of the citing cases listed in *Shepard's* for a cited case like yours are also cases like yours. If you have found a case that you know is exactly like, or similar to, your case, you can shepardize it, and check out each case listed as a citing case. About 50% of the time—more if you're lucky, less if you're not—the citing case will be like yours. Because *Shepard's* systematically lists all the citing cases for a cited case, no editorial judgment is involved. You can often find cases like yours using *Shepard's* that didn't make it into an annotation, digest, encyclopedia, or other law book, because they didn't have to meet stricter editorial standards.

Unlike a case citing another case, when a case cites a statute it is highly probable that the statute is important to the case. You can assume that 75% of the citing cases listed in *Shepard's* statute edition for a cited statute like your case are also cases like yours. Because *Shepard's* statute edition systematically lists all the citing cases for a cited statute or ordinance, no editorial judgment is involved. You can often find cases like yours using *Shepard's* statute edition that didn't make it into an annotated code or other law book, because they didn't have to meet stricter editorial standards.

Again, *Shepard's* is an imperfect case finder. You have to consider your chances of success. *Shepard's* may list hundreds of citing cases for a cited case like yours, and about 50% will *not* be cases like yours. In a given case, using *Shepard's* as a case finder may not be worth the time and effort involved.

Shepard's on LEXIS or WESTLAW

Selected *Shepard's Citations* are available on the LEXIS (SHEP command) and WESTLAW (SH command) computer-assisted legal research systems, to be discussed in the next chapter. The principal advantage of using *Shepard's* on-line is that the bound volume and pamphlet lists of citing cases are automatically merged for each cited case. In addition, analysis abbreviations are spelled out in *Shepard's* on-line, and you can quickly retrieve a citing case from the computer-assisted legal research system.

11–2 Other Citators

While *Shepard's Citations* uniquely lists all the citing cases for a cited case, there are other useful citators that simply list parallel citations for a cited case and/or list all the cites to a single case as it has made its way through the court system.

The path a legal controversy has taken through the court system is known as its **case history.**

Parallel Cites

As discussed in the previous chapter, it is necessary to find the appropriate parallel cites to a case, if any, to properly cite the case in Bluebook style. There are often more practical reasons for finding a parallel cite. Law libraries, particularly law firm libraries, do not always contain the same sets of books. As a result, you must be able to find and use alternative sources. For example, in the early stages of your research you may have only the cite to a case in a state reporter, but need to find the case in the West regional reporter, or you may have only the cite to the case in the West regional reporter, but need to find the case in a state reporter.

Until computers were commonly used in legal research (see Auto-Cite and Insta-Cite discussed below), the most common way to get back and forth between state reporters and the National Reporter System was to use West's *National Reporter Blue Book* (not to be confused with *The Bluebook: A Uniform System of Citation*) and the appropriate West's state "Blue and White Book."

The *National Reporter Blue Book,* as its name suggests, is a blue book. Its tables list state citations for each state and give for each the parallel citations in the National Reporter System. The state "Blue and White Book" (e.g., *Ohio Blue and White*), as its name suggests, is a blue and white book. The blue pages repeat the parallel citation information found in the *National Reporter Blue Book* for that state. The white pages have tables that list the National Reporter citations for the state and give for each the parallel citations in the state reporters.

Besides *Shepard's,* other historic methods of finding parallel cites included searching tables of cases in volumes and digests, checking for cross-reference tables in volumes, thumbing through running heads, and other trickery. These methods are now overshadowed by two computer case history citators: Auto-Cite and Insta-Cite.

Auto-Cite

The first commercial computer case history citator was Auto-Cite, introduced directly to the public by the Lawyers Co-operative Publishing Co. (LCP) in 1982. Its origins date back to the preparation of *Lawyers' Reports Annotated* (L.R.A.) from 1888–1918, and include a citation service once offered by the company at no charge.

In 1913, LCP began "The Co-op. Citation Bureau" to help promote L.R.A. A legal researcher could send a case cite to LCP and LCP would return, at no charge, by mail or "telegraph collect" (1) the citations to "All the cases which have ever cited that case," (2) where, if at all, the case was reported in a "leading selected case series" (such as LCP's L.R.A.), and (3) where, if at all, the case was cited in an L.R.A. annotation, insofar as all of the above had already been found by LCP editors in preparing L.R.A. and other texts. The "Citation Bureau" was based on a card file of approximately 1.4 million cards on which LCP editors had checked and noted the histories of cases before citing them in L.R.A.

The free "Citation Bureau" faded out of existence, but as L.R.A. became A.L.R., LCP editors continued to keep case history file cards. Of course, until 1977, LCP never saw the need to publish the cards, because A.L.R. theoretically contained all its case analysis. Theoretically, A.L.R. readers did not need

Shepard's, because A.L.R. editors picked up the value of case precedents reading all the on-point cases in the course of preparing annotations. Instead of a few analysis abbreviations, A.L.R. provided a detailed narrative analytical treatment of all the case law on the point annotated, with complete case summaries set out for all relevant cites.

As will be discussed in the next chapter, by 1977, LCP was looking for a way to get into "electronic publishing." The pages of LCP's books were then being composed by computer, and the company had begun to look into computerizing other aspects of the manufacturing process. One aspect was editorial "testing." A clerical staff assisted LCP editors in checking the validity of cases cited in LCP publications using the LCP's case history collection. LCP decided to computerize its "testing" department. The new computer system was known as Auto-Cite (Automated Citation Testing Service).

In 1977, LCP entered into talks with Mead Data Central, publisher of the LEXIS computer-assisted legal research system. On January 22, 1979, the companies signed a royalty agreement whereby LCP's Auto-Cite system would be provided to LEXIS subscribers. LEXIS had already demonstrated that information could be economically entered into a computer database, and with the development of personal computers, acoustic couplers (a device in which a telephone receiver can be inserted), and modems, customers could be linked to an electronic publisher over telephone lines.

By 1982, LCP had collected nearly four million case histories. LCP decided to once again provide "testing" services not only to its own editors and LEXIS subscribers, but to its own customers as well, this time for a fee.

Auto-Cite allows the user to make an electronic citation search. Enter a cite by volume, reporter abbreviation, and page, and Auto-Cite displays the full citation to the case, including title, court (if necessary), date, parallel cites, references in A.L.R. annotations, and case history citations, all in an easy-to-read "sentence."

Auto-Cite is *not*, however, the same as *Shepard's*. *Shepard's* has all the citing cases for a cited case, and so is useful in both case review and case finding. *Shepard's* covers both the history and the treatment of a cited case. Auto-Cite covers only the history of the cited case and leaves case reviewing and case finding to A.L.R.

Auto-Cite has three main features: citation verification, parallel case referencing, and A.L.R. referencing.

Other than a check of citation information (e.g., the title of the case; the year of decision), the citation verification of Auto-Cite extends only to a determination of whether a case has become bad law as a result of its own history in the courts (e.g., reversed by a higher court). Auto-Cite's citation verification is not a determination of whether the case has become bad law as a result of its treatment by other courts, unless another case explicitly states that the cited case was affected by another case (an "as stated in" reference). Otherwise, the treatment of a case by other courts is still left to A.L.R. Auto-Cite does have an advantage over *Shepard's* in that its collection of case history information is all in one place.

Auto-Cite also has an advantage over *Shepard's* with regard to parallel citations. Auto-Cite displays collect in one place parallel cites for both the cited case and the history cases. To find the history case parallel cites in *Shepard's*, you have to make separate searches.

Auto-Cite also has some slight advantages over *Shepard's* in citing A.L.R. annotations. *Shepard's* gives only volume-series-page cites to citing annotations, and the annotations themselves are not shepardized. Auto-Cite includes full A.L.R. titles and section number references for citing annotations, and it returns cites to related annotations if an annotation cite is entered.

Auto-Cite also has greater coverage, in terms of both breadth (number) and depth (reach back in time), of case reporters and administrative decisions than its competitor, Insta-Cite (discussed below), including an extensive coverage of the Bureau of National Affairs (BNA), Commerce Clearing House (CCH), and other non-West reporters, in addition to those included in West's National Reporter System.

As discussed in the next chapter, direct access to Auto-Cite from LCP ceased on April 1, 1991, after a 10-year run. Thus, again, Auto-Cite is available only to LCP editors and LEXIS subscribers. LEXIS subscribers can also purchase *CheckCite* software from Jurisoft, a division of Mead Data Central, Inc., to automatically use Auto-Cite and *Shepard's* to check citations in a word-processing document on their personal computers.

Insta-Cite

As discussed in the next chapter, Insta-Cite, introduced in 1983, was West's WESTLAW response to Auto-Cite on LEXIS. Compared with Auto-Cite's history dating back to the 1800s, West created Insta-Cite from scratch, for purely competitive reasons.

Similar to Auto-Cite, Insta-Cite has three main features: case history, parallel citations, and citation verification. Insta-Cite's case history is case history: the ability to determine whether a case has become bad law as a result of its own history in the courts. Insta-Cite's parallel citations emphasize parallel citations to units of the National Reporter System. Insta-Cite's citation verification is simply case information (title, year of decision, etc.). While Insta-Cite includes citations to A.L.R. reported cases, it does not include citations to A.L.R. annotations.

Insta-Cite also has more current coverage of case reporters than its competitor, Auto-Cite, because Insta-Cite principally covers the National Reporter System, and West obviously has access to its own reporters before its competitors.

Insta-Cite is available only on the WESTLAW computer-assisted legal research system, to be discussed in the next chapter. WESTLAW subscribers can also purchase *WestCheck* software to automatically use Insta-Cite, *Shepard's*, and Shepard's Preview (to be discussed in the next chapter) to check citations in word-processing documents on their personal computers.

LEXIS or WESTLAW as a Citator

As discussed in the next chapter, LEXIS or WESTLAW can be used as a citator by using the cited case's cite as a word search for citing cases.

SUMMARY

11–1

It takes a lot of mental work to be objective. Because of human nature, a legal researcher may seize on and cite the inaccurate statement without checking it out. Because of the march of time, a legal researcher may suffer the greatest embarrassment in advocacy: unwittingly arguing the opponent's case. Bad law is precedent without authority. Starting in 1873, Frank Shepard provided the service of systematically noting every time an earlier case was cited by a later case. *Shepard's Citations* quickly became a standard legal research tool, leading a group of books and other media known as citators. In listing parallel cites, citators list cites to a target case, known as the *cited case*. In listing cites of cases that refer to a target case, citators list referring cases, known as *citing cases*. *Shepard's* is a book of tables uniquely listing all the citing cases for a cited case. When legal researchers shepardize a case, they review all the citing cases for a cited case to make sure the cited case is not bad law or to help find other cases like the cited case. There are *Shepard's* sets covering virtually every set of court reports published in the United States, including every major unit of the National Reporter System. A statute edition lists all the citing cases for a particular statute or ordinance. A legal researcher using *Shepard's* can review all the citing cases for a cited case. With help from analysis abbreviations for case history and treatment, the legal researcher can determine whether the cited case is bad law. A legal researcher can also use *Shepard's* as an imperfect case finder to find other cases like the cited case. Selected *Shepard's Citations* are available on the LEXIS and WESTLAW computer-assisted legal research services.

11–2

Until Auto-Cite and Insta-Cite were developed, the most common way to get back and forth between state reporters and the National Reporter System was to use West's *National Reporter Blue Book* and the appropriate West's state "Blue and White Book." The first commercial computer case history citator was Auto-Cite, introduced directly to the public by LCP in 1982. Auto-Cite allows the user to make an electronic citation search. Enter a cite by volume, reporter abbreviation, and page, and Auto-Cite displays the full citation to the case, including title, court (if necessary), date, parallel cites, references in A.L.R. annotations, and case history citations, all in an easy-to-read "sentence." Auto-Cite has three main features: citation verification, parallel case referencing, and A.L.R. referencing. Other than a check of citation information, the citation verification of Auto-Cite extends only to a determination of whether a case has become bad law as a result of its own history in the courts (e.g., reversed by a higher court). Since April 1, 1991, Auto-Cite is available only on the LEXIS computer-assisted legal research system. LEXIS subscribers can purchase *CheckCite* software to automatically use Auto-Cite and *Shepard's* to check citations in a word-processing document on their personal computer. Insta-Cite is West's WESTLAW response to Auto-Cite on LEXIS. Similar to Auto-Cite, Insta-Cite has three main features: case history, parallel citations, and citation verification. Insta-Cite's citation verification is simply case information. Insta-Cite is available only on the WESTLAW computer-assisted legal research system. WESTLAW subscribers can purchase *WestCheck* software to automatically use Insta-Cite, *Shepard's*, and Shepard's Preview to check citations in a word-processing document on their personal computer. In addition, LEXIS or WESTLAW can be used as a citator by using the cited case cite itself as a word search for citing cases.

REVIEW

Key Terms

Before proceeding, review the key terms listed below to be sure you understand each one. If necessary, read over the corresponding section of the chapter. When you are ready to test your understanding, answer the Review Questions.

bad law
case history
citators
cited case
citing cases
good law
Shepard's
shepardize
statute edition

Questions for Review and Discussion

1. Why is it hard for human beings to be objective while performing legal research?
2. Why should you hesitate to cite a case you found in a 20-year-old law book?
3. What is the greatest embarrassment in advocacy?
4. Where are parallel citations located in *Shepard's*?
5. What important feature of *Shepard's* do you find on the cover of its pamphlets?
6. What are *Shepard's* analysis abbreviations for?
7. Why is *Shepard's* an "imperfect" case finder?
8. What are West's state "Blue and White" books used for?
9. What are the main features of Auto-Cite?
10. What are the main features of Insta-Cite?

Activities

1. Locate the *Shepard's* sets in your local law library. Referring to the "What Your Library Should Contain" information on the covers of the pamphlets, determine if all the pamphlets have been properly shelved. Have superseded volumes and pamphlets been properly removed?
2. Shepardize a U.S. Supreme Court case decided in the 1960s. How many cases did you find?
3. If you dare, completely shepardize a U.S. Supreme Court case. That is, shepardize the case, then shepardize each of the cases you found. After eliminating duplicates, how many cites did you find? Are you impressed, overwhelmed, or both?

PART FIVE

USING COMPUTERS AND OTHER TECHNOLOGIES

Chapter 12
Computer-Assisted Legal Research

Chapter 13
Microforms, Floppy Disks, CD-ROM, and Computer-Organized Legal Research

CHAPTER 12 Computer-Assisted Legal Research

OUTLINE

12–1 Understanding Computer-Assisted Legal Research
    The Data Corporation's Concordance
    Computer-Assisted Legal Research Takes Off
12–2 LEXIS
12–3 WESTLAW
12–4 Other Databases
12–5 The Advantages and Disadvantages of Computer-Assisted Legal Research

COMMENTARY

The mayor and law director are pleased with your memorandum. By following your "advice," the diverse public religious display the city erects, balanced by nonreligious elements, survives the Christmas holiday season without objection. Now, you are hit by a "bolt from the blue." The U.S. senator from your state has died and the governor has appointed the mayor to fill the Senate seat. You are asked to join the new senator's staff in Washington, D.C., and you accept. The senator becomes a member of the Judiciary Committee just before the President nominates a U.S. Court of Appeals judge to be the next Associate Justice of the Supreme Court. Your assignment is to find all of the judge's opinions, analyze them for any unexplained changes or contradictions, and prepare the senator for the judge's testimony before the committee.

OBJECTIVES

In this chapter you will learn about the use of computer-modem technology to aid in the search of legal materials. Emphasis is placed on the two leading computer-assisted legal research systems: LEXIS and WESTLAW. After reading this chapter, you should be able to:

1. Describe the events preceding the discovery of CALR.
2. Understand the logic of a computer word search.
3. Describe the events since the discovery of CALR.
4. Describe the organization and use of LEXIS.
5. List the principal advantages of using LEXIS.
6. Describe the organization and use of WESTLAW.
7. List the principal advantages of using WESTLAW.
8. Recognize CALR systems other than LEXIS and WESTLAW.

9. Describe the advantages of CALR.
10. Describe the disadvantages of CALR.

12–1 Understanding Computer-Assisted Legal Research

Computer-assisted legal research (CALR) is the use of computer-modem systems to automate the search of legal materials as an aid in legal research. The search is made upon a collection of information placed in the computer's memory, known as a **database.**

The Data Corporation's Concordance

In 1965, Ohio State Bar Association executives became interested in developing a CALR system for Ohio lawyers. In 1966, a computer software company, Data Corporation of Beavercreek, Ohio, learned of the project and offered to build it. In 1977, a nonprofit corporation, Ohio Bar Automated Research (OBAR), was formed. OBAR entered into a contract with Data Corporation to build the system, also named OBAR. Ohio law was entered into Data Corporation's computer, and search software (a modification of software previously created for the Air Force called Central) was developed. The software allowed the user to make a **word search,** a computer search of the words likely to have been used to describe the information sought. Although OBAR could perform some searches faster and better than they could be performed manually, the system was slow, unreliable, and limited in scope. Since neither OBAR nor Data Corporation had sufficient funds to make additional changes, the project appeared doomed.

The project gained new life, however, in 1969, when Data Corporation was purchased by Mead Corporation (Mead) of Dayton, Ohio. Mead, a billion-dollar paper and forest products company, made the purchase in order to acquire a new printing process. The word search software just happened to come with the package. In 1970, Mead formed a subsidiary, Mead Data Central (MDC), to take over the OBAR project, and bought out OBAR corporation's interest.

The heart of MDC's system is a computer-generated **concordance,** an index of words. Unlike an ordinary index, which refers a reader to the location of concepts in a book by short entries and page references, a concordance is a literal alphabetical listing of the principal words of a book, with precise references to where in the book each word is used.

Many concordances, for example, have been made for the Bible. If biblical researchers want to find where the word *light* is used in the Bible, they can look the word up in a concordance for precise references by chapter and verse.

Most significant for legal research, however, is the fact that a concordance can be used to find relational concepts. For example, if you want to read about the biblical relationship between *mercy* and *sacrifice,* you can use a concordance to find a reference the words have in common. Since words are ordinarily used for the concepts they stand for, a convergence of those words likely involves a convergence of their concepts as well.

As cases and other documents are loaded on MDC's computer, the computer builds a concordance. While loading cases, the computer notes, for example, that the word *death* appears in the 15th case as the 89th word, in the 31st case as the 25th word, and in the 55th case as 17th word. The computer also notes that the word *penalty* appears in the 23rd case as the 40th word, in the 31st case as the 75th word, in the 55th case as the 20th word, in the 93th case as the 64th word, and so on. It is then relatively simple for a legal researcher trying to find "death penalty" cases to ask the computer—with its lightning-fast math, search, and sort capabilities—to compare the references to the words *death* (15–89, 31–25, 55–17) and *penalty* (23–40, 31–75, 55–20, 93–64) and return the full text of the cases in which both words appear (31 and 55), or the portion of the text where the word *death* appears within five words of the word *penalty* (case 55, from word 17 to word 20).

It is important to understand how CALR word searching is unique. Instead of using an existing index, digest, or annotation, CALR word searching allows legal researchers to make their own index of the material searched.

The system depends on the assumption that the words the judge used in a given opinion correspond to what the case is about and that a legal researcher can make educated guesses about what words the judge used in describing the case and their relationships in the opinion. The computer takes the legal researcher's words and the relationships, and searches its concordance. If the legal researcher makes good educated guesses and the desired words and relationships exist in cases in the database, the system returns the cases like the legal researcher's where the person like the researcher won.

The software MDC developed is **user-friendly** (easy to use). Once you are in the appropriate case file, if you want to search for the words *death* and *penalty* in the same case, all you have to do is type *death* and *penalty* and hit the enter key.

MDC had custom computer terminals and printers manufactured, and by 1973, the commercially viable system was ready to be put **on-line** (accessible by a modem-equipped computer using telephone lines).

Computer-Assisted Legal Research Takes Off

In April 1973, MDC introduced the LEXIS computer-assisted legal research system, and "electronic" law publishing was born. LEXIS was a pseudo-acronym (LEgal X Information Service?), based on market research indicating people had a favorable reaction to names with an *X* (e.g., Exxon). Lacking a door-to-door sales force, LEXIS was slow to catch on, but wherever it was sold, it was a hit.

Since the database originally included New York and Ohio cases, LEXIS was initially marketed in New York and Ohio. MDC rushed to add cases from other states because every time it did, it found more customers. By 1976, MDC had added a federal library, cases from several states, and thousands of users. As LEXIS grew, MDC grew, and the profits were plowed back into the system. MDC hired scores of data entry people to work around-the-clock. By 1979, LEXIS had the full text of almost every case—state and federal—on-line. In 1979, MDC continued its growth by starting NEXIS, a computer-assisted research system for news and business information.

West Publishing Company (West) was caught off-guard. For the first time in decades, West's monopoly over a lawyer's access to case law was broken. Like West, MDC had the cases too. And MDC had something West didn't: a computer system for the computer age.

West competed with MDC the only way it could: it poured money into the development of its own CALR system. To catch up with LEXIS' growing database, West created its own around-the-clock data entry department. In 1975, West introduced WESTLAW.

The original WESTLAW contained only West's case summaries (e.g., synopses and headnotes). It wasn't until July 1977 that West announced its intention to include the full text of all cases in its database. However, WESTLAW began to distinguish itself from LEXIS, since only WESTLAW contained both the full text of cases and West's case summaries.

For West, it was vitally important that WESTLAW succeed. For MDC, it was equally important that LEXIS maintain its advantage. The competition became intense. Each company looked for new features to distinguish its service, and each company tried to match any features added by its competitor.

For example, West began to make the same argument that the Lawyers Co-operative Publishing Company (LCP) had always made against West. LCP argued that although West had the cases, LCP had the analysis in A.L.R. Now West argued that although LEXIS had the cases on computer, WESTLAW had the analysis on computer. As early as 1978, West advertised its case summaries on WESTLAW with the slogan "Full Text Plus." West argued that a word search might not pick up a case in LEXIS, which contained only the opinions, because the court might not use the words searched, but the words might be in the West case summary, leading to the discovery of the case. For example, a judge might draft an opinion in a death penalty case, but not use the words *death penalty* in the opinion. However, a headnote for the case might indicate that it was a death penalty case. If a legal researcher was searching "death penalty" on LEXIS and WESTLAW, the argument went, the legal researcher would find the case with WESTLAW but not with LEXIS.

Meanwhile, LCP executives became concerned. It was clear that the future of law publishing was in *electronic publishing*, and LCP wasn't in the game. As discussed in the last chapter, LCP developed a computer citation system, Auto-Cite, and offered it to the general public in 1982. Noting that Auto-Cite gave citations to *American Law Reports* (A.L.R.) annotations, an LCP editor quipped: "We've put A.L.R. into CALR."

MDC executives anticipated the need to have a comeback to West's Full Text Plus campaign. In 1979, after two years of talks with LCP executives, LCP agreed to put Auto-Cite on LEXIS. To press its Full Text Plus advantage, West had to counter Auto-Cite on LEXIS. West poured money into the development of its own computer citation service, and in 1983, Insta-Cite, discussed in Chapter 11, was born. With Insta-Cite to answer Auto-Cite, West was again on the offensive.

In 1984, LEXIS remained in the lead. Nevertheless, MDC needed another comeback to West's persistent Full Text Plus campaign. MDC needed to add case analysis to LEXIS that West couldn't counter. LCP needed something to counter Insta-Cite on WESTLAW, and access to cases on computer.

In 1985, MDC and LCP made another agreement: a joint venture. MDC and LCP cooperated in putting A.L.R. (except First Series) on LEXIS. MDC got the leading book of case analysis, A.L.R., on LEXIS. LCP formed an "electronic" subsidiary, Veracorp, to sell Veralex (in Latin: "truth word"), consisting of Auto-Cite, A.L.R. on-line, and access to the cases on LEXIS, each accessible by **citation search** (i.e., entering a citation).

Introduced in February 1986, A.L.R. on LEXIS was a hit for MDC, which advertised the fact with full-page advertisements in national publications. LEXIS was set up so that in any combined file search of federal case law or state case law, A.L.R. would also automatically be searched. The implicit argument was that A.L.R. annotations were better than West's case summaries.

Veralex, introduced in January 1986 by LCP's Veracorp, was targeted at small and medium-sized firms. It had limited success. Many users did not understand or appreciate the citation search format. Without word search capability, Veralex was dwarfed by LEXIS and WESTLAW. A second agreement, in which LCP traded access to its sales force for access to LEXIS itself, led to the creation of Veralex 2. It failed. In 1991, Veralex 2 ceased operation, ending direct access to Auto-Cite as well.

Entering the 1990s, the competition between West and MDC balanced out.

Entering the 1990s, the competition between West and MDC balanced out. LEXIS has advantages over WESTLAW, and WESTLAW has advantages over LEXIS. LCP remains in the market with its production of Auto-Cite and A.L.R. for LEXIS.

12–2 LEXIS

Discussing every aspect and feature of LEXIS is beyond the scope of this textbook; however, the publisher has developed CALR tutorial software to accompany this text that provides instruction in searching LEXIS and reinforces the concepts presented on the following pages. You should also know that Mead Data Central publishes a number of excellent guides to using LEXIS, including the pamphlet *Learning LEXIS: A Handbook for Modern Legal Research* and the newsletter "LEXIS Brief."

You should carefully study this chapter and use the software that accompanies this text, as well as referring to Mead Data Central's LEXIS guides and the latest *Library Contents and Alphabetical List*, before accessing LEXIS on a subscriber line.

In summary, subscribers can access LEXIS through a dedicated UBIQ terminal or personal computer 24 hours-a-day (except Sunday). Using a modem, the user is connected with the MDC computer in Dayton, Ohio. At the

LEXIS/NEXIS

"Welcome to LEXIS" screen, the user transmits an identification number. After entering client information, the user selects the part of the database to search. The LEXIS database is divided into "services," "libraries," "files," "documents," "segments," and "words." A search is made by entering the desired terms and alternatives, along with **connectors** (codes to indicate the desired logical and numerical relationships among the terms). The results can be displayed in full, with the "key words in context" **(kwic),** or as a list of citations. The search can be modified as desired. Cases can be checked with Auto-Cite and *Shepard's.* Cases and statutes can be viewed via their citations using "LEXSEE" and "LEXSTAT" commands. There are a variety of options for printing search results. LEXIS also features "Dot Commands" (e.g., .kw) and "SHORT CUT," allowing the user to make a series of commands in one step, to speed through the usual command-return sequences.

The principal advantage of using LEXIS is the size of its database. LEXIS/NEXIS is the largest commercially available full-text computer database in the world. It has over 85 million documents available for reading and research.

In 1990, several hundred LEXIS files that were unavailable on WESTLAW were available on MDC. LEXIS is the sole source of several non-West publications, including many published by LCP. Only LEXIS provides access to the nation's most complete case-history citation service, Auto-Cite, and the leading book of case analysis (A.L.R.).

12–3 WESTLAW

Discussing every aspect and feature of WESTLAW is beyond the scope of this textbook; however, the publisher has developed CALR tutorial software to accompany this text that provides instruction in searching WESTLAW and reinforces the concepts presented on the following pages. You should also know that West publishes a number of excellent guides to using WESTLAW, including the pamphlet *Introductory Guide to Legal Research* and the newsletter "Password."

You should carefully study this chapter and use the software that accompanies this text, as well as referring to West's guides and the latest *Database List,* before accessing WESTLAW on a subscriber line.

In summary, WESTLAW can be accessed by subscribers through a WALT (West's Automated Law Terminal) or a personal computer 24 hours a day (except Sunday). Using a modem, the user is connected with the West computer in St. Paul, Minnesota. At the WESTLAW "logo" screen, the user transmits an identification number. After entering client information, the user selects the part of the database to search. The WESTLAW database is divided into "services," "databases," "documents," "fields," and words. A word search (i.e., **query**) is made by entering the desired terms and alternatives, along with connectors. The results can be browsed by page **(page mode)** or by search term **(term mode),** or a list of citations can be displayed. Cases can be checked with Insta-Cite, *Shepard's,* or Shepard's Preview (discussed below). Cases and statutes can be viewed via their citations using the "Find" service. There are many options for printing search results. WESTLAW also features EZ ACCESS, a slower but easier-to-use menu-driven version of WESTLAW.

The principal advantage of using WESTLAW is the ability to make computerized digest searches by searching West's case summaries on-line. Along with Insta-Cite and Star Paging, WESTLAW also features West publications like *Black's Law Dictionary* and *United States Code Annotated* (U.S.C.A.). In addition, the Shepard's Preview service on WESTLAW provides the most recent *Shepard's*

WESTLAW

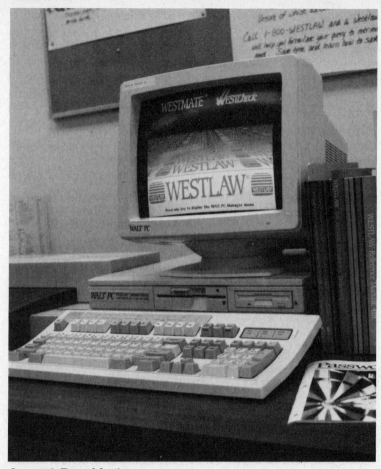

Source: © Doug Martin.

citations for cases in the National Reporter System before their publication by Shepard's/McGraw-Hill, Inc., in bound volumes and pamphlets. WESTLAW's Quick-Cite updates Shepard's Preview by automatically using WESTLAW as a citator.

12–4 Other Databases

LEXIS and WESTLAW are unusual in providing full-text data accessible by word search. Other computer database systems generally provide abstracted information accessible by citation, list, or index. Some of the systems available independently of LEXIS and WESTLAW are mentioned in the following paragraphs.

DIALOG, "the world's largest card catalog," is prepared by Dialog Information Services Inc., a subsidiary of the Lockheed Corporation. Along with the Congressional Research Service, DIALOG's coverage includes business information, copyrights, engineering, medicine, patents and trademarks, science, and other subjects. DIALOG can also be accessed through WESTLAW.

ELISS, the Electronic Legislative Search Service prepared by Commerce Clearing House (CCH), contains up-to-date federal and state legislative information.

FLITE (Federal Legal Information Through Electronics) and JURIS (Justice Retrieval and Inquiry System) are systems available to employees of the federal government.

PHINet, the Prentice-Hall Information Network, was a full-text collection of Prentice-Hall's comprehensive tax and pension publications. PHINet is now part of TAXRIA.

12–5 The Advantages and Disadvantages of Computer-Assisted Legal Research

CALR has a number of advantages over research in books. The user may save money by being charged only for what is needed. CALR can eliminate the need for printed sources (unless they are cheaper in print) and save shelf space. Information on CALR is more current, doesn't physically deteriorate, and can be accessed from a variety of locations.

The principal advantage of CALR is the ability to perform a computer word search. Computer word searching is great when searching for uniquely identifiable information (e.g., a docket number) that must be found quickly and that cannot, as a practical matter, be found another way. For example, suppose you are getting married tomorrow to a person with an unusual name. Before you "tie the knot," you want to find out if your spouse-to-be has ever been involved in a court case, and why. You can use CALR to word search the name of your spouse-to-be. You may find, in an unreported opinion from a state court thousands of miles away, that your spouse-to-be successfully appealed a conviction on a "technicality." Such a search would, as a practical matter, be impossible without the word search capability of CALR.

On the other hand, CALR can be useless when you are searching for information described in common terms, involving sophisticated analysis. For example, if you search for exceptions to the rule that an acquittal in a criminal case does not collaterally estop (preclude) litigating the same issues in a civil case, and search the words *acquittal*, *civil*, *criminal*, *collateral*, and *estoppel*, in different relationships, you will find hundreds of irrelevant cases. In such a situation, where sentences are more important than words, you need to use a source organized, written, and indexed by human beings who understand the issue and exercise judgment. A search of *American Jurisprudence, Second* (Am. Jur. 2d), for example, would lead you to 46 Am. Jur. 2d, *Judgments* § 618 entitled "Denial of doctrine; exceptions and limitations," and the cases cited therein.

The problem is that computer word searches are "extremely literal." The computer merely searches a concordance. It works on the assumption that the user can make educated guesses about what words the writer of a document used in describing the concepts the researcher wants to find. Even an educated user can guess wrong, and the less educated the user, the poorer the guess.

Synonymous words are a major problem. If users search for the word *doctor*, they will get all the "doctor" cases, but they won't get all the "physician" cases unless they search for the word *physician* as well. One person can be described in several different ways (e.g., attorney, author, father, genius, guardian, lawyer, man, plaintiff, professor, teacher, uncle, victim, witness).

Another problem is ambiguity. Because words can have several denotations and connotations, word searches often lead to irrelevant, even comical, results. A researcher looking for a person named *John* may find a case involving a bathroom. One story involves a products liability lawyer who was searching for cases involving the female hormone drug diethylstilbestrol, commonly known as DES. He searched "DES" in an "all states" database. He found hundreds of cases—none involving the drug DES—from Des Moines, Iowa.

Because of ambiguity, include date restrictions in your searches wherever you can. If you know what you're looking for happened in 1990, a search restricted to 1990 avoids retrieving irrelevant results from other years. Similarly, if what you are looking for will be found in a particular LEXIS "segment" or WESTLAW "field" (e.g., case title or judge-author), just search that segment or field.

Another problem involves the nature of the computer systems. If you make an identical word search in both LEXIS and WESTLAW, you will not always get the same result. You will find that each system's database contains typographical errors. The errors may be errors repeated from the original document or that occur as a result of errors in data entry. If a searcher is looking for one word spelled one way and that word has been misspelled, the system will not return the case containing that word. West has tried to make a positive feature out of this by correcting typos made by the court on WESTLAW. MDC, taking the view that the opinion of the court is the opinion of the court and that its editors are not above the law, does not correct typos made by the court on LEXIS.

There are other reasons an identical word search in LEXIS and WESTLAW will not always get the same result. Each system automatically searches for certain plurals and equivalencies (e.g., *child* also retrieves *children*) and excludes commonly used words (called ***noise words*** in LEXIS, ***stop words*** in WESTLAW), such as *as, be, and,* and *the*. While the programming is similar, the words included or excluded by each system, and the system's operation, are not identical. For example, in a **proximity search** (i.e., is one word within a specified number of words from another) LEXIS does not count noise words, but WESTLAW does count stop words.

Another significant limitation of CALR is the cost. Word search systems are expensive. While schools can obtain the use of LEXIS and WESTLAW at discount prices (allowing students to use the services for free), in the real world you have to pay for it. Although the different systems have different pricing structures and charges, the average researcher making typical searches on LEXIS or WESTLAW can expect to pay over $200 per hour. Because of the cost, it is foolish to do any more reading than necessary while using CALR.

Other disadvantages to CALR include the fact that CALR systems generally do not contain historical materials, that determining what the CALR systems contain requires effort, and that CALR systems generally require considerable training and practice for effective use. Unreasonable resistance also exists to computer use by some people, especially among those born before the computer age. They are simply more familiar with, and prefer to use, books.

Understand that CALR has many advantages over books as a finding tool, but very few advantages over books as a reading tool. As a finding tool, CALR is a wonder and a joy. It is errorless, tireless, and incredibly fast. As a reading tool, it is a headache; sometimes literally so.

Under existing technology, computer monitors cannot be economically made to display sharp black figures on a white background (like a book). Black and white provides maximum contrast for greatest reading ease. On the other hand, looking at the glowing letters on a glare-filled screen causes most people to squint and strain, and eventually gives them a headache.

With the typical CALR display, you can view only a small part of a given document at a given time. For example, a screen of text on WESTLAW covers less than half of a page in a West reporter. Since you can see two pages of a book when it is open in front of you, a screen of WESTLAW covers less than a quarter of what you can see in a book. Although a CALR system may let you search through a result, you cannot scan it as if it were printed in a book.

Understand that while CALR was a great invention, books were too. Books continue to be a great invention. They collect a large amount of information in a single place. They're reasonably permanent, easy to carry, easy to handle, easy to use, and easy on the eyes. They don't use electricity or need special programming, and they usually don't break if you drop them. You can thumb through them, dog-ear them, and mark them up. Books are an incredible bargain. Buy a book and you can use it as often as you want, as long as you want, and wherever you want, at no additional cost, other than storage.

At present, the ideal use of CALR is to carefully prepare an effective search strategy before you start (West publishes "Query Planner" forms for this purpose). When you're ready, go on-line, quickly make your search, print the results, and get off. Study your results off-line. This procedure allows you to take advantage of the unique power of CALR—to make a computer word search—without bankrupting you or your employer. In general, use books as a reading tool and CALR as a finding tool, and you will do fine.

SUMMARY

12–1

Computer-assisted legal research (CALR) is the use of computer-modem systems to automate the search of legal materials as an aid in legal research. In 1973, Mead Data Central (MDC) of Dayton, Ohio, came on the scene with the first commercial CALR system, LEXIS. Featuring word search software based on a concordance, LEXIS was a hit, allowing researchers to make their own indexes of the material searched. WESTLAW was introduced in 1975. It took a long time for WESTLAW to catch up to LEXIS. However, WESTLAW began to distinguish itself from LEXIS, since only WESTLAW allowed a search of both the full text of cases and West's case summaries, advertised by West as "Full Text Plus." When LCP created the citation history service Auto-Cite in the late 1970s, Mead put it on LEXIS, forcing West to create its own citation history service, Insta-Cite, to put on WESTLAW. In 1985, MDC and LCP cooperated in putting A.L.R. on LEXIS. Entering the 1990s, the competition between West and MDC has balanced out. LEXIS has some advantages over WESTLAW, and WESTLAW has some advantages over LEXIS. LCP remains in the market with its production of Auto-Cite and A.L.R. for LEXIS.

12–2

The publisher of this text has developed CALR tutorial software that provides instruction in searching LEXIS. MDC publishes excellent guides to using LEXIS, including the pamphlet *Learning LEXIS: A Handbook for Modern Legal Research*. You should carefully study MDC's guides including the latest *Library Contents and Alphabetical List*, as well as use the software accompanying this text, before using LEXIS. The principal advantage of using LEXIS is that LEXIS/NEXIS is the largest commercially available full-text computer database in the world. LEXIS has several hundred files not available on WESTLAW, and it is the sole source of several non-West publications, including many published by LCP.

12–3

The publisher of this text has developed CALR tutorial software that provides instruction in searching WESTLAW. West publishes excellent guides to using WESTLAW, including the pamphlet *Introductory Guide to Legal Research*. You should carefully study West's guides including the latest *Database List*, as well as use the software accompanying this text, before using WESTLAW. The principal advantage of using WESTLAW is the ability to make a computer digest search by searching West's case summaries online.

12–4

CALR systems available independently of LEXIS and WESTLAW include DIALOG, ELISS, FLITE, JURIS, and TAXRIA.

12–5

CALR has several advantages over research in books. CALR can eliminate the need for printed sources and save shelf space. Information on CALR is more current, doesn't physically deteriorate, and can be accessed from a variety of locations. The principal advantage of CALR is the ability to perform a computer word search. Computer word searching is great if you are searching for uniquely identifiable information that must be found quickly and that cannot, as a practical matter, be found in any other way. However, CALR can be useless when you are searching for information described in common terms, involving sophisticated analysis. Computer word searches are "extremely literal." Synonyms are a major problem, as is ambiguity. If a searcher is looking for a particular word spelled in a particular way and that word has been misspelled, the system will not return the case containing that word. While their programming is similar, the words included or excluded by each system, and the systems' operation, are not identical. The average researcher making typical searches on LEXIS or WESTLAW will be expected to pay over $200 per hour.

Other disadvantages to CALR include the fact that CALR systems generally do not contain historical materials, that determining what the CALR systems do contain requires some effort, and that CALR systems generally require considerable training and practice for effective use. CALR has many advantages over books as a finding tool, but very few advantages over books as a reading tool. While CALR was a great invention, books were also a great invention, and continue to be a great invention. Books collect a large amount of information in a single place, and they are reasonably permanent, easy to use, and easy on the eyes. Once you buy a book, you can use it as much as you want, wherever and whenever you want, at no additional cost, other than storage. The ideal use of CALR is to carefully prepare an effective search strategy before you start. When you're ready, go on-line, quickly make your search, print the results, and get off. Study your results off-line. Take advantage of the power of CALR without bankrupting you or your employer. Use books as a reading tool and CALR as a finding tool.

REVIEW

Key Terms

Before proceeding, review the key terms listed below to be sure you understand each one. If necessary, read over the corresponding section of the chapter. When you are ready to test your understanding, answer the Review Questions.

citation search
computer-assisted legal research (CALR)
concordance
connectors
database
kwic
noise words
on-line
page mode
proximity search
query
stop words
term mode
user-friendly
word search

Questions for Review and Discussion

1. How did LCP compete with West before CALR?
2. How does LEXIS search millions of pages of text without searching all of it each time a user makes a search request?
3. What role did Auto-Cite, Veralex, and Veralex 2 play in the competition between LEXIS and WESTLAW?
4. What MDC publications explain the use of LEXIS?
5. What is the principal advantage of using LEXIS?
6. What West publications explain the use of WESTLAW?
7. What is the principal advantage of using WESTLAW?
8. What is DIALOG?
9. What are some of the advantages of using CALR?
10. What are some of the disadvantages of using CALR?

Activities

1. Obtain information about LEXIS from MDC. If at all possible, get LEXIS training. At a minimum, observe a trained user using LEXIS.
2. Obtain information about WESTLAW from West. If at all possible, get WESTLAW training. At a minimum, observe a trained user using WESTLAW.
3. Look up LEXIS and WESTLAW in the index to *The Bluebook: A Uniform System of Citation* (15th ed). Both entries guide you to page 68 and Rule 10.8.1(b). Note that a citation to LEXIS or WESTLAW is required only when a case is unreported.

CHAPTER 13 Microforms, Floppy Disks, CD-ROM, and Computer-Organized Legal Research

OUTLINE

13–1 Microforms
13–2 Floppy Disks
13–3 CD-ROM
13–4 Computer-Organized Legal Research
      Searching and Sorting a Database
      Word Processing
      The Advantages of Information on Computer
      COLR Products

COMMENTARY

After making effective searches on LEXIS and WESTLAW, you have collected all of the judge's opinions and are ready to begin to analyze them for any unexplained changes or contradictions. Can this be done in a systematic way? Can technology help? What about that computer sitting in front of you?

OBJECTIVES

In this chapter you will learn about the use of technology, other than computer-modem systems, to aid in the search for legal materials and to organize the results of legal research. Emphasis is placed on the power of searching and sorting a computer database. After reading this chapter, you should be able to:

1. Recognize the use of microforms in legal research.
2. Recognize the use of floppy disks in legal research.
3. Recognize the use of CD-ROM in legal research.
4. Describe the effect created when information is organized.
5. Distinguish COLR from CALR.
6. Compare and contrast COLR and litigation support.
7. Explain how COLR puts "new" information at a legal researcher's fingertips.
8. Use basic database terminology.
9. List the advantages of having information on computer.
10. Recognize the use of COLR products in legal research.

13–1 Microforms

Computer-modem technology is not the only way that technology has been used to aid in the search of legal materials. When law books began to overflow their shelves, lawyers, librarians, and other law office managers began to explore ways to solve the problem. Firms renting space in downtown office buildings, paying rent by the square foot, were particularly interested in cutting overhead by reducing the amount of space taken up by their books.

Although law publishers were not about to stop selling books, they did begin to recognize the problem. The Lawyers Co-operative Publishing Company (LCP) was the leader, until it got burned. In 1939, an LCP advertisement (45#2 Case & Com., inside back cover [Oct. 1939]) pointed out that LCP's selective annotated reporter, *American Law Reports* (A.L.R.), provided the benefit of "Economy of Space." In 1952, LCP ads bluntly declared that A.L.R. "saves you shelf space." Then, in 1955, LCP announced Microlex.

Microlex was a product of the Microlex Corporation, a joint venture of LCP and the inventor of a microprint process, Sidney Teiser. In 1950, market research indicated that some firms were not purchasing LCP sets because they didn't have enough space for them. Believing that **microforms,** the reproduction of printed matter in greatly reduced size, was the wave of the future, LCP poured money into Microlex. A.L.R., *United States Supreme Court Reports, Lawyers' Edition* (L. Ed.), and *Lawyers' Reports Annotated* (L.R.A.) were put on **microfiche,** file-card-sized sheets of film containing miniature pictures of printed pages. "Microlex Editions" contained 200 printed pages per card.

To the horror of LCP executives, Microlex was an Edsel-like flop. Microlex Corporation could not develop an adequate magnifier/reader for the cards, and only a few hundred sets were ever sold. Inconvenient to use, Microlex was also ahead of its time. Saving space alone wasn't enough to make lawyers give up the advantages of books. Cutting heavy losses, LCP dismantled the operation.

Adequate readers of microfiche and **microfilm** (reels or cassettes of film containing miniature pictures of printed pages) have since been developed, but they remain bulky and inconvenient. Space is a more important consideration than ever, but microforms are not frequently used outside of library research.

Microforms are a common source of the briefs and records of federal and state appellate courts. Microforms are also a common source of governmental documents and records. More than half of the documents published by the Government Printing Office are available in microform. Check with your local law library to find out what microforms are available there.

Only a few major publications are published in microform. Since 1973, West has published an "Ultra Fiche Edition" of the entire First Series of the National Reporter System, along with selected Second Series volumes. In 1985, LCP quietly announced the availability of A.L.R. and A.L.R.2d on microfiche. All of these microforms are designed to provide access to out-of-print volumes.

13–2 Floppy Disks

Out of the computer technology of the 1980s came the ordinary floppy disk. One floppy disk can contain hundreds of pages of information. Using a personal computer, a researcher can make a computer search of the information on disk and download or print it, without the time pressure and expense of a computer-modem system. Disks can be marketed like a book, a periodical

Microfiche

Source: © Doug Martin.

subscription, or a home video. Indeed, the only advantage a computer-modem system has over disks is the ability to access current "time-sensitive" information, such as a slip opinion or market quote. If information is not that time-sensitive, it can be put on disk.

Floppy disk publishing is in its infancy. Only a few legal publications have appeared on floppy disk. Commerce Clearing House (CCH) offers its *Master Tax Guide* on floppy disk (for transfer to the user's hard disk). As explained in a CCH advertising mailer:

> All information can be accessed instantly by key word or phrase searching, walking through subject menus or using a combination of the two. Also, a lightning-quick LINK command lets you leap from any paragraph reference within the text or topical index to the paragraph itself. Once there, a RELATE command brings up a list of related documents.

In a similar manner, Tax Analysts of Arlington, Virginia, publishes *The Internal Revenue Code on Diskette.*

A publisher of college educational material, South-Western Publishing Co., offers *The Legal Tutor on Contracts* and *The Legal Tutor on Sales* on floppy disk. In addition, the LEXIS simulation *Learning LEXIS: A Computer-based Training Course* and the WESTLAW simulation *PC WESTrain II* are offered on floppy disk.

Floppy Disk

Source: The Image Bank/Jeffrey M. Spielman.

13–3 CD-ROM

The "hot" technology of the 1990s is high-density **CD-ROM** (compact disk with read-only memory). One CD-ROM can contain thousands of pages of information. As with ordinary floppy disks, a researcher using a personal computer equipped with a CD-ROM reader can make a computer search of the

CD-ROM

Source: The Image Bank/J. Brousseau.

information on the disk and download or print it, without the time pressure and expense of a computer-modem system.

As with ordinary floppy disks, CD-ROM publishing is in its infancy. The first major legal publication on CD-ROM, circa 1986, was the Information Access Corporation's LegalTrac system. As discussed in Chapter 9, LegalTrac is the *Legal Resource Index* on CD-ROM.

In 1988, West began publication of "CD-ROM Libraries," including *Bankruptcy Library*, *Delaware Corporation Law Library*, *Federal Civil Practice Library*, *Federal Tax Library*, and *Government Contracts Library*. The *Federal Tax Library* includes the Bureau of National Affairs' (BNA) *Tax Management* portfolios.

In 1990, Martindale-Hubbell announced the *Martindale-Hubbell Law Directory on CD-ROM*. The Michie Company published *New Mexico Statutes Annotated* on CD-ROM, and in 1991, it published the *Code of Virginia* on CD-ROM.

In 1991, Matthew Bender & Co., Inc., announced the publication of its "Search Master" compact disk libraries, including *Collier Bankruptcy*, *Intellectual Property*, *Business Law*, *Federal Practice*, *Tax*, *Personal Injury*, *California Practice*, and *Texas Practice*.

13–4 Computer-Organized Legal Research

While computers can be used to search for legal materials as an aid in legal research, they can also be used to organize the information found. When the information found is organized, there is a **synergistic** ("a whole greater than the sum of its parts") effect. Information is created that is not available from any other source.

The purpose of this section is to identify and label this synergistic effect, an inherent aspect of legal research, as magnified by the use of computers. **Computer-organized legal research (COLR)** is hereby defined as the use of computers to automate the organization of the search results as an aid in legal research.

Litigation paralegals will recognize COLR as being analogous to litigation support. **Litigation support** involves the organization of case information, particularly from discovery, to aid an attorney in the trial of a case. Several litigation support computer software packages are available that are specifically designed for that purpose.

For example, a litigation paralegal might be asked to **digest** (extract significant information from) a deposition transcript. The paralegal, perhaps using a computer program, will index and (if desired) summarize the testimony of a particular witness, so that a busy attorney can quickly locate and review what the witness said about any given subject. This is particularly important if the attorney plans to use the deposition to rebut the testimony of a witness at trial.

The deposition digest may reveal things nobody realized; things nobody had put together before. Early in the deposition the witness said she was at "A" at 11 p.m. Later in the deposition the witness said she was at "B" at 11 p.m. Putting this testimony together, the paralegal provides the lawyer with a "juicy" fact: the witness said she was in two different places at the same time. The digest might also reveal a pattern of "forgetfulness" indicating that the witness didn't talk about what she was doing from 11 p.m. to midnight, and so on.

It is important to recognize that *but for* the creation of the digest, it is unlikely the discovered facts would have been available from any other source. The discovered facts would have been buried in the deposition.

Similarly, COLR is finding information like the legal researcher's from the results of an initial search to find cases like the legal researcher's where the person like the legal researcher won. COLR puts "new" information, discovered information, at the legal researcher's fingertips. COLR comes after CALR, but before and during legal writing.

Searching and Sorting a Database

As noted in Chapter 12, a computer search is made upon a collection of information placed in its memory, known as a database. In this loose sense, a **database** is any collection of information capable of being searched by a computer, no matter how disorganized that information is.

In this chapter the term *database* is used in its technical sense, as a collection of information specially organized for rapid search and retrieval. In such a database, information is organized into defined categories known as **fields.** The variable items in the database, known as **records,** contain the categorical information for each item. (See Figure 13–1.)

A simple example of a database is a telephone book. The fields are name, address, and telephone number. The records are the listed subscribers: Andrews, John, at 123 Main Street with the number 987–6543; Bacon, Richard, at 987 Market Avenue with the number 123–4567; and so on, alphabetically by last name. The telephone book is a database because it is specially organized (in fields and alphabetically by last name) for the rapid search and retrieval of someone's telephone number by his or her name.

Figure 13–1 Databases

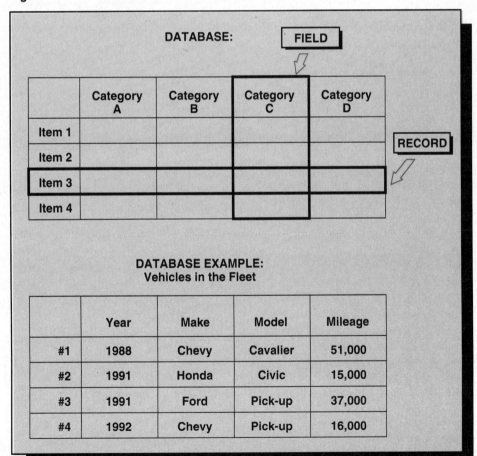

Because a telephone book is not a computer database, it is difficult to search its information in unintended ways. It is difficult, for example, to find the address for a telephone number (e.g., the way 911 operators send ambulances to the scene of an accident).

When the information in a telephone book is put on computer, it becomes a relatively simple matter to have the computer quickly search for the telephone number in the telephone field, then pick up the address from the address field of the desired record.

While a computer can search for a desired record by searching for information in the record, the computer's awesome power is the ability to quickly **sort** (put in alphanumeric order) records by a given field. Thus, the computer could sort the records by the telephone number field, allowing a human (like a computer) to quickly search for the telephone number in the telephone number field, then pick up the address from the address field of the desired record.

Moreover, multiple sorts can be made of the records by different fields to organize the records by category in whatever priority is desired. For example, a sort by telephone number field, then by address field, and finally by name field, will return the database to its original arrangement: by name, then by address, and finally by telephone number.

Suppose you work for a large law firm and you want to predict which associates are going to make partner because you want to work with a rising star. You can make an educated guess by making a database. A knowledge of Lotus 1–2–3 or any other software that allows you to create your own database now comes in handy.

Suppose there are 30 partners and 15 associates, and that for the last 30 years the firm has published a **house organ** (an in-house periodical) announcing, among other things, all new associates with their biographies and all promotions to partner, including the new partner's activities in the firm.

A house organ is a gold mine of information that can be put into a database. You have a number of fields of personal information to organize: last name, first name, month of birth, day of birth, year of birth, college attended, law school attended, name of spouse, hobbies, and so on. Now add to the database fields of employment information: month of start date, day of start date, year of start date, department assigned to, supervising partner, months to promotion, and so on. Dust off the old house organs and fill in the records of everyone, including former associates who never made partner and left the firm.

If the house organ left something out, you'll have a blank field to fill. Ask around. For instance, Ms. Hill's secretary knows her birthday. Be observant. Mr. Thomas just celebrated his 25th anniversary with the firm, and so on.

When the database is complete, start sorting. Want a list of attorneys by age? Sort by day of birth, month of birth, year of birth. Want a list of attorneys by seniority? Sort by day of start date, month of start date, year of start date. Want to find out about that "Bob" your friend mentioned, who works in the litigation department? Sort by name and department.

Keep sorting and checking your records and you'll discover a lot of things. If associates don't make partner within five years, they never do. All the partners in the corporate department play golf. All the associates promoted to partner in two years or less either had Mr. Johnson for a supervisor or attended the local state university. Fascinating information, valuable information, found in a simple database.

The techniques described above can be applied to legal research. As you search legal materials, you can enter the information you find into a database. The database will lead you to the discovery of additional information.

A case law database, for example, could include such fields as citation, court,

court level, date, type of case, type of plaintiff, type of defendant, winner, key fact, second fact, *ratio decidendi*, holding, and so on. Sorting the database, you could quickly determine, for example, if a banker was ever held liable, and under what circumstances. You could quickly determine if the plaintiff had ever won a case in California, and so on.

COLR varies greatly with the needs of the researcher. The bigger the research project, the more it makes sense to build a database. Experiment. Be creative. If you succeed, you'll be far ahead of the competition.

Word Processing

One of the most common uses of a computer is for **word processing,** which includes the electronic display, correction, and revision of text before printing. Word processing improves writing because the ability to make quick revisions encourages revision, which is the heart of writing. Word processing can also improve legal research.

Professional word-processing software, such as WordPerfect, includes the search and sorting power discussed above, and may also include the ability to program a series of commands and keyboard strokes known in WordPerfect as a **macro.** Macros can automate portions of the legal research and writing process.

For example, a legal researcher can use word processing to prepare a list of sources to be preliminarily searched and to record the results. Case citations listed in the results can be extracted, duplicate citations can be eliminated, and the remaining citations can be expanded to include parallel citations and case history. The list of case citations can also be sorted by court level for effective reading and numbered in sequence.

As the cases are read, information from the cases can be referenced to the case list, and an outline can be made (and altered as necessary) for the legal writing being prepared. Citations found within the cases can be checked against the citations the legal researcher had already found, to ensure accuracy and completeness. A macro can automatically prepare a rough draft by reading the outline and calling case citations and case information from other documents. Of course, word processing can be used to revise the rough draft and create a final version of the legal writing being prepared.

Again, COLR varies greatly with the needs of the researcher. The bigger the research project, the more it makes sense to use word processing. Experiment. Be creative. If you succeed, you'll be far ahead of the competition.

The Advantages of Information on Computer

The more you use COLR, the more you will realize the advantages of having information on a computer. Information on a computer can be copied, deleted, formatted, merged, moved, printed, reformatted, replaced, revised, searched, sorted, and spell checked, among other things.

Develop the habit of putting as much information on a computer as you can. The only exception is "fast" facts (such as a telephone number given in a radio or television advertisement) for which you only have enough time to jot down notes on paper. Even then, you will probably want to record the notes on a computer as soon as possible.

COLR Products

For the most part, COLR is something you design yourself, using general computer software like Lotus 1-2-3 and WordPerfect. However, a few commercial "COLR" software products do exist. More will come in the future.

Anderson Publishing Co. sells a legal document creation system known as *Lawriter*. The software allows the user to merge client information with legal forms found in forms modules in the computer's memory. The available forms modules include *Couse's Ohio Will Forms*, *Couse's Ohio Incorporation Forms*, and *Personal Injury Settlement Forms*. The software also allows the user to alter text databases to create custom documents. The text databases include Ohio court rules and *Ohio Jury Instructions, Software Version*.

Jurisoft, a division of Mead Data Central, Inc., sells *FullAuthority* software that finds cites in a word-processing document and automatically builds a table of authorities.

SUMMARY

13-1

In 1950, market research indicated that some firms were not purchasing LCP sets because they didn't have enough space for them. Believing that microforms, the reproduction of printed matter in greatly reduced size, was the wave of the future, LCP poured money into "Microlex Editions" of A.L.R., L. Ed., and L.R.A. on microfiche, in 1955. However, Microlex flopped. Inconvenient to use, Microlex was also ahead of its time. Saving space alone wasn't enough to make lawyers give up the advantages of books. Microform readers remain bulky and inconvenient. Although space is now a more important consideration than ever, microforms are not often used outside of law library research. Microforms are a common source of the briefs and records of federal and state appellate courts. Microforms are also a common source of governmental documents and records. West publishes an "Ultra Fiche Edition" of the National Reporter System, and LCP publishes A.L.R. and A.L.R.2d on microfiche, all designed to provide access to out-of-print volumes.

13-2

One floppy disk can contain hundreds of pages of information. Using a personal computer, a researcher can make a computer search of the information on disk, and download or print it, without the time pressure and expense of a computer-modem system. If information is not time-sensitive, it can be put on disk. Only a few legal publications have appeared on floppy disk. CCH offers its *Master Tax Guide* on floppy disk. Both the LEXIS simulation and the WESTLAW simulation are offered on floppy disk.

13-3

The "hot" technology for the 1990s is high-density CD-ROM. One CD-ROM disk can contain thousands of pages of information. As with ordinary floppy disks, CD-ROM publishing is in its infancy. The first major legal publication on disk, circa 1986, was the Information Access Corporation's *Legal Trac* system. In 1989, West announced the publication of "CD-ROM Libraries." In 1990, Martindale-Hubbell announced the *Martindale-Hubbell Law Directory on CD-ROM*. In 1991, Matthew Bender announced the publication of its "Search Master" compact disk libraries.

13-4

When information is organized, there is a synergistic effect. Information is created that is not available from any other source. Computer-organized legal research (COLR) is the use of computers to automate the organization of the search results as an aid in legal research. COLR is analogous to litigation support. COLR is putting together information that would have been buried in the results of the initial search. COLR comes after CALR, but before and during legal writing. In the technical sense, a database is a collection of information specially organized for rapid search and retrieval. Information is organized into defined categories known as *fields*. Variable items in the database, records, contain the categorical information for each item. While a computer can search for a desired record by searching for information in the record, the computer's awesome power is the ability to quickly sort records by a given field. Multiple sorts can be made of the records by different fields to organize the records by category in whatever priority is desired. As you search legal materials, you can enter the information you find into a database. The database will lead you to the discovery of additional information. The bigger the research project, the more it makes sense to build a database. One of the most common uses of a computer is for word processing, which includes the electronic display, correction, and revision of text before printing. Word processing can also improve legal research. Macros can automate portions of the legal research process. COLR varies greatly with the needs of the researcher. The bigger the research project, the more it makes sense to use word processing. Information on a computer can be copied, deleted, formatted, merged, moved, printed, reformatted, replaced, revised, searched, sorted, and spell checked, among other things. A few commercial COLR products exist. Anderson Publishing Co. sells a legal document creation system known as *Lawriter*. Jurisoft sells *FullAuthority* software that finds cites in a word-processing document and automatically builds a table of authorities.

REVIEW

Key Terms

Before proceeding, review the key terms listed below to be sure you understand each one. If necessary, read over the corresponding section of the chapter. When you are ready to test your understanding, answer the Review Questions.

CD-ROM
computer-organized legal research (COLR)
database
digest
fields
house organ
litigation support
macro
microfiche
microfilm
microforms
records
sort
synergistic
word processing

Questions for Review and Discussion

1. What major publications are available in microform?
2. Can you name a publication available on floppy disk?
3. What was the first major publication available on CD-ROM?
4. What is a synergistic effect?
5. How is COLR different from CALR?
6. How is COLR analogous to litigation support?
7. How does COLR put "new" information at a legal researcher's fingertips?
8. What are database fields?
9. What are the advantages of having information on computer?
10. Can you name a COLR product?

Activities

1. Learn to type (keyboard). The principal way COLR users enter data into a computer, both today and for the foreseeable future, is through a typewriter-like keyboard. The ability to type (keyboard) is one of the most useful skills you can have and a practical necessity for COLR.
2. Learn to use professional spreadsheet software, such as Lotus 1–2–3. Learn to set up a database and use the sort commands. Use your abilities to find out what you want to know.
3. Learn to use professional word-processing software like WordPerfect. Learn how to create "macros" to speed your way through your work.

PART SIX

RESEARCH STRATEGIES

Chapter 14
Legal Research Strategies

CHAPTER 14 Legal Research Strategies

OUTLINE

14-1 Ready for Legal Research
    Get the Facts
    Analyze the Facts
14-2 Basic Search Strategy
    Select the Sovereign
    Search Mandatory "Statutory" Authority
    Search Mandatory Case Authority
    Search Persuasive Case Authority
    Search Persuasive Secondary Authority
14-3 Basic Search Procedure
    Find the Law
    Read the Law
    Review the Law
    Stop the Search
14-4 Comprehensive Search Strategy
    Background and Citations
    Quick Read and Outline
    Second Read and First Draft
    Review and Final Draft
14-5 Limited Search Strategies
    Instant Answers
14-6 Mastering Legal Research

COMMENTARY

Just as the Judiciary Committee's work is winding down and it appears that the judge will be confirmed, a crisis occurs. A law professor has come forward to allege that the judge sexually harassed her 10 years ago when they worked together at a federal agency. The judge vehemently denies the allegation. The senator asks you to find out absolutely everything you can about the law of sexual harassment, for obvious reasons.

OBJECTIVES

In this chapter you will learn to organize your knowledge of Chapters 1 to 13 into effective legal research strategies. Emphasis is placed on the basic strategy of searching mandatory "statutory" authority, mandatory case authority, persuasive case authority, and persuasive secondary authority. After reading this chapter you should be able to:

1. Outline the materials used in legal research.
2. Recognize the importance of getting the facts.

3. Develop appropriate entry terms.
4. Describe search strategy.
5. Describe search methods.
6. Read and analyze the results of a search.
7. Stop a search when it is reasonably complete.
8. Perform a comprehensive search.
9. Perform a limited search.
10. Master legal research.

14–1 Ready for Legal Research

If you have read and studied this book through Chapter 13, you are ready to do legal research. Like Daniel in the movie *The Karate Kid*, you've learned all the fundamentals, even if you don't realize it yet.

This book develops the subject of legal research from a **bibliographic** approach, emphasizing detailed descriptions of the various books used. When bibliographic books describe a particular book among others, they explain the purpose of the book: why it exists. When you know the purpose of the book, you ought to know *when* to use it: for its purpose. When bibliographic books describe a particular book, they explain the structure of the book: how it is organized. When you know the structure of the book, you ought to know *how* to use it: by its structure.

By now you've acquired a good deal of background knowledge and insight. You've experienced the jargon of legal research in context. You've developed an understanding of the purpose and structure of law books and other media. You've also seen the limitations of law books and other media, a valuable "negative image," a warning of dangers and pitfalls, bringing the positive image, the true purpose and structure, into sharp focus. In this final chapter, you get the benefit of experience: strategies with which to apply the tactics already learned.

Take a moment to consider, to outline, all the tactics available to you in achieving your goal of finding a case (or other law) like yours where the person like you won. Billions of dollars, centuries of human effort, and waves of technology have combined to create a vast array of law books and other media that you can use. The law of the United States is probably the most recorded, organized, and analyzed body of knowledge in the world.

Researching federal law? All the primary sources are covered. The Constitution of the United States, the statutes of Congress, and court rules can be located in U.S.C.A., U.S.C.S., and other sources. Administrative regulations can be located in the *Federal Register*, C.F.R., and other sources. Supreme Court opinions can be located in U.S., L. Ed. & L. Ed. 2d, S. Ct., and other sources. Lower court opinions are located in F.2d, F. Supp., and other sources. Need help? Consider all the secondary sources. To get an overview, read Am. Jur. 2d, C.J.S., treatises, and other sources. To find more cases, use federal digests, A.L.R. Fed., and other sources. And whatever you do, don't forget looseleaf services, form books, law reviews, *Shepard's*, Auto-Cite, Insta-Cite, LEXIS, WESTLAW, and other sources.

Researching state law? There is a similar array: state codes, state administrative codes, official state reporters, National Reporter System regional reporters, state digests, A.L.R., and other sources.

As a legal researcher you can "stand on the shoulders" of judges, justices, lawyers, and law professors, and all other legal writers, authors, and editors in order to find a case (or other law) like yours where the person like you won to use to win your case.

Get the Facts

Of course, your vast knowledge of legal research sources is useless if you don't know what you are looking for. As the old saying goes, "If you don't know where you are going, any road will take you there." If you are doing legal research and suddenly don't know what to do next, there is a good chance you forgot what you were looking for. Refresh your memory and go on, renewed in the understanding that a necessary part of legal research is to gather the facts about the case you are researching, both before you begin and as needed along the way.

Analyze the Facts

After you have gathered the facts (or have been given the facts as an assignment), you must analyze them. You must identify the legal issues that need to be researched and the relative importance of each issue. You must come up with the terms you will use as entry points in digests, indexes, and tables of contents, or in a computer word search.

Your ability to analyze the facts will increase with experience. The more law you know and the more familiar you become with law books and other media, the easier it will be to identify the legal issues that need to be researched and their relative importance, along with appropriate terms to use as entry points.

One well-known rule of thumb for analyzing fact patterns, and for generating entry terms, is the "TAPP Rule" used by indexers at the Lawyers Cooperative Publishing Company (LCP). The **TAPP Rule** is that legal researchers should be able find the law they are looking for by looking up terms representing the thing, act, person, or place involved in the case. For example, if an automobile is damaged when it hits a hole in a parking lot, a researcher should be able to find the relevant law by looking up things like "automobile" or "vehicle," acts like "maintenance" or "negligence," persons like "driver" or "property owner," and places like "parking lot" or even "hole."

There are several similar rules of thumb. Writing in J. Myron Jacobstein and Roy M. Mersky's *Fundamentals of Legal Research,* 5th ed. (Westbury, NY: Foundation Press, 1990), on page 16, Steven M. Barkan suggests the "TARP Rule," consisting of the *"Thing* or subject matter," the "Cause of *action* or ground of defense," the *"Relief* sought," and the *"Persons* or *parties* involved." Forgoing a catchy acronym, West Publishing Company (West) in its *West's Law Finder* (1991), on p. 18, and its *Sample Pages,* 3rd ed. (1986), on pp. vii–viii, suggests the following analysis: "Parties," "Places and Things," "Basis of Action or Issue," "Defense," and "Relief Sought."

The types of legal issues that arise, and their relative importance, generally mirror the litigation process. Does the court have jurisdiction? Has the statute of limitations run? Have all other procedural requirements been met? Does the plaintiff have a sound theory on which to sue? Does the defendant have a sound defense? Were the rules of evidence followed at trial? What relief is appropriate?

Many researchers find it useful to write out each issue they are researching in a complete sentence.

In collecting appropriate entry terms for a search in a variety of sources, consider synonyms and near synonyms (e.g., apartment, dwelling, home, homestead, house, residence, unit), understanding that your issue may be organized and indexed differently in different sources. William P. Statsky, in his *Legal Research and Writing: Some Starting Points,* 3rd ed. (St. Paul, MN: West

Publishing Co., 1986), on pp. 98–101, recommends the routine word-associating of each major term you identify around a "cartwheel" of broader terms, narrower terms, synonyms, antonyms, "closely related terms," procedural terms, agencies and courts, and "long shots."

When the facts and issues are reasonably clear, and appropriate entry terms have come to mind, you are ready to find the law.

14–2 Basic Search Strategy

The basic legal research strategy for each issue has five overlapping phases or steps: (1) select the sovereign, (2) search mandatory "statutory" authority ("statutes in the sovereign"), (3) search mandatory case authority ("cases in the sovereign"), (4) search persuasive case authority ("cases in other sovereigns"), and (5) search persuasive secondary authority. (See Figure 14–1.)

Select the Sovereign

The first step is to determine whether the issue is a matter of federal law or state law, and if of state law, of what state.

Because law is the command of a sovereign, you must first select the appropriate sovereign's law to search. And as a practical matter, most law books cover either federal law or state law, or the law of a particular state. By selecting the appropriate sovereign's law to search, you avoid the mistake of searching another sovereign's law as mandatory authority.

Determining whether the issue is a matter of federal law or of state law is not always easy. Indeed, some issues may involve both federal law and state law.

Figure 14–1 Basic Search Strategy

With experience, you will develop the knack of recognizing which is which.

In general, federal law is law that relates to the Constitution of the United States, the federal government, or the powers granted to Congress in Article I, Section 8. State laws cover everything else. One twist is that the Constitution of the United States and the decisions of the U.S. Supreme Court interpreting the Constitution of the United States are, via the supremacy clause, mandatory authority for the states. When in doubt, search both federal law and state law.

Search Mandatory "Statutory" Authority

The second step is to search for relevant constitutional provisions, statutes, administrative regulations, and court rules in the appropriate sovereign, and any relevant federal treaties. Unless your issue is of constitutional import, involves a court rule, or is affected by a treaty, as a practical matter you need search only for statutes in the sovereign. An enabling statute, or a cross-reference in an annotated code, should indicate the existence of any relevant administrative regulations. If you expect to find constitutional provisions, court rules, treaties, or administrative regulations, search for them.

There are at least three reasons why searching for statutes in the sovereign is the second step: (1) you want to find primary authority—the law itself—as soon as possible; (2) you want to find mandatory authority—the law that must be followed within the sovereign—as soon as possible; and (3) the existence (or nonexistence) of statutes on your issue will direct the next step: the search for cases in the sovereign.

Remember that statutes are usually enacted either to fill in where there is no case precedent or to overrule existing case precedent. If the statute fills in where there was no case precedent, you only need to search for cases in the sovereign from the date of the statute (obviously). Likewise, if the statute overruled existing case precedent, you know that precedent is bad law, and, again, you only need to search for cases in the sovereign from the date of the statute. Moreover, if there is a statute in the sovereign, the case summaries in an annotated code will help you to find relevant cases in the sovereign from the date of the statute. If there is no statute in the sovereign, you know you must search for cases in the sovereign from as far back as the creation of the sovereign. Of course, the most authoritative precedents will be those from the most recent decisions from the higher-level courts with the most similarities to the case at bar.

In a similar fashion, administrative regulations will direct a search for administrative decisions.

Search Mandatory Case Authority

The third step is to search for relevant cases and administrative decisions in the sovereign, for the same reasons that searching for statutes in the sovereign is the second step. You want to find primary authority and mandatory authority as soon as possible, and the existence (or nonexistence) of statutes or administrative regulations in the sovereign will direct the search for cases or administrative decisions in the sovereign.

Remember that cases are more important than statutes because they can interpret statutes. Thus, the third step, the search for cases in the sovereign, must be completed after the second step, the search for statutes in the sovereign.

Find as many cases as you can. In the ideal search, you might find three types of cases to cite in support of your case: the landmark case, the leading case, and the local case. The **landmark case** is the first significant case, often the case of first impression for your issue, decided in your favor. The **leading case,** which may also be the landmark case, is the case opinion that reads like an A.L.R. annotation or treatise, laying out all the precedent on your issue, pro and con, and deciding in your favor. The **local case** is the most recent case from your local jurisdiction decided in your favor, pointing out that your local jurisdiction follows the precedent established by the landmark case and reaffirmed by the leading case.

The third step, the search for cases in the sovereign, completes the search for mandatory authority. Remember that *dicta,* dissenting opinions, and precedent from equal or lower courts are not mandatory authority, but may be considered persuasive authority. Thus, insofar as the third step—the search for cases in the sovereign—discovers *dicta,* dissenting opinions, and precedent from equal or lower courts, it begins the fourth step, the search for persuasive case authority.

Search Persuasive Case Authority

If sufficient authority has not been found after the third step, the fourth step is to search for the remaining persuasive primary authority: the common law at large. The fourth step is to search for relevant cases in other jurisdictions and sovereigns that trace their origin to the Norman Conquest in 1066, as far back as the creation of that other sovereign, or, in the case of English law, as far back as the Norman Conquest in 1066. The most authoritative precedents will be those from the most recent cases from the higher-level courts with the most similarities to the case at bar.

Remember that statutes in other sovereigns are not considered persuasive authority because other sovereigns' legislatures can "dream up" whatever law they want. However, the existence of similar statutes in other sovereigns may support a policy argument based on the existence of a nationwide pattern or a trend.

The fourth step, the search for cases in the other sovereigns, completes the search for primary authority.

Search Persuasive Secondary Authority

If sufficient authority has not been found after the fourth step, the fifth step is to search for the remaining persuasive authority: secondary authority. Among secondary authorities, the most authoritative are well-reasoned law review articles and treatises, but, by definition, a court may be persuaded by other persuasive secondary authorities as well. For example, A.L.R.'s claim to fame is as the nation's most-cited law book (not simply a reporter). Nonlegal texts may also be cited. In fact, when courts decide a case of first impression, they may cite almost anything that supports their decision.

14–3 Basic Search Procedure

The basic legal research procedure is to find the law, read the law, review the law, and stop the search.

Find the Law

The most stressful task of a legal researcher is to go into the library (or get on-line) and, under time pressure, actually find the law desired in books and other media, based on the basic legal research strategy.

There are four basic methods of finding the law in a particular law book or in law books generally: the topic method, the case method, the statute method, and the index method. (See Figure 14–2.) The use of these methods requires cleverness, creativity, and patience.

The **topic method** can be used if you know the topic you want to search. It involves a search of the law book's table of contents, if any, and going to all references. In addition, scan the text for your topic. The "known topic" method is best used by experienced researchers who are confident they know exactly what they are looking for.

A basic strategy search using the topic method begins with the selection of the appropriate title and section of the sovereign's annotated code to check for statutes in the sovereign and to pick up cases from the case summaries. Cases are found by selecting the appropriate topics in the appropriate digest and using the A.L.R. Digest method of locating A.L.R. annotations.

Using CALR, the topic method allows the user to search a specialized database. Using LEXIS, A.L.R. annotations can be searched by topic, by searching A.L.R. titles and scope sections. Using WESTLAW, specific West digest Topics and Key Numbers can be searched.

The **case method** can be used if you know at least one case like yours (e.g., it is cited in your opponent's brief) and you want to search for more. This method involves a search of the law book's table of cases, if any, and going to the references. If you know only the popular name of the case, use a table of cases by popular names to convert it to a citation or search the name by CALR. Knowing the importance of cases in U.S. law, the "known case" method is a favorite of professional researchers.

A basic strategy search using the case method begins by checking the statutes cited in the case and in the sovereign's annotated code, and picking up cases from the case summaries. Cases can be found by picking up digest Topics and Key Numbers from the headnotes for the case and using Auto-Cite to locate A.L.R. annotations. And, of course, looking for cases from a case cite just "cries out" for shepardizing the case, using *Shepard's* as an imperfect case finder.

Using CALR, the case method allows the user to use *Shepard's* electronically or to use the CALR system as a citator. Using LEXIS, A.L.R. annotations can be searched by finding the case within an annotation. Using WESTLAW, Shepard's Preview can also be searched.

The **statute method** can be used if you know at least one statute like yours (e.g., it is cited in your opponent's brief) and you want to search for more law. This method involves a search of the law book's code finding table, if any, and going to the references. If you know only the popular name of the statute, use a table of statutes by popular names to convert it to a citation or search the name by CALR. Remember that many annotated codes give cross-references to related statutes within the sovereign and to comparative statutes from other sovereigns.

A basic strategy search using the statute method begins with a check of the statute in the sovereign's annotated code. Cases can be found by picking up the case summaries for the statute. If available for the sovereign's statutes, you can also shepardize the statute, using *Shepard's* as an imperfect case finder.

Using CALR, the statute method calls for the use of the CALR system as a citator.

The **index method** involves using your entry terms to search the law book's index, if any, and going to the references. If there is no index, use your entry terms to search the law book's table of contents, if any, and go to all references.

Figure 14-2 Methods of Finding the Law

	TOPIC METHOD (Table of Contents)	CASE METHOD (Known Relevant Case)	STATUTE METHOD (Known Relevant Statute)	INDEX METHOD (Entry Terms)
Statutes via Codes	Search appropriate title and contents	Search statutes cited in the case	Search the known relevant statute	Search the indexes
Cases via Digests	Search appropriate Topic from Outline	Search Topics and Key Numbers in the case	Search appropriate Topic from Outline	Search Descriptive Word Indexes
Cases via A.L.R.	Search A.L.R. digests	Auto-Cite on LEXIS or annotation (if any) following case in A.L.R.	Use code finding table for U.S.C., and search A.L.R. Digests	Search *Index to Annotations* and *A.L.R. First Series Quick Index*
Cases via *Shepard's*		Shepardize the case using *Shepard's* as an imperfect case finder	Shepardize the statute (if available) as an imperfect case finder	
Cases via LEXIS	Search specialized database and A.L.R. by title and scope	Shepardize, and use LEXIS as a citator, including for A.L.R.	Use LEXIS as a citator	Word search (including A.L.R.)
Cases via WESTLAW	Search specialized database and West Topics and Key Numbers	Shepardize, Shepard's Preview, Quick-Cite, and WESTLAW as a citator	Use Quick-Cite, and WESTLAW as a citator	Word search (including West's case summaries)

When in doubt, or as a double check, always use the "descriptive word or fact"/index method.

A basic strategy search using the index method begins with a search of the indexes of the sovereign's annotated code to check for statutes in the sovereign and to pick up cases from the case summaries. Cases can be found by searching the descriptive word indexes in digests to find the appropriate Topics and Key

14-3 Basic Search Procedure   249

Numbers in the appropriate digest, and using the *Index to Annotations* and *A.L.R First Series Quick Index* method of locating A.L.R. annotations.

Using CALR, the index method is the classic word search, allowing you to create your own index of the material searched. In addition to cases found by searching the full text of the opinions, LEXIS can pick up cases caught by A.L.R. annotations and WESTLAW can pick up cases caught by West's case summaries.

Of course, by now you realize that all of these methods overlap each other. In executing the basic strategy, you can use any method, or any combination of methods, to get the job done. Also remember that if one publisher's products aren't helping you in a given search, switch to the competitor's products. No law book is perfect, so you have to know the alternatives.

Read the Law

As a legal researcher, your most intellectual task comes after finding the law. You must carefully read and analyze *all* of the law you have found to determine just how relevant it is to your case. You must read the law both literally, as it is actually written, and figuratively, as it might be construed.

Every case you have found must be read in order to evaluate how similar it is to your case, including to what extent the case might be analogized to your case. Similarly, you must read every statute that you found to evaluate how similar each statute is to your case. This includes evaluating the extent of the legislature's intent in enacting the statute to include your case.

You must sort through all the law, noting anything that might be relevant and discarding the rest. If it's relevant, you must decide if it will help your case or hurt it, and to what degree. The ability to read and analyze the law "separates the contenders from the pretenders." Legal researchers extract gems from legal minds.

Review the Law

As discussed in Chapter 11, the powerful forces of human nature and time can deceive any legal researcher, no matter how experienced. The law that is found and read must also be reviewed to make sure that it is correct and up to date. New material generated by a review must also be found, read, and reviewed.

If a legal source has a supplement, such as a "developments" section, pamphlet, or pocket part, you must check it every time you use the source. Make it a habit. Check the supplement.

The importance of checking the supplement cannot be overstated. Legal research is required, in part, because the law changes. The main body or bound volume of a source may be several years out of date and overdue for replacement. The thicker the supplement, the greater the likelihood of disaster if you don't check it.

Often a researcher is looking for exactly what the supplement contains: the latest law on the subject. To impress students with the importance of checking the supplement, some legal research instructors give assignments in which every correct answer is found in the supplement.

As discussed in Chapter 11, the importance of reviewing cases cited in a memorandum or a brief—to make sure that the cases cited are not bad law—cannot be overstated. Use *Shepard's*, Auto-Cite, and Insta-Cite as much as possible. Don't let the person judging your work or your opponent catch a mistake that you should have caught. You should also check your opponent's work for mistakes that can be cited to your advantage.

Supplement in the Form of Pocket Part

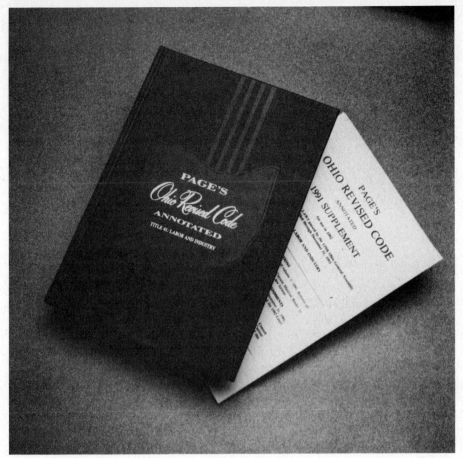

Source: © Doug Martin.

Stop the Search

A question that often arises in legal research is when to stop. "When you are done" is not always a satisfactory answer because it can be hard to know when you're done. Sometimes you search, but you can't find what you're looking for. Is it because what you're looking for isn't there or because you couldn't find it?

The practical answer is that legal research takes time, and time is money. At some point, you can't afford *not* to stop. There is no sense in doing $1,000 worth of research on a $500 case. In a world in which the typical personal injury lawyer collects a contingent fee of 33% of the money recovered, in one out of two cases of equal earning potential, the lawyer who wants to pay bills and make a profit *cannot possibly* afford legal research costing more than 16.5% of the money expected to be recovered. The practical limit, reduced by the lawyer's bills and profit, is much less.

Nevertheless, you must be wary of seizing on the first thing that meets your expectations. You have to learn how to be patient and objective, and strong enough to accept bad news, if that is what you find. When in doubt about stopping your search, don't. But if your search has become repetitive, such that you are merely going in circles, then stop.

Maybe the best answer is to think of yourself as the legal detective you are. You search through law books and other media for clues that will lead you to the answer to your problem. As you collect clues, you should progress toward the answer to your problem. You must believe that after a thorough search, the clues will shed light on, and focus on, a suspect. If a suspect is in sight, continue the search. If no suspect is in sight, stop the search.

14–4 Comprehensive Search Strategy

On occasion, situations arise where money is no object. A life or lifestyle is on the line, and for whatever reason, fame (e.g., the Supreme Court has granted *certiorari*) or fortune (e.g., the client is rich) allows you to make an **exhaustive search,** a search through every source. This section briefly discusses a strategy to use when you are asked to find out everything you can about a given topic.

Background and Citations

Begin by preparing a legal pad (or a COLR system) to keep a record of your search. The record fields should include "source," "other source," "other source searched," and "case cites." (See Figure 14–3.)

Begin by searching secondary sources for background information and for every apparently relevant cite. You can start anywhere. Record every source you search in the "source" field. If that source refers to another secondary source, record that other source in the "other source" field. When the source cites

Figure 14–3   Search Record

Source	Other Source	Other Source Searched	Case Cites

primary authority other than cases, also record that other source's cite in the "other source" field. Whenever the source cites a case, record the cite in the "case cites" field.

Work your way through every secondary source available to you. If there are competitive sources on the same topic (e.g., an Am. Jur. 2d article and a C.J.S. article), search *both*. It may seem redundant, and to a large extent it will be, but you want to make sure you capture all the other sources and case cites uniquely found in each source. As you are searching, make sure that you have searched every "other source" as a source, by checking off every "other source" in the appropriate "other source searched" field.

Continue by searching every available noncase primary source as a source, checking off each "other source" as appropriate. Eventually you will have searched every secondary source and every noncase primary source. Moreover, you can be confident that you searched every noncase source because you checked off every noncase source cited by a secondary source or a noncase primary source.

Having read all the secondary sources and noncase primary sources relevant to your problem, you will be well prepared to read and understand the most important law: the cases. You will also have a very long list of case cites.

Before reading the apparently relevant cases, you must process your list of case cites. Go through the list (or have your COLR system go through the list) and eliminate all the duplicate cites. Sort (or have your COLR system sort) the cites chronologically by court level and jurisdiction.

"Chronologically by court level" means, for example, that the first federal case cite will be for the oldest U.S. Supreme Court case, followed by the next-oldest case, and so on, down to the most recent case. Next is the oldest court of appeals case, the next-oldest, and so on, followed by district court cases. By "jurisdiction" means, for example, that all the First Circuit cases are grouped together, followed by all the Second Circuit cases, and so on.

Reading cases by court level, like searching statutes before cases, will save you time and effort. If, on a particular issue, a higher court has reversed a lower court, you know that the lower court precedent on that issue is bad law. And even if the higher court has affirmed the lower court, the higher court's opinion is more authoritative than the lower court's. If the higher court's opinion is more comprehensive than the lower court's opinion, it may not even be necessary to read the lower court's opinion. Of course, if the lower court has decided an issue or has provided information not touched on by the higher court, the lower court's opinion is authoritative and must be read.

The cases are read chronologically by jurisdiction to easily capture and understand the historical development of the law in each jurisdiction. Some researchers read the cases in reverse chronological order to catch when courts reverse themselves, but that advantage is outweighed by having a historical understanding of the reversal.

Quick Read and Outline

After your list of case cites is processed, quickly skim through all the cases, understanding that your list of cites is just a list of apparently relevant cases. As you skim through the cases, you will find that many are irrelevant to your problem. Quickly note them for what they are worth and discard them. For each case relevant to your problem, quickly record the reasons why on your list (or on your COLR system).

When you have completed your quick read of the cases, you will have a complete record of every case relevant to your problem and why. Sort the whys, and you can make a good tentative outline of what you have found for a memorandum or brief. Do so.

Second Read and First Draft

With your case list and outline in hand, read the relevant cases again, slowly and carefully, looking for every nuance in every detail, to extract the gems. Sift and sort and analyze, as you write down what you have found in your first draft, according to your outline.

Part of the genius of this strategy is that as you carefully read the cases, you can check (or use your COLR system to check) if you've found everything cited in each and every case. You'll discover that cases frequently cite law that was not found, and could not be found, in any other source. The unsupported claim of first-year law school professors turns out to be true: *the law is in the cases.* That's why you should research everything you find in a case.

Review and Final Draft

After the second reading you will have a complete first draft according to your tentative outline. Review it, revise it, and put it in proper form, and you will have your final draft. Both your legal research and your legal writing will be complete.

14–5 Limited Search Strategies

Most legal research—everyday legal research—is a limited quick search for specific information. The search strategy is simple and obvious. Search the appropriate sources for the appropriate information.

Examples of quick searches could be given endlessly. Looking for the text of U.S. Supreme Court case *Roe v. Wade?* You could use the L. Ed. Digest's Table of Cases to find the L. Ed. 2d cite, and use L. Ed. 2d to look up the case. Want to find out, for federal tax purposes, when the meals provided by an employer can be excluded from the employee's income? You could search the index for Title 26 of U.S.C.A., or a looseleaf federal tax service, for the appropriate code section. What days are legal holidays in your state? Use the index to your state's statutory code to find the appropriate code section, and look it up. How has a given word or phrase been legally defined? Examine West's *Words and Phrases*, and so on.

Instant Answers

In a crunch, reasonably reliable answers can be found by quickly searching secondary sources, and perhaps using CALR. Well-written A.L.R. annotations, encyclopedias, treatises, and law review articles can be reasonably reliable sources.

For example, if you want to know why Congress created the U.S. Court of Veterans Appeals (see 38 U.S.C. § 4051 et seq.) in 1988, you might guess that there was a law review article written about it somewhere. A search of LegalTrac under the topic "Veterans" would quickly lead you to several articles, including an excellent article by the Chair of the Veterans' Law Committee of the Federal Bar Association, Barton F. Stichman. [Barton F. Stichman, *The Veterans' Judicial Review Act of 1988: Congress Introduces Courts and Attorneys to Veterans' Benefits Proceedings*, 41 Admin. L. Rev. 365 (1989).]

Of course, the danger in making quick searches for instant answers is that it can become a sloppy habit, leading to malpractice. Beware of people who quote from legal encyclopedias without any supporting cases. Don't forget the difference between primary authority and secondary authority.

14–6 Mastering Legal Research

Many students are surprised to discover that legal research is a skill. Like any other skill, it can be mastered with knowledge and disciplined self-critical practice. The old story about the man who asked a conductor for directions to Carnegie Hall, but was mistaken for a promising young musician, applies here. "How do you get to Carnegie Hall?" he asked. The answer: "Practice, practice, practice."

You cannot earn a black belt in legal research. No matter what you have done in your life, someone will question your credentials. The only real reward is self-satisfaction. Only you will know when you have mastered legal research.

You have mastered legal research when you walk into a law library and take the right book off the shelf without even thinking about it.

You have mastered legal research when, if you are right-handed, you automatically take a book off the shelf with your left hand, so you can flip the pages with your right hand, or vice versa.

You have mastered legal research when you are comfortable with every legal source and can give each the credit, and the criticism, due.

You have mastered legal research when you are comfortable with every strategy and method of legal research and can use whatever strategy and method, or combination of strategies and methods, appropriate to get the job done.

You have mastered legal research when you can find whatever you are looking for, unless it's not there. If it's not there, you have mastered legal research when you have the confidence to say, "I have looked, and it's not there."

In short, you have mastered legal research when you have mastered the *art* of legal research.

As the captain told his crew in the movie *Away All Boats*. "Good luck, and good hunting."

Source: Reprinted with special permission of King Features Syndicate.

SUMMARY

14–1

If you have read and studied this book through Chapter 13, you are ready to do legal research. By this final chapter, you are given the benefit of experience: strategies with which to apply the tactics already learned. As a legal researcher, you can "stand on the shoulders" of justices, judges, lawyers, and law professors, and all other legal writers, authors, and editors, to find a case (or other law) like yours where the person like you won. Of course, your vast knowledge of legal research sources is useless if you don't know what you are looking for. If you are doing legal research and suddenly don't know what to do next, there is a good chance you forgot what you were looking for. After you have gathered the facts (or have been given the facts as an assignment), you must analyze them. You must identify the legal issues that need to be researched and the relative importance of each issue. You must come up with the terms you will use as entry points in digests, indexes, and tables of contents, or in a computer word search. The types of legal issues that arise, and their relative importance, generally mirror the litigation process. When the facts and issues are reasonably clear, and appropriate entry terms have come to mind, you are ready to find the law.

14–2

The basic legal research strategy for each issue has five overlapping phases or steps: (1) select the sovereign, (2) search mandatory "statutory" authority ("statutes in the sovereign"), (3) search mandatory case authority ("cases in the sovereign"), (4) search persuasive case authority ("cases in other sovereigns"), and (5) search persuasive secondary authority. The first step is to determine whether the issue is a matter of federal law or state law, and if of state law, of what state. One twist is that the Constitution of the United States and the decisions of the U.S. Supreme Court interpreting the Constitution of the United States are, via the supremacy clause, mandatory authority for the states. The second step is to search for relevant constitutional provisions, statutes, administrative regulations, and court rules in the appropriate sovereign, and any relevant federal treaties. There are three reasons why searching for statutes in the sovereign is the second step: (1) you want to find primary authority; (2) you want to find mandatory authority; and (3) the existence (or nonexistence) of statutes on your issue will direct the third step: the search for cases and administrative decisions in the sovereign. Find as many cases as you can, including landmark cases, leading cases, and local cases. Remember that *dicta*, dissenting opinions, and precedent from equal or lower courts are not mandatory authority, although they may be considered persuasive authority. If sufficient authority has not been found after the third step, the fourth step is to search for the remaining persuasive primary authority: relevant cases in other sovereigns that trace their origin to the Norman Conquest in 1066, as far back as the creation of that other sovereign, or, in the case of English law, as far back as the Norman Conquest in 1066. If sufficient authority has not been found after the fourth step, the fifth step is to search for the remaining persuasive authority: secondary authority.

14–3

The basic legal research procedure is to find the law, read the law, review the law, and stop the search. There are four basic methods of finding the law in a particular law book or in law books generally: the topic method, the case method, the statute method, and the index method. The topic method is used if you know the topic you want to search. It involves a search of the law book's table of contents, if any, and going to all references. The case method is used if you know at least one case like yours and you want to search for more. It involves a search of the law book's table of cases, if any, and going to the references. The statute method is used if you know at least one statute like yours and you want to search for more law. It involves a search of the law book's code finding table, if any, and going to the references. The index method involves using your entry terms to search the law book's index, if any, and going to the references. When in doubt, or as a double check, always use the index method. Using CALR, the index method is the classic word search. It allows you to create your own index of the material searched. In executing the basic strategy, you, as a legal researcher, can use any method, or any combination of methods, to get the job done. The law found must be carefully read and analyzed. You must sort through all the law, noting anything that might be relevant, and discard the rest. Legal researchers extract gems from legal minds. The law that is found and read must also be reviewed to make sure that it is correct and up to date. New material generated by a review must also be found, read, and reviewed. The importance of checking the supplement and of reviewing cites in a memorandum or brief to make sure that the cases cited are not bad law cannot be overstated. Stop when you are done, understanding that at some point, you can't afford not to stop. Nevertheless, you must be wary of seizing on the first thing that meets your expectations. Think of yourself as the legal detective that you are. As you collect clues, you should progress toward the answer to your problem. If a suspect is in sight, continue the search. If no suspect is in sight, stop the search.

14-4

On occasion, situations will arise allowing you to make an exhaustive search. Begin by searching secondary sources for background information and for every apparently relevant cite. Record every source you search. If that source refers to another secondary source, record that other source. When the source cites primary authority other than cases, also record that. Whenever the source cites a case, record the cite. Work your way through every available secondary source and noncase primary source as a source, checking off each "other source" as appropriate. Before reading the apparently relevant cases, eliminate all the duplicate cites and sort the remaining cites chronologically by court level and by jurisdiction. Quickly skim through all the cases. You will find that many are irrelevant to your problem. Quickly note them for what they are worth and discard them. For each case relevant to your problem, quickly record the reasons why. When you have completed your quick read of the cases, sort the whys, and make a tentative outline of what you have found. With your case list and outline in hand, read the relevant cases again, slowly and carefully, looking for every nuance in every detail, to extract the gems. Sift and sort and analyze, as you write down what you have found in your first draft, according to your outline. You'll discover that cases frequently cite law that couldn't be found in any other source; that the law is in the cases. Review your first draft, revise it as necessary, and you will have your final draft.

14-5

Most legal research—everyday legal research—is a limited quick search for specific information. The search strategy is simple and obvious. Search the appropriate sources for the appropriate information. In a crunch, reasonably reliable answers can be found by quickly searching secondary sources. The danger in making quick searches for instant answers is that it can become a sloppy habit, leading to malpractice. Don't forget the difference between primary authority and secondary authority.

14-6

Legal research is skill that can be mastered with knowledge and disciplined self-critical practice. You have mastered legal research when you walk into a law library and take the right book off the shelf without even thinking about it; when you are comfortable with every legal source; and when you are comfortable with every strategy and every method of legal research. You have mastered legal research when you can find whatever you are looking for, unless it's not there and you have the confidence to say, "I have looked, and it's not there."

You have mastered legal research when you have mastered the *art* of legal research.

REVIEW

Key Terms
Before proceeding, review the key terms listed below to be sure you understand each one. If necessary, read over the corresponding section of the chapter. When you are ready to test your understanding, answer the Review Questions.

bibliographic
case method
exhaustive search
index method
landmark case
leading case
local case
statute method
TAPP Rule
topic method

Questions for Review and Discussion
1. What are the principal sources of federal case law?
2. What can happen if you do legal research before you have all the facts?
3. What is the importance of the "TAPP Rule" and other similar rules of thumb?
4. What should you search first, cases or statutes? Why?
5. What methods can you use to find the law in law books?
6. How should the results of a search be read and analyzed?
7. When should you stop a search?
8. How do you make a comprehensive search?
9. What danger is there in making a limited search?
10. How do you know when you have mastered legal research?

Activities
1. Practice. Make legal research a habit. Whenever you catch yourself saying, "I wonder," find out the answer.
2. As a matter of professional curiosity, compare and contrast other books on legal research. Look for mistakes. Look for faulty organization. Look for bias and prejudice. Decide which authors have thoroughly thought through the process of legal research, and follow their advice.
3. Share your knowledge of legal research with others. Extract their gems and discard their mistakes. Never stop learning.

APPENDIX I The Constitution of the United States

WE THE PEOPLE of the United States, in Order to form a more perfect Union, establish Justice, insure domestic Tranquility, provide for the common defence, promote the general Welfare, and secure the Blessings of Liberty to ourselves and our Posterity, do ordain and establish this Constitution for the United States of America.

ARTICLE I

Section 1. All legislative powers herein granted shall be vested in a Congress of the United States, which shall consist of a Senate and House of Representatives.

Section 2. **[1]** The House of Representatives shall be composed of Members chosen every second Year by the People of the several States, and the Electors in each State shall have the Qualifications requisite for Electors of the most numerous Branch of the State Legislature.

[2] No Person shall be a Representative who shall not have attained to the Age of twenty-five Years, and been seven Years a Citizen of the United States, and who shall not, when elected, be an Inhabitant of that State in which he shall be chosen.

[3] Representatives [and direct Taxes] {see 16th Amendment} shall be apportioned among the several States which may be included within this Union, according to their respective Numbers, [which shall be determined by adding to the whole Number of free Persons, including those bound to Service for a Term of Years, and excluding Indians not taxed, three fifths of all other Persons.] {See 14th Amendment.} The actual Enumeration shall be made within three Years after the first Meeting of the Congress of the United States, and within every subsequent Term of ten Years, in such Manner as they shall by Law direct. The Number of Representatives shall not exceed one for every thirty Thousand, but each State shall have at Least one Representative; and until such enumeration shall be made, the State of New Hampshire shall be entitled to choose three, Massachusetts eight, Rhode Island and Providence Plantations one, Connecticut five, New York six, New Jersey four, Pennsylvania eight, Delaware one, Maryland six, Virginia ten, North Carolina five, South Carolina five, and Georgia three.

[4] When vacancies happen in the Representation from any State, the Executive Authority thereof shall issue Writs of Election to fill such Vacancies.

[5] The House of Representatives shall chuse their Speaker and other Officers; and shall have the sole Power of Impeachment.

Section 3. **[1]** The Senate of the United States shall be composed of two Senators from each State, [chosen by the Legislature thereof,] {see 17th Amendment} for six Years; and each Senator shall have one Vote.

[2] Immediately after they shall be assembled in Consequence of the first Election, they shall be divided as equally as may be into three Classes. The Seats of the Senators of the first Class shall be vacated at the Expiration of the Second Year, of the second Class at the Expiration of the fourth Year, and of the third Class at the Expiration of the sixth Year, so that one third may be chosen every second Year; and if Vacancies happen by Resignation, or otherwise, during the Recess of the Legislature of any State, the Executive thereof may make temporary Appointments until the next Meeting of the Legislature, which shall then fill such Vacancies. {See 17th Amendment.}

[3] No person shall be a Senator who shall not have attained to the Age of thirty Years, and been nine Years a Citizen of the United States, and who shall not, when elected, be an Inhabitant of that State for which he shall be chosen.

[4] The Vice President of the United States shall be President of the Senate, but shall have no Vote, unless they be equally divided.

[5] The Senate shall choose their other Officers, and also a President pro tempore, in the Absence of the Vice President, or when he shall exercise the Office of the President of the United States.

[6] The Senate shall have the sole Power to try all Impeachments. When sitting for that Purpose, they shall be on Oath or Affirmation. When the President of the United States is tried, the Chief Justice shall preside: And no Person shall be convicted without the Concurrence of two thirds of the Members present.

[7] Judgment in Cases of Impeachment shall not extend further than to removal from Office, and disqualifications to hold and enjoy any Office of honor, Trust or Profit under the United States: but the Party convicted shall nevertheless be liable and subject to Indictment, Trial, Judgment, and Punishment, according to Law.

Section 4. **[1]** The Times, Places and Manner of holding Elections for Senators and Representatives, shall be prescribed in each State by the legislature thereof; but the Congress may at any time by Law make or alter such Regulations, except as to the Places of chusing Senators.

[2] The Congress shall assemble at least once in every Year, and such Meeting shall be on the first Monday in December, {see 20th Amendment} unless they shall by Law appoint a different Day.

Section 5. **[1]** Each House shall be the Judge of the Elections, Returns and Qualifications of its own Members, and a Majority of each shall constitute a Quorum to do Business; but a smaller Number may adjourn from day to day, and may be authorized to compel the Attendance of absent Members, in such Manner, and under such Penalties as each House may provide.

[2] Each House may determine the Rules of its Proceedings, punish its Members for disorderly Behavior, and, with the Concurrence of two thirds, expel a Member.

[3] Each House shall keep a Journal of its Proceedings, and from time to time publish the same, excepting such Parts as may in their Judgment require Secrecy; and the Yeas and Nays of the Members of either House on any question shall, at the Desire of one fifth of those Present, be entered on the Journal.

[4] Neither House, during the Session of Congress, shall, without the Consent of the other, adjourn for more than three days, nor to any other Place than that in which the two Houses shall be sitting.

Section 6. **[1]** The Senators and Representatives shall receive a Compensation for their Services, to be ascertained by Law, and paid out of the Treasury of the United States. They shall in all Cases, except Treason, Felony and Breach of the Peace, be privileged from Arrest during their Attendance at the Session of their respective Houses, and in going to and returning from the same; and for any Speech or Debate in either House, they shall not be questioned in any other Place.

[2] No Senator or Representative shall, during the Time for which he was elected, be appointed to any civil Office under the Authority of the United States, which shall have been created, or the Emoluments whereof shall have been increased during such time; and no Person holding any Office under the United States shall be a Member of either House during his Continuance in Office.

Section 7. **[1]** All Bills for raising Revenue shall originate in the House of Representatives; but the Senate may propose or concur with Amendments as on other Bills.

[2] Every Bill which shall have passed the House of Representatives and the Senate, shall, before it becomes a Law, be presented to the President of the United States; if he approve he shall sign it, but if not he shall return it, with his Objections to that House in which it shall have originated, who shall enter the Objections at large on their Journal, and proceed to reconsider it. If after such Reconsideration two thirds of that House shall agree to pass the Bill, it shall be sent together with the Objections, to the other House, by which it shall likewise be reconsidered, and if approved by two thirds of that House, it shall become a Law. But in all such Cases the Votes of both Houses shall be determined by Yeas and Nays, and the Names of the Persons voting for and against the Bill shall be entered on the Journal of each House respectively. If any Bill shall not be returned by the President within ten Days (Sundays excepted) after it shall have been presented to him, the Same shall be a Law, in like Manner as if he had signed it, unless the Congress by their Adjournment prevent its Return, in which Case it shall not be a Law.

[3] Every Order, Resolution, or Vote to Which the Concurrence of the Senate and the House of Representative may be necessary (except on a question of Adjournment) shall be presented to the President of the United States; and before the Same shall take Effect, shall be approved by him, or being disapproved by him, shall be repassed by two thirds of the Senate and House of Representatives, according to the Rules and Limitations prescribed in the Case of a Bill.

Section 8. The Congress shall have the Power

[1] To lay and collect Taxes, Duties, Imposts and Excises, to pay the Debts and provide for the common Defence and general Welfare of the United States; but all Duties, Imposts and Excises shall be uniform throughout the United States;

[2] To borrow money on the credit of the United States;

[3] To regulate Commerce with foreign Nations, and among the several States, and with the Indian Tribes;

[4] To establish a uniform Rule of Naturalization, and uniform Laws on the subject of Bankruptcies throughout the United States;

[5] To coin Money, regulate the Value thereof, and of foreign Coin, and fix the Standard of Weights and Measures;

[6] To provide for the Punishment of counterfeiting the Securities and current Coin of the United States;

[7] To Establish Post Offices and Post Roads;

[8] To promote the Progress of Science and useful Arts, by securing for limited Times to Authors and Inventors the exclusive Right to their respective Writings and Discoveries;

[9] To constitute Tribunals inferior to the supreme Court;

[10] To define and punish Piracies and Felonies committed on the high Seas, and Offenses against the Law of Nations;

[11] To declare War, grant Letters of Marque and Reprisal, and make Rules concerning Captures on Land and Water;

[12] To raise and support Armies, but no Appropriation of Money to that Use shall be for a longer Term than two Years;

[13] To provide and maintain a Navy;

[14] To make Rules for the Government and Regulation of the land and naval Forces;

[15] To provide for calling forth the Militia to execute the Laws of the Union, suppress Insurrections and repel Invasions;

[16] To provide for organizing, arming, and disciplining the Militia, and for governing such Part of them as may be employed in the Service of the United States, reserving to the States respectively, the Appointment of the Officers, and the Authority of training the Militia according to the discipline prescribed by Congress;

[17] To exercise exclusive Legislation in all Cases whatsoever, over such District (not exceeding ten Miles square) as may, by Cession of particular States, and the Acceptance of Congress, become the Seat of the Government of the United States, and to exercise like Authority over all Places purchased by the Consent of the Legislature of the State in which the Same shall be, for the Erection of Forts, Magazines, Arsenals, dock-Yards, and other needful Buildings;—And

[18] To make all Laws which shall be necessary and proper for carrying into Execution the foregoing Powers, and all other Powers vested by this Constitution in the Government of the United States, or in any Department or Officer thereof.

Section 9. **[1]** The Migration or Importation of Such Persons as any of the States now existing shall think proper to admit, shall not be prohibited by the Congress prior to the Year one thousand eight hundred and eight, but a Tax or duty may be imposed on such Importation, not exceeding ten dollars for each Person.

[2] The privilege of the Writ of Habeas Corpus shall not be suspended, unless when in Cases of Rebellion or Invasion the public Safety may require it.

[3] No Bill of Attainder or ex post facto Law shall be passed.

[4] No Capitation, or other direct, Tax shall be laid, unless in Proportion to the Census or Enumeration herein before directed to be taken. {See 16th Amendment.}

[5] No Tax or Duty shall be laid on Articles exported from any State.

[6] No Preference shall be given by any Regulation of Commerce or Revenue to the Ports of one State over those of another: nor shall Vessels bound to, or from, one State be obliged to enter, clear, or pay Duties in another.

[7] No money shall be drawn from the Treasury, but in Consequence of Appropriations made by Law; and a regular Statement and Account of the Receipts and Expenditures of all public Money shall be published from time to time.

[8] No Title of Nobility shall be granted by the United States: And no Person holding any Office of Profit or Trust under them, shall, without the Consent of the Congress, accept of any present, Emolument, Office, or Title, of any kind whatever, from any King, Prince, or foreign State.

Section 10. [1] No State shall enter into any Treaty, Alliance, or Confederation; grant Letters of Marque and Reprisal; coin Money; emit Bills of Credit; make any Thing but gold and silver Coin a Tender in Payment of Debts; pass any Bill of Attainder, ex post facto Law, or Law impairing the Obligation of Contracts, or grant any Title of Nobility.

[2] No State shall, without the Consent of the Congress, lay any Imposts or Duties on Imports or Exports, except what may be absolutely necessary for executing its inspection Laws; and the net Produce of all Duties and Imposts laid by any State on Imports or Exports, shall be for the Use of the Treasury of the United States; and all such Laws shall be subject to the Revision and Control of the Congress.

[3] No State shall, without the Consent of the Congress, lay any Duty of Tonnage, keep Troops, or Ships of War in time of Peace, enter into any Agreement or Compact with another State, or with a foreign Power, or engage in War, unless actually invaded, or in such imminent Danger as will not admit of delay.

ARTICLE II

Section 1. [1] The executive Power shall be vested in a President of the United States of America. He shall hold his Office during the Term of four Years, and, together with the Vice President, chosen for the same Term, be elected as follows:

[2] Each State {see 23rd Amendment} shall appoint, in such Manner as the Legislature thereof may direct, a Number of Electors, equal to the whole Number of Senators and Representatives to which the State may be entitled in the Congress: but no Senator or Representative, or Person holding an Office of Trust or Profit under the United States, shall be appointed an Elector.

[3] [The Electors shall meet in their respective States, and vote by Ballot for two Persons, of whom one at least shall not be an Inhabitant of the same State with themselves. And they shall make a List of all the Persons voted for, and of the Number of Votes for each; which List they shall sign and certify, and transmit sealed to the Seat of the Government of the United States, directed to the President of the Senate. The President of the Senate shall, in the Presence of the Senate and House of Representatives, open all the Certificates, and the Votes shall then be counted. The Person having the greatest Number of Votes shall be the President, if such Number be a Majority of the whole Number of Electors appointed; and if there be more than one who shall have such Majority, and have an equal Number of Votes, then the House of Representatives shall immediately chuse by Ballot one of them for President; and if no Person have a Majority, then from the five highest on the List the said House shall in like Manner chuse the President. But in chusing the President, the Votes shall be taken by States, the Representation from each State having one Vote; a quorum for this Purpose shall consist of a Member or Members from two thirds of the States, and a Majority of all the States shall be necessary to a Choice. In every Case, after the Choice of the President, the Person having the greatest Number of Votes of the Electors shall be the Vice President. But if there should remain two or more who have equal Votes, the Senate shall chuse from them by Ballot the Vice President.] {See 12th Amendment.}

[4] The Congress may determine the Time of chusing the Electors, and the Day on which they shall give their Votes; which Day shall be the same throughout the United States.

[5] No person except a natural born Citizen, or a Citizen of the United States, at the time of the Adoption of this Constitution, shall be eligible to the Office of President; neither shall any Person be eligible to that Office who shall not have attained to the Age of thirty-five Years, and been fourteen Years a Resident within the United States.

[6] In case of removal of the President from Office, or of his Death, Resignation or Inability to discharge the Powers and Duties of the said Office, the Same shall devolve on the Vice President, and the Congress may by Law provide for the Case of Removal, Death, Resignation or Inability, both of the President and Vice President, declaring what Officer shall then act as President, and such Officer shall act accordingly, until the Disability be removed, or a President shall be elected. {See 25th Amendment.}

[7] The President shall, at stated Times, receive for his Services a Compensation, which shall neither be increased nor diminished during the Period for which he shall have been elected, and he shall not re-

ceive within that Period any other Emolument from the United States, or any of them.

[8] Before he enter on the Execution of his Office, he shall take the following Oath or Affirmation:—"I do solemnly swear (or affirm) that I will faithfully execute the Office of President of the United States, and will to the best of my Ability, preserve, protect and defend the Constitution of the United States."

Section 2. [1] The President shall be Commander in Chief of the Army and Navy of the United States, and of the militia of the several States, when called into the actual Service of the United States; he may require the Opinion, in writing, of the principal Officer in each of the Executive Departments, upon any Subject relating to the Duties of their Respective Offices, and he shall have Power to grant Reprieves and Pardons for Offenses against the United States, except in Cases of Impeachment.

[2] He shall have Power, by and with the Advice and Consent of the Senate, to make Treaties, provided two thirds of the Senators present concur; and he shall nominate, and by and with the Advice and Consent of the Senate, shall appoint Ambassadors, other public Ministers and Consuls, Judges of the supreme Court, and all other Officers of the United States, whose Appointments are not herein otherwise provided for, and which shall be established by Law: but the Congress may by Law vest the Appointment of such inferior Officers, as they think proper, in the President alone, in the Courts of Law, or in the Heads of Departments.

[3] The President shall have Power to fill up all Vacancies that may happen during the Recess of the Senate, by granting Commissions which shall expire at the End of their next Session.

Section 3. He shall from time to time give to the Congress Information of the State of the Union, and recommend to their Consideration such Measures as he shall judge necessary and expedient; he may, on extraordinary Occasions, convene both Houses, or either of them, and in Case of Disagreement between them with Respect to the Time of Adjournment, he may adjourn them to such Time as he shall think proper; he shall receive Ambassadors and other public Ministers; he shall take Care that the Laws be faithfully executed, and shall Commission all the Officers of the United States.

Section 4. The President, Vice President, and all civil Officers of the United States, shall be removed from Office on Impeachment for, and Conviction of, Treason, Bribery, or other high Crimes and Misdemeanors.

ARTICLE III

Section 1. The judicial Power of the United States shall be vested in one supreme Court, and in such inferior Courts as the Congress may from time to time ordain and establish. The Judges, both of the supreme and inferior Courts, shall hold their Offices during good Behavior, and shall, at stated Times, receive for their Services, a Compensation, which shall not be diminished during their Continuance in Office.

Section 2. [1] The judicial Power shall extend to all Cases, in Law and Equity, arising under this Constitution, the Laws of the United States, and Treaties made, or which shall be made, under their Authority;—to all Cases affecting Ambassadors, other public Ministers and Consuls;—to all Cases of admiralty and maritime Jurisdiction;—to Controversies to which the United States shall be a Party;—to Controversies between two or more States;—between a State and Citizens of another State; {see 11th Amendment}—between Citizens of different States;—between Citizens of the same State claiming Lands under Grants of different States, and between a State, or the Citizens thereof, and foreign States, Citizens or Subjects.

[2] In all Cases affecting Ambassadors, other public Ministers and Consuls, and those in which a State shall be a Party, the supreme Court shall have original Jurisdiction. In all the other Cases before mentioned, the supreme Court shall have appellate Jurisdiction, both as to Law and Fact, with such Exceptions, and under such Regulations as the Congress shall make.

[3] The trial of all Crimes, except in Cases of Impeachment, shall be by Jury; and such Trial shall be held in the State where the said Crimes shall have been committed; but when not committed within any State, the Trial shall be at such Place or Places as the Congress may by law have directed.

Section 3. [1] Treason against the United States shall consist only in levying War against them, or, in adhering to their Enemies, giving them Aid and Comfort. No Person shall be convicted of Treason unless on the Testimony of two Witnesses to the same overt Act, or on Confession in open Court.

[2] The Congress shall have Power to declare the Punishment of Treason, but no Attainder of Treason shall work Corruption of Blood, or Forfeiture except during the Life of the Person attained.

ARTICLE IV

Section 1. Full Faith and Credit shall be given in each State to the public Acts, Records, and judicial Proceedings of every other State. And the Congress may by general Laws prescribe the Manner in which such Acts, Records, and Proceedings shall be proved, and the Effect thereof.

Section 2. **[1]** The Citizens of each State shall be entitled to all Privileges and Immunities of Citizens in the several States. {See 14th Amendment.}

[2] A Person charged in any State with Treason, Felony, or other Crime, who shall flee from Justice, and be found in another State, shall on demand of the executive Authority of the State from which he fled, be delivered up to be removed to the State having Jurisdiction of the Crime.

[3] No Person held to Service or Labor in one State under the Laws thereof, escaping into another, shall, in Consequence of any Law or Regulation therein, be discharged from such Service or Labor, but shall be delivered up on Claim of the Party to whom such Service or Labor may be due. {See 13th Amendment.}

Section 3. **[1]** New States may be admitted by the Congress into this Union; but no new State shall be formed or erected within the Jurisdiction of any other State; nor any State be formed by the Junction of two or more States, or Parts of States, without the Consent of the Legislatures of the States concerned as well as of the Congress.

[2] The Congress shall have Power to dispose of and make all needful Rules and Regulations respecting the Territory or other Property belonging to the United States; and nothing in this Constitution shall be so construed as to Prejudice any Claims of the United States, or of any particular State.

Section 4. The United States shall guarantee to every State in this Union a Republican Form of Government, and shall protect each of them against Invasion; and on Application of the Legislature, or of the Executive (when the Legislature cannot be convened) against domestic Violence.

ARTICLE V

The Congress, whenever two thirds of both Houses shall deem it necessary, shall propose Amendments to this Constitution, or, on the Application of the Legislatures of two thirds of the several States, shall call a Convention for proposing Amendments, which in either Case, shall be valid to all Intents and Purposes, as part of this Constitution, when ratified by the Legislatures of three fourths of the several States, or by Conventions in three fourths thereof, as the one or the other Mode of Ratification may be proposed by Congress; Provided that no Amendment which may be made prior to the year One thousand eight hundred and eight shall in any Manner affect the first and fourth Clauses in the Ninth Section of the first Article; and that no State, without its Consent, shall be deprived of its equal Suffrage in the Senate.

ARTICLE VI

[1] All Debts contracted and Engagements entered into, before the Adoption of this Constitution, shall be valid against the United States under this Constitution, as under the Confederation.

[2] This Constitution, and the Laws of the United States which shall be made in Pursuance thereof; and all Treaties made, or which shall be made, under the Authority of the United States, shall be the supreme Law of the Land; and the Judges in every State shall be bound thereby, any Thing in the Constitution or laws of any State to the Contrary notwithstanding.

[3] The Senators and Representatives before mentioned, and the Members of the several State Legislatures, and all executive and judicial Officers, both of the United States and of the several States, shall be bound by Oath or Affirmation, to support this Constitution; but no religious Test shall ever be required as a Qualification to any Office or public Trust under the United States.

ARTICLE VII

The Ratification of the Conventions of nine States shall be sufficient for the Establishment of this Constitution between the States so ratifying the Same.

DONE in Convention by the Unanimous Consent of the States present the Seventeenth Day of September in the Year of our Lord one thousand seven hundred and Eighty-seven, and of the Independence of the United States of America the Twelfth. IN WITNESS whereof we have hereunto subscribed our Names.

[AMENDMENTS]

ARTICLE I [1791]

Congress shall make no law respecting an establishment of religion, or prohibiting the free exercise thereof; or abridging the freedom of speech, or of the press; or the right of the people peaceably to assemble, and to petition the Government for a redress of grievances.

ARTICLE II [1791]

A well regulated Militia, being necessary to the security of a free State, the right of the people to keep and bear Arms, shall not be infringed.

ARTICLE III [1791]

No Soldier shall, in time of peace be quartered in any house, without the consent of the Owner, nor in time of war, but in a manner to be prescribed by law.

ARTICLE IV [1791]

The right of the people to be secure in their persons, houses, papers, and effects, against unreasonable searches and seizures, shall not be violated, and no Warrants shall issue, but upon probable cause, supported by Oath or affirmation, and particularly describing the place to be searched, and the person or things to be seized.

ARTICLE V [1791]

No person shall be held to answer for a capital, or otherwise infamous crime, unless on a presentment or indictment of a Grand Jury, except in cases arising in the land or naval forces, or in the Militia, when in actual service in time of War or public danger; nor shall any person be subject for the same offence to be twice put in jeopardy of life or limb; nor shall be compelled in any criminal case to be a witness against himself, nor be deprived of life, liberty, or property, without due process of law; nor shall private property be taken for public use, without just compensation.

ARTICLE VI [1791]

In all criminal prosecutions, the accused shall enjoy the right to a speedy and public trial, by an impartial jury of the State and district wherein the crime shall have been committed, which district shall have been previously ascertained by law, and to be informed of the nature and cause of the accusation; to be confronted with the witnesses against him; to have compulsory process for obtaining witnesses in his favor, and to have the Assistance of Counsel for his defence.

ARTICLE VII [1791]

In Suits at common law, where the value in controversy shall exceed twenty dollars, the right of trial by jury shall be preserved, and no fact tried by jury, shall be otherwise re-examined in any Court of the United States, than according to the rules of the common law.

ARTICLE VIII [1791]

Excessive bail shall not be required, nor excessive fines imposed, nor cruel and unusual punishments inflicted.

ARTICLE IX [1791]

The enumeration in the Constitution, of certain rights, shall not be construed to deny or disparage others retained by the people.

ARTICLE X [1791]

The powers not delegated to the United States by the Constitution, nor prohibited by it to the States, are reserved to the States respectively, or to the people.

ARTICLE XI [1798]

The Judicial power of the United States shall not be construed to extend to any suit in law or equity, commenced or prosecuted against one of the United States by Citizens of another State, or by Citizens or Subjects of any Foreign State.

ARTICLE XII [1804]

The Electors shall meet in their respective states and vote by ballot for President and Vice-President, one of whom, at least, shall not be an inhabitant of the same state with themselves; they shall name in their ballots the person voted for as President, and in distinct ballots the person voted for as Vice-President, and they shall make distinct lists of all persons voted for as President, and of all persons voted for as Vice-President, and of the number of votes for each, which lists they shall sign and certify, and transmit sealed to the seat of the government of the United States, directed to the President of the Senate;—The President of the Senate shall, in the presence of the Senate and House of Representatives, open all the certificates and the votes shall then be counted;—The person having the greatest number of votes for President, shall be the President, if such number be a majority of the whole number of Electors appointed; and if no person have such majority, then from the persons having the highest numbers not exceeding three on the list of those voted for as President, the House of Representatives shall choose immediately, by ballot, the President. But in choosing the President, the votes shall be taken by states, the representation of each state having one vote; a quorum for this purpose shall consist of a member or members from two-thirds of the states, and a majority of all the states shall be necessary to a choice. And if the House of Representatives shall not choose a President whenever the right of choice shall devolve upon them before the fourth day of March {see 20th Amendment} next following, then the Vice-President shall act as President, as in the case of the death or other constitutional disability of the President.—The person having the greatest number of votes as Vice-President, shall be the Vice-President, if such number be a majority of the whole number of Electors appointed, and if no person have a majority, then from the two highest numbers on the list, the Senate shall choose the Vice-President; a quorum for the purpose shall consist of two-thirds of the whole number of Senators, and a majority of the whole number shall be necessary to a choice. But no person constitutionally ineligible to the office of President shall be eligible to that of Vice-President of the United States.

ARTICLE XIII [1865]

Section 1. Neither slavery nor involuntary servitude, except as a punishment for crime whereof the party shall have been duly convicted, shall exist within the United States, or any place subject to their jurisdiction.

Section 2. Congress shall have power to enforce this article by appropriate legislation.

ARTICLE XIV [1868]

Section 1. All persons born or naturalized in the United States, and subject to the jurisdiction thereof, are citizens of the United States and of the State wherein they reside. No State shall make or enforce any law which shall abridge the privileges or immunities of citizens of the United States; nor shall any State deprive any person of life, liberty, or property, without due process of law; nor deny to any person within its jurisdiction the equal protection of the laws.

Section 2. Representatives shall be apportioned among the several States according to their respective numbers, counting the whole number of persons in each State excluding Indians not taxed. But when the right to vote at any election for the choice of electors for President and Vice President of the United States, Representatives in Congress, the Executive and Judicial officers of a State, or the members of the Legislature thereof, is denied to any of the male inhabitants of such State, being twenty-one years of age, and citizens of the United States, or in any way abridged, except for participation in rebellion, or other crime, the basis of representation therein shall be reduced in the proportion which the number of such male citizens shall bear to the whole number of male citizens twenty-one years of age in such State.

Section 3. No person shall be a Senator or Representative in Congress, or elector of President and Vice President, or hold any office, civil or military, under the United States, or under any State, who having previously taken an oath, as a member of Congress, or as an officer of the United States, or as a member of any State legislature, or as an executive or judicial officer of any State, to support the Constitution of the United States, shall have engaged in insurrection or rebellion against the same, or given aid or comfort to the enemies thereof. But Congress may by a vote of two-thirds of each House, remove such disability.

Section 4. The validity of the public debt of the United States, authorized by law, including debts incurred for payment of pensions and bounties for services in suppressing insurrection or rebellion, shall not be questioned. But neither the United States nor any State shall assume or pay any debt or obligation incurred in aid of insurrection or rebellion against the United States, or any claim for the loss or emancipation of any slave; but all such debts, obligations and claims shall be held illegal and void.

Section 5. The Congress shall have power to enforce, by appropriate legislation, the provisions of this article.

ARTICLE XV [1870]

Section 1. The right of citizens of the United States to vote shall not be denied or abridged by the United States or by any State on account of race, color, or previous condition of servitude.

Section 2. The Congress shall have power to enforce this article by appropriate legislation.

ARTICLE XVI [1913]

The Congress shall have power to lay and collect taxes on incomes, from whatever source derived, without apportionment among the several States, and without regard to any census or enumeration.

ARTICLE XVII [1913]

[1] The Senate of the United States shall be composed of two Senators from each State, elected by the people thereof, for six years; and each Senator shall have one vote. The electors in each State shall have the qualifications requisite for electors of the most numerous branch of the State legislatures.

[2] When vacancies happen in the representation of any State in the Senate, the executive authority of such State shall issue writs of election to fill such vacancies: Provided, That the legislature of any State may empower the executive thereof to make temporary appointments until the people fill the vacancies by election as the legislature may direct.

[3] This amendment shall not be so construed as to affect the election or term of any Senator chosen before it becomes valid as part of the Constitution.

ARTICLE XVIII [1919]

[repealed by 21st Amendment]

Section 1. After one year from the ratification of this article the manufacture, sale, or transportation of intoxicating liquors within, the importation thereof into, or the exportation thereof from the United States and all territory subject to the jurisdiction thereof for beverage purposes is hereby prohibited.

Section 2. The Congress and the several States shall have concurrent power to enforce this article by appropriate legislation.

Section 3. This article shall be inoperative unless it shall have been ratified as an amendment to the Constitution by the legislatures of the several States, as provided in the Constitution, within seven years from the date of the submission hereof to the States by the Congress.

ARTICLE XIX [1920]

[1] The right of citizens of the United States to vote shall not be denied or abridged by the United States or by any State on account of sex.

[2] Congress shall have power to enforce this article by appropriate legislation.

ARTICLE XX [1933]

Section 1. The terms of the President and Vice President shall end at noon on the 20th day of January, and the terms of Senators and Representatives at noon on the 3d day of January, of the years in which such terms would have ended if this article had not been ratified; and the terms of their successors shall then begin.

Section 2. The Congress shall assemble at least once in every year, and such meeting shall begin at noon on the 3d day of January, unless they shall by law appoint a different day.

Section 3. If, at the time fixed for the beginning of the term of the President, the President elect shall have died, the Vice President elect shall become President. If the President shall not have been chosen before the time fixed for the beginning of his term, or if the President elect shall have failed to qualify, then the Vice President elect shall act as President until a President shall have qualified; and the Congress may by law provide for the case wherein neither a President elect nor a Vice President elect shall have qualified, declaring who shall then act as President, or the manner in which one who is to act shall be selected, and such person shall act accordingly until a President or Vice President shall have qualified.

Section 4. The Congress may by law provide for the case of the death of any of the persons from whom the House of Representatives may choose a President whenever the right of choice shall have devolved upon them, and for the case of the death of any of the persons from whom the Senate may choose a Vice President whenever the right of choice shall have devolved upon them.

Section 5. Sections 1 and 2 shall take effect on the 15th day of October following the ratification of this article.

Section 6. This article shall be inoperative unless it shall have been ratified as an amendment to the Constitution by the legislatures of three-fourths of the several States within seven years from the date of its submission.

ARTICLE XXI [1933]

Section 1. The eighteenth article of amendment to the Constitution of the United States is hereby repealed.

Section 2. The transportation or importation into any State, Territory, or possession of the United States for delivery or use therein of intoxicating liquors, in violation of the laws thereof, is hereby prohibited.

Section 3. This article shall be inoperative unless it shall have been ratified as an amendment to the Constitution by conventions in the several States, as provided in the Constitution, within seven years from the date of the submission hereof to the States by the Congress.

ARTICLE XXII [1951]

Section 1. No person shall be elected to the office of the President more than twice, and no person who has held the office of President, or acted as President, for more than two years of a term to which some other person was elected President shall be elected to the office of President more than once. But this Article shall not apply to any person holding the office of President when this Article was proposed by the Congress, and shall not prevent any person who may be holding the office of President, or acting as President, during the term within which this Article becomes operative from holding the office of President or acting as President during the remainder of such term.

Section 2. This article shall be inoperative unless it shall have been ratified as an amendment to the Constitution by the legislatures of three-fourths of the several States within seven years from the date of its submission to the States by the Congress.

ARTICLE XXIII [1961]

Section 1. The District constituting the seat of Government of the United States shall appoint in such manner as the Congress may direct:

A number of electors of President and Vice President equal to the whole number of Senators and Representatives in Congress to which the District would be entitled if it were a State, but in no event more than the least populous state; they shall be in addition to those appointed by the states, but they shall be considered, for the purposes of the election of President and Vice President, to be electors appointed by a state; and they shall meet in the District and perform such duties as provided by the twelfth article of amendment.

Section 2. The Congress shall have power to enforce this article by appropriate legislation.

ARTICLE XXIV [1964]

Section 1. The right of citizens of the United States to vote in any primary or other election for President or Vice President, for electors for President or Vice President, or for Senator or Representative in Congress, shall not be denied or abridged by the United States, or any State by reason of failure to pay any poll tax or other tax.

Section 2. The Congress shall have power to enforce this article by appropriate legislation.

ARTICLE XXV [1967]

Section 1. In case of the removal of the President from office or of his death or resignation, the Vice President shall become President.

Section 2. Whenever there is a vacancy in the office of the Vice President, the President shall nominate a Vice President who shall take office upon confirmation by a majority vote of both Houses of Congress.

Section 3. Whenever the President transmits to the President pro tempore of the Senate and the Speaker of the House of Representatives his written declaration that he is unable to discharge the powers and duties of his office, and until he transmits to them a written declaration to the contrary, such powers and duties shall be discharged by the Vice President as Acting President.

Section 4. Whenever the Vice President and a majority of either the principal officers of the executive departments or of such other body as Congress may by law provide, transmit to the President pro tempore of the Senate and the Speaker of the House of Representatives their written declaration that the President is unable to discharge the powers and duties of his office, the Vice President shall immediately assume the powers and duties of the office as Acting President.

Thereafter, when the President transmits to the President pro tempore of the Senate and the Speaker of the House of Representatives his written declaration that no inability exists, he shall resume the powers and duties of his office unless the Vice President and a majority of either the principal officers of the executive department or of such other body as Congress may by law provide, transmit within four days to the President pro tempore of the Senate and the Speaker of the House of Representatives their written declaration that the President is unable to discharge the powers and duties of his office. Thereupon Congress shall decide the issue, assembling within forty-eight hours for that purpose if not in session. If the Congress, within twenty-one days after receipt of the latter written declaration, or, if Congress is not in session, within twenty-one days after Congress is required to assemble, determines by two-thirds vote of both Houses that the President is unable to discharge the power and duties of his office, the Vice President shall continue to discharge the same as Acting President; otherwise, the President shall resume the powers and duties of his office.

ARTICLE XXVI [1971]

Section 1. The right of citizens of the United States, who are eighteen years of age or older, to vote shall not be denied or abridged by the United States or by any State on account of age.

Section 2. The Congress shall have power to enforce this article by appropriate legislation.

ARTICLE XXVII [1992]*

No law, varying the compensation for the services of the Senators and Representatives, shall take effect, until an election of Representatives shall have intervened.

---

*This amendment was certified by the Archivist of the United States on May 18, 1992.

APPENDIX II Table of Parallel Volume References, U.S. Supreme Court Reporters

Term or Year of Decision	Government Printing Office	Nominative Reporters & West	LCP
1790	1 U.S.	1 Dall.	1 L. Ed.
1791	2 U.S.	2 Dall.	1 L. Ed.
1794	3 U.S.	3 Dall.	1 L. Ed.
1799	4 U.S.	4 Dall.	1 L. Ed.
1801	5 U.S.	1 Cranch	2 L. Ed.
1804	6 U.S.	2 Cranch	2 L. Ed.
1805	7 U.S.	3 Cranch	2 L. Ed.
1807	8 U.S.	4 Cranch	2 L. Ed.
1809	9 U.S.	5 Cranch	3 L. Ed.
1810	10 U.S.	6 Cranch	3 L. Ed.
1812	11 U.S.	7 Cranch	3 L. Ed.
1814	12 U.S.	8 Cranch	3 L. Ed.
1815	13 U.S.	9 Cranch	3 L. Ed.
1816	14 U.S.	1 Wheat.	4 L. Ed.
1817	15 U.S.	2 Wheat.	4 L. Ed.
1818	16 U.S.	3 Wheat.	4 L. Ed.
1819	17 U.S.	4 Wheat.	4 L. Ed.
1820	18 U.S.	5 Wheat.	5 L. Ed.
1821	19 U.S.	6 Wheat.	5 L. Ed.
1822	20 U.S.	7 Wheat.	5 L. Ed.
1823	21 U.S.	8 Wheat.	5 L. Ed.
1824	22 U.S.	9 Wheat.	6 L. Ed.
1825	23 U.S.	10 Wheat.	6 L. Ed.
1826	24 U.S.	11 Wheat.	6 L. Ed.
1827	25 U.S.	12 Wheat.	6 L. Ed.
1828	26 U.S.	1 Pet.	7 L. Ed.
1829	27 U.S.	2 Pet.	7 L. Ed.
1830	28 U.S.	3 Pet.	7 L. Ed.
1830	29 U.S.	4 Pet.	7 L. Ed.
1831	30 U.S.	5 Pet.	8 L. Ed.
1832	31 U.S.	6 Pet.	8 L. Ed.
1833	32 U.S.	7 Pet.	8 L. Ed.
1834	33 U.S.	8 Pet.	8 L. Ed.
1835	34 U.S.	9 Pet.	9 L. Ed.
1836	35 U.S.	10 Pet.	9 L. Ed.
1837	36 U.S.	11 Pet.	9 L. Ed.
1838	37 U.S.	12 Pet.	9 L. Ed.
1839	38 U.S.	13 Pet.	10 L. Ed.
1840	39 U.S.	14 Pet.	10 L. Ed.
1841	40 U.S.	15 Pet.	10 L. Ed.
1842	41 U.S.	16 Pet.	10 L. Ed.
1843	42 U.S.	1 How.	11 L. Ed.
1844	43 U.S.	2 How.	11 L. Ed.
1845	44 U.S.	3 How.	11 L. Ed.
1846	45 U.S.	4 How.	11 L. Ed.

Term or Year of Decision	Government Printing Office	Nominative Reporters & West	LCP
1847	46 U.S.	5 How.	12 L. Ed.
1848	47 U.S.	6 How.	12 L. Ed.
1849	48 U.S.	7 How.	12 L. Ed.
1850	49 U.S.	8 How.	12 L. Ed.
1850	50 U.S.	9 How.	13 L. Ed.
1850	51 U.S.	10 How.	13 L. Ed.
1850	52 U.S.	11 How.	13 L. Ed.
1851	53 U.S.	12 How.	13 L. Ed.
1851	54 U.S.	13 How.	14 L. Ed.
1852	55 U.S.	14 How.	14 L. Ed.
1853	56 U.S.	15 How.	14 L. Ed.
1853	57 U.S.	16 How.	14 L. Ed.
1854	58 U.S.	17 How.	15 L. Ed.
1855	59 U.S.	18 How.	15 L. Ed.
1856	60 U.S.	19 How.	15 L. Ed.
1857	61 U.S.	20 How.	15 L. Ed.
1858	62 U.S.	21 How.	16 L. Ed.
1859	63 U.S.	22 How.	16 L. Ed.
1859	64 U.S.	23 How.	16 L. Ed.
1860	65 U.S.	24 How.	16 L. Ed.
1861	66 U.S.	1 Black	17 L. Ed.
1862	67 U.S.	2 Black	17 L. Ed.
1863	68 U.S.	1 Wall.	17 L. Ed.
1864	69 U.S.	2 Wall.	17 L. Ed.
1865	70 U.S.	3 Wall.	18 L. Ed.
1866	71 U.S.	4 Wall.	18 L. Ed.
1866	72 U.S.	5 Wall.	18 L. Ed.
1867	73 U.S.	6 Wall.	18 L. Ed.
1868	74 U.S.	7 Wall.	19 L. Ed.
1868	75 U.S.	8 Wall.	19 L. Ed.
1869	76 U.S.	9 Wall.	19 L. Ed.
1869	77 U.S.	10 Wall.	19 L. Ed.
1870	78 U.S.	11 Wall.	20 L. Ed.
1870	79 U.S.	12 Wall.	20 L. Ed.
1871	80 U.S.	13 Wall.	20 L. Ed.
1871	81 U.S.	14 Wall.	20 L. Ed.
1872	82 U.S.	15 Wall.	21 L. Ed.
1872	83 U.S.	16 Wall.	21 L. Ed.
1872	84 U.S.	17 Wall.	21 L. Ed.
1873	85 U.S.	18 Wall.	21 L. Ed.
1873	86 U.S.	19 Wall.	22 L. Ed.
1873	87 U.S.	20 Wall.	22 L. Ed.
1874	88 U.S.	21 Wall.	22 L. Ed.
1874	89 U.S.	22 Wall.	22 L. Ed.
1874	90 U.S.	23 Wall.	23 L. Ed.
1875	91 U.S.		23 L. Ed.
1875	92 U.S.		23 L. Ed.
1876	93 U.S.		23 L. Ed.
1876	94 U.S.		24 L. Ed.
1877	95 U.S.		24 L. Ed.
1877	96 U.S.		24 L. Ed.
1878	97 U.S.		24 L. Ed.
1878	98 U.S.		25 L. Ed.
1878	99 U.S.		25 L. Ed.
1879	100 U.S.		25 L. Ed.
1879	101 U.S.		25 L. Ed.
1880	102 U.S.		26 L. Ed.
1880	103 U.S.		26 L. Ed.
1881	104 U.S.		26 L. Ed.
1881	105 U.S.		26 L. Ed.
1882	106 U.S.	1 S. Ct.	27 L. Ed.
1882	107 U.S.	1 S. Ct.	27 L. Ed.
1882	107 U.S.	2 S. Ct.	27 L. Ed.

Term or Year of Decision	Government Printing Office	Nominative Reporters & West	LCP
1882	108 U.S.	2 S. Ct.	27 L. Ed.
1883	109 U.S.	3 S. Ct.	27 L. Ed.
1883	110 U.S.	3 S. Ct.	28 L. Ed.
1883	110 U.S.	4 S. Ct.	28 L. Ed.
1883	111 U.S.	4 S. Ct.	28 L. Ed.
1884	112 U.S.	5 S. Ct.	28 L. Ed.
1884	113 U.S.	5 S. Ct.	28 L. Ed.
1884	114 U.S.	5 S. Ct.	29 L. Ed.
1884	115 U.S.	5 S. Ct.	29 L. Ed.
1885	115 U.S.	6 S. Ct.	29 L. Ed.
1885	116 U.S.	6 S. Ct.	29 L. Ed.
1885	117 U.S.	6 S. Ct.	29 L. Ed.
1886	118 U.S.	7 S. Ct.	30 L. Ed.
1886	119 U.S.	7 S. Ct.	30 L. Ed.
1886	120 U.S.	7 S. Ct.	30 L. Ed.
1886	121 U.S.	7 S. Ct.	30 L. Ed.
1887	122 U.S.	7 S. Ct.	30 L. Ed.
1887	123 U.S.	8 S. Ct.	31 L. Ed.
1887	124 U.S.	8 S. Ct.	31 L. Ed.
1887	125 U.S.	8 S. Ct.	31 L. Ed.
1887	126 U.S.	8 S. Ct.	31 L. Ed.
1887	127 U.S.	8 S. Ct.	32 L. Ed.
1888	128 U.S.	9 S. Ct.	32 L. Ed.
1888	129 U.S.	9 S. Ct.	32 L. Ed.
1888	130 U.S.	9 S. Ct.	32 L. Ed.
1888	131 U.S.	9 S. Ct.	33 L. Ed
1889	132 U.S.	10 S. Ct.	33 L. Ed.
1889	133 U.S.	10 S. Ct.	33 L. Ed.
1889	134 U.S.	10 S. Ct.	33 L. Ed.
1889	135 U.S.	10 S. Ct.	34 L. Ed.
1889	136 U.S.	10 S. Ct.	34 L. Ed.
1890	137 U.S.	11 S. Ct.	34 L. Ed.
1890	138 U.S.	11 S. Ct.	34 L. Ed.
1890	139 U.S.	11 S. Ct.	35 L. Ed.
1890	140 U.S.	11 S. Ct.	35 L. Ed.
1891	141 U.S.	11 S. Ct.	35 L. Ed.
1891	141 U.S.	12 S. Ct.	35 L. Ed.
1891	142 U.S.	12 S. Ct.	35 L. Ed.
1891	143 U.S.	12 S. Ct.	36 L. Ed.
1891	144 U.S.	12 S. Ct.	36 L. Ed.
1891	145 U.S.	12 S. Ct.	36 L. Ed.
1892	146 U.S.	13 S. Ct.	36 L. Ed.
1892	147 U.S.	13 S. Ct.	37 L. Ed.
1892	148 U.S.	13 S. Ct.	37 L. Ed.
1892	149 U.S.	13 S. Ct.	37 L. Ed.
1893	150 U.S.	14 S. Ct.	37 L. Ed.
1893	151 U.S.	14 S. Ct.	38 L. Ed.
1893	152 U.S.	14 S. Ct.	38 L. Ed.
1893	153 U.S.	14 S. Ct.	38 L. Ed.
1893	154 U.S.	14 S. Ct.	38 L. Ed.
1894	155 U.S.	15 S. Ct.	39 L. Ed.
1894	156 U.S.	15 S. Ct.	39 L. Ed.
1894	157 U.S.	15 S. Ct.	39 L. Ed.
1894	158 U.S.	15 S. Ct.	39 L. Ed.
1895	159 U.S.	15 S. Ct.	40 L. Ed.
1895	159 U.S.	16 S. Ct.	40 L. Ed.
1895	160 U.S.	16 S. Ct.	40 L. Ed.
1895	161 U.S.	16 S. Ct.	40 L. Ed.
1895	162 U.S.	16 S. Ct.	40 L. Ed.
1895	163 U.S.	16 S. Ct.	41 L. Ed.
1896	164 U.S.	17 S. Ct.	41 L. Ed.
1896	165 U.S.	17 S. Ct.	41 L. Ed.
1896	166 U.S.	17 S. Ct.	41 L. Ed.

Term or Year of Decision	Government Printing Office	Nominative Reporters & West	LCP
1896	167 U.S.	17 S. Ct.	42 L. Ed.
1897	168 U.S.	18 S. Ct.	42 L. Ed.
1897	169 U.S.	18 S. Ct.	42 L. Ed.
1897	170 U.S.	18 S. Ct.	42 L. Ed.
1898	171 U.S.	18 S. Ct.	43 L. Ed.
1898	171 U.S.	19 S. Ct.	43 L. Ed.
1898	172 U.S.	19 S. Ct.	43 L. Ed.
1898	173 U.S.	19 S. Ct.	43 L. Ed.
1898	174 U.S.	19 S. Ct.	43 L. Ed.
1899	175 U.S.	20 S. Ct.	44 L. Ed.
1899	176 U.S.	20 S. Ct.	44 L. Ed.
1899	177 U.S.	20 S. Ct.	44 L. Ed.
1899	178 U.S.	20 S. Ct.	44 L. Ed.
1900	178 U.S.	21 S. Ct.	44 L. Ed.
1900	179 U.S.	21 S. Ct.	45 L. Ed.
1900	180 U.S.	21 S. Ct.	45 L. Ed.
1900	181 U.S.	21 S. Ct.	45 L. Ed.
1901	182 U.S.	22 S. Ct.	45 L. Ed.
1901	183 U.S.	22 S. Ct.	46 L. Ed.
1901	184 U.S.	22 S. Ct.	46 L. Ed.
1901	185 U.S.	22 S. Ct.	46 L. Ed.
1901	186 U.S.	22 S. Ct.	46 L. Ed.
1902	186 U.S.	23 S. Ct.	46 L. Ed.
1902	187 U.S.	23 S. Ct.	47 L. Ed.
1902	188 U.S.	23 S. Ct.	47 L. Ed.
1902	189 U.S.	23 S. Ct.	47 L. Ed.
1902	190 U.S.	23 S. Ct.	47 L. Ed.
1903	190 U.S.	24 S. Ct.	47 L. Ed.
1903	191 U.S.	24 S. Ct.	48 L. Ed.
1903	192 U.S.	24 S. Ct.	48 L. Ed.
1903	193 U.S.	24 S. Ct.	48 L. Ed.
1903	194 U.S.	24 S. Ct.	48 L. Ed.
1903	195 U.S.	24 S. Ct.	49 L. Ed.
1904	195 U.S.	25 S. Ct.	49 L. Ed.
1904	196 U.S.	25 S. Ct.	49 L. Ed.
1904	197 U.S.	25 S. Ct.	49 L. Ed.
1904	198 U.S.	25 S. Ct.	49 L. Ed.
1904	199 U.S.	25 S. Ct.	50 L. Ed.
1905	199 U.S.	26 S. Ct.	50 L. Ed.
1905	200 U.S.	26 S. Ct.	50 L. Ed.
1905	201 U.S.	26 S. Ct.	50 L. Ed.
1905	202 U.S.	26 S. Ct.	50 L. Ed.
1906	203 U.S.	27 S. Ct.	51 L. Ed.
1906	204 U.S.	27 S. Ct.	51 L. Ed.
1906	205 U.S.	27 S. Ct.	51 L. Ed.
1906	206 U.S.	27 S. Ct.	51 L. Ed.
1907	207 U.S.	28 S. Ct.	52 L. Ed.
1907	208 U.S.	28 S. Ct.	52 L. Ed.
1907	209 U.S.	28 S. Ct.	52 L. Ed.
1907	210 U.S.	28 S. Ct.	52 L. Ed.
1908	211 U.S.	29 S. Ct.	53 L. Ed.
1908	212 U.S.	29 S. Ct.	53 L. Ed.
1908	213 U.S.	29 S. Ct.	53 L. Ed.
1908	214 U.S.	29 S. Ct.	53 L. Ed.
1909	215 U.S.	30 S. Ct.	54 L. Ed.
1909	216 U.S.	30 S. Ct.	54 L. Ed.
1909	217 U.S.	30 S. Ct.	54 L. Ed.
1909	218 U.S.	30 S. Ct.	54 L. Ed.
1910	218 U.S.	31 S. Ct.	54 L. Ed.
1910	219 U.S.	31 S. Ct.	55 L. Ed.
1910	220 U.S.	31 S. Ct.	55 L. Ed.
1910	221 U.S.	31 S. Ct.	55 L. Ed.
1911	222 U.S.	32 S. Ct.	56 L. Ed.

Term or Year of Decision	Government Printing Office	Nominative Reporters & West	LCP
1911	223 U.S.	32 S. Ct.	56 L. Ed.
1911	224 U.S.	32 S. Ct.	56 L. Ed.
1911	225 U.S.	32 S. Ct.	56 L. Ed.
1912	226 U.S.	33 S. Ct.	57 L. Ed.
1912	227 U.S.	33 S. Ct.	57 L. Ed.
1912	228 U.S.	33 S. Ct.	57 L. Ed.
1912	229 U.S.	33 S. Ct.	57 L. Ed.
1912	230 U.S.	33 S. Ct.	57 L. Ed.
1913	231 U.S.	34 S. Ct.	58 L. Ed.
1913	232 U.S.	34 S. Ct.	58 L. Ed.
1913	233 U.S.	34 S. Ct.	58 L. Ed.
1913	234 U.S.	34 S. Ct.	58 L. Ed.
1914	235 U.S.	35 S. Ct.	59 L. Ed.
1914	236 U.S.	35 S. Ct.	59 L. Ed.
1914	237 U.S.	35 S. Ct.	59 L. Ed.
1914	238 U.S.	35 S. Ct.	59 L. Ed.
1915	239 U.S.	36 S. Ct.	60 L. Ed.
1915	240 U.S.	36 S. Ct.	60 L. Ed.
1915	241 U.S.	36 S. Ct.	60 L. Ed.
1916	242 U.S.	37 S. Ct.	61 L. Ed.
1916	243 U.S.	37 S. Ct.	61 L. Ed.
1916	244 U.S.	37 S. Ct.	61 L. Ed.
1917	245 U.S.	38 S. Ct.	62 L. Ed.
1917	246 U.S.	38 S. Ct.	62 L. Ed.
1917	247 U.S.	38 S. Ct.	62 L. Ed.
1918	248 U.S.	39 S. Ct.	63 L. Ed.
1918	249 U.S.	39 S. Ct.	63 L. Ed.
1918	250 U.S.	39 S. Ct.	63 L. Ed.
1919	250 U.S.	40 S. Ct.	63 L. Ed.
1919	251 U.S.	40 S. Ct.	64 L. Ed.
1919	252 U.S.	40 S. Ct.	64 L. Ed.
1919	253 U.S.	40 S. Ct.	64 L. Ed.
1920	254 U.S.	41 S. Ct.	65 L. Ed.
1920	255 U.S.	41 S. Ct.	65 L. Ed.
1920	256 U.S.	41 S. Ct.	65 L. Ed.
1921	257 U.S.	42 S. Ct.	66 L. Ed.
1921	258 U.S.	42 S. Ct.	66 L. Ed.
1921	259 U.S.	42 S. Ct.	66 L. Ed.
1922	260 U.S.	43 S. Ct.	67 L. Ed.
1922	261 U.S.	43 S. Ct.	67 L. Ed.
1922	262 U.S.	43 S. Ct.	67 L. Ed.
1923	263 U.S.	44 S. Ct.	68 L. Ed.
1923	264 U.S.	44 S. Ct.	68 L. Ed.
1923	265 U.S.	44 S. Ct.	68 L. Ed.
1924	266 U.S.	45 S. Ct.	69 L. Ed.
1924	267 U.S.	45 S. Ct.	69 L. Ed.
1924	268 U.S.	45 S. Ct.	69 L. Ed.
1925	269 U.S.	46 S. Ct.	70 L. Ed.
1925	270 U.S.	46 S. Ct.	70 L. Ed.
1925	271 U.S.	46 S. Ct.	70 L. Ed.
1926	272 U.S.	47 S. Ct.	71 L. Ed.
1926	273 U.S.	47 S. Ct.	71 L. Ed.
1926	274 U.S.	47 S. Ct.	71 L. Ed.
1927	275 U.S.	48 S. Ct.	72 L. Ed.
1927	276 U.S.	48 S. Ct.	72 L. Ed.
1927	277 U.S.	48 S. Ct.	72 L. Ed.
1928	278 U.S.	49 S. Ct.	73 L. Ed.
1928	279 U.S.	49 S. Ct.	73 L. Ed.
1929	280 U.S.	50 S. Ct.	74 L. Ed.
1929	281 U.S.	50 S. Ct.	74 L. Ed.
1930	282 U.S.	51 S. Ct.	75 L. Ed.
1930	283 U.S.	51 S. Ct.	75 L. Ed.
1931	284 U.S.	52 S. Ct.	76 L. Ed.

Term or Year of Decision	Government Printing Office	Nominative Reporters & West	LCP
1931	285 U.S.	52 S. Ct.	76 L. Ed.
1931	286 U.S.	52 S. Ct.	76 L. Ed.
1932	287 U.S.	53 S. Ct.	77 L. Ed.
1932	288 U.S.	53 S. Ct.	77 L. Ed.
1932	289 U.S.	53 S. Ct.	77 L. Ed.
1933	290 U.S.	54 S. Ct.	78 L. Ed.
1933	291 U.S.	54 S. Ct.	78 L. Ed.
1933	292 U.S.	54 S. Ct.	78 L. Ed.
1934	293 U.S.	55 S. Ct.	79 L. Ed.
1934	294 U.S.	55 S. Ct.	79 L. Ed.
1934	295 U.S.	55 S. Ct.	79 L. Ed.
1935	296 U.S.	56 S. Ct.	80 L. Ed.
1935	297 U.S.	56 S. Ct.	80 L. Ed.
1935	298 U.S.	56 S. Ct.	80 L. Ed.
1936	299 U.S.	57 S. Ct.	81 L. Ed.
1936	300 U.S.	57 S. Ct.	81 L. Ed.
1936	301 U.S.	57 S. Ct.	81 L. Ed.
1937	302 U.S.	58 S. Ct.	82 L. Ed.
1937	303 U.S.	58 S. Ct.	82 L. Ed.
1937	304 U.S.	58 S. Ct.	82 L. Ed.
1938	305 U.S.	59 S. Ct.	83 L. Ed.
1938	306 U.S.	59 S. Ct.	83 L. Ed.
1938	307 U.S.	59 S. Ct.	83 L. Ed.
1939	308 U.S.	60 S. Ct.	84 L. Ed.
1939	309 U.S.	60 S. Ct.	84 L. Ed.
1939	310 U.S.	60 S. Ct.	84 L. Ed.
1940	311 U.S.	61 S. Ct.	85 L. Ed.
1940	312 U.S.	61 S. Ct.	85 L. Ed.
1941	313 U.S.	61 S. Ct.	85 L. Ed.
1941	314 U.S.	62 S. Ct.	86 L. Ed.
1941	315 U.S.	62 S. Ct.	86 L. Ed.
1942	316 U.S.	62 S. Ct.	86 L. Ed.
1942	317 U.S.	63 S. Ct.	87 L. Ed.
1942	318 U.S.	63 S. Ct.	87 L. Ed.
1942	319 U.S.	63 S. Ct.	87 L. Ed.
1943	320 U.S.	63 S. Ct.	87 L. Ed.
1943	320 U.S.	63 S. Ct.	88 L. Ed.
1943	320 U.S.	64 S. Ct.	88 L. Ed.
1943	321 U.S.	64 S. Ct.	88 L. Ed.
1943	322 U.S.	64 S. Ct.	88 L. Ed.
1944	323 U.S.	65 S. Ct.	89 L. Ed.
1945	324 U.S.	65 S. Ct.	89 L. Ed.
1945	325 U.S.	65 S. Ct.	89 L. Ed.
1945	326 U.S.	65 S. Ct.	89 L. Ed.
1945	326 U.S.	65 S. Ct.	90 L. Ed.
1945	326 U.S.	66 S. Ct.	90 L. Ed.
1946	327 U.S.	66 S. Ct.	90 L. Ed.
1946	328 U.S.	66 S. Ct.	90 L. Ed.
1946	329 U.S.	67 S. Ct.	91 L. Ed.
1947	330 U.S.	67 S. Ct.	91 L. Ed.
1947	331 U.S.	67 S. Ct.	91 L. Ed.
1947	332 U.S.	67 S. Ct.	91 L. Ed.
1947	332 U.S.	67 S. Ct.	92 L. Ed.
1947	332 U.S.	68 S. Ct.	92 L. Ed.
1948	333 U.S.	68 S. Ct.	92 L. Ed.
1948	334 U.S.	68 S. Ct.	92 L. Ed.
1948	335 U.S.	68 S. Ct.	92 L. Ed.
1948	335 U.S.	69 S. Ct.	93 L. Ed.
1949	336 U.S.	69 S. Ct.	93 L. Ed.
1949	337 U.S.	69 S. Ct.	93 L. Ed.
1949	338 U.S.	69 S. Ct.	93 L. Ed.
1949	338 U.S.	69 S. Ct.	94 L. Ed.
1949	338 U.S.	70 S. Ct.	94 L. Ed.

Term or Year of Decision	Government Printing Office	Nominative Reporters & West	LCP
1950	339 U.S.	70 S. Ct.	94 L. Ed.
1950	340 U.S.	71 S. Ct.	95 L. Ed.
1951	341 U.S.	71 S. Ct.	95 L. Ed.
1951	342 U.S.	72 S. Ct.	96 L. Ed.
1952	343 U.S.	72 S. Ct.	96 L. Ed.
1952	344 U.S.	73 S. Ct.	97 L. Ed.
1953	345 U.S.	73 S. Ct.	97 L. Ed.
1953	346 U.S.	73 S. Ct.	97 L. Ed.
1953	346 U.S.	74 S. Ct.	98 L. Ed.
1954	347 U.S.	74 S. Ct.	98 L. Ed.
1954	348 U.S.	75 S. Ct.	99 L. Ed.
1955	349 U.S.	75 S. Ct.	99 L. Ed.
1955	350 U.S.	76 S. Ct.	100 L. Ed.
1956	351 U.S.	76 S. Ct.	100 L. Ed.
1956	352 U.S.	77 S. Ct.	1 L. Ed. 2d
1957	353 U.S.	77 S. Ct.	1 L. Ed. 2d
1957	354 U.S.	77 S. Ct.	1 L. Ed. 2d
1957	355 U.S.	78 S. Ct.	2 L. Ed. 2d
1958	356 U.S.	78 S. Ct.	2 L. Ed. 2d
1958	357 U.S.	78 S. Ct.	2 L. Ed. 2d
1958	358 U.S.	78 S. Ct.	3 L. Ed. 2d
1958	358 U.S.	79 S. Ct.	3 L. Ed. 2d
1959	359 U.S.	79 S. Ct.	3 L. Ed. 2d
1959	360 U.S.	79 S. Ct.	3 L. Ed. 2d
1959	361 U.S.	80 S. Ct.	4 L. Ed. 2d
1960	362 U.S.	80 S. Ct.	4 L. Ed. 2d
1960	363 U.S.	80 S. Ct.	4 L. Ed. 2d
1960	364 U.S.	80 S. Ct.	4 L. Ed. 2d
1960	364 U.S.	81 S. Ct.	5 L. Ed. 2d
1961	365 U.S.	81 S. Ct.	5 L. Ed. 2d
1961	365 U.S.	81 S. Ct.	6 L. Ed. 2d
1961	366 U.S.	81 S. Ct.	6 L. Ed. 2d
1961	367 U.S.	81 S. Ct.	6 L. Ed. 2d
1961	368 U.S.	82 S. Ct.	7 L. Ed. 2d
1962	369 U.S.	82 S. Ct.	7 L. Ed. 2d
1962	369 U.S.	82 S. Ct.	8 L. Ed. 2d
1962	370 U.S.	82 S. Ct.	8 L. Ed. 2d
1962	371 U.S.	83 S. Ct.	9 L. Ed. 2d
1963	372 U.S.	83 S. Ct.	10 L. Ed. 2d
1963	373 U.S.	83 S. Ct.	10 L. Ed. 2d
1963	374 U.S.	83 S. Ct.	10 L. Ed. 2d
1963	375 U.S.	84 S. West	11 L. Ed. 2d
1964	376 U.S.	84 S. Ct.	11 L. Ed. 2d
1964	376 U.S.	84 S. Ct.	12 L. Ed. 2d
1964	377 U.S.	84 S. Ct.	12 L. Ed. 2d
1964	378 U.S.	84 S. Ct.	12 L. Ed. 2d
1964	379 U.S.	85 S. Ct.	13 L. Ed. 2d
1965	380 U.S.	85 S. Ct.	13 L. Ed. 2d
1965	380 U.S.	85 S. Ct.	14 L. Ed. 2d
1965	381 U.S.	85 S. Ct.	14 L. Ed. 2d
1965	382 U.S.	86 S. Ct.	15 L. Ed. 2d
1966	383 U.S.	86 S. Ct.	15 L. Ed. 2d
1966	383 U.S.	86 S. Ct.	16 L. Ed. 2d
1966	384 U.S.	86 S. Ct.	16 L. Ed. 2d
1966	385 U.S.	87 S. Ct.	17 L. Ed. 2d
1967	386 U.S.	87 S. Ct.	17 L. Ed. 2d
1967	386 U.S.	87 S. Ct.	18 L. Ed. 2d
1967	387 U.S.	87 S. Ct.	18 L. Ed. 2d
1967	388 U.S.	87 S. Ct.	18 L. Ed. 2d
1967	389 U.S.	88 S. Ct.	19 L. Ed. 2d
1968	390 U.S.	88 S. Ct.	19 L. Ed. 2d
1968	390 U.S.	88 S. Ct.	20 L. Ed. 2d
1968	391 U.S.	88 S. Ct.	20 L. Ed. 2d

Term or Year of Decision	Government Printing Office	Nominative Reporters & West	LCP
1968	392 U.S.	88 S. Ct.	20 L. Ed. 2d
1968	393 U.S.	89 S. Ct.	21 L. Ed. 2d
1969	393 U.S.	89 S. Ct.	22 L. Ed. 2d
1969	394 U.S.	89 S. Ct.	22 L. Ed. 2d
1969	394 U.S.	89 S. Ct.	23 L. Ed. 2d
1969	395 U.S.	89 S. Ct.	23 L. Ed. 2d
1969	396 U.S.	90 S. Ct.	24 L. Ed. 2d
1970	397 U.S.	90 S. Ct.	25 L. Ed. 2d
1970	398 U.S.	90 S. Ct.	26 L. Ed. 2d
1970	399 U.S.	90 S. Ct.	26 L. Ed. 2d
1970	400 U.S.	91 S. Ct.	27 L. Ed. 2d
1971	401 U.S.	91 S. Ct.	27 L. Ed. 2d
1971	401 U.S.	91 S. Ct.	28 L. Ed. 2d
1971	402 U.S.	91 S. Ct.	28 L. Ed. 2d
1971	402 U.S.	91 S. Ct.	29 L. Ed. 2d
1971	403 U.S.	91 S. Ct.	29 L. Ed. 2d
1971	404 U.S.	92 S. Ct.	30 L. Ed. 2d
1971	404 U.S.	92 S. Ct.	31 L. Ed. 2d
1972	405 U.S.	92 S. Ct.	30 L. Ed. 2d
1972	405 U.S.	92 S. Ct.	31 L. Ed. 2d
1972	406 U.S.	92 S. Ct.	31 L. Ed. 2d
1972	406 U.S.	92 S. Ct.	32 L. Ed. 2d
1972	407 U.S.	92 S. Ct.	32 L. Ed. 2d
1972	407 U.S.	92 S. Ct.	33 L. Ed. 2d
1972	408 U.S.	92 S. Ct.	33 L. Ed. 2d
1972	409 U.S.	93 S. Ct.	34 L. Ed. 2d
1973	409 U.S.	93 S. Ct.	35 L. Ed. 2d
1973	410 U.S.	93 S. Ct.	35 L. Ed. 2d
1973	410 U.S.	93 S. Ct.	36 L. Ed. 2d
1973	411 U.S.	93 S. Ct.	36 L. Ed. 2d
1973	412 U.S.	93 S. Ct.	36 L. Ed. 2d
1973	412 U.S.	93 S. Ct.	37 L. Ed. 2d
1973	413 U.S.	93 S. Ct.	37 L. Ed. 2d
1973	414 U.S.	94 S. Ct.	38 L. Ed. 2d
1974	414 U.S.	94 S. Ct.	39 L. Ed. 2d
1974	415 U.S.	94 S. Ct.	39 L. Ed. 2d
1974	416 U.S.	94 S. Ct.	39 L. Ed. 2d
1974	416 U.S.	94 S. Ct.	40 L. Ed. 2d
1974	417 U.S.	94 S. Ct.	40 L. Ed. 2d
1974	417 U.S.	94 S. Ct.	41 L. Ed. 2d
1974	418 U.S.	94 S. Ct.	41 L. Ed. 2d
1974	419 U.S.	95 S. Ct.	42 L. Ed. 2d
1975	420 U.S.	95 S. Ct.	42 L. Ed. 2d
1975	420 U.S.	95 S. Ct.	43 L. Ed. 2d
1975	421 U.S.	95 S. Ct.	43 L. Ed. 2d
1975	421 U.S.	95 S. Ct.	44 L. Ed. 2d
1975	422 U.S.	95 S. Ct.	44 L. Ed. 2d
1975	422 U.S.	95 S. Ct.	45 L. Ed. 2d
1975	423 U.S.	96 S. Ct.	46 L. Ed. 2d
1976	424 U.S.	96 S. Ct.	46 L. Ed. 2d
1976	424 U.S.	96 S. Ct.	47 L. Ed. 2d
1976	425 U.S.	96 S. Ct.	47 L. Ed. 2d
1976	425 U.S.	96 S. Ct.	48 L. Ed. 2d
1976	426 U.S.	96 S. Ct.	48 L. Ed. 2d
1976	426 U.S.	96 S. Ct.	49 L. Ed. 2d
1976	427 U.S.	96 S. Ct.	49 L. Ed. 2d
1976	428 U.S.	96 S. Ct.	49 L. Ed. 2d
1976	429 U.S.	97 S. Ct.	50 L. Ed. 2d
1977	429 U.S.	97 S. Ct.	51 L. Ed. 2d
1977	430 U.S.	97 S. Ct.	51 L. Ed. 2d
1977	430 U.S.	97 S. Ct.	52 L. Ed. 2d
1977	431 U.S.	97 S. Ct.	52 L. Ed. 2d
1977	431 U.S.	97 S. Ct.	53 L. Ed. 2d

Term or Year of Decision	Government Printing Office	Nominative Reporters & West	LCP
1977	432 U.S.	97 S. Ct.	53 L. Ed. 2d
1977	433 U.S.	97 S. Ct.	53 L. Ed. 2d
1977	434 U.S.	98 S. Ct.	54 L. Ed. 2d
1978	434 U.S.	98 S. Ct.	55 L. Ed. 2d
1978	435 U.S.	98 S. Ct.	55 L. Ed. 2d
1978	435 U.S.	98 S. Ct.	56 L. Ed. 2d
1978	436 U.S.	98 S. Ct.	56 L. Ed. 2d
1978	437 U.S.	98 S. Ct.	57 L. Ed. 2d
1978	438 U.S.	98 S. Ct.	57 L. Ed. 2d
1978	439 U.S.	99 S. Ct.	58 L. Ed. 2d
1979	439 U.S.	99 S. Ct.	59 L. Ed. 2d
1979	440 U.S.	99 S. Ct.	59 L. Ed. 2d
1979	441 U.S.	99 S. Ct.	60 L. Ed. 2d
1979	442 U.S.	99 S. Ct.	60 L. Ed. 2d
1979	442 U.S.	99 S. Ct.	61 L. Ed. 2d
1979	443 U.S.	99 S. Ct.	61 L. Ed. 2d
1979	444 U.S.	100 S. Ct.	62 L. Ed. 2d
1980	444 U.S.	100 S. Ct.	63 L. Ed. 2d
1980	445 U.S.	100 S. Ct.	63 L. Ed. 2d
1980	446 U.S.	100 S. Ct.	64 L. Ed. 2d
1980	447 U.S.	100 S. Ct.	64 L. Ed. 2d
1980	447 U.S.	100 S. Ct.	65 L. Ed. 2d
1980	448 U.S.	100 S. Ct.	65 L. Ed. 2d
1980	449 U.S.	101 S. Ct.	66 L. Ed. 2d
1981	450 U.S.	101 S. Ct.	67 L. Ed. 2d
1981	451 U.S.	101 S. Ct.	67 L. Ed. 2d
1981	451 U.S.	101 S. Ct.	68 L. Ed. 2d
1981	452 U.S.	101 S. Ct.	68 L. Ed. 2d
1981	452 U.S.	101 S. Ct.	69 L. Ed. 2d
1981	453 U.S.	101 S. Ct.	69 L. Ed. 2d
1981	454 U.S.	102 S. Ct.	70 L. Ed. 2d
1982	455 U.S.	102 S. Ct.	70 L. Ed. 2d
1982	455 U.S.	102 S. Ct.	71 L. Ed. 2d
1982	456 U.S.	102 S. Ct.	71 L. Ed. 2d
1982	456 U.S.	102 S. Ct.	72 L. Ed. 2d
1982	457 U.S.	102 S. Ct.	72 L. Ed. 2d
1982	457 U.S.	102 S. Ct.	73 L. Ed. 2d
1982	458 U.S.	102 S. Ct.	73 L. Ed. 2d
1982	459 U.S.	103 S. Ct.	74 L. Ed. 2d
1983	460 U.S.	103 S. Ct.	74 L. Ed. 2d
1983	460 U.S.	103 S. Ct.	75 L. Ed. 2d
1983	461 U.S.	103 S. Ct.	75 L. Ed. 2d
1983	461 U.S.	103 S. Ct.	76 L. Ed. 2d
1983	462 U.S.	103 S. Ct.	76 L. Ed. 2d
1983	462 U.S.	103 S. Ct.	77 L. Ed. 2d
1983	463 U.S.	103 S. Ct.	77 L. Ed. 2d
1983	463 U.S.	104 S. Ct.	77 L. Ed. 2d
1983	464 U.S.	104 S. Ct.	78 L. Ed. 2d
1984	465 U.S.	104 S. Ct.	79 L. Ed. 2d
1984	466 U.S.	104 S. Ct.	80 L. Ed. 2d
1984	467 U.S.	104 S. Ct.	81 L. Ed. 2d
1984	468 U.S.	104 S. Ct.	82 L. Ed. 2d
1984	468 U.S.	105 S. Ct.	82 L. Ed. 2d
1984	469 U.S.	105 S. Ct.	83 L. Ed. 2d
1985	470 U.S.	105 S. Ct.	84 L. Ed. 2d
1985	471 U.S.	105 S. Ct.	85 L. Ed. 2d
1985	472 U.S.	105 S. Ct.	86 L. Ed. 2d
1985	473 U.S.	105 S. Ct.	87 L. Ed. 2d
1985	473 U.S.	106 S. Ct.	87 L. Ed. 2d
1985	474 U.S.	106 S. Ct.	88 L. Ed. 2d
1986	475 U.S.	106 S. Ct.	89 L. Ed. 2d
1986	476 U.S.	106 S. Ct.	90 L. Ed. 2d
1986	477 U.S.	106 S. Ct.	91 L. Ed. 2d

Term or Year of Decision	Government Printing Office	Nominative Reporters & West	LCP
1986	478 U.S.	106 S. Ct.	92 L. Ed. 2d
1986	478 U.S.	107 S. Ct.	92 L. Ed. 2d
1986	479 U.S.	107 S. Ct.	93 L. Ed. 2d
1987	480 U.S.	107 S. Ct.	94 L. Ed. 2d
1987	481 U.S.	107 S. Ct.	95 L. Ed. 2d
1987	482 U.S.	107 S. Ct.	96 L. Ed. 2d
1987	483 U.S.	107 S. Ct.	97 L. Ed. 2d
1987	484 U.S.	108 S. Ct.	98 L. Ed. 2d
1988	485 U.S.	108 S. Ct.	99 L. Ed. 2d
1988	486 U.S.	108 S. Ct.	100 L. Ed. 2d
1988	487 U.S.	108 S. Ct.	101 L. Ed. 2d
1988	488 U.S.	109 S. Ct.	102 L. Ed. 2d
1989	489 U.S.	109 S. Ct.	103 L. Ed. 2d
1989	490 U.S.	109 S. Ct.	104 L. Ed. 2d
1989	491 U.S.	109 S. Ct.	105 L. Ed. 2d
1989	492 U.S.	109 S. Ct.	106 L. Ed. 2d
1989	493 U.S.	110 S. Ct.	107 L. Ed. 2d
1990	494 U.S.	110 S. Ct.	108 L. Ed. 2d
1990	495 U.S.	110 S. Ct.	109 L. Ed. 2d
1990	496 U.S.	110 S. Ct.	110 L. Ed. 2d
1990	497 U.S.	110 S. Ct.	111 L. Ed. 2d
1990	498 U.S.	111 S. Ct.	112 L. Ed. 2d
1991	499 U.S.	111 S. Ct.	113 L. Ed. 2d
1991	500 U.S.	111 S. Ct.	114 L. Ed. 2d
1991	501 U.S.	111 S. Ct.	115 L. Ed. 2d

APPENDIX III Table of Selected State Law Sources

ALABAMA (AL) {Ala.}†

Federal Circuit: Eleventh {11th Cir.} (Atlanta, GA)
Federal Districts: Northern, Middle, Southern
All Courts:
    West Region: Southern Reporter {So. 2d.}
    On LEXIS: ALA;CASES
    On WESTLAW: AL-CS
High Court:
*Supreme Court {Ala.}
    Official Reporter: Southern Reporter {So. 2d}
Intermediate Courts:
*Court of Civil Appeals {Ala. Civ. App.}
    Official Reporter: Southern Reporter {So. 2d}
*Court of Criminal Appeals {Ala. Crim. App.}
    Official Reporter: Southern Reporter {So. 2d}
Statutory Code:
*Code of Alabama (Michie) {Ala. Code § x (19xx)}
    On LEXIS: ALA;ALCODE
    On WESTLAW: AL-ST-ANN
Administrative Code:
*Alabama Administrative Code {Ala. Admin. Code r. x (19xx)}

ALASKA (AK) {Alaska}

Federal Circuit: Ninth {9th Cir.} (San Francisco, CA)
Federal District: Alaska
All Courts:
    West Region: Pacific Reporter {P.2d}
    On LEXIS: ALAS;CASES
    On WESTLAW: AK-CS
High Court:
*Supreme Court {Alaska}
    Official Reporter: Pacific Reporter {P.2d}
Intermediate Court:
*Court of Appeals {Alaska Ct. App.}
    Official Reporter: Pacific Reporter {P.2d}
Statutory Code:
*Alaska Statutes (Michie) {Alaska Stat. § x (19xx)}
    On LEXIS: ALAS;AKCODE
    On WESTLAW: AK-ST-ANN
Administrative Code:
*Alaska Administrative Code {Alaska Admin. Code tit. x, § x (month 19xx)}

†{ } = *The Bluebook: A Uniform System of Citation* Abbreviation

ARIZONA (AZ) {Ariz.}

Federal Circuit: Ninth {9th Cir.} (San Francisco, CA)
Federal District: Arizona
All Courts:
    West Region: Pacific Reporter {P.2d}
    On LEXIS: ARIZ;CASES
    On WESTLAW: AZ-CS
High Court:
*Supreme Court {Ariz.}
    Official Reporter: Arizona Reports {Ariz.}
Intermediate Court:
*Court of Appeals {Ariz. Ct. App.}
    Official Reporter: Arizona Reports {Ariz.}
Statutory Codes:
*Arizona Revised Statutes
    On LEXIS: ARIZ;AZCODE
*Arizona Revised Statutes Annotated (West) {Ariz. Rev. Stat. Ann. § x (19xx)}
    On WESTLAW: AZ-ST-ANN
Administrative Code:
*Official Compilation Administrative Rules and Regulations {Ariz. Comp. Admin. R. & Regs. x (19xx)}

ARKANSAS (AR) {Ark.}

Federal Circuit: Eighth {8th Cir.} (St. Louis, MO)
Federal Districts: Eastern, Western
All Courts:
    West Region: South Western Reporter {S.W.2d.}
    On LEXIS: ARK;CASES
    On WESTLAW: AR-CS
High Court:
*Supreme Court {Ark.}
    Official Reporter: Arkansas Reports {Ark.}
Intermediate Court:
*Court of Appeals {Ark. Ct. App.}
    Official Reporter: Arkansas Appellate Reports {Ark. App.}
Statutory Code:
*Arkansas Code of 1987 Annotated, Official Edition (Michie) {Ark. Stat. Ann. § x (19xx)}
    On LEXIS: ARK;ARCODE
    On WESTLAW: AR-ST-ANN
Administrative Code: none

CALIFORNIA (CA) {Cal.}

Federal Circuit: Ninth {9th Cir.} (San Francisco, CA)
Federal Districts: Central, Eastern, Northern, Southern
All Courts:
    West Region: Pacific Reporter {P.2d.},
              California Reporter {Cal. Rptr.}
    On LEXIS: CAL;CASES
    On WESTLAW: CA-CS
High Court:
*Supreme Court {Cal.}
    Official Reporter: California Reports {Cal. 3d}

Intermediate Court:
*Court of Appeal {Cal. Ct. App.}
    Official Reporter: California Appellate Reports {Cal. App. 3d}
Statutory Codes:
*Deering's Annotated California Code (BW) {Cal. [subject] Code § x (Deering 19xx)}
    On LEXIS: CAL;CACODE
*West's Annotated California Code {Cal. [subject] Code § x (West 19xx)}
    On WESTLAW: CA-ST-ANN
Administrative Code:
*California Administrative Code {Cal. Admin. Code tit. x, § x (19xx)}
Encyclopedia: California Jurisprudence 3d (LCP)

COLORADO (CO) {Colo.}

Federal Circuit: Tenth {10th Cir.} (Denver, CO)
Federal District: Colorado
All Courts:
    West Region: Pacific Reporter {P.2d}
    On LEXIS: COLO;CASES
    On WESTLAW: CO-CS
High Court:
*Supreme Court {Colo.}
    Official Reporter: Pacific Reporter {P.2d}
Intermediate Court:
*Court of Appeals {Colo. Ct. App.}
    Official Reporter: Pacific Reporter {P.2d}
Statutory Codes:
*Colorado Revised Statutes (Bradford) {Colo. Rev. Stat. § x (19xx)}
    On LEXIS: COLO;COCODE
*Colorado Revised Statutes Annotated (West)
    On WESTLAW: CO-ST-ANN
Administrative Code:
*Code of Colorado Regulations {x Colo. Code Regs. § x (19xx)}

CONNECTICUT (CT) {Conn.}

Federal Circuit: Second {2d Cir.} (New York, NY)
Federal District: Connecticut
All Courts:
    West Region: Atlantic Reporter {A.2d}
    On LEXIS: CONN;CASES
    On WESTLAW: CT-CS
High Court:
*Supreme Court {Conn.}
    Official Reporter: Connecticut Reports {Conn.}
Intermediate Court:
*Appellate Court {Conn. App. Ct.}
    Official Reporter: Connecticut Appellate Reports {Conn. App.}
Statutory Codes:
*Connecticut General Statutes Annotated (West) {Conn. Gen. Stat. Ann. § x (West 19xx)}
    On WESTLAW: CT-ST-ANN
*General Statutes of Connecticut {Conn. Gen. Stat. § x (19xx)}
    On LEXIS: CONN;CTCODE
Administrative Code:
*Regulations of Connecticut State Agencies {Conn. Agencies Regs. § x (19xx)}

DELAWARE (DE) {Del.}

Federal Circuit: Third {3d Cir.} (Philadelphia, PA)
Federal District: Delaware
All Courts:
    West Region: Atlantic Reporter {A.2d}
    On LEXIS: DEL;CASES
    On WESTLAW: DE-CS
High Court:
*Supreme Court {Del.}
    Official Reporter: Atlantic Reporter {A.2d}
Intermediate Court: none
Statutory Code:
*Delaware Code Annotated (Michie) {Del. Code. Ann. tit. x, § x (19xx)}
    On LEXIS: DEL;DECODE
    On WESTLAW: DE-ST-ANN
Administrative Code: none

DISTRICT OF COLUMBIA (DC) {D.C.}

Federal Circuit: District of Columbia {D.C. Cir.}
Federal District: District of Columbia
All Courts:
    West Region: Atlantic Reporter {A.2d}
    On LEXIS: DC;DCAPP
    On WESTLAW: DC-CS
High Court:
*Court of Appeals {D.C.}
    Official Reporter: Atlantic Reporter {A.2d}
Intermediate Court: none
Statutory Code:
*District of Columbia Code (Michie) {D.C. Code Ann. § x (19xx)}
    On WESTLAW: DC-ST-ANN
Administrative Code: none

FLORIDA (FL) {Fla.}

Federal Circuit: Eleventh {11th Cir.} (Atlanta, GA)
Federal Districts: Northern, Middle, Southern
All Courts:
    West Region: Southern Reporter {So. 2d}
    On LEXIS: FLA;CASES
    On WESTLAW: FL-CS
High Court:
*Supreme Court {Fla.}
    Official Reporter: Southern Reporter {So. 2d}
Intermediate Court:
*District Courts of Appeals {Fla. Dist. Ct. App.}
    Official Reporter: Southern Reporter {So. 2d}
Statutory Codes:
*Florida Statutes {Fla. Stat. § x (19xx)}
    On LEXIS: FLA;FLCODE
*West's Florida Statutes Annotated {Fla. Stat. Ann. § x (West 19xx)}
    On WESTLAW: FL-ST-ANN
Administrative Code:
*Florida Administrative Code Annotated {Fla. Admin. Code Ann. r. x (19xx)}
Encyclopedia: Florida Jurisprudence 2d (LCP)

GEORGIA (GA) {Ga.}

Federal Circuit: Eleventh {11th Cir.} (Atlanta, GA)
Federal Districts: Northern, Middle, Southern
All Courts:
    West Region: Southern Reporter {So. 2d}
    On LEXIS: GA;CASES
    On WESTLAW: GA-CS
High Court:
*Supreme Court {Ga.}
    Official Reporter: Georgia Reports {Ga.}
Intermediate Court:
*Court of Appeals {Ga. Ct. App.}
    Official Reporter: Georgia Appeals Reports {Ga. App.}
Statutory Codes:
*Official Code of Georgia Annotated (Michie) {Ga. Code Ann. § x (19xx)}
    On LEXIS: GA;GACODE
*Code of Georgia Annotated (Harrison) {Ga. Code Ann. § x (Harrison 19xx)}
    On WESTLAW: GA-ST-ANN
Administrative Code:
*Official Compilation: Rules and Regulations of the State of Georgia {Ga. Comp. R. & Regs. r. x (19xx)}

HAWAII (HI) {Haw.}

Federal Circuit: Ninth {9th Cir.} (San Francisco, CA)
Federal District: Hawaii
All Courts:
    West Region: Pacific Reporter {P.2d}
    On LEXIS: HAW;CASES
    On WESTLAW: HI-CS
High Court:
*Supreme Court {Haw.}
    Official Reporter: Hawaii Reports {Haw.}
Intermediate Court:
*Intermediate Court of Appeals {Haw. Ct. App.}
    Official Reporter: Hawaii Appellate Reports {Haw. App.}
Statutory Code:
*Hawaii Revised Statutes Annotated (Michie) {Haw. Rev. Stat. § x (19xx)}
    On LEXIS: HAW;HICODE
    On WESTLAW: HI-ST-ANN
Administrative Code: none

IDAHO (ID) {Idaho}

Federal Circuit: Ninth {9th Cir.} (San Francisco, CA)
Federal District: Idaho
All Courts:
    West Region: Pacific Reporter {P.2d}
    On LEXIS: IDA;CASES
    On WESTLAW: ID-CS
High Court:
*Supreme Court {Idaho}
    Official Reporter: Idaho Reports {Idaho}

Intermediate Court:
*Court of Appeals {Idaho Ct. App.}
    Official Reporter: Idaho Reports {Idaho}
Statutory Code:
*Idaho Official Code (Michie) {Idaho Code § x (19xx)}
    On LEXIS: IDA;IDCODE
    On WESTLAW: ID-ST-ANN
Administrative Code: none

ILLINOIS (IL) {Ill.}

Federal Circuit: Seventh {7th Cir.} (Chicago, IL)
Federal Districts: Northern, Central, Southern
All Courts:
    West Region: North Eastern Reporter {N.E.2d}
    On LEXIS: ILL;CASES
    On WESTLAW: IL-CS
High Court:
*Supreme Court {Ill.}
    Official Reporter: Illinois Reports {Ill. 2d}
Intermediate Court:
*Appellate Court {Ill. App. Ct.}
    Official Reporter: Illinois Appellate Reports {Ill. App. 3d}
Statutory Codes:
*Illinois Revised Statutes {Ill. Rev. Stat. ch. x, para. x (19xx)}
    On LEXIS: ILL;ILCODE
*Smith-Hurd Illinois Annotated Statutes (West) {Ill. Ann. Stat. ch. x, para. x (Smith-Hurd 19xx)}
    On WESTLAW: IL-ST-ANN
Administrative Code:
*Illinois Administrative Code {Ill. Admin. Code tit. x, § x (19xx)}
Encyclopedia: Illinois Law and Practice (West)

INDIANA (IN) {Ind.}

Federal Circuit: Seventh {7th Cir.} (Chicago, IL)
Federal Districts: Northern, Southern
All Courts:
    West Region: North Eastern Reporter {N.E.2d}
    On LEXIS: IND;CASES
    On WESTLAW: IN-CS
High Court:
*Supreme Court {Ind.}
    Official Reporter: North Eastern Reporter {N.E.2d}
Intermediate Court:
*Court of Appeals {Ind. Ct. App.}
    Official Reporter: North Eastern Reporter {N.E.2d}
Statutory Codes:
*Burns Indiana Statutes Annotated (Michie) {Ind. Code Ann. § x (Burns 19xx)}
    On LEXIS: IND;INCODE
    On WESTLAW: IN-STB-ANN
*Indiana Code {Ind. Code Ann. § x (19xx)}
*West's Annotated Indiana Code {Ind. Code Ann. § x (West 19xx)}
    On WESTLAW: IN-ST-ANN
Administrative Code:
*Indiana Administrative Code {Ind. Admin. Code tit. x, r. x (19xx)}

State Law Sources

IOWA (IA) {Iowa}

Federal Circuit: Eighth {8th Cir.} (St. Louis, MO)
Federal Districts: Northern, Southern
All Courts:
    West Region: North Western Reporter {N.W.2d}
    On LEXIS: IOWA;CASES
    On WESTLAW: IA-CS
High Court:
*Supreme Court {Iowa}
    Official Reporter: North Western Reporter {N.W.2d}
Intermediate Court:
*Court of Appeals {Iowa Ct. App.}
    Official Reporter: North Western Reporter {N.W.2d}
Statutory Codes:
*Code of Iowa {Iowa Code § x (19xx)}
    On LEXIS: IOWA;IACODE
*Iowa Code Annotated (West) {Iowa Code Ann. § x (West 19xx)}
    On WESTLAW: IA-ST-ANN
Administrative Code:
*Iowa Administrative Code {Iowa Admin. Code r. x-x.x (19xx)}

KANSAS (KS) {Kan.}

Federal Circuit: Tenth {10th Cir.} (Denver, CO)
Federal District: Kansas
All Courts:
    West Region: Pacific Reporter {P.2d}
    On LEXIS: KAN;CASES
    On WESTLAW: KS-CS
High Court:
*Supreme Court {Kan.}
    Official Reporter: Kansas Reports {Kan.}
Intermediate Court:
*Court of Appeals {Kan. Ct. App.}
    Official Reporter: Kansas Court of Appeals Reports {Kan. App.}
Statutory Codes:
*Kansas Statutes Annotated {Kan. Stat. Ann. § x (19xx)}
    On LEXIS: KAN;KSCODE
*Vernon's Kansas Statutes Annotated (West) {varies}
Administrative Code:
*Kansas Administrative Regulations {Kan. Admin. Regs. x (19xx)}

KENTUCKY (KY) {Ky.}

Federal Circuit: Sixth {6th Cir.} (Cincinnati, OH)
Federal Districts: Eastern, Western
All Courts:
    West Region: South Western Reporter {S.W.2d}
    On LEXIS: KY;CASES
    On WESTLAW: KY-CS
High Court:
*Supreme Court {Ky.}
    Official Reporter: South Western Reporter {S.W.2d}
Intermediate Court:

*Court of Appeals {Ky. Ct. App.}
    Official Reporter: South Western Reporter {S.W.2d}
Statutory Codes:
*Baldwin's Official Edition, Kentucky Revised Statutes Annotated
(Banks-Baldwin) {Ky. Rev. Stat. Ann. § x (Baldwin 19xx)}
    On LEXIS: KY;KYCODE
    On WESTLAW: KY-ST-ANN
*Kentucky Revised Statutes Annotated, Official Edition (Michie) {Ky. Rev.
Stat. Ann. § x (Michie/Bobbs-Merrill 19xx)}
    On LEXIS: KY;KYSTAT
Administrative Code:
*Kentucky Administrative Regulations Service {x Ky. Admin. Regs. x:x (19xx)}
Encyclopedia: Kentucky Jurisprudence (LCP)

LOUISIANA (LA) {La.}

Federal Circuit: Fifth {5th Cir.} (New Orleans, LA)
Federal Districts: Eastern, Middle, Western
All Courts:
    West Region: Southern Reporter {So. 2d}
    On LEXIS: LA;CASES
    On WESTLAW: LA-CS
High Court:
*Supreme Court {La.}
    Official Reporter: none {cite to So. 2d}
Intermediate Court:
*Court of Appeal {La. Ct. App.}
    Official Reporter: none {cite to So. 2d}
Statutory Codes:
*Louisiana Statutes
    On LEXIS: LA;LACODE
*West's Louisiana Statutes Annotated {La. Rev. Stat. Ann. § x (West 19xx)}
    On WESTLAW: LA-ST-ANN
Administrative Code:
*Louisiana Administrative Code {La. Admin. Code tit. x, § x (19xx)}

MAINE (ME) {Me.}

Federal Circuit: First {1st Cir.} (Boston, MA)
Federal District: Maine
All Courts:
    West Region: Atlantic Reporter {A.2d}
    On LEXIS: ME;ME
    On WESTLAW: ME-CS
High Court:
*Supreme Judicial Court {Me.}
    Official Reporter: Atlantic Reporter {A.2d}
Intermediate Court: none
Statutory Codes:
*Maine Revised Statutes
    On LEXIS: ME;MECODE
*Maine Revised Statutes Annotated (West) {Me. Rev. Stat. Ann. tit. x, § x
(19xx)}
    On WESTLAW: ME-ST-ANN
Administrative Code: none

MARYLAND (MD) {Md.}

Federal Circuit: Fourth {4th Cir.} (Richmond, VA)
Federal District: Maryland
All Courts:
> West Region: Atlantic Reporter {A.2d}
> On LEXIS: MD;CASES
> On WESTLAW: MD-CS

High Court:
*Court of Appeals {Md.}
> Official Reporter: Maryland Reports {Md.}

Intermediate Court:
*Court of Special Appeals {Md. Ct. Spec. App.}
> Official Reporter: Maryland Appellate Reports {Md. App.}

Statutory Code:
*Annotated Code of Maryland (Michie) {Md. [subject] Code Ann. § x (19xx)}
> On LEXIS: MD;MDCODE
> On WESTLAW: MD-ST-ANN

Administrative Code:
*Code of Maryland Regulations {Md. Regs. Code tit. x, § x (19xx)}
Encyclopedia: Maryland Law and Practice (West)

MASSACHUSETTS (MA) {Mass.}

Federal Circuit: First {1st Cir.} (Boston, MA)
Federal District: Massachusetts
All Courts:
> West Region: North Eastern Reporter {N.E.2d}
> On LEXIS: MASS;CASES
> On WESTLAW: MA-CS

High Court:
*Supreme Judicial Court {Mass.}
> Official Reporter: Massachusetts Reports {Mass.}

Intermediate Court:
*Appeals Court {Mass. App. Ct.}
> Official Reporter: Massachusetts Appeals Court Reports {Mass. App. Ct.}

Statutory Codes:
*Annotated Laws of Massachusetts (LCP) {Mass. Ann. Laws ch. x, § x (Law. Co-op. 19xx)}
*General Laws of the Commonwealth of Massachusetts (LCP) {Mass. Gen. L. ch. x, § x (19xx)}
*Massachusetts General Laws Annotated (West) {Mass. Gen. Laws Ann. ch. x, § x (West 19xx)}
> On WESTLAW: MA-ST-ANN

Administrative Code:
*Code of Massachusetts Regulations {Mass. Regs. Code tit. x, § x (19xx)}

MICHIGAN (MI) {Mich.}

Federal Circuit: Sixth {6th Cir.} (Cincinnati, OH)
Federal Districts: Eastern, Western
All Courts:
> West Region: North Western Reporter {N.W.2d}
> On LEXIS: MICH;CASES
> On WESTLAW: MI-CS

High Court:
*Supreme Court {Mich.}
    Official Reporter: Michigan Reports {Mich.}
Intermediate Court:
*Court of Appeals {Mich. Ct. App.}
    Official Reporter: Michigan Appeals Reports {Mich. App.}
Statutory Codes:
*Michigan Compiled Laws {Mich. Comp. Laws § x (19xx)}
    On LEXIS: MICH;MICODE
*Michigan Compiled Laws Annotated (West) {Mich. Comp. Laws Ann. § x (West 19xx)}
    On WESTLAW: MI-ST-ANN
*Michigan Statutes Annotated (Callaghan) {Mich. Stat. Ann. § x (Callaghan 19xx)}
Administrative Code:
*Michigan Administrative Code {Mich. Admin. Code r. x (19xx)}
Encyclopedia: Michigan Law and Practice (West)

MINNESOTA (MN) {Minn.}

Federal Circuit: Eighth {8th Cir.} (St. Louis, MO)
Federal District: Minnesota
All Courts:
    West Region: North Western Reporter {N.W.2d}
    On LEXIS: MINN;CASES
    On WESTLAW: MN-CS
High Court:
*Supreme Court {Minn.}
    Official Reporter: North Western Reporter {N.W.2d}
Intermediate Court:
*Court of Appeals {Minn. Ct. App.}
    Official Reporter: North Western Reporter {N.W.2d}
Statutory Codes:
*Minnesota Statutes {Minn. Stat. § x (19xx)}
    On LEXIS: MINN;MNCODE
*Minnesota Statutes Annotated (West) {Minn. Stat. Ann. § x (West 19xx)}
    On WESTLAW: MN-ST
Administrative Code:
*Minnesota Rules {Minn. R. x.x (19xx)}

MISSISSIPPI (MS) {Miss.}

Federal Circuit: Fifth {5th Cir.} (New Orleans, LA)
Federal Districts: Northern, Southern
All Courts:
    West Region: Southern Reporter {So.2d}
    On LEXIS: MISS;MISS
    On WESTLAW: MS-CS
High Court:
*Supreme Court {Miss.}
    Official Reporter: Southern Reporter {So. 2d}
Intermediate Court: none
Statutory Code:
*Mississippi Code Annotated (LCP) {Miss. Code Ann. § x (19xx)}
Administrative Code: none

MISSOURI (MO) {Mo.}

Federal Circuit: Eighth {8th Cir.} (St. Louis, MO)
Federal Districts: Eastern, Western
All Courts:
    West Region: South Western Reporter {S.W.2d}
    On LEXIS: MO;CASES
    On WESTLAW: MO-CS
High Court:
*Supreme Court {Mo.}
    Official Reporter: South Western Reporter {S.W.2d}
Intermediate Court:
*Court of Appeals {Mo. Ct. App.}
    Official Reporter: South Western Reporter {S.W.2d}
Statutory Codes:
*Missouri Revised Statutes {Mo. Rev. Stat. § x (19xx)}
    On LEXIS: MO;MOCODE
*Vernon's Annotated Missouri Statutes (West) {Mo. Ann. Stat. § x (Vernon 19xx)}
    On WESTLAW: MO-ST-ANN
Administrative Code:
*Missouri Code of State Regulations {Mo. Code Regs. tit. x, § x-x.x (19xx)}

MONTANA (MT) {Mont.}

Federal Circuit: Ninth {9th Cir.} (San Francisco, CA)
Federal District: Montana
All Courts:
    West Region: Pacific Reporter {P.2d}
    On LEXIS: MONT;CASES
    On WESTLAW: MT-CS
High Court:
*Supreme Court {Mont.}
    Official Reporter: Montana Reports {Mont.}
Intermediate Court: none
Statutory Code:
*Montana Code Annotated {Mont. Code Ann. § x (19xx)}
    On LEXIS: MONT;MTCODE
Administrative Code:
*Administrative Rules of Montana {Mont. Admin. R. x (19xx)}

NEBRASKA (NE) {Neb.}

Federal Circuit: Eighth {8th Cir.} (St. Louis, MO)
Federal District: Nebraska
All Courts:
    West Region: North Western Reporter {N.W.2d}
    On LEXIS: NEB;NEB
    On WESTLAW: NE-CS
High Court:
*Supreme Court {Neb.}
    Official Reporter: Nebraska Reports {Neb.}
Intermediate Court: none

Statutory Code:
*Revised Statutes of Nebraska {Neb. Rev. Stat. § x (19xx)}
    On LEXIS: NEB;NECODE
    On WESTLAW: NE-ST
Administrative Code:
*Nebraska Administrative Rules & Regulations {Neb. Admin. R. & Regs. x (19xx)}

NEVADA (NV) {Nev.}

Federal Circuit: Ninth {9th Cir.} (San Francisco, CA)
Federal District: Nevada
All Courts:
    West Region: Pacific Reporter {P.2d}
    On LEXIS: NEV;NEV
    On WESTLAW: NV-CS
High Court:
*Supreme Court {Nev.}
    Official Reporter: Nevada Reports {Nev.}
Intermediate Court: none
Statutory Codes:
*Nevada Revised Statutes {Nev. Rev. Stat. § x (19xx)}
    On WESTLAW: NV-ST-ANN
*Nevada Revised Statutes Annotated (Michie) {Nev. Rev. Stat. Ann. § x (Michie 19xx)}
    On LEXIS: NEV;NVCODE
Administrative Code:
*Nevada Administrative Code {Nev. Admin. Code ch. x, § x (19xx)}

NEW HAMPSHIRE (NH) {N.H.}

Federal Circuit: First {1st Cir.} (Boston, MA)
Federal District: New Hampshire
All Courts:
    West Region: Atlantic Reporter {A.2d}
    On LEXIS: NH;CASES
    On WESTLAW: NH-CS
High Court:
*Supreme Court {N.H.}
    Official Reporter: New Hampshire Reports {N.H.}
Intermediate Court: none
Statutory Code:
*New Hampshire Revised Statutes Annotated (Equity) {N.H. Rev. Stat. Ann. § x (19xx)}
    On WESTLAW: NH-ST-ANN
Administrative Code:
*New Hampshire Code of Administrative Rules {N.H. Code Admin. R. [abbrev. dep't name] x.x (19xx)}

NEW JERSEY (NJ) {N.J.}

Federal Circuit: Third {3d Cir.} (Philadelphia, PA)
Federal District: New Jersey

All Courts:
    West Region: Atlantic Reporter {A.2d}
    On LEXIS: NJ;CASES
    On WESTLAW: NJ-CS
High Court:
*Supreme Court {N.J.}
    Official Reporter: New Jersey Reports {N.J.}
Intermediate Court:
*Appellate Division, Superior Court {N.J. Super. Ct. App. Div.}
    Official Reporters:*New Jersey Superior Court Reports {N.J. Super.}
                       *New Jersey Equity Reports {N.J. Eq.}
Statutory Codes:
*New Jersey Statutes {N.J. Rev. Stat. § x (19xx)}
    On LEXIS: NJ;NJCODE
*New Jersey Statutes Annotated (West) {N.J. Stat. Ann. § x (West 19xx)}
    On WESTLAW: NJ-ST-ANN
Administrative Code:
*New Jersey Administrative Code {N.J. Admin. Code tit. x, § x-x.x (19xx)}

NEW MEXICO (NM) {N.M.}

Federal Circuit: Tenth {10th Cir.} (Denver, CO)
Federal District: New Mexico
All Courts:
    West Region: Pacific Reporter {P.2d}
    On LEXIS: NM;CASES
    On WESTLAW: NM-CS
High Court:
*Supreme Court {N.M.}
    Official Reporter: New Mexico Reports {N.M.}
Intermediate Court:
*Court of Appeal {N.M. Ct. App.}
    Official Reporter: New Mexico Reports {N.M.}
Statutory Code:
*New Mexico Statutes Annotated (Michie) {N.M. Stat. Ann. § x (19xx)}
    On LEXIS: NM;NMCODE
    On WESTLAW: NM-ST-ANN
Administrative Code: none

NEW YORK (NY) {N.Y.}

Federal Circuit: Second {2d Cir.} (New York, NY)
Federal Districts: Eastern, Northern, Southern, Western
All Courts:
    West Region: North Eastern Reporter {N.E.2d},
            West's New York Supplement {N.Y.S.2d}
    On LEXIS: NY;CASES
    On WESTLAW: NY-CS
High Court:
*Court of Appeals {N.Y.}
    Official Reporter: New York Reports {N.Y.}
Intermediate Court:
*Appellate Division, Supreme Court {N.Y. App. Div.}
    Official Reporter: Appellate Division Reports {A.D.2d}

Statutory Codes:
*McKinney's Consolidated Laws of New York Annotated (West) {N.Y. [subject] Law § x (McKinney 19xx)}
    On WESTLAW: NY-ST-ANN
*New York Consolidated Laws (Michie) {N.Y. [subject] Law § x (Consol. 19xx)}
    On LEXIS: NY;NYCODE
*New York Consolidated Laws Service (LCP) {N.Y. [subject] Law § x (Consol. 19xx)}
Administrative Code:
*Official Compilation of Codes, Rules & Regulations of the State of New York {N.Y. Comp. Codes R. & Regs. tit. x, § x (19xx)}
Encyclopedia: New York Jurisprudence 2d (LCP)

NORTH CAROLINA (NC) {N.C.}

Federal Circuit: Fourth {4th Cir.} (Richmond, VA)
Federal Districts: Eastern, Middle, Western
All Courts:
    West Region: South Eastern Reporter {S.E.2d}
        On LEXIS: NC;CASES
        On WESTLAW: NC-CS
High Court:
*Supreme Court {N.C.}
    Official Reporter: North Carolina Reports {N.C.}
Intermediate Court:
*Court of Appeals {N.C. Ct. App.}
    Official Reporter: N.C. Court of Appeals Reports {N.C. App.}
Statutory Code:
*General Statutes of North Carolina (Michie) {N.C. Gen. Stat. § x (19xx)}
    On LEXIS: NC;NCCODE
    On WESTLAW: NC-ST-ANN
Administrative Code:
*North Carolina Administrative Code (microfiche) {N.C. Admin. Code tit. x, r. xx.xxxx (month 19xx)}

NORTH DAKOTA (ND) {N.D.}

Federal Circuit: Eighth {8th Cir.} (St. Louis, MO)
Federal District: North Dakota
All Courts:
    West Region: North Western Reporter {N.W.2d}
        On LEXIS: ND;CASES
        On WESTLAW: ND-CS
High Court:
*Supreme Court {N.D.}
    Official Reporter: North Western Reporter {N.W.2d}
Intermediate Court: none
Statutory Code:
*North Dakota Century Code Annotated (Michie) {N.D. Cent. Code § x (19xx)}
Administrative Code:
*North Dakota Administrative Code {N.D. Admin. Code § x (month 19xx)}

OHIO (OH) {Ohio}

Federal Circuit: Sixth {6th Cir.} (Cincinnati, OH)
Federal Districts: Northern, Southern

All Courts:
    West Region: North Eastern Reporter {N.E.2d.}
    On LEXIS: OHIO;CASES
    On WESTLAW: OH-CS
High Court:
*Supreme Court {Ohio}
    Official Reporter: Ohio Official Reports {Ohio St. 3d}
Intermediate Court:
*Court of Appeals {Ohio Ct. App.}
    Official Reporter: Ohio Official Reports {Ohio App. 3d}
Statutory Codes:
*Baldwin's Ohio Revised Code Annotated (Banks-Baldwin) {Ohio Rev. Code Ann. § x (Baldwin 19xx)}
    On LEXIS: OHIO;OHCODE
*Page's Ohio Revised Code Annotated (Anderson) {Ohio Rev. Code Ann. § x (Anderson 19xx)}
    On WESTLAW: OH-ST-ANN
Administrative Code:
*Ohio Administrative Code {Ohio Admin. Code § x (19xx)}
    On LEXIS: OHIO;OHADMIN
Encyclopedia: Ohio Jurisprudence 3d (LCP)

OKLAHOMA (OK) {Okla.}

Federal Circuit: Tenth {10th Cir.} (Denver, CO)
Federal Districts: Eastern, Northern, Western
All Courts:
    West Region: Pacific Reporter {P.2d.}
    On LEXIS: OKLA;CASES
    On WESTLAW: OK-CS
High Courts:
*Supreme Court {Okla.}
    Official Reporter: Pacific Reporter {P.2d}
*Court of Criminal Appeals {Okla. Crim. App.}
    Official Reporter: Pacific Reporter {P.2d}
Intermediate Court:
*Court of Appeals {Okla. Ct. App.}
    Official Reporter: Pacific Reporter {P.2d}
Statutory Codes:
*Oklahoma Statutes {Okla. Stat. tit. x, § x (19xx)}
    On LEXIS: OKLA;OKCODE
*Oklahoma Statutes Annotated (West) {Okla. Stat. Ann. tit. x, § x (West 19xx)}
    On WESTLAW: OK-ST-ANN
Administrative Code: none

OREGON (OR) {Or.}

Federal Circuit: Ninth {9th Cir.} (San Francisco, CA)
Federal District: Oregon
All Courts:
    West Region: Pacific Reporter {P.2d}
    On LEXIS: ORE;CASES
    On WESTLAW: OR-CS
High Court:
*Supreme Court {Or.}
    Official Reporter: Oregon Reports {Or.}

Intermediate Courts:
*Court of Appeals {Or. Ct. App.}
    Official Reporter: Oregon Reports, Court of Appeals {Or. App.}
*Tax Court {Or. T.C.}
    Official Reporter: Oregon Tax Reports {Or. Tax}
Statutory Code:
*Oregon Revised Statutes {Or. Rev. Stat. § x (19xx)}
    On LEXIS: ORE;ORCODE
    On WESTLAW: OR-ST
Administrative Code:
*Oregon Administrative Rules {Or. Admin. R. x (19xx)}

PENNSYLVANIA (PA) {Pa.}

Federal Circuit: Third {3d Cir.} (Philadelphia, PA)
Federal Districts: Eastern, Middle, Western
All Courts:
    West Region: Atlantic Reporter {A.2d}
    On LEXIS: PA;CASES
    On WESTLAW: PA-CS
High Court:
*Supreme Court {Pa.}
    Official Reporter: Pennsylvania State Reports {Pa.}
Intermediate Courts:
*Commonwealth Court {Pa. Commw. Ct.}
    Official Reporter: Pennsylvania Commonwealth Court Reports {Pa. Commw.}
*Superior Court {Pa. Super. Ct.}
    Official Reporter: Pennsylvania Superior Court Reports {Pa. Super.}
Statutory Codes:
*Pennsylvania Consolidated Statutes {x Pa. Cons. Stat. § x (19xx)}
    On LEXIS: PA;PACODE
*Purdon's Pennsylvania Statutes Annotated and Consolidated Statutes Annotated (Bissel/West) {x Pa. Cons. Stat. Ann. § x (Purdon 19xx)}
    On WESTLAW: PA-ST-ANN
Administrative Code:
*Pennsylvania Code {x Pa. Code § x (19xx)}

RHODE ISLAND (RI) {R.I.}

Federal Circuit: First {1st Cir.} (Boston, MA)
Federal District: Rhode Island
All Courts:
    West Region: Atlantic Reporter {A.2d}
    On LEXIS: RI;RI
    On WESTLAW: RI-CS
High Court:
*Supreme Court {R.I.}
    Official Reporter: Atlantic Reporter {A.2d}
Intermediate Court: none
Statutory Code:
*General Laws of Rhode Island (Michie) {R.I. Gen. Laws § x (19xx)}
    On LEXIS: RI;RICODE
    On WESTLAW: RI-ST-ANN
Administrative Code: none

SOUTH CAROLINA (SC) {S.C.}

Federal Circuit: Fourth {4th Cir.} (Richmond, VA)
Federal District: South Carolina
All Courts:
    West Region: South Eastern Reporter {S.E.2d}
    On LEXIS: SC;CASES
    On WESTLAW: SC-CS
High Court:
*Supreme Court {S.C.}
    Official Reporter: South Carolina Reports {S.C.}
Intermediate Court:
*Court of Appeals {S.C. Ct. App.}
    Official Reporter: South Carolina Reports {S.C.}
Statutory Code:
*Code of Laws of South Carolina Annotated (LCP) {S.C. Code Ann. § x (Law. Co-op. 19xx)}
Administrative Code:
*Code of Laws of South Carolina Annotated, Code of Regulations (LCP) {S.C. Code Regs. x (19xx)}

SOUTH DAKOTA (SD) {S.D.}

Federal Circuit: Eighth {8th Cir.} (St. Louis, MO)
Federal District: South Dakota
All Courts:
    West Region: North Western Reporter {N.W.2d}
    On LEXIS: SD;SD
    On WESTLAW: SD-CS
High Court:
*Supreme Court {S.D.}
    Official Reporter: North Western Reporter {N.W.2d}
Intermediate Court: none
Statutory Code:
*South Dakota Codified Laws Annotated (Michie) {S.D. Codified Laws Ann. § x (19xx)}
    On LEXIS: SD;SDCODE
    On WESTLAW: SD-ST-ANN
Administrative Code:
*Administrative Rules of South Dakota {S.D. Admin. R. x (19xx)}

TENNESSEE (TN) {Tenn.}

Federal Circuit: Sixth {6th Cir.} (Cincinnati, OH)
Federal Districts: Eastern, Middle, Western
All Courts:
    West Region: South Western Reporter {S.W.2d}
    On LEXIS: TENN;CASES
    On WESTLAW: TN-CS
High Court:
*Supreme Court {Tenn.}
    Official Reporter: South Western Reporter {S.W.2d}
Intermediate Courts:
*Court of Appeals {Tenn. Ct. App.}
    Official Reporter: South Western Reporter {S.W.2d}

*Court of Criminal Appeals {Tenn. Crim. App.}
    Official Reporter: South Western Reporter {S.W.2d}
Statutory Code:
*Tennessee Code Annotated (Michie) {Tenn. Code Ann. § x (19xx)}
    On LEXIS: TENN;TNCODE
    On WESTLAW: TN-ST-ANN
Administrative Code:
*Official Compilation: Rules & Regulations of the State of Tennessee {Tenn. Comp. R. & Regs. tit. x, ch. x (19xx)}

TEXAS (TX) {Tex.}

Federal Circuit: Fifth {5th Cir.} (New Orleans, LA)
Federal Districts: Eastern, Northern, Southern, Western
All Courts:
    West Region: South Western Reporter {S.W.2d}
    On LEXIS: TEX;CASES
    On WESTLAW: TX-CS
High Courts:
*Supreme Court {Tex.}
    Official Reporter: none {cite to S.W.2d}
*Court of Criminal Appeals {Tex. Crim. App.}
    Official Reporter: none {cite to S.W.2d}
Intermediate Court:
*Court of Appeals {Tex. Ct. App.}
    Official Reporter: none {cite to S.W.2d}
Statutory Codes:
*Texas Statutes and Codes
    On LEXIS: TEX;TXCODE
*Vernon's Annotated Texas Statutes and Codes (West) {Tex. [subject] Code Ann. § x (Vernon 19xx)}
    On WESTLAW: TX-ST-ANN
Administrative Code:
*Texas Administrative Code {Tex. Admin. Code tit. x, § x (19xx)}
Encyclopedia: Texas Jurisprudence 3d (LCP)

UTAH (UT) {Utah}

Federal Circuit: Tenth {10th Cir.} (Denver, CO)
Federal District: Utah
All Courts:
    West Region: Pacific Reporter {P.2d}
    On LEXIS: UTAH;CASES
    On WESTLAW: UT-CS
High Court:
*Supreme Court {Utah}
    Official Reporter: none {cite to P.2d}
Intermediate Court:
*Court of Appeals
    Official Reporter: none {cite to P.2d}
Statutory Code:
*Utah Code Annotated (Michie) {Utah Code Ann. § x (19xx)}
    On LEXIS: UTAH;UTCODE
    On WESTLAW: UT-ST-ANN

State Law Sources

Administrative Code:
*Administrative Rules of the State of Utah {Utah Admin. R. x (19xx)}

VERMONT (VT) {Vt.}

Federal Circuit: Second {2d Cir.} (New York, NY)
Federal District: Vermont
All Courts:
    West Region: Atlantic Reporter {A.2d}
    On LEXIS: VT;CASES
    On WESTLAW: VT-CS
High Court:
*Supreme Court {Vt.}
    Official Reporter: Vermont Reports {Vt.}
Intermediate Court: none
Statutory Code:
*Vermont Statutes Annotated (Equity) {Vt. Stat. Ann. tit. x, § x (19xx)}
    On WESTLAW: VT-ST-ANN
Administrative Code:
*Vermont Administrative Procedures Compilation {Vt. Admin. Proc. Comp. [agency] r. [or §] x (19xx)}

VIRGINIA (VA) {Va.}

Federal Circuit: Fourth {4th Cir.} (Richmond, VA)
Federal Districts Eastern, Western
All Courts:
    West Region: South Eastern Reporter {S.E.2d}
    On LEXIS: VA;CASES
    On WESTLAW: VA-CS
High Court:
*Supreme Court {Va.}
    Official Reporter: Virginia Reports {Va.}
Intermediate Court:
*Court of Appeals {Va. Ct. App.}
    Official Reporter: Virginia Court of Appeals Reports {Va. App.}
Statutory Code:
*Code of Virginia Annotated (Michie) {Va. Code Ann. § x (19xx)}
    On LEXIS: VA;VACODE
    On WESTLAW: VA-ST-ANN
Administrative Code: none

WASHINGTON (WA) {Wash.}

Federal Circuit: Ninth {9th Cir.} (San Francisco, CA)
Federal Districts Eastern, Western
All Courts:
    West Region: Pacific Reporter {P.2d.}
    On LEXIS: WASH;CASES
    On WESTLAW: WA-CS
High Court:
*Supreme Court {Wash.}
    Official Reporter: Washington Reports {Wash. 2d}

Intermediate Court:
*Court of Appeals {Wash. Ct. App.}
    Official Reporter: Washington Appellate Reports {Wash. App.}
Statutory Codes:
*Revised Code of Washington {Wash. Rev. Code § x (19xx)}
    On LEXIS: WASH;WACODE
*West's Revised Code of Washington Annotated {Wash. Rev. Code Ann. § x (19xx)}
    On WESTLAW: WA-ST-ANN
Administrative Code:
*Washington Administrative Code {Wash. Admin. Code § x (19xx)}

WEST VIRGINIA (WV) {W. Va.}

Federal Circuit: Fourth {4th Cir.} (Richmond, VA)
Federal Districts: Northern, Southern
All Courts:
    West Region: South Eastern Reporter {S.E.2d}
    On LEXIS: WVA;CASES
    On WESTLAW: WV-CS
High Court:
*Supreme Court {W. Va.}
    Official Reporter: South Eastern Reporter {S.E.2d}
Intermediate Court: none
Statutory Code:
*West Virginia Code Annotated (Michie) {W. Va. Code § x (19xx)}
    On LEXIS: WVA;WVCODE
    On WESTLAW: WV-ST-ANN
Administrative Code: none

WISCONSIN (WI) {Wis.}

Federal Circuit: Seventh {7th Cir.} (Chicago, IL)
Federal Districts: Eastern, Western
All Courts:
    West Region: North Western Reporter {N.W.2d}
    On LEXIS: WISC;CASES
    On WESTLAW: WI-CS
High Court:
*Supreme Court {Wis.}
    Official Reporter: Wisconsin Reports {Wis. 2d}
Intermediate Court:
*Court of Appeals {Wis. Ct. App.}
    Official Reporter: Wisconsin Reports {Wis. 2d}
Statutory Codes:
*West's Wisconsin Statutes Annotated {Wis. Stat. Ann. § x (West 19xx)}
    On WESTLAW: WI-ST-ANN
*Wisconsin Statutes {Wis. Stat. § x (19xx)}
    On LEXIS: WISC;WICODE
Administrative Code:
*Wisconsin Administrative Code {Wis. Admin. Code § [agency] x (month 19xx)}

WYOMING (WY) {Wyo.}

Federal Circuit: Tenth {10th Cir.} (Denver, CO)
Federal District: Wyoming
All Courts:
    West Region: Pacific Reporter {P.2d}
    On LEXIS: WYO;CASES
    On WESTLAW: WY-CS
High Court:
*Supreme Court {Wyo.}
    Official Reporter: Pacific Reporter {P.2d}
Intermediate Court: none
Statutory Code:
*Wyoming Statutes Annotated (Michie) {Wyo. Stat. § x (19xx)}
    On LEXIS: WYO;WYCODE
    On WESTLAW: WY-ST-ANN
Administrative Code: none

APPENDIX IV Law Library Classification

A **library,** by definition, is an organized collection of books and other media kept for their use. As a practical matter, books and other media in a library can be used only if they can be found in the collection. A library, to be worthy of the name, must be organized to facilitate the finding of books and other media.

A **law library** is an organized collection of law books and other media. Legal research is the art of the effective use of law books and other media generally found in a law library. To find books and other media in a law library, a legal researcher must have a basic understanding of the organization of books and other media in a law library.

The arrangement of books and other media in a library is known as **classification.** Classification brings related books and other media together in sequence from general to specific. Classification is usually according to the predominant subject of an item, then to its form, then to its most useful place in the collection. Over the years, many different systems of classification have been developed, but almost every library in the United States uses either the Dewey Decimal system or the Library of Congress system. In addition, government publications are usually organized according to the Superintendent of Documents system.

The **Dewey Decimal Classification** system was devised by Melvil Dewey in 1876. Dewey's system, entirely numerical, was devised around standard divisions and subdivisions, with the social sciences classified in the 300s, and law starting at 340. The Dewey system is generally used in public, primary school, and secondary school libraries.

The **Library of Congress Classification** system was devised in the early 1900s by Librarian of Congress Herbert Putnam and his Chief Cataloger, Charles Martel, replacing the previous system, which had become inadequate. Their letter-number classification system reflected the actual content of the Library of Congress at the time. After preparing the main classifications, they called in subject specialists to prepare the subclassifications. The resulting classification schedules are periodically reviewed by committees and are published as needed. Many of the classification schedules have gone through several editions. Because of its expansive and flexible format, the Library of Congress Classification is generally used in large government, university, and research libraries, including law school and other law libraries. It is used in the U.S. Supreme Court Library, and, of course, in the Library of Congress Law Library.

The **Superintendent of Documents Classification** system is often used for collections of governmental documents. Its essential feature is the grouping of publications by the issuing governmental agency. The issuing governmental agency is indicated by a letter or letter combination prefix. Numbers follow indicating the subordinate bureau within the agency, the title designation, and the year of publication (e.g., C 61.34:987). Common prefixes include:

A	Agriculture Department
C 3.	Census Bureau (Commerce Department)
D	Defense Department
E	Energy Department
ED	Education Department
GA	General Accounting Office
GS	General Services Administration
HE	Health and Human Services Department
I	Interior Department
I 19.	U.S. Geological Survey (Interior Department)
J	Justice Department
JU	Judiciary
L	Labor Department
LC	Library of Congress
NAS	National Aeronautics and Space Administration
S	State Department
SI	Smithsonian Institution
T 22.	Internal Revenue Service (Treasury Department)
X, Y	Congress
Y 4.	Congressional Committees

The LC Classification Scheme

Because it is the classification system used in most law libraries, legal researchers should have an intimate knowledge of the Library of Congress Classification system (LC). There are 21 main classifications, lettered from A to Z (except for I, O, W, X, and Y). A second letter, or a second and third letter, each from A to Z, is used to indicate a subclassification. The Library of Congress Classification includes published schedules covering the following subjects:

A	General Works; Polygraphy
B-BJ	Philosophy; Psychology
BL-BX	Religion
C	Auxiliary Sciences of History
D	General and Old World History
E-F	American History
G	Geography; Maps; Anthropology; Recreation
H-HJ	Economics
HM-HX	Sociology
J	Political Science
K	Law (General)
KD	Law of the United Kingdom and Ireland
KDZ, KG-KH	Law of the Americas, Latin America, and the West Indies
KE	Law of Canada

KF	Law of the United States
KK-KKC	Law of Germany
L	Education
M	Music
N	Fine Arts
P	Language
Q	Science
R	Medicine
S	Agriculture
T	Technology
U	Military Science
V	Naval Science
Z	Bibliography; Library Science

Note that political science (which includes international law) is covered in the J classification, law is covered in the K classification, and law of the United States is covered in the KF subclassification.

KF Subclassification

The KF subclassification covers the law of the United States in general. The law of each state, alphabetically by state, is covered in subclasses KFA-KFW. The law of each city, alphabetically by city, is covered in subclass KFX. The law of each territory, alphabetically by territory, is covered in subclass KFZ.

The KF subclassification is broken down numerically from 1 to 9760. The class number assignments may be summarized as follows:

KF		Law of the United States.
1–	8	Bibliography.
16–	49	Legislative documents.
50–	90	Statutes and administrative regulations.
101–	152	Law reports and related materials.
154		Encyclopedias.
156		Law dictionaries. "Words and Phrases."
159		Legal maxims. Quotations.
165		Uniform State laws.
170		Form books.
175		Periodicals.
178		Yearbooks.
180–	185	Judicial statistics.
190–	195	Directories.
200		Society and bar association journals and yearbooks.
202		Congresses.
209–	224	Collections.
209		-Monographic series.
210–	211	-Several authors.
213		-Individual authors.

Law Library Classification

220– 224	-Criminal trials.
228	Records and briefs of individual civil suits.
240– 246	Legal research. Legal bibliography.
250– 251	Legal composition and draftsmanship.
255	Law reporting.
260	Cases and materials.
262– 292	Legal education.
294	Law societies, A–Z.
297– 334	The legal profession.
320	Legal Assistantship/Paralegalism.
336– 337	Legal aid. Legal aid societies.
338	Lawyer referral services.
350– 375	History.
379– 384	Jurisprudence and philosophy of American law.
384	Criticism. Legal reform. General "administration of justice."
385– 391	General and comprehensive works.
394– 395	Common law in the U.S.
398– 400	Equity.
410– 418	Conflict of laws.
420	Retroactive law.
425– 435	General principles and concepts.
445– 450	Concepts applying to several branches of law.
465– 553	Persons.
465– 485	-General. Status. Capacity.
501– 550	-Domestic relations. Family law.
553	-Guardian and ward.
560– 720	Property.
560– 562	-General. Ownership.
566– 698	-Real property. Land law.
701– 720	-Personal property.
726– 745	Trusts and trustees.
746– 750	Estate planning.
753– 780	Succession upon death.
801–1241	Contracts.
801– 805	-General and comprehensive works.
807– 839	-General principles.
841– 869	-Government contracts.
871–1241	-Particular contracts.
871– 890	--Comprehensive. Commercial law. Mercantile transactions.
894	--Contract of service. Master and servant.
898– 905	--Contract for work and labor. Independent contractors.
911– 935	--Sale of goods.
939– 951	--Contracts involving bailments.
956– 962	--Negotiable instruments.
966–1032	--Banking.

1033	--Foreign exchange brokerage.
1035–1040	--Loan of money.
1045	--Suretyship. Guaranty.
1046–1062	--Secured transactions.
1066–1083	--Marketing of securities. Investments. Stock exchange transactions.
1085–1086	--Commodity exchanges. Produce exchanges.
1091–1137	--Carriers. Carriage of goods and passengers.
1091	---General. Liability.
1092	---Carriage by land.
1093	---Carriage by air.
1096–1114	---Carriage by sea. Maritime commercial law. Admiralty.
1121–1132	---Maritime labor law.
1135–1137	---Marine insurance.
1146–1238	--Insurance.
1241	--Aleatory contracts.
1244	Restitution. Quasi contracts. Unjust enrichment.
1246–1327	Torts.
1341–1348	Agency.
1355–1480	Associations.
1355–1359	-General.
1361–1380	-Unincorporated associations.
1361–1362	--General.
1365–1380	--Business associations. Partnership.
1384–1480	-Corporations.
1384–1386	--General.
1388–1389	--Nonprofit corporations.
1396–1477	--Business corporations.
1480	--Government-owned corporations and business organizations.
1501–1548	Insolvency and bankruptcy. Creditors' rights.
1600–2940	Regulation of industry, trade, and commerce. Occupational law.
1600	-General and comprehensive.
1601–1666	-Trade regulation. Control of trade practices.
1601–1611	--General. Unfair trade practices.
1614–1617	--Advertising.
1619–1620	--Labeling.
1624–1625	--Restraint of trade.
1626–1629	--Price fixing.
1631–1657	--Monopolies. Antitrust laws.
1659	--"Small business."
1661	--Trade associations.
1663	--State jurisdiction. "Trade barriers."
1665–1666	--Weights and measures. Containers.
1681–1873	-Primary production. Extractive industries.
1681–1750	--Agriculture. Forestry.

1770–1773	--Fishery.
1801–1873	--Mining. Quarrying. Oil and gas.
1875–1893	-Manufacturing industries.
1900–1944	-Food processing industries.
1950	-Construction and building industry.
1970–2057	-Trade and commerce.
2076–2140	-Public utilities.
2161–2849	-Transportation and communication.
2901–2940	-The professions.
2971–3192	Intellectual property.
2971–2980	-General.
2986–3080	-Copyright.
3084	-Author and publisher. The publishing contract.
3086	-Design protection.
3091–3192	-Patent law and trade marks.
3195–3198	Unfair competition.
3300–3750	Social legislation.
3300	-General.
3301–3580	-Labor law.
3600–3686	-Social insurance.
3720–3745	-Public welfare. Public assistance.
3750	-Disaster relief.
3775–3813	Public health. Sanitation.
3821–3829	Medical legislation.
3832	Eugenics. Sterilization.
3835–3838	Veterinary laws. Veterinary hygiene.
3841–3845	Prevention of cruelty to animals.
3861–3894	Food. Drugs. Cosmetics.
3901–3925	Liquor control. Prohibition.
3941–3977	Public safety.
3941–3942	-Weapons. Firearms. Munitions.
3945–3965	-Hazardous articles and processes.
3970	-Accident control.
3975–3977	-Fire prevention and control. Explosives.
3985–3995	Control of social activities.
3985	-General.
3987	-Amusements.
3989	-Sports. Prize-fighting.
3992	-Lotteries.
3995	-Other.
4101–4258	Education.
4270–4330	Science and the arts. Research.
4270	-General.
4280	-Particular branches and subjects. A–Z.
4288–4302	-The arts.
4305	-Museums and galleries.
4310–4312	-Historical buildings and documents.

4315-4319	-Libraries.
4325	-Archives. Historical documents.
4330	-Educational, scientific, and cultural exchanges.
4501-5130	Constitutional law.
4501-4515	-Sources.
4520	-Works on legislative history of the constitution.
4525-4528	-Texts of the Constitution.
4530	-State constitutions (Collections).
4541-4545	-Constitutional history of the United States.
4546-4554	-General works (History, theory, and interpretation of constitutional law).
4555	-Amending process.
4558	-Particular amendments.
4565-4578	-Separation of powers. Delegation of powers.
4581-4583	-Sources and relationships of law.
4600-4629	-Structure of government. Federal and State relations. Jurisdiction.
4635	-National territory. Noncontiguous territories.
4650-4694	-Foreign relations.
4695	-Public policy. Police power.
4700-4856	-Individual and state.
4700-4720	--Nationality and citizenship.
4741-4783	--Civil and political rights and liberties.
4788	--Political parties.
4791-4856	--Control of individuals.
4791	---Identification.
4794	---Passports.
4800-4848	---Aliens.
4850-4856	---Internal security.
4865-4869	-Church and state.
4880-5130	-Organs of the government.
4880-4921	--The people. Election law.
4930-5005	--The legislature.
5050-5125	--The executive branch.
5130	--The judiciary. Judicial power.
5150	National emblems. Flag. Seal. Seat of government. National anthem.
5152	Patriotic customs and observances.
5153-5154	Decorations of honor. Awards.
5155-5156	Commemorative medals.
5300-5332	Local government.
5336-5398	Civil service. Government officials and employees.
5399	Police and power of the police.
5401-5425	Administrative organization and procedure.
5500-5865	Public property. Public restraints on private property.
5500-5501	-General.
5505-5508	-Conservation of natural resources.

5521–5536	-Roads.
5540–5541	-Bridges.
5551–5590	-Water resources. Watersheds. Rivers. Lakes. Water courses.
5594	-Weather control. Meteorology. Weather stations.
5599	-Eminent domain.
5601–5646	-Public land law.
5660–5662	-Indian lands.
5670–5673	-Homesteads.
5675–5677	-Land grants.
5691–5710	-Regional and city planning. Zoning. Building.
5721–5740	-Housing. Slum clearance. City development.
5750–5857	-Government property.
5750–5755	--Administration. Powers and controls.
5760–5810	--Land and real property.
5820–5857	--Personal property.
5865	-Public works.
5900–6075	Government measures in time of war, national emergency, or economic crisis. Emergency economic legislation.
6200–6795	Public finance.
6200	-General.
6201–6219	-Money. Currency. Coinage.
6221–6225	-Budget. Government expenditures.
6231–6236	-Expenditure control. Public auditing and accounting.
6241–6245	-Public debts. Loans. Bond issues.
6251–6708	-National revenue.
6251–6256	--History.
6260	--General.
6265–6708	--Particular sources of revenue.
6265	---Charges.
6271–6645	---Taxation.
6651–6708	---Tariff. Trade agreements. Customs.
6720–6795	--State and local finance.
7201–7755	National defense. Military law.
7201–7225	-Comprehensive. General.
7250–7680	-The military establishment. Armed Forces.
7250–7298	--General.
7305–7479	--Particular branches of service.
7485–7488	--Auxiliary services during war or emergency.
7590	--Military discipline.
7595–7596	--Law enforcement. Criminal investigation.
7601–7679	--Military criminal law and procedure.
7680	--Civil status of members of the Armed Forces.
7683	-Other defense agencies, A–Z.

7685	-Civil defense.
7695	-Other topics, A–Z.
7701–7755	-War veterans.
8201–8228	Indians.
8700–9075	Courts. Procedure.
8700–8707	-Administration of justice. Organization of the judiciary.
8711–8807	-Court organization and procedure.
8810–9075	-Civil procedure.
9085	Arbitration and award. Commercial arbitration.
9201–9461	Criminal law.
9601–9760	Criminal procedure.

Note that books on legal research are classified at KF240, and books on legal assistantship are classified at KF320 (more precisely: KF320.L4).

LC Cataloging

Books are cataloged in the Library of Congress Classification system beginning with the **class notation:** a main classification letter, then a subclassification may be indicated by additional letters, then a class number assignment (e.g., KF 320). Then comes a letter-number (and perhaps letter-number-letter-number) designation treated as a decimal, known as a **cutter number,** named after its originator, Charles Ammi Cutter. The tables for the assignment of cutter numbers are beyond the scope of this book, but generally a cutter number identifies a book's author by the initial letter of the author's last name, followed by a number representing the remaining letters of the author's last name (e.g., Carter is .C37).

In a library using the Library of Congress Classification system, the **call number** of a book, the place on the shelf where the book may be found, consists of the class notation, the cutter number, followed by the year of publication (e.g., KF320.C37 1990). Books are then shelved alpha-numeric-chronologically by their call number. The genius of the system is the idea that two books on the same subject are rarely written by two authors with the same name in the same year.

Interestingly, you don't need a Master's Degree in Library Science in order to arrange a small collection of books according to the Library of Congress Classification system. Skipping the details of (and, of course, the benefits of) true cataloging, you can engage in a portion of what is known as **copy cataloging,** whereby you pick up a book's call number by finding it, by whatever means, in a library using the Library of Congress Classification system, and copy the call number given it by the librarian.

Better yet, you can copy the preliminary call numbers used by the Library of Congress. More and more major publishers are participating in the **Library of Congress Cataloging-in-Publication Data** program. Manuscripts are sent to the Library of Congress just prior to publication. The Library of Congress librarians then catalog the book, and the publisher includes the preliminary data, including the call number, on the reverse side of the title page.

Using the Card Catalog

Like the card catalog in an ordinary library, the card catalog in a law library can be very useful in helping you find what you're looking for. Most libraries now have some type of on-line (i.e., computer) catalog. Nevertheless, three cards are usually inserted for each book: an author card, a title card, and a subject card. Thus, using a card catalog, you can search for a book by author, title, or subject. An on-line catalog may also allow you to search for particular terms in the catalog. From the appropriate card, you pick up the call number of the book. With the call number you then locate the book on the shelf. Of course, you can locate other books on your subject by scanning the books shelved next to the book you've located.

Key Terms
call number
class notation
classification
copy cataloging
cutter number
Dewey Decimal Classification
law library
library
Library of Congress Cataloging-in-Publication Data
Library of Congress Classification
Superintendent of Documents Classification

GLOSSARY

Act: Bill considered and passed by one house of the Congress of the United States.

Adjudication: Deciding of a case by judgment and/or decree.

Administrative agency: Generally, a specialized governmental entity. Narrowly, a governmental entity distinct from the branches of government, created to independently regulate a limited specialized area of law.

Administrative codes: Topical collections of regulations.

Administrative decision: Decision of, or written explanation of the decision of, an administrative law judge.

Administrative law judge: Generally, the decision maker in an administrative hearing.

Administrative order: Formal exercise of discretionary power by the administrator of an administrative agency.

Advance sheets: Temporary pamphlets of court opinions.

Affirm: Decision of an appellate court that it agrees with the decision of the lower court and that the party who won in the lower court wins.

Annotate: To note or to mark up.

Annotated: With a careful editorial compilation of the authorities on important points raised by the decisions.

Annotated code: Code containing case summaries of how the courts have interpreted each statute.

Annotated constitution: Version of a constitution containing case summaries of how the courts have interpreted it.

Annotation: Method of finding cases in a specialized collection of the law (e.g., an A.L.R. annotation).

Appellant: Party who appealed.

Appellee: Party who answered the appeal.

Attorney general: Chief lawyer for a sovereign.

Bad law: Overruled (or otherwise discredited) precedent. Precedent without authority.

Bar journal: Law journal published by a bar association.

Bibliographic: Approach emphasizing detailed descriptions of the various books used.

Bill: Proposed permanent law introduced in a house of Congress.

Bill of Rights: First 10 amendments to the Constitution of the United States.

Binding authority: Authority that a court must follow.

Bluebook: Abbreviated form for *The Bluebook: A Uniform System of Citation*, 15th edition (1991), and earlier editions.

Bluebook style: Citation style suggested by *The Bluebook*.

BNA: Acronym for the Bureau of National Affairs, Inc., of Washington, D.C.

Brief: Formal written argument to a court.

BW: Acronym for the Bancroft-Whitney Company of San Francisco, California, a long-time subsidiary of the Lawyers Co-operative Publishing Company.

Call number: In Library of Congress Classification system, place on the shelf where a book may be found, consisting of the class notation, cutter number, and year of publication (e.g., KF320.C37 1990).

CALR: Acronym for computer-assisted legal research. Use of computer-modem systems to automate the search of legal materials.

Canned briefs: Guides to law school casebooks in which each major case is preanalyzed for the reader.

Case at bar: Actual legal controversy to be decided.

Case history: Path, noted by citations, a legal controversy has taken through the court system.

Case in point: Previous case like the case at bar.

Case law: Law from the judicial branch.

Case method: Method of legal research whereby if you know at least one case like yours, you can search the law book's table of cases, if any, and go to the references.

Case of first impression: A case without precedent.

Casebook: Law school textbook containing a series of selected cases on each topic to be covered.

Casenotes: Case summaries in the *United States Code Service* (U.S.C.S.).

Cases: Actual legal controversies.

CCH: Acronym for the Commerce Clearing House, Inc., of Chicago, Illinois.

CD-ROM: Acronym for compact disk with read-only memory.

***Certiorari*, writ of:** Written order of an appellate court with discretionary jurisdiction stating that it chooses to review a lower court decision and directing the lower court to produce its records for review.

Charter: Documents that form a government. The fundamental law of a local government.

Chronologically: In or by real-time sequence.

Citation: Reference to the location at which a case opinion may be found in a reporter. In dictionary making, a sample of the actual use of a word in context.

Citation-based: Standard for creating a dictionary in which a fair sample of actual uses of each word in context are collected, allowing the editor to authoritatively determine whether each word is current or archaic, and its spelling, etymology, meaning, and usage.

Citation search: Computer search made by entering a citation, rather than a word.

Citation style: How cited legal materials should be abbreviated to avoid confusing readers.

Citators: Books and other media that primarily list legal citations.

Cite: To point out the location of legal authority for the law that supports your case. Reference to the location at which a case opinion may be found in a reporter.

Cited case: Case being cited by other courts. The target case.

Citing cases: Cases that make reference to the cited case.

Class notation: In Library of Congress Classification system, beginning main classification letter, any subclassification indicated by additional letters, and a class number assignment (e.g., KF 320).

Classification: Arrangement of books and other media in a library.

Code: Topical collection of statutes.

Codification: Process of collecting permanent public statutes topically, adding amendments, and deleting expired, repealed, or superseded statutes.

COLR: Acronym for computer-organized legal research. Use of computers to automate the organization of search results.

Comments: Articles written by law professors, prominent practitioners, or outstanding students that are published in law reviews.

Common law: Rules of law common to all of medieval England. The law made by judges in deciding actual cases. A legal system emphasizing case law.

Computer-assisted legal research (CALR): Use of computer-modem systems to automate the search of legal materials.

Computer-organized legal research (COLR): Use of computers to automate the organization of search results.

Concordance: Index of words. A literal alphabetical listing of the principal words of a book, with precise references to where in the book each word is used.

Concurrent resolution: Proposed *administrative* (not legislative) statement of Congress.

Concurring opinion: Opinion of a justice who agrees with the decision of the court, but does not fully agree with the opinion of the court.

Congress: Two-year period in which the Congress of the United States meets, mirroring the two-year term of a representative.

Connectors: Codes used to indicate the desired logical and numerical relationships among the terms in a computer word search.

Considered *dicta*: Serious extra comment made by a court in its opinion, not necessary to the decision.

Constitution: Written fundamental law of a sovereign (e.g., the Constitution of the United States).

Constitution of the United States: Written fundamental law of the United States of America.

Constitutional law: Any aspect of law directly derived from the written fundamental law of a sovereign.

Copy cataloging: Mimicking the cataloging used by an existing library.

Cross-references: In an index, references to other entries.

Cutter number: In Library of Congress Classification system, after the class notation, the letter-number designation treated as a decimal (e.g., .C37).

Database: Generally, collection of information placed in a computer's memory and capable of being searched by the computer. Technically, collection of information especially organized for rapid computer search and retrieval.

Decision: Outcome of a case (i.e., who wins).

Decree: Determination of the rights and duties of the parties (e.g., in a divorce).

Defendant: Person or legal entity responding to the claim of a plaintiff.

Definitions: Meanings of a word.

Dewey Decimal Classification: Entirely numerical system of library classification devised by Melvil Dewey in 1876 (law starts at 340).

Dicta: Extra comments made by a court in its opinion, not necessary to the decision.

Dictionary: Book containing an alphabetical list of words, along with information about each word, usually including its spelling, pronunciation, etymology, definitions, forms, and uses.

Dictum: Single extra comment made by a court in its opinion, not necessary to the decision.

Digest: Specialized index of reported cases. Case summary used as an entry in such an index. In litigation support, extraction of significant information from a deposition transcript or other document.

Digest paragraphs: Case summaries used as entries in a digest.

Directory: List of names and certain other information, such as addresses, telephone numbers, and the like.

Dissenting opinion: Opinion of a justice who disagrees with the decision of the court.

Docket number: The court's serial number.

Enabling act: Statute creating and/or empowering a local government or agency.

Enactment: Legislative process resulting in the making of a statute.

Encyclopedia: Comprehensive work, usually a narrative summary, that covers all of the subjects within a particular branch of knowledge (or all branches of knowledge).

Engrossed bill: Final, officially signed copy of an act.

Enrolled bill: Final, officially signed copy on parchment of a bill that has passed both houses of Congress.

Entries: In an index, words or phrases used to note key concepts, words, and phrases in the text indexed.

Et seq.: Latin for "and the following."

Etymology: Word origin.

Ex post facto: Latin for "after the fact." A criminal law with retroactive effect. Such laws are prohibited by the Constitution of the United States.

Executive: Branch of government that enforces the law.

Executive agreement: President's agreement with a foreign country that, because it is without the advice and consent of the Senate, is not nation-binding.

Executive departments: Under the executive branch, groups of specialists organized to assist the executive in carrying out the functions of the executive branch.

Executive order: Executive's formal announcement of the exercise of a discretionary power.

Exhaustive annotations: Annotations collecting every case on the point annotated.

Exhaustive search: A search through every source.

Federal Depository Library: Library that gets copies of federal government publications at little or no cost. By federal law, such a library must be open to the public.

Federalism: Concept that the federal government of the United States is a limited sovereign, having only the powers explicitly or implicitly granted it in the Constitution; all other powers being retained by the states.

Feudalism: Legal system in medieval England in which the king parceled out the use of the land in exchange for services to his kingdom.

Fields: Defined categories of information in a database.

Form books: Collections of sample legal documents used by lawyers and paralegals.

Good law: Case precedent that has not been overruled (or otherwise discredited). Precedent with authority.

Headnotes: Brief editor-made summaries of the major points of law in an opinion that appear before the court's opinion (and generally falling at the top or "head" of a page).

Holding: Rule of law found in a case.

Hornbook: One of a series of one-volume treatises for students published by West Publishing Company, named after teaching tablets with handles used from the late 1400s to the middle 1700s, which held a sheet of paper protected by a sheet of translucent horn.

House organ: In-house periodical.

In point: Case that covers an issue explicitly, or exactly.

Index: A-to-Z list that refers a reader to the location of concepts in a book or other text by short entries and page references.

Index method: Method of legal research using entry terms to search the law book's index, if any, and go to the references.

Infra: Below or after this point in the text.

International law: Rules governing sovereign countries by their consent, the law of nations.

Joint resolution: Proposed temporary (time-oriented) law.

Judges: Individuals with the power to decide actual legal disputes in the name of the sovereign.

Judgment: Final decision of a court entered into its records.

Judicial: Branch of government that interprets the law.

Judicial review: Doctrine that the clauses of the Constitution, like statutes, are subject to interpretation by the courts, and in particular, by the U.S. Supreme Court.

Jump cite: Reference to a specific succeeding page, after the first page, of an opinion (also known as a pinpoint cite).

Jur table: "Table of Jurisdictions Represented" in an A.L.R. annotation.

Jurisprudence: The philosophy of law. The law collectively.

Justices: Appellate court judges.

Key Number: West Publishing Company's term for the numerical designation of a line in a Topic outline.

KWIC: Acronym for the "key word in context" display of the results of a word search on LEXIS.

Landmark case: First significant case, often the case of first impression for your issue, decided in your favor.

Law: The command of a sovereign.

Law dictionary: Book containing a list of words unique to the legal profession, words often used by the legal profession, and ordinary words with a legal meaning.

Law journal: Legal periodical emphasizing current events.

Law library: Organized collection of law books and other media.

Law review: Scholarly periodical published by a law school.

Lawyer: Legal expert.

LCP: Acronym for the Lawyers Co-operative Publishing Company, of Rochester, New York, which became the Lawyers Cooperative Publishing Division of Thomson Legal Publishing Inc.

Leading case: Case opinion that reads like an A.L.R. annotation or treatise, laying out all the precedent on your issue, pro and con, and deciding in your favor.

Legal directory: Guide to lawyers, law firms, and/or government agencies.

Legal forms: Samples of legally effective documents, such as contracts, deeds, and wills.

Legislative: Branch of government that makes the law.

Legislative departments: Under the legislative branch, groups of specialists organized to assist the legislature in carrying out the functions of the legislative branch.

Legislative history: Committee reports, floor debates, and other information considered by the legislature in enacting a bill or joint resolution, which may be reviewed by a court in an attempt to determine the intent of the legislature in enacting a statute.

LEXIS: Mead Data Central, Inc.'s computer-assisted legal research system, which includes access to A.L.R.

Library: Collection of books and other media kept for their use. An organized collection of books and other media.

Library of Congress Cataloging-in-Publication Data: Results of a program by which manuscripts are sent to the Library of Congress just prior to publication. Library of Congress librarians catalog them, and publishers include the preliminary data for each book, including the call number, on the reverse side of the title page.

Library of Congress Classification: Letter-number system of library classification devised in the early 1900s by Librarian of Congress Herbert Putnam and his Chief Cataloger, Charles Martel (law of the United States is subclassification KF).

Litigation support: Organization of case information, particularly from discovery, to aid an attorney in the trial of a case.

Local case: Most recent case from your local jurisdiction decided in your favor, pointing out that your local jurisdiction follows established precedent.

Looseleaf service: Law publication, usually a set of books, issued in notebook form.

Macro: User-made program of a series of commands and keyboard strokes in WordPerfect.

Majority opinion: Opinion of the court in which a majority of the justices join.

Mandatory authority: Authority that a court must follow.

MB: Abbreviated form for the Matthew Bender & Company of New York, New York.

MDC: Acronym for Mead Data Central, Inc., of Dayton, Ohio.

Memorandum of law: Written discussion of a legal question, objectively reporting the law favoring each side in the fact pattern, as found after researching the topic.

Memorandum opinion: A brief opinion.

Michie: Abbreviated form for The Michie Company of Charlottesville, Virginia, now a subsidiary of Mead Data Central, Inc.

Microfiche: File-card-sized sheets of film containing miniature pictures of printed pages.

Microfilm: Reels or cassettes of film containing miniature pictures of printed pages.

Microforms: Reproductions of printed matter in greatly reduced size.

National Reporter System: System of reporters published by West Publishing Company covering all the appellate courts in the United States.

Noise words: Set of commonly used words that cannot be searched on LEXIS.

Nominative reporters: Reporter volumes compiled by individuals; especially the initial reporters who covered the U.S. Supreme Court.

Norman Conquest: Event in English history to which the U.S. legal system can be traced. In 1066, William the Conqueror, living on the Normandy coast of France, crossed the English Channel and deposed the reigning king, Harold.

Notes: Short book, case, or subject reviews that are published in law reviews.

Nutshells: Series of paperback textbooks published by West Publishing Company.

Obiter dicta: Irrelevant extra comment made by a court in its opinion, not necessary to the decision.

Official reports: Reports designated by the high court (or the legislature) as the official version of its opinions.

On-line: Accessible by a modem-equipped computer using telephone lines. Available on a computer system.

On point: Case that covers an issue implicitly, or by analogy, if not explicitly, or exactly.

Opinion: Court's written explanation of its decision.

Order: Preliminary decision of a court (e.g., a ruling on a motion).

Ordinance: Legislation of a local government.

Outline: Summary showing the pattern of subordination of one thought to another.

P-H: Acronym for Prentice-Hall, Inc., a division of Simon & Schuster, Inc., Paramus, New Jersey.

Page mode: Browsing by page feature on WESTLAW.

Parallel citation/cite: Alternate location reference for a case opinion.

Per curiam **opinion:** "By the court" opinion. A joint anonymous opinion of the court.

Periodical: Work that is published at regular intervals.

Persuasive authority: Authority that a court may follow.

Petitioner: Party who appealed. A plaintiff, especially a plaintiff expecting to be unopposed.

Pinpoint cite: Reference to a specific succeeding page, after the first page, of an opinion (also known as a jump cite).

Plaintiff: Person or legal entity that sought relief in the trial court.

Plaintiff in error: A defendant-appellant.

Pleading and practice forms: Samples of documents used in actually litigating a case, such as complaints, answers, replies, interrogatories, motions, and judgments.

Plurality opinion: Opinion of the court where a majority of the justices agree on a decision, but a majority is unable to agree on the reasoning behind it.

Pocket veto: Untimely nonreturn of a bill presented to the President. Since, in such a case, the houses of Congress have adjourned, the veto cannot be overridden.

Positive law: Codified law passed as a statute. The law "actually enacted."

Practice pointers: Part of an A.L.R. annotation that contains "useful hints" on how to handle a case involving the point annotated.

Preamble: Introductory statement of legal intent (e.g., the "We the People . . ." portion of the Constitution of the United States).

Precedent: Preceding similar case. A case like yours.

Prima facie: Accepted on its face, but not irrebuttably.

Primary authority: The law itself. The authoritative acts of the sovereign (e.g., the constitution, statutes, executive orders, court decisions, and administrative regulations).

Private law: Law that applies only to an individual or to a few individuals.

Proclamations: Executive orders having no continuing legal effect, such as declaring a certain day to be "National Whatever Day."

Promulgated: Made official and public.

Proximity search: CALR word search for one word within a specified number of words from another.

Public law: Law that applies to everyone.

Query: A word search on WESTLAW.

Ratio decidendi: Distinction or point on which a case turns.

Records: Variable items in a database containing the categorical information for each item.

References: In an index, page numbers indicating the location in the text at which key concepts, words, or phrases appear.

Regulates: Makes regulations.

Regulations: Laws made by an administrative agency.

Related matters: Part of an A.L.R. annotation that lists similar, related annotations, along with a token sample of law review articles and treatises on the point annotated.

Remand: Decision of an appellate court that the proceedings in a lower court were not fair or complete, returning the case to lower court for a new decision to be made after a fair and complete proceeding.

Reporter: A set of reports.

Reports: Books that collect court opinions.

Respondent: Party who answered the appeal. A defendant, especially a defendant opposing a petitioner.

Restatement: Systematic exposition of the common law as if it were a codified statutory code.

Reversal: Decision of an appellate court that it disagrees with the decision of the lower court and that the party who lost in the lower court wins.

Reverse: Decision of an appellate court that it disagrees with the decision of the lower court, and that either the party who lost in the lower court wins or the case itself is dismissed.

RIA: Acronym for the Research Institute of America of New York, New York, a long-time subsidiary of the Lawyers Co-operative Publishing Company.

Rulemaking: Process of making administrative rules and regulations.

Scheme: Detailed logical section-numbered outline of an A.L.R. annotation.

Scope: Part of an A.L.R. annotation that states the purported contents of the annotation.

Secondary authority: Anything that is not primary authority. Any assertion about the law that is not the law itself.

Sections: Organizing subdivision of statutes under each title of a code.

Separation of powers: Concept that the powers of the federal government of the United States are divided by the Constitution into three branches—legislative, executive, and judicial—to avoid the tyranny of a king.

Session: One of the yearly meeting periods of the Congress of the United States.

Session law: Bill or joint resolution that has become law during a particular session of the legislature.

Setout: Paragraph sketch of a case in an A.L.R. annotation.

Shepard's: Abbreviated form for any or all of the *Shepard's Citations* sets published by Shepard's/McGraw Hill, Inc., of Colorado Springs, Colorado. A book of tables listing all the citing cases for a cited case.

Shepardize: To review all the citing cases for a cited case using *Shepard's Citations* to make sure the cited case is not bad law or to help find other cases like the cited case. Also, to review all the cases cited in the brief or other legal writing using *Shepard's Citations* to make sure the brief or other legal writing does not cite bad law or to help find other cases like the case cited to use in a reply or revision.

Simple resolution: Proposed *administrative* (not legislative) statement of one house of Congress.

Slip law: Copy of a particular law passed during a session of the legislature.

Slip opinion: Individual court opinion published separately from bound volumes.

Sort: Put in alphanumeric order.

Sovereign: Entity with the power to command.

Star pagination: Notation of the pagination of one text (e.g., an official reporter) in another text (e.g., an unofficial reporter).

Stare decisis: Custom or doctrine of following precedent.

Statute edition: Volume of *Shepard's Citations* that lists all the citing cases for a statute or ordinance.

Statute method: Method of legal research whereby if you know at least one statute like yours, you can search the law book's code finding table, if any, and go to the references.

Statutes: Laws the legislative branch makes.

Statutory law: Law from the legislative branch.

Stop words: Set of commonly used words that cannot be searched on WESTLAW.

Superintendent of Documents Classification: Letter-number system of library classification often used for collections of governmental documents.

Superseding annotation: Annotation that replaces another annotation.

Supplementing annotation: Annotation that provides additional cases on a point already annotated.

Supra: Above or before this point in the text.

Syllabus: Official summary or list of the major legal points made in an opinion.

Synergistic: Having "a whole greater than the sum of its parts" effect.

Synopsis: Short paragraph summary of an entire case.

TAPP Rule: Rule of thumb used by indexers at the Lawyers Co-operative Publishing Company for analyzing fact patterns and for generating entry terms. It is based on the premise that legal researchers should be able to find the law they are looking for by looking up terms representing the thing, act, person, or place involved.

TCSL Box: Part of an A.L.R. annotation that lists cross-references to other units of the LCP's Total Client Service Library.

Term mode: Browsing by search term feature on WESTLAW.

Textbook: Book that contains the principles of a given subject; thus it is useful in the study of that subject.

Thesauri: Books of words and their synonyms and near synonyms. The singular form is "thesaurus."

Titles: Major topical division of a code (e.g., the 50 titles of the *United States Code*).

TLPI: Acronym for Thomson Legal Publishing Inc., of Rochester, New York, of which the Lawyers Cooperative Publishing division is the successor to the Lawyers Co-operative Publishing Company.

Topic method: Method of legal research whereby if you know the topic you want to search, you can search the law book's table of contents, if any, and go to all references, and scan the text for your topic.

Topically: By subject or by topic.

Topics: The central divisions, the subdivisions of the subdivisions of the seven main divisions, in the outline of the law used for digests published by West Publishing Company.

Total Client Service Library (TCSL): LCP's marketing slogan for its national law book sets, which are thoroughly cross-referenced with each other.

Treatise: Systematic scholarly discussion, or treatment, of the principles of a given subject; thus it is especially useful in the study of that subject.

Treaty: Nation-binding agreement with a foreign country.

Trial and practice books: Books that guide a lawyer or a paralegal through the proof of contentions at trial, often with samples of litigation aids and trial testimony.

Unconstitutional: Fundamentally illegal.

Unofficial reports: Reports not designated by the high court (or the legislature) as the official version of its opinions.

User-friendly: A computer system that is easy to use.

Vacating: Decision of an appellate court that it disagrees with the decision of the lower court, and that the case is dismissed.

Veto: Return to Congress of a bill without the President's signature that had been presented to the President by Congress. A vetoed bill is not law unless the veto is overridden by a two-thirds vote of each house.

West: Abbreviated form for West Publishing Company of St. Paul, Minnesota.

WESTLAW: West Publishing Company's computer-assisted legal research system, which includes access to West's case summaries.

Word processing: Electronic display, correction, and revision of text before printing.

Word search: Computer search of the words likely to have been used to describe the information sought.

INDEX

ABA Journal (A.B.A.J.), 185–186
   excerpt from, 187
Abbreviations, of reporters, 33
Acronyms for government agencies, in *U.S. Government Manual*, 140, 142
Act, 104
Adjudication (judgment or decree), 22
Administrative agencies, 7, 137–140, 142
Administrative codes, 143, 145
Administrative decisions, 146
Administrative law judge, 146
Administrative orders, 145
Administrative Procedure Act, 139
Administrative regulations, 140, 142
   citation style for, 198
Advance sheets, 32
Affirming of decision, 29
A.F.T.R. *See American Federal Tax Reports*
Agencies, administrative, 7, 137–140, 142
Alabama, law sources for, 280
Alaska, law sources for, 280
Allegheny County v. *ACLU*, 202
A.L.R. *See American Law Reports*
A.L.R. annotations, 77, 83, 84–86
   and *American Jurisprudence*, 96, 156
   citation style for, 198
   limitations of, 99
   parts and sections of, 86–93
   preparation of, 93–94
   sample of, 87–92
   as shortcut, 84
   tools for finding, 94–97
   in topic method, 248, 249
A.L.R. annotation supplementation, 97–99
A.L.R. Blue Book of Supplemental Decisions, 98
A.L.R. digests, 96, 248, 249
A.L.R. Federal (A.L.R. Fed.), 86, 97
A.L.R. First Series Quick Index, 94, 249, 250
A.L.R. help line, 96
A.L.R. indexes, 94, 95, 249, 250
A.L.R. latest-case service, 98

A.L.R. 2d Later Case Service, 98
Ambiguity, in word search, 225–226
American Annotated Cases, 83
"American Casebook Series," 50
American Decisions, 81
American Digest System, 72–73
   weakness in, 82
American and English Annotated Cases, 82, 83
American Federal Tax Reports (A.F.T.R.), 40
American Federal Tax Reports, Second Series (A.F.T.R.2d), 40, 149
American Jurisprudence (Am. Jur.), 84, 96, 156
American Jurisprudence, Second Series (Am. Jur.2d), 74, 96, 156, 159
   citation style of, 195, 198
   excerpt from, 160
American Jurisprudence Legal Forms 2d, 96, 178
   excerpt from, 179–180
American Jurisprudence Pleading and Practice Forms, Revised, 97, 181
American Jurisprudence Proof of Facts 2d, 97, 181–182
   excerpts from, 183–184
American Jurisprudence Trials, 97, 181–182
American Law Institute (ALI), 174
American Law Reports (A.L.R.), 83, 177, 182. *See also* A.L.R. annotations
   and Auto-Cite, 212–214
   on LEXIS, 221
   on microfiche, 231
American Law of Torts, The, 173
American Lawyer, The, 186
American Reports, 81
American State Reports, 81, 83
Analogy, legal reasoning by, 22–25
Anderson, William S., 165
Anderson's Ohio Civil Practice With Forms, 181
Anderson Publishing Company (Anderson), 9, 40, 130, 165, 168, 178, 181, 238

Annotated codes, 111–113
Annotated constitutions, 129–130
Annotated court rules, 132
Annotated treaties, 134
Annotation history table, 98–99, 100
Annotations, 81. *See also* A.L.R. annotations
   exhaustive, 82
   origin of, 81–84
   use of, 84
Appellant, 29
Appellate courts, 31–32
   federal, 38
   opinions of, 29, 30, 32, 43
Appellee, 29
Arizona, law sources for, 281
Arkansas, law sources for, 281
Art of Advocacy, 182
Atlantic Digest, Second Series, 73
Atlantic Reporter (A., A.2d), 41–42
Attorney general, 146
Attorney's Pocket Dictionary, The (Sodhi), 165
Authority
   and commercial law outline, 161
   and digests, 59
   inherent (of courts), 131
   mandatory (binding), 23, 246–247
   persuasive, 23, 182, 247
   primary, 12, 50, 195–198, 246
   secondary, 12–13, 50, 77, 198–199 (*see also* Secondary authority or sources)
Auto-Cite computer research system, 87, 97, 212–214
   and A.L.R., 221
   and LEXIS, 223
   and search procedure, 249, 250

Bad law, 203
Bailey, F. Lee, 174
Baldwin's Ohio Civil Practice, 181
Baldwin's Ohio Legal Forms, 178
Ballentine, James A., 165
Ballentine's Law Dictionary, 161–162, 163, 165
Bancroft, Hubert Howe, 8, 81
Bancroft-Whitney Company (BW), 8, 9, 81, 82–84
Bankruptcy Citations, 209
Bankruptcy Library, on CD-ROM, 234
Bankruptcy Reporter (Bankr.), 39
Bankruptcy Service, Lawyers' Edition, 97
Banks-Baldwin Law Publishing Company, 9, 44, 178, 181
Bar journal, 185
Barkan, Steven M., 244
Bender, Matthew, 8. *See also* Matthew Bender & Company
Bender's Federal Practice Forms, 181
Bender's Forms of Discovery, 181
Bibliographic approach, 243
Bill, 104

Bill of Rights, 129
Binding authority. *See* Mandatory authority
Black, Henry Campbell, 163
Black, J. S., 36
Black Letter Series, West's, 161
Black's Law Dictionary, 72, 161–163
Bluebook style, 193–195
   computer checking for, 199
   vs. *Shepard's*, 204
   technical rules of, 195–199
Bluebook: A Uniform System of Citation, The, 15th ed., 193–194
BNA (Bureau of National Affairs, Inc.), 9, 40, 148, 214, 234
Boardroom Reports, Inc., 186
Bodenheimer, Edgar, 173
Books, vs. computer database, 226–227
Books, law. *See* Law books
Bouvier's Law Dictionary, 165
Briefs, 52
   canned, 161
   excerpts from, 53–58
Briggs, James E., 8, 36
Briggs, William H., 36
Brown, Gordon W., 174
Brumbaugh, Jesse Franklin, 76
Bureau of National Affairs, Inc. (BNA), 9, 40, 148, 214, 234
Burr, Aaron, 11
Business law, and looseleaf services, 148
Business Laws, Inc., 9
Business Law: With UCC Applications, 7th ed., 173–174
Business Lawyer, The, 186
Business Lawyer Update, The, 186
BW (Bancroft-Whitney Company), 8, 9, 81, 82–84
Byers, Edward E., 174

California, law sources for, 280–281
California Reporter (Cal. Rptr.), 42
Call number, 309
Cambridge Law Study Aids, 161
Canned briefs, 161
Card catalog, use of, 310
Case(s), 7
   citation of, 49–50, 195–197
   cited and citing, 204
   classification of, 76
   importance of in research, 254
   landmark, 246–247
   leading, 246–247
   local, 246–247
   search for (search strategy), 246–247
Case at bar, 22
Casebook (Socratic) method, 50, 161
Casebooks, 50–51
Case & Comment magazine, 97
Case finders, 49, 77
   A.L.R annotation, 77, 83, 84–94

A.L.R. annotation finders, 94–97
A.L.R. annotation supplementation, 97–99
annotations, 81–84
briefs, 52, 53–58
casebooks, 50–51
computer-assisted legal research, 77, 219–222 (see also Computer-assisted legal research)
digests, 33, 52, 59–76 (see also Digests)
lawyers as, 51
memorandums, 52
secondary authority, 12–13, 50, 77 (see also Secondary authority or sources)
Shepard's Citations, 77, 211
Case of first impression, 23
and legislative history, 105
Case history, 212
and Auto-Cite, 213
computer citators of, 212–214
in Insta-Cite, 214
and *Shepard's*, 209, 213
Case law, 7
Case method of finding law, 248, 249
Casenote Legal Briefs, 161
Casenotes, 114
Case in point, 23, 24
Case on point, 24
Case reviewer, *Shepard's* as, 209–211
Case treatment, and *Shepard's*, 209, 213
Catholic Lawyer, 186
CCH Congressional Index, 107
CD-ROM, 233–234
Century Digest, 72, 73
Charter
of government, 128
of local government agency, 130
CheckCite software, 214
CheckRite software, 199
CIS (Congressional Information Service, Inc.), 107, 142
CIS Federal Register Index, 142
CIS Index (*Congressional Information Service Index*), 107
Citation-based dictionary, 163
Citations (cites), 49–50, 193
parallel, 49, 196, 212
Citation search, 221
Citation style, 193–195
for cases, 49–50, 195–197
computer-assisted, 199
for primary sources, 195–198
for secondary sources, 198–199
specific court requirements on, 199
for statutes, 197–198
Citators, 204
Auto-Cite, 87, 97, 212–214, 221, 223, 249, 250
"Blue and White Books," 212
Insta-Cite, 214, 221, 223, 250
National Reporter Blue Book, 212
Shepard's Citations, 77, 203–211 (see also *Shepard's Citations*)
Cited cases, 204
Citing cases, 204
Citing & Typing the Law: A Guide to Legal Citation & Style, 194
C.J. (*Corpus Juris*), 156
C.J.S. See *Corpus Juris Secundum*
Clark, George L., 159
Clark Boardman Callaghan (CBC), 9
Classification, 301. See also Law library classification
Class notation, 309
Cl. Ct. See *United States Claim Court Reporter*; U.S. Claims Court
Cochran's Law Lexicon, 165
Code of Federal Regulations (C.F.R.), 113, 114, 143, 145
Title 3 of, 145
Code of Federal Regulations (Citations), 209
Code finding tables, 14, 249
Codes, 108. See also Legislation
administrative, 143, 145
annotated, 111–113
of court rules, 132
federal, 108, 110–114
limitations of, 114
local, 124
and search procedure, 249
state, 114, 120, 124
Code of Virginia, on CD-ROM, 234
Codification, 108
Codification of Presidential Proclamations and Executive Orders, 145
Collections, 49
Colorado, law sources for, 282
COLR (computer-organized legal research), 234–238
Comments (law review), 182
Commerce Clearing House, Inc. (CCH), 9, 33
and Auto-Cite, 214
and ELISS, 224
and legislative history, 107
looseleaf services by, 148
and tax law, 40, 134, 148–149, 232
and treaties, 134
Commerce Clearing House, Tax Treaties, 134
Common law, 3–5, 7
and court sovereignty, 21
restatements of, 174, 177
Compacts, interstate, 124
Compleat Lawyer, The, 186
Computer-assisted citation style, 199
Computer-assisted legal research (CALR), 77, 219–222. See also Software
advantages and disadvantages of, 225–227
Auto-Cite, 87, 97, 212–214, 221, 223, 249, 250
best way of using, 227
EZ ACCESS, 223

and federal court of appeal opinions, 38
　Insta-Cite, 214, 221, 223, 250
　LEXIS, 77, 220–223 (see also LEXIS system)
　WESTLAW, 77, 220–221, 223–224 (see also WESTLAW system)
Computer databases, 147, 235–237
Computer-organized legal research (COLR), 234–238
Computer word search, 219–220, 221, 225–226, 249
Concordance, 219–220, 225
Concurrent resolution, 105
Concurring opinion, 30
Congress, meetings of, 104
Congressional Directory, 168
Congressional Information Service, Inc. (CIS), 107, 142
Congressional Information Service Index (CIS Index), 107
Congressional Record (Cong. Rec.), 107
Congressional Record Index, History of Bills and Resolution part of, 107
Congressional Research Service, 224
Connecticut, law sources for, 282
Connectors, 223
Considered *dicta*, 24
Constitution(s), 128
　citation style for, 198
　federal, 128–129 (see also Constitution of the United States)
　state and local, 130
Constitutional law, 5, 128–130
Constitution of the United States, 5, 128–129
　annotated versions of, 129–130
　on creation of federal courts, 131
　on interstate compacts, 120, 124
　on procedure for bill, 105
　and separation of powers, 6–8
　Tenth Amendment of, 5
　text of, 259–269 (Appendix I)
　on treaties, 132–133
　Twentieth Amendment of, 104
Constitution of the United States of America, The, 130
Constitutions of the United States: National and State, 130
Contracts, mailbox rule of, 4
Copy cataloging, 309
Corbin, Arthur Linton, 174
Corbin on Contracts, 174
Corley, Robert N., 174
Corpus Juris (C.J.), 156
Corpus Juris Secundum (C.J.S.), 72, 156
　citation style of, 195
　excerpt from, 158
Court of International Trade Reports (Ct. Int'l. Trade), 40
Court rules, 131–132
　annotated, 132
　citation style for, 198

Courts of appeal. *See* Appellate courts
Court sovereignty, 21–22
Court systems, levels of, 30–32
Couse's Ohio Form Book, 178
Couse's Ohio Incorporation Forms, 238
Couse's Ohio Will Forms, 238
Cranch, William, 33, 36
Cross-references, 59
Ct. Int'l. Trade (*Court of International Trade Reports*), 40
Current Law Index, 188
Current Legal Forms With Tax Analysis, 178
Customs Bulletin and Decisions (Cust. B. & Dec.), 40
Cutter, Charles Ammi, 309
Cutter number, 309

Dallas, Alexander J., 36
Danner, Douglas, 173
Databases, computer, 147, 219, 235
　on CD-ROM, 234
　DIALOG, 188, 224
　ELISS, 224
　FLITE, 225
　JURIS, 225
　PHINet, 225
　search of, 236
　search of (LEXIS), 223
　search of (WESTLAW), 223
　sorting of, 236–237
　typographical errors in, 226
Data Corporation, 219
Decennial digest, 72
Decision, 22
　administrative, 146
　appellate court actions on, 29
Decree, 22
Defendant, 22, 25
Delaware, law sources for, 283
Delaware Corporation Law Library, on CD-ROM, 234
Department of State Bulletin, 134
Descriptive-Word Index, 70, 71
　and search procedure, 249
Desk Book (Am. Jur. 2d), 159
Dewey, Melvil, 301
Dewey Decimal Classification system, 301
DIALOG, 188, 224
Dialog Information Services Inc., 224
Dicta, 24
Dictionaries, law, 161–165
　citation-based, 163
Digesting of document, 234
Digest paragraphs, 59, 69, 76
Digests (of cases), 33, 52, 59–60, 70, 72
　A.L.R., 96
　American Digest System, 72–73
　cumulative annual pocket parts as supplementing, 72
　Descriptive-Word Index for, 70, 71
　limitations of, 74, 76

326　Index

other, 73–74
outline of the law for, 59–60, 61–68
paragraphs for, 59, 69, 76
topic outlines for, 60, 67–68
Digests of laws (*Martindale-Hubbell*), 167
Digest of United States Supreme Court Reports, 73, 75
Directories, legal, 165, 167–168
Directory of Law Teachers, 168
Discovery, and litigation support, 234
Disks, floppy, 231–233
Dissenting opinion, 30
District of Columbia, law sources for, 283
Docket number, 26, 29
Dworsky, Alan L., 194

Edward Thomson Company (ET), 82, 83, 84
ELISS (Electronic Legislative Search Service), 224
Emanuel, Steven L., 161
Emanuel Law Outlines, 161
Enabling act, 124
Enactment, 104
Encyclopedias, 155–161
  citation style for, 198
  and quick searches, 255
Engrossed bill, 104
Enrolled bill, 105
Entries (index), 59
ET (Edward Thomson Company), 82, 83, 84
Etymology, 161
Executive agreement, 133
Executive branch, 7
Executive departments, 139
Executive order, 7, 145
Exhaustive annotations, 82
Exhaustive search, 252–254
"Ex parte" (in title of case), 29
"Ex post facto" ("after the fact") clauses of the Constitution, 6
EZ ACCESS, 223

F. See *Federal Reporter*
Feazel, E. A., 40
Federal Cases (F. Cas.), 37, 72
Federal Civil Practice Library, on CD-ROM, 234
Federal constitution. See Constitution of the United States
Federal court reports, 36–40
Federal courts of appeals, 38
Federal Criminal Code and Rules, 132
Federal Depository Library Program, 15–16
Federalism, 5–6
Federal Labor Law Citations, 209
Federal law, 108, 110–114
  legislative history of, 107
  researching of, 243, 246
Federal Procedural Forms, Lawyers' Edition, 97, 181
Federal Procedure, Lawyers' Edition, 97, 181

Federal Register (Fed. Reg.), 140, 142, 143, 145
  excerpt from, 144
Federal Reporter (F.), 32, 38
Federal Reporter, Second Series (F.2d), 32, 38
Federal Rules Decisions (F.R.D.), 38
Federal Rules Service (Fed. R. Serv.), 38–39
Federal Rules Service, Second Series (Fed. R. Serv. 2d), 39
Federal Supplement (F. Supp.), 38
Federal Tax Citations, 209
Federal Tax Coordinator 2d, 148, 149
Federal Taxes 2d, 149
Federal Tax Library, on CD-ROM, 234
Federal Trial Handbook 2d, 182
Federal Yellow Book, 140
Feudalism, 4
Fields, in database, 235
First impression, case of, 23
FLITE (Federal Legal Information Through Electronics), 225
Floppy disks, 231–233
Florida, law sources for, 283
Floyd, Charles F., 174
Form books, 178–182
Forms
  legal, 178
  pleading and practice, 178, 181
Foundation Press, Inc., 9
  casebooks by, 50
FullAuthority software, 238
Fundamentals of Criminal Advocacy, 174
Fundamentals of Legal Research, 5th ed., 244

Gans, Alfred W., 159, 173
General Digest (LCP), 82
General Digest (West), 72
General Digest, American and English, Annotated (LCP), 82
Georgia, law sources for, 284
Gifis, Steven H., 165
Gilbert Law Summaries, 161
Gilmer, Wesley, Jr., 165
Good, C. Edward, 194
Good law, 209
Government Contracts Library, on CD-ROM, 234
Government Printing Office, 36, 40, 107, 108, 111, 140, 143, 146
Great Depression, 9
Guide to American Law, 156
  excerpt from, 157

Handbook of the Law of Torts, 4th ed., 174
Hawaii, law sources for, 284
Headnotes, 26, 29, 59–60, 76
  and word search, 221
Help line, A.L.R., 96
High (final) court, 32
Hitchcock, Ernest, 36
Holding (rule of law), 23
Hornbook(s), 72, 174

excerpt from, 175–176
House organ, 236
Howard, Benjamin C., 36
How to Prepare a Legal Citation, 194
Hunter, Robert S., 182
Hypothetical legal question, and court's power, 21

Idaho, law sources for, 284–285
Illinois, law sources for, 285
Index to Annotations, 94, 97
   Annotation History Table in, 98–99, 100
   and search procedure, 249, 250
Indexes, 49
   A.L.R., 94, 95, 249, 250
   and digests, 49, 52, 59–60
   periodical, 186, 188
Index to Legal Periodicals, 186, 188
Index method, 248–250
Indiana, law sources for, 285
Indian Affairs, Laws and Treaties, 134
Information Access Corporation, 188, 234
Info Trac CD-ROM system, 188
Inherent authority, 131
"*In re*" (in title of case), 29
In re Copland, 21
Insta-Cite, 214, 221
   and search procedure, 250
   and WESTLAW, 214, 223
Intermediate appellate courts, 31–32
Internal Revenue Bulletin (I.R.B.), 186
Internal Revenue Code on Diskette, The, 232
International law, 132
International Thomson Organization Ltd., 9, 84
International Trade Reporter Decisions (I.T.R.D.), 40
Interstate compacts, 124
Iowa, law sources for, 286
Israel, Jerold H., 50

Jacobstein, J. Myron, 244
Johnson, Mark H., 178
Joint resolution, 105
   sample of, 106
Journals, law, 185–186
Judges, under Norman administration, 4
Judgment, 22
Judicial branch, 7
Judicial opinions. *See* Opinions
Judicial power, 21–25
Judicial reports. *See* Reports and reporters
Judicial review, 129
Jump cite, 49
JURIS (Justice Retrieval and Inquiry System), 225
Jurisoft, 199, 214
Jurisprudence, 3
Jurisprudence: The Philosophy and Method of the Law, 173

"Jur table," in A.L.R. annotations, 89, 93
Justices (Supreme Court), 13

Kamisar, Yale, 50
Kansas, law sources for, 286
Kappler, C., 134
Kentucky, law sources for, 286–287
Key Number, 60
   and search procedure, 249
KF subclassification to LC Library scheme, 303–309
Kimbrough, Robert T., 159
"Known topic" method, 248
Krause, Charles F., 173
KWIC (key words in context), 223

LaFave, Wayne R., 50
Landmark case, 246–247
Langdell, Christopher Columbus, 50
Language of the Law, The, 173
Later-case service, A.L.R., 98
Latest-case service, A.L.R., 98
Law(s). *See also* Legislation
   analyzing of, 250
   bad, 203
   as command of sovereign, 3, 5, 11–12
   common-law origins of, 3–5, 7
   constitutional, 5, 128–130
   good, 209
   international, 132
   positive, 108, 111
   as seamless web, 155
   uniform, 177
Law books, 13–14
   forewords or prefaces of, 13
   publishers of, 8–10
Law and Business Publications Inc., 165
Law Dictionary (Gifis), 165, 166
Law Dictionary, The (Gilmer), 165
Law of Evidence, 2d ed., 174
Law journals, 185–186
Law libraries, 14–16, 301
   and microforms, 231
Law library classification, 173, 301–302
   and card catalog, 310
   Library of Congress scheme, 173, 301, 302–303
   Library of Congress scheme (cataloging), 309
   Library of Congress scheme (KF subclassification), 303–309
   and looseleaf services, 148
Law Library Journal, 186
Lawlor, Mary Ann, 174
Law outlines. *See* Outlines, law
Law publishing, 8–10
   and National Reporter System, 33
Law Review Citations, 209
Law reviews, 182, 185
   in quick search example, 254–255
Lawriter, 238

Lawyers, as case finders, 51
Lawyers Co-operative Publishing Company (LCP), 8, 9
   and A.L.R., 77, 82–84, 94 (see also American Law Reports; A.L.R. annotations)
   and BW, 82–84
   and computer-assisted research, 212–214, 221
   citation style of, 195
   dictionary of, 161, 165
   digests by, 73
   encyclopedias of, 73–74, 96, 155, 156, 159, 161
   legal forms from, 178
   looseleaf services of, 147
   and Microlex, 231
   pleading and practice forms of, 181
   purchase of, 9, 84
   and Supreme Court reports, 36–37, 271–279
   trial and practice books of, 181–182
   United States Code Service, 97, 111, 114, 120, 121–123, 130
   and unofficial reports, 32
Lawyers Reports Annotated (L.R.A.), 82, 212
   on microfiche, 231
LCP. *See* Lawyers Co-operative Publishing Company
LCP-BW, 83–84
Leading case, 246–247
L. Ed. *See United States Supreme Court Reports, Lawyers' Edition*
L. Ed. 2d. *See United States Supreme Court Reports, Lawyers' Edition, Second Series*
Legal directories, 165, 167–168
Legal Directories Publishing Company, Inc., 168
Legal Economics, 186
Legal forms, 178
Legalines, 161
Legal reasoning, 22–25
Legal Reference Services Quarterly, 186
Legal research
   bibliographic approach to, 243
   and chronological vs. topical ordering of cases, 49, 82
   computer-organized, 234–238
   deceptive forces working against, 203
   journals on, 186
   and law books, 13–14
   and law libraries, 14–16
   and legislative history, 105
   mastery of, 255
   National Reporter System backbone of, 33
   on opponent's work, 250
   purpose of, 10–13
   question of when to stop in, 251–252
   readiness for, 243–244
   synergy in, 234
   and unreported opinions, 43–44, 99
   word search vs. analysis in, 225
Legal research, strategies in. *See* Search strategies in legal research
Legal Research and Writing: Some Starting Points, 3d ed., 244–245
Legal Resource Index, 188
Legal system, U.S., 3–8
Legal Thesaurus (Burton), 165
Legal Thesaurus/Dictionary (Statsky), 165
Legal Times, 186
Legal Trac system, 188, 234
Legal Tutor on Contracts, 232
Legal Tutor on Sales, 232
Legislation, 104–108
   local codes, 124
   federal, 107, 108, 110–114, 243, 246
   state, 107, 114, 120, 124, 243, 246, 280–300
Legislative branch, 6
Legislative departments, 139
Legislative history, 105, 107
Legislative History Service, 107
LEXIS system, 77, 220, 222–223
   A.L.R. on, 221
   and A.L.R. annotations, 97
   attorney-general opinions on, 146
   and Auto-Cite, 213, 223
   and case method, 248, 249
   C.F.R. on, 143
   federal court opinions on, 38, 39, 40
   Federal Register on, 142
   floppy-disk simulation of, 232
   Legal Resource Index on, 188
   legislative history materials on, 107
   Martindale-Hubbell on, 167
   Shepard's Citations on, 211
   specialized directories on, 168
   state court opinions on, 42
   state laws on, 280–300 (Appendix III)
   statute databases on, 120
   Supreme Court opinions on, 37
   unreported opinions on, 44
   U.S.C.S. on, 114
   and WESTLAW, 221, 222
Library, 301
Library, law. *See* Law libraries
Library of Congress Cataloging-in-Publication Data program, 309
Library of Congress Classification system, 173, 301, 302–303
   cataloging under, 309
   KF subclassification of, 303–309
   and looseleaf services, 148
Litigation support, 234
Little, Brown and Company, 9, 50
Local case, 246–247
Local codes, 124
Local constitutions, 130
Local directories, 168
Local legal newspapers, 186
Louisiana, law sources for, 287

Looseleaf services, 146–148
  and state statutes, 120
Lotus 1–2–3, 236, 238
L.R.A. See *Lawyers' Reports Annotated*
LSA: List of CFR Sections Affected, 143
Lynch v. Donnelly, 20, 48, 202

McCarthy, J. Thomas, 173
McCormick, Charles T., 174
McKinney, William Mark, 9
Macro, 237
Maier, Elaine C., 194
Maine, law sources for, 287
Majority opinion, 30
Mandatory authority, 23
  and search strategy, 246–247
Markus, Richard M., 182
Marquis Who's Who, Macmillan Directory Division, 168
Martel, Charles, 301
Martindale-Hubbell division, Reed Publishing Inc., 167, 234
Martindale-Hubbell Law Directory, 120, 167
Martindale-Hubbell Law Directory on CD-ROM, 234
Maryland, law sources for, 288
Massachusetts, law sources for, 288
Master Federal Tax Manual, 149
Master Tax Guide (U.S. Master Tax Guide), 148, 232
Matthew Bender & Company, Inc. (MB), 8, 9, 178, 181, 182, 234
Mead Corporation (Mead), 219
Mead Data Central (MDC), 9, 199, 213, 214, 219, 220, 221, 222, 226, 238
Mellinkoff, David, 173
Memorandum Decisions of the Tax Court (T.C.M.), 149
Memorandum of law, 52
Memorandum opinion, 30, 43
Mersky, Roy M., 244
Michie Company (Michie), 9, 234
Michigan, law sources for, 288–289
Michigan courts, citation requirements for, 199
Microforms, 231
  microfiche, 231
  microfilms, 231
Microlex, 231
Microlex Corporation, 231
Military Justice Citations, 209
Military Justice Digest, 74
Military Justice Reporter (M.J.), 39
Minnesota, law sources for, 289
Mississippi, law sources for, 289
Missouri, law sources for, 290
M.J. (*Military Justice Reporter*), 39
Monitor Publishing Co., 140
Montana, law sources for, 290
Moore's Federal Practice, 181

National Conference of Commissioners on Uniform State Laws, 177
National Law Journal, 186
National Reporter Blue Book, 212
National Reporter System, 33, 37–38, 40, 41–43
  and Auto-Cite, 214
  citation style of, 195
  and digests, 59
  and Insta-Cite, 214
  and *Shepard's*, 207
  "Ultra Fiche Edition" of, 231
Nebraska, law sources for, 290–291
Nemeth, Charles P., 173
Nevada, law sources for, 291
New Hampshire, law sources for, 291
New Jersey, law sources for, 291–292
New Mexico, law sources for, 292
New Mexico Statutes Annotated, on CD-ROM, 234
Newsletters, 186
Newspapers, 186
New Topic Service (Am. Jur. 2d), 159
New York, law sources for, 292–293
New York Supplement (N.Y.S., N.Y.S.2d), 42
NEXIS, 220
Nimmer, Melville B., 173
Nimmer on Copyright, 173
Noise words, 226
Nominative reporters, 36
  in table of parallel volume references, 270–271
Norman Conquest, 3–4, 247
North Carolina, law sources for, 293
North Dakota, law sources for, 293
North Eastern Reporter (N.E., N.E.2d), 41
North Western Digest, Second Series, 73
North Western Reporter (N.W., N.W.2d), 33, 41
Notes (law review), 182
Nutshells, 174

Obiter dicta, 24
Official reports, 32
Ohio, law sources for, 293–294
Ohio Appellate Decisions Index, 44
Ohio Appellate Reports, 41
Ohio Bar Automated Research (OBAR), 219
Ohio Court of Appeals, citation requirements for, 199
Ohio court rules, in *Lawriter*, 238
Ohio Forms: Legal and Business, 178
Ohio Forms of Pleading and Practice, 181
Ohio Jury Instructions, Software Version, 238
Ohio Lawyer, 186
Ohio Miscellaneous, 41
Ohio Official Reports, 40–41
Ohio Opinions (Ohio Op.), 40
Ohio Opinions, Second Series (Ohio Op. 2d), 40
Ohio Opinions, Third Series (Ohio Op. 3d), 40

Ohio State Bar Association Report, 186
Ohio State Reports, 41
Ohio State Tax Report, 186
Ohio Supreme Court, citation requirements for, 199
Ohio Transaction Guide—Legal Forms, 178
Oklahoma, law sources for, 294
On-line system, 220
Opinions, 25
  of attorneys general, 146
  parts of, 25–29
  reported, 32–33
  unreported, 43–44, 99
Opinions, types of
  concurring, 30
  dissenting, 30
  majority, 30
  memorandum, 30, 43
  per curiam ("by the court"), 30
  plurality, 30
Order(s), 22
  administrative, 145
  executive, 7, 145
Ordinance, 124
Oregon, law sources for, 294–295
Outlines, law, 161
  and search procedure, 249
  by West, 59–60, 61–68
Oxford Law Dictionary (proposed), 163

Pacific Digest, Third Series, 73
Pacific Reporter (P., P.2d), 41
Page mode, 223
Page's Ohio Revised Code Annotated, 130
Panama Refining Co. v. Ryan, 140
Paragraphs, digest, 59, 69, 76
Paralegal Resource Manual, The, 173
Parallel citations (cites), 49, 212
  style for, 196
Parallel volume references, for U.S. Supreme Court reporters, 270–279
Patents, in *West's Federal Practice*, 73
Pattern Deposition Checklists, 2d ed., 173
Pennsylvania, law sources for, 295
Per curiam ("by the court") opinion, 30
Periodical indexes, 186, 188
Periodicals, 182, 185–186
  citation style for, 198–199
Personal Injury Settlement Forms, 238
Persuasive authority, 23
  law review articles as, 182
  and search strategy, 247
Peters, Richard, 36
Petitioner, 22, 29
PHINet (Prentice-Hall Information Network), 225
Pike & Fischer, Inc., 9
Pinpoint cite, 49
Plaintiff, 22, 25, 29
Plaintiff in error, 29

Pleading and practice forms, 178, 181
Plurality opinion, 30
Pocket supplementation, for A.L.R. volumes, 98
Pocket veto, 105
Positive law, 108, 111
Practical Lawyer, 186
Practical Tax Lawyer, 186
Practice pointers, in A.L.R. annotations, 86, 91, 93
Preamble to Constitution, 128
Precedent, 4
  as bad law, 203
Prentice-Hall Information Services (P-H), 9, 40, 148, 149
Prima facie evidence, 108
Primary authority or sources, 12, 50
  citation style for, 195–198
  and search strategy, 246
Private law, 107
Procedure for legal research, 247–252
Proclamations, 145
Professional Responsibility Citations, 209
Profiles of Ohio Lawyers, 168
Promulgation of constitution, 130
Prosser, William L., 174
Proximity search, 226
Public law, 107
Public Laws—Legislative Histories Microfiche, 107
Putnam, Herbert, 301

Query, 223
Quick-Cite, 224, 249

Rabkin, Jacob, 178
Ratio decidendi, 23
Real Estate and the Law, 174
Reasoning, legal, 22–25
Record
  in database, 235
  for search, 252
References (index), 59
Regulations of administrative agencies, 7, 140, 142
"Related matters," in A.L.R. annotations, 89, 93
Remanding of decision, 29
Reporter of Decisions, 29
Reports and reporters, 13, 30, 32–33. *See also specific reporters*
  and chronological vs. topical order, 49, 82
  on federal courts, 36–40
  National System of, 33, 37–38, 40, 41–43 (*see also* National Reporter System)
  of state courts, 40–43
  useful features of, 33
Reports of the United States Tax Court (T.C.), 40
Research, legal. *See* Legal research
Research Institute of America (RIA), 9, 148

Index 331

Resolution (Congress), 105
Respondent, 22, 29
Restatement Citations, 209
Restatement in the Courts, 177
Restatements, 174, 177
Reversal of decision, 29
Reviews, law, 182, 185
Revised Statutes of 1875, 108, 110
Rhode Island, law sources for, 295
Riding a circuit, 4
Rose, Walter, 36
Rothblatt, Henry B., 174
Rulemaking, by administrative agency, 140
Rules, of Bluebook style, 195–199
Rules, court, 131–132
Rule of thumb for analyzing fact patterns, 244
Ruling Case Law, 156
Ryan Law Capsules, 161

Sample Pages, 3d ed., 244
Scheme, in A.L.R. notation, 86
Schopler, Ernest Hugo, 36
Scope, in A.L.R. annotations, 89, 93
S. Ct. *See Supreme Court Reporter*
Search
 citation, 221
 of database, 223, 236
 word search, 219–220, 221, 225–226, 249
"Search Master" compact disc libraries, 234
Search procedure, basic, 247–252
Search strategies in legal research
 basic, 245–247
 comprehensive, 252–254
 and fact-acquisition, 244
 and fact-analysis, 244–245
 limited, 254
 procedure in, 247–252
Secondary authority or sources, 12–13, 50
 as case finder, 77
 citation style for, 198–199
 dictionaries, 161–165
 encyclopedias, 155–161, 198, 255
 periodicals, 182, 185–188, 198–199
 and search strategy, 247
 textbooks, 172–174, 198
 treatises, 172–177, 198
Sections of U.S. Code, 111
Separation of powers, 6–8
 and court sovereignty, 21
 and origin of law, 12
Session law, 107
Setout, in A.L.R. annotations, 93
Shedd, Peter J., 174
Shepard, Frank, and Frank Shepard Company, 8, 203
Shepardizing of case, 204, 248, 249
Shepard's Citations, 77, 97, 203–211
 attorney-general opinions in, 146
 vs. Auto-Cite, 213
 and case method, 248, 249
 citation style of, 195
 pamphlets with, 207
 sample page of, 205
 and search procedure, 250
 and WESTLAW, 223
Shepard's/McGraw Hill, Inc. (Shepard's), 9, 195, 204, 207
Shepard's Preview service, 223–224
Shepard's United States Citations, 207
Shepard's United States Citations (Statute Edition), 207
Simple justice, 4, 10, 25
Simple resolution, 105
Slip law, 107–108, 109, 114
Slip opinion, 32
Smith's Review Series, 161
Socratic (casebook) method, 50, 161
Sodhi, Datinder S., 165
Software. *See also* Computer-assisted legal research
 CheckCite, 214
 CheckRite, 199
 for computer-organized research, 238
 Lotus 1–2–3, 236, 238
 user-friendly, 220
 WestCheck, 214
 word-processing, 237
Sorting
 chronologically by court level, 253
 of database, 236–237
Sources of Compiled Legislative Histories, 107
South Carolina, law sources for, 296
South Dakota, law sources for, 296
South Eastern Digest, Second Series, 73
South Eastern Reporter (S.E., S.E.2d), 32–33, 42
Southern Reporter (So., So.2d), 42
South Western Reporter (S.W., S.W.2d), 42
Sovereign
 under federalism (U.S.), 5–6
 law as command of, 3, 5, 11–12
 as plaintiff, 25
 and search strategy, 245–246
Speiser, Stuart M., 173
Spelling, and database search, 226
Standard Federal Tax Reporter, 148, 149
Stare decisis, 4, 21, 22
Star pagination, 37
State administrative and executive orders, 145
State administrative regulations, 145
State constitutions, 130
State court reports, 40–43
State directories, 168
State encyclopedias, 159, 161
"State ex. rel." (in title of case), 29
State legislation, 114, 120, 124
 legislative history of, 107
 and local codes, 124
 researching of, 243, 246
 table of selected sources of, 280–300 (Appendix III)

State Public Defender Report, 186
Statsky, William, 165, 244–245
Statute edition of *Shepard's,* 207, 209, 211
Statute method, 248, 249
Statutes, 6–7, 104. *See also* Legislation
   citing of, 197–198
   and search strategy, 246, 249
Statutes at Large, United States, 108, 110
Statutory law, 7, 104
Stichman, Barton F., 255
Stop words, 226
Strategies for searching. *See* Search strategies in legal research
Style, citation, 193–195
Summary of American Law, 159
Sum & Substance (law outline), 161
Superintendent of Documents Classification, 301–302
Superseding annotation, 98
Supplementing annotation, 98
Supplements
   to A.L.R. annotations, 97–99
   to digests, 72
   in review of law, 250
   to *Shepard's Citations,* 207, 208
Supreme court, 32
Supreme Court, Ohio (citation requirements for), 199
Supreme Court, U.S., 36
   opinion process in, 30
Supreme Court Library, classification scheme in, 301
Supreme Court Reporter (S. Ct.), 36–37
   Shepard's table for, 207
Supreme Court reporters, 36–37, 270–279. *See also specific reporters*
Syllabus (in opinion), 29
Synergy, 234
Synonyms, in word search, 225
Synopsis of case, 26, 29

Table of Key Numbers Section for Century Digest, 73
Tables of information, 14, 33
   on cases reported (sample), 35
   on judges (sample), 34
Table of Statutes and Rules Cited (Am. Jur. 2d.), 159
TAPP Rule, 244
TARP Rule, 244
Tax Action Coordinator, 149
Tax Analysts (company), 232
Tax Court Memorandum Decisions (T.C.M.), 40, 148
Tax courts and tax law, 40, 148–149, 232, 234
   and legal forms, 178
   periodicals on, 186
   and treaties, 134
Tax Guide, 149
Tax HOTline, 186

Tax Management portfolios (BNA), 234
Tax Practitioner Newsletter, 186
Tax services, 148–149
T.C. (*Reports of the United States Tax Court*), 40
"TCSL Box," 86. *See also* Total Client Service Library
Technical rules, of Bluebook style, 195–199
Teiser, Sidney, 231
Tennessee, law sources for, 296–297
Tenth Amendment, 5
Term model, 223
Texas, law sources for, 297
Textbooks, 172–174
   citation style for, 198
Thesaurus of Legal Fact Words and Concepts, 97
Thesauri, legal, 165
Thomson Legal Publishing Inc. (TLPI), 9, 84
Thomson Professional Publishing, 9
Title of case, 25
Titles, of U.S. Code, 110
Topic method, 248, 249
Topic outlines, 60, 67–68
Topics
   and search procedure, 249
   in West's outline, 60
Total Client Service Library, 74, 86, 97
Trademarks, in *West's Federal Practice,* 73
Trademarks and Unfair Competition, 2d ed., 173
Trade names, in *West's Federal Practice,* 73
Treaties, 7, 132–134
Treaties in Force, 134
Treaties and Other International Acts Series (T.I.A.S.), 133
Treatises, 172–177
   citation style for, 198
Trial courts, 30–31
Trial Handbook for Ohio Lawyers, Second Edition, 182
Trial and practice books, 181
Trinity Series, 81
Twentieth Amendment, 104

Unconstitutional act, 21
Uniform Commercial Code (U.C.C.), 177
Uniform Commercial Code Citations, 209
Uniform laws, 177
Uniform Laws Annotated, Master Edition, 177
United States Claims Court Reporter (Cl. Ct.), 39
United States Code (U.S.C.), 110–111
United States Code Annotated (U.S.C.A.), 72, 111, 113–114, 115–119, 130, 132
United States Code Congressional and Administrative News (U.S. Code Cong. & Admin. News), 107, 145
United States Code Service (U.S.C.S.), 97, 111, 114, 120, 121–123, 130, 132, 181
   advance pamphlets to, 145
   treaties in, 134
United States Law Week (U.S.L.W.), 37

United States Reporter, 33
United States Reports (U.S.), 36, 37
   Shepard's table for, 207
   in table of parallel volume references, 270–279
United States Statutes at Large (Stat.), 108, 110, 124, 133, 145
United States Supreme Court Bulletin (S. Ct. Bull.), 37
United States Supreme Court Reports, Lawyers' Edition (L. Ed.), 32, 33, 36, 84
   Digest for, 74
   on microfiche, 231
   Shepard's table for, 207
United States Supreme Court Reports, Lawyers' Edition, Second Series (L. Ed. 2d), 32, 36, 37, 84, 130, 181
   Shepard's table for, 207
United States Tax Cases (U.S.T.C.), 33, 40, 148
United States Treaties and Other International Agreements (U.S.T.), 133
United States Treaties and Other International Agreements Cumulative Index, 133
Unofficial reports, 32
Unreported opinions, 43–44, 99
U.S. *See* United States Reports
U.S.C. (*United States Code*), 110–111
U.S. Claims Court (Cl. Ct.), 38, 39
U.S. Claims Court Digest, 74
U.S.C.S. *See* United States Code Service
User-friendly software, 220
User's Guide to A Uniform System of Citation: The Cure for the Bluebook Blues, 194
U.S. Government Manual, 139–140
   excerpts from, 141–142
U.S. Government Printing Office, 36, 40, 107, 108, 111, 140, 143, 146
U.S. Master Tax Guide, 148
   on floppy disk, 232
U.S. Supreme Court Digest, 73
U.S. Supreme Court Digest, Lawyers' Edition, 73, 75
Utah, law sources for, 297–298

Vacating of decision, 29
Veralex, 221
Vermont, law sources for, 298
Veto, 105
Virginia, law sources for, 298

Wallace, John William, 36
Washington, law sources for, 298–299
Weekly Compilation of Presidential Documents, 145
Weinstein, Martin, 159
West, Horatio D., 33
West, John B., 8, 33, 76
WestCheck software, 214
West Digest System, and A.L.R., 84, 93–94
WESTLAW system, 77, 220–221, 223–224
   attorney-general opinions on, 146
   and case method, 248, 249
   C.F.R. on, 143
   and DIALOG, 224
   federal courts of appeal opinions on, 38, 39
   Federal Register on, 142
   floppy-disk simulation of, 232
   Insta-Cite on, 214, 223
   Legal Resource Index on, 188
   legislative history materials on, 107
   and LEXIS, 221, 222
   reporters and digests searches through, 72, 76
   Shepard's Citations on, 211
   specialized directories on, 168
   specialized federal court opinions on, 40
   state court opinions on, 42
   state laws on, 280–300 (Appendix III)
   statute databases on, 120
   Supreme Court opinions on, 37
   unreported opinions on, 44
   U.S.C.A. on, 114
West Publishing Company (West), 8, 9, 33, 72
   blue/white books of, 212
   casebooks of, 50
   and computer-assisted research, 220–221 (*see also* WESTLAW)
   dictionary of, 161–163, 165
   digests of, 52, 59–73, 82
   encyclopedias of, 155, 156
   and federal court opinions, 38–39
   and Federal Reporter, 32
   hornbooks of, 72, 174
   and Insta-Cite, 214
   legal forms by, 178
   and National Reporter System, 33, 37–38, 40, 41–43 (*see also* National Reporter System)
   and National Reporter System (microform), 231
   "nutshells" of, 174
   outline of the law by, 59–60, 61–68
   rules of court by, 132
   and Supreme Court, 36–37, 271–279
   United States Code Annotated, 111, 113–114, 115–119, 130 [inv]
   United States Code Congressional and Administrative News, 107
West's Black Letter Series, 161
West's Bankruptcy Digest, 74
West's Education Law Digest, 74
West's Federal Forms, 181
West's Federal Practice Digest, 3d, 73
West's Federal Practice Digest, 4th, 73
West's Federal Practice Manual, 181
West's Illinois Decisions, 42
West's Law Finder, 60, 70, 244
West's Legal Directory, 168
West Virginia, law sources for, 299
Wheaton, Henry, 36

White, Robert D., 162–163
Whitney, Summer, 81
Who's Who in American Law, 168
William the Conqueror, 3–4
Wilson, H. W., Company, 186
Wilsondisc CD-ROM system, 188
Wisconsin, law sources for, 299
WordPerfect, 237, 238
Word processing, 237

Word searching, 219–220, 221, 225–226, 249
Words and Phrases, 163
  excerpt from, 164
Writ of *certiorari*, 30
Wyoming, law sources for, 300

"Yellow Book" directories, for federal
  government, 140